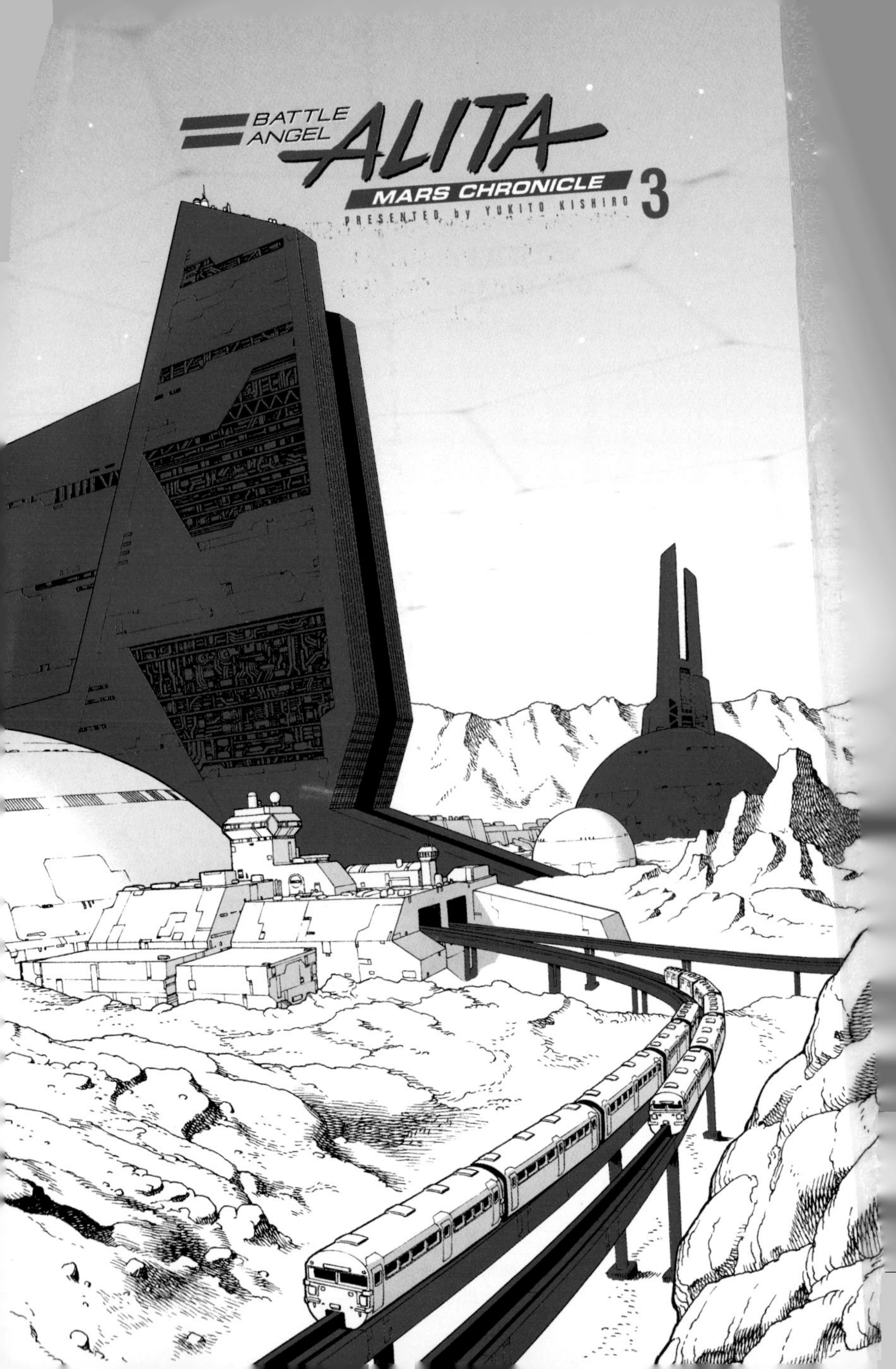
BATTLE ANGEL ALITA
MARS CHRONICLE 3
PRESENTED by YUKITO KISHIRO

BATTLE ANGEL ALITA MARS CHRONICLE
PRESENTED by YUKITO KISHIRO

CONTENTS

ADDITIONAL STAFF:
TSUTOMU KISHIRO / EMIYA KINARI

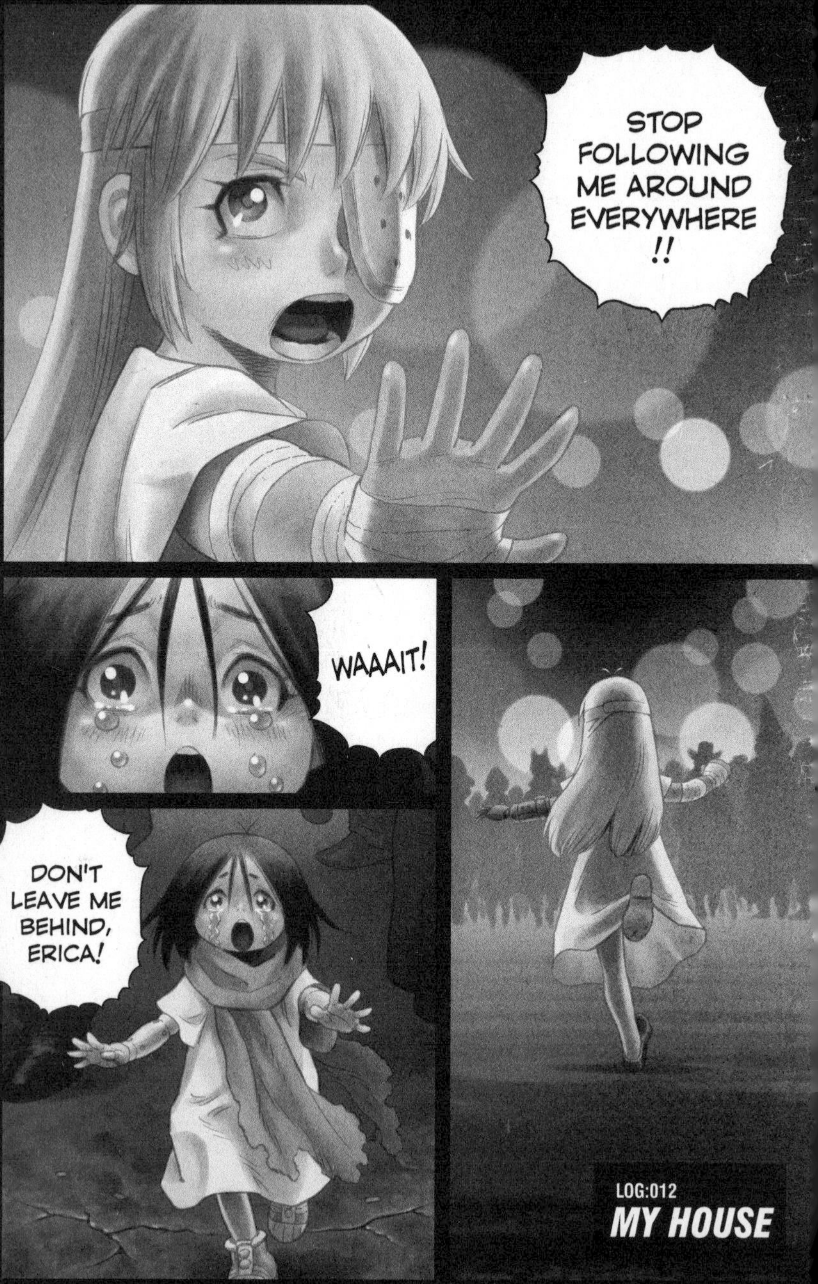
STOP FOLLOWING ME AROUND EVERYWHERE!!
LOG:012
MY HOUSE
WAAAIT!
DON'T LEAVE ME BEHIND, ERICA!

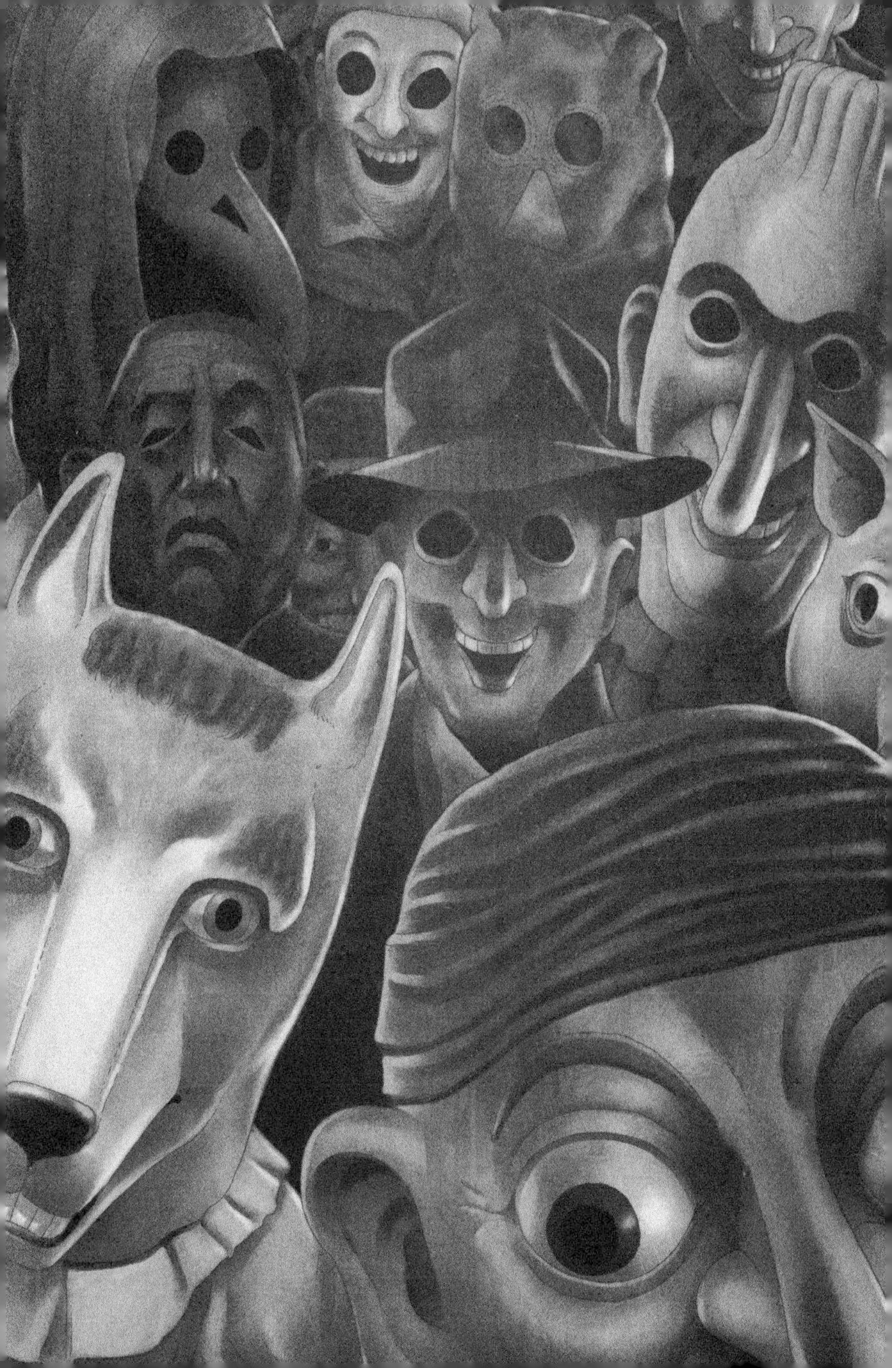

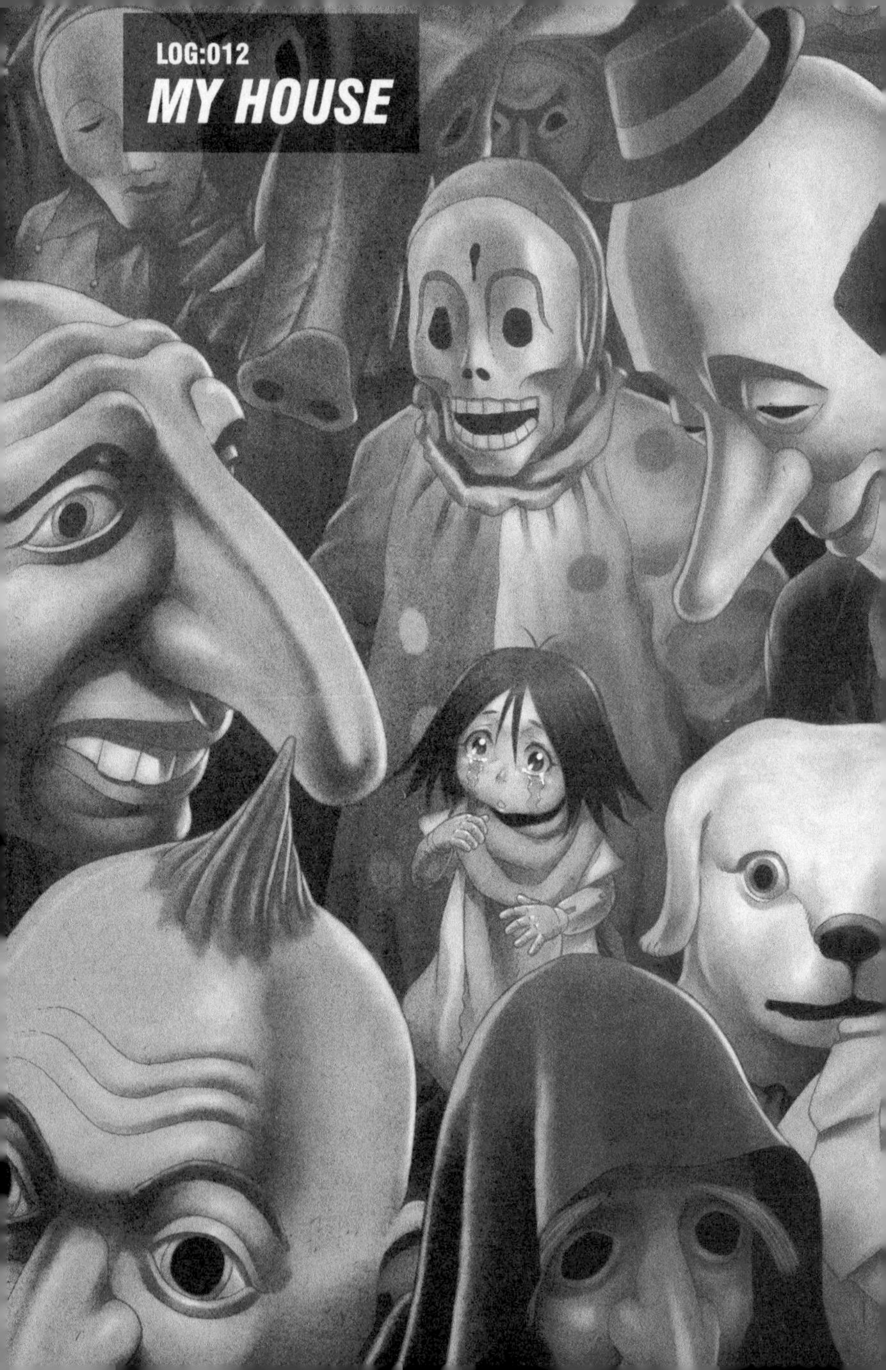
LOG:012
MY HOUSE

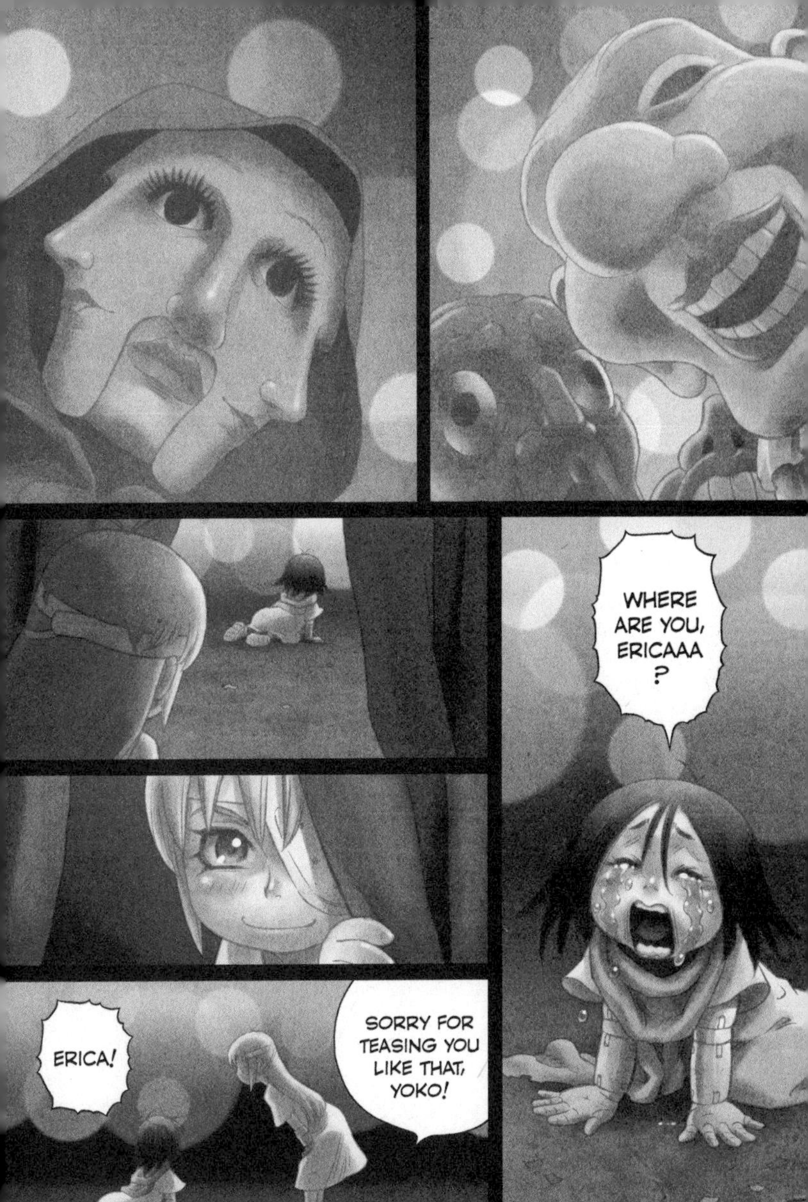
WHERE ARE YOU, ERICAAA?
SORRY FOR TEASING YOU LIKE THAT, YOKO!
ERICA!

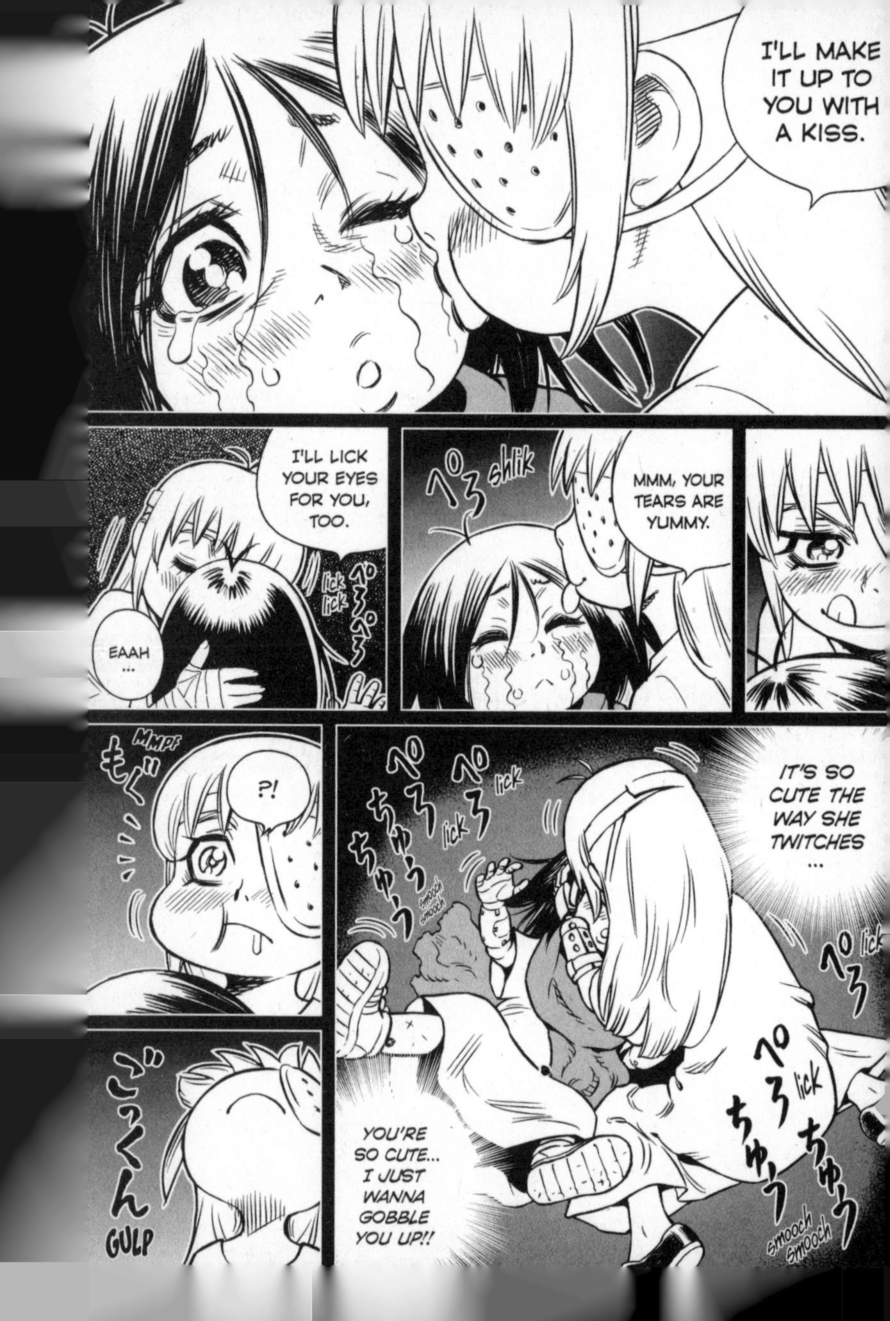
I'LL MAKE IT UP TO YOU WITH A KISS.
ぺろ shlik
MMM, YOUR TEARS ARE YUMMY.
I'LL LICK YOUR EYES FOR YOU, TOO.
ぺろぺろ lick lick
EAAH ...
IT'S SO CUTE THE WAY SHE TWITCHES ...
ぺろ lick
ぺろ lick
ちゅうちゅう smooch smooch
ぺろ lick
ぺろ lick
ちゅうちゅう smooch smooch
YOU'RE SO CUTE... I JUST WANNA GOBBLE YOU UP!!
もぐ MMPF
?!
ごっくん GULP

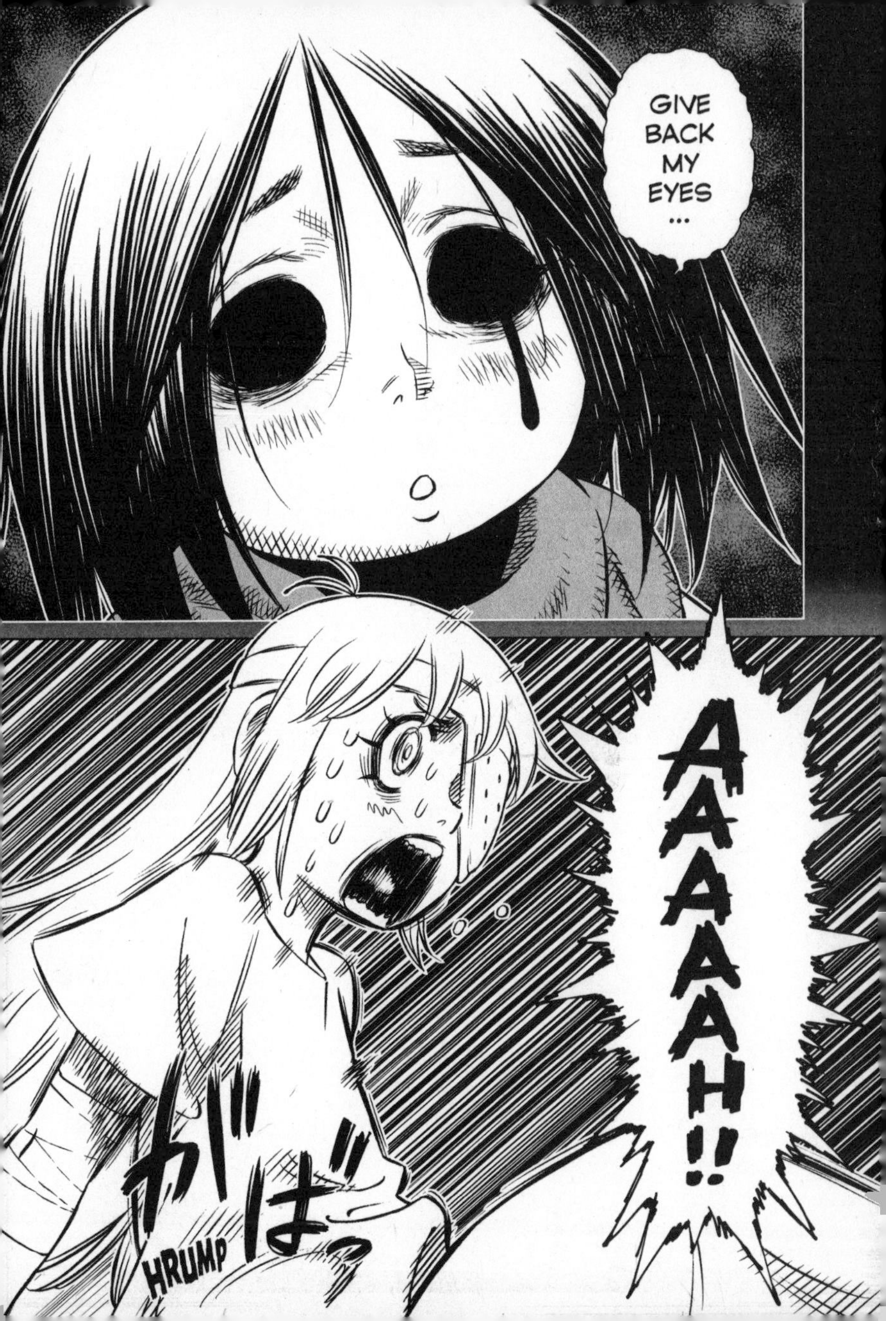
GIVE BACK MY EYES ...
AAAAAH!!
がばっ
HRUMP

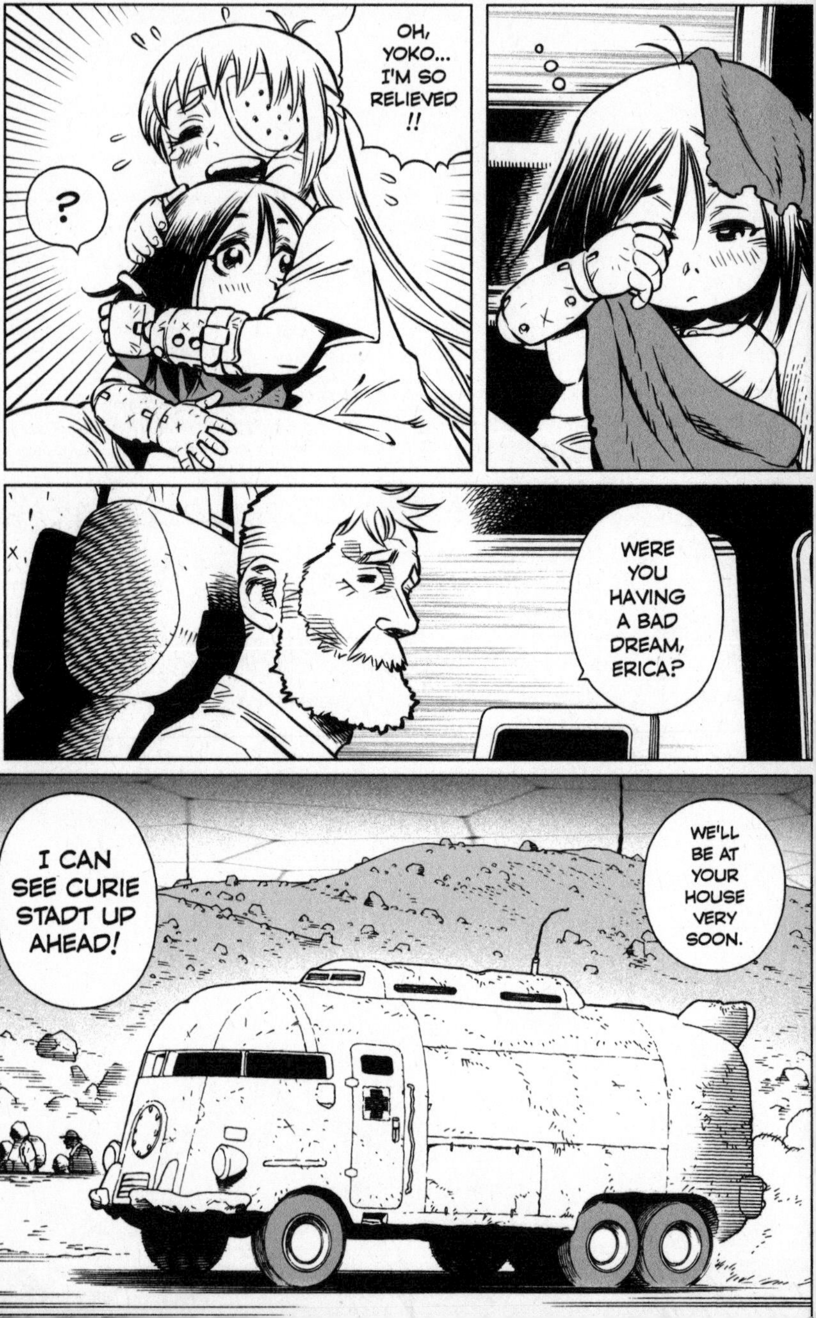
OH, YOKO... I'M SO RELIEVED !!
?
WERE YOU HAVING A BAD DREAM, ERICA?
WE'LL BE AT YOUR HOUSE VERY SOON.
I CAN SEE CURIE STADT UP AHEAD!

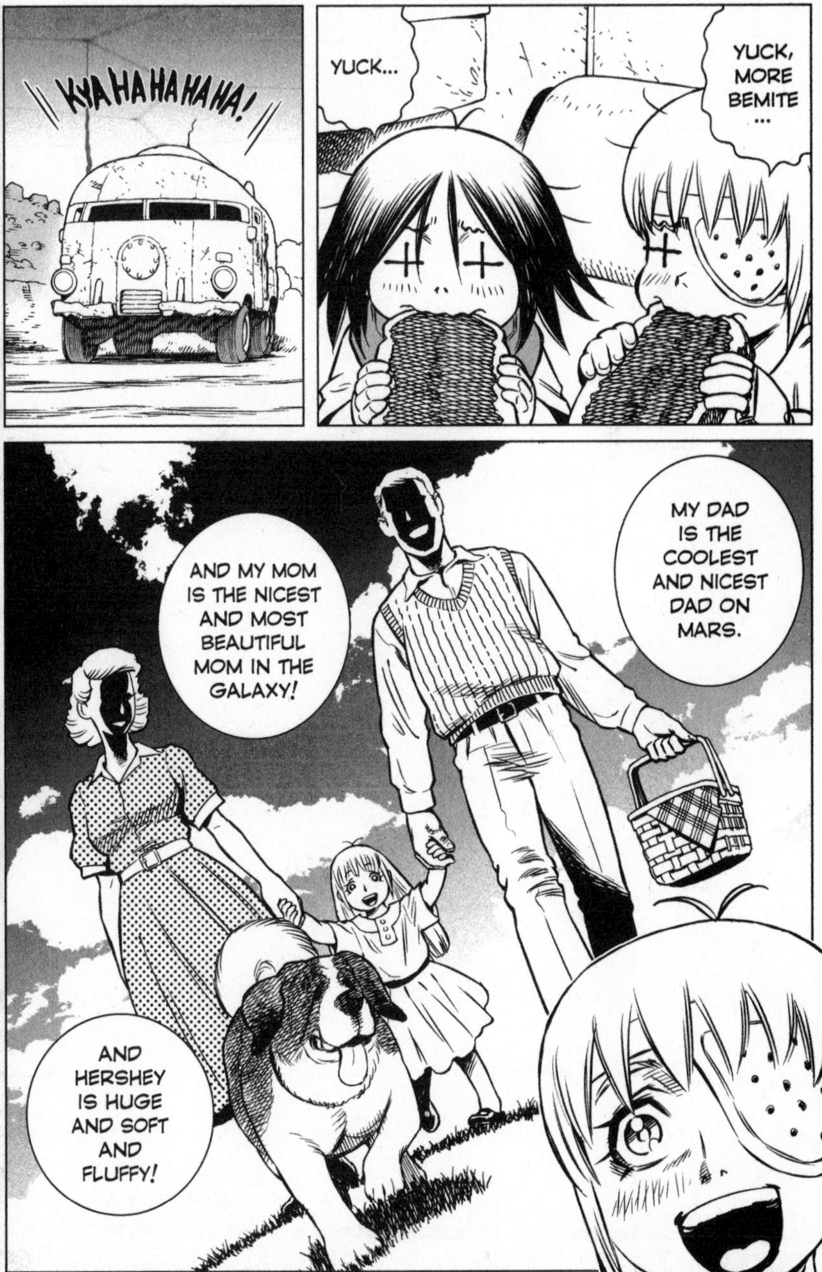
YUCK, MORE BEMITE ...
YUCK...
KYAHAHAHAHAHA!
MY DAD IS THE COOLEST AND NICEST DAD ON MARS.
AND MY MOM IS THE NICEST AND MOST BEAUTIFUL MOM IN THE GALAXY!
AND HERSHEY IS HUGE AND SOFT AND FLUFFY!

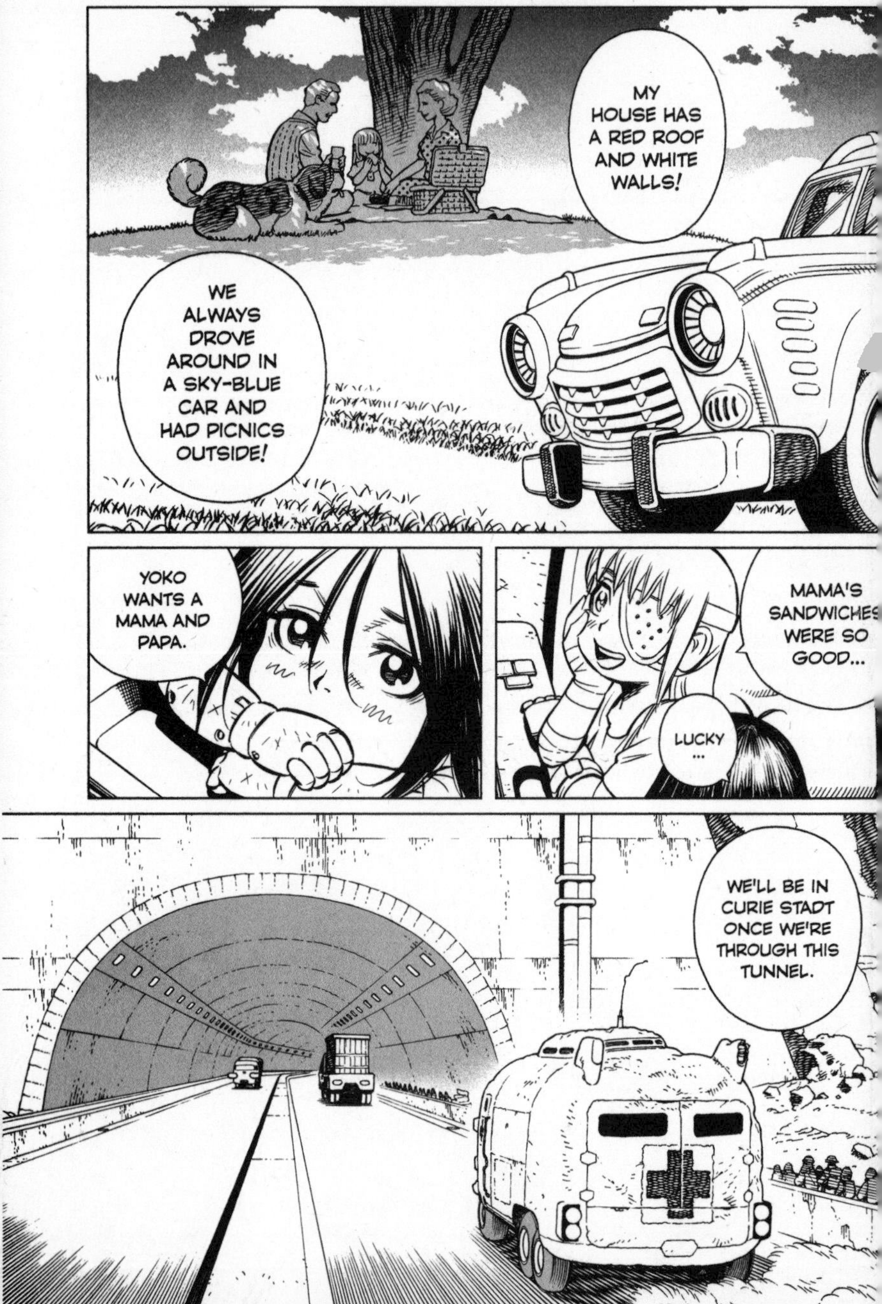
MY HOUSE HAS A RED ROOF AND WHITE WALLS!
WE ALWAYS DROVE AROUND IN A SKY-BLUE CAR AND HAD PICNICS OUTSIDE!
MAMA'S SANDWICHES WERE SO GOOD...
LUCKY ...
YOKO WANTS A MAMA AND PAPA.
WE'LL BE IN CURIE STADT ONCE WE'RE THROUGH THIS TUNNEL.

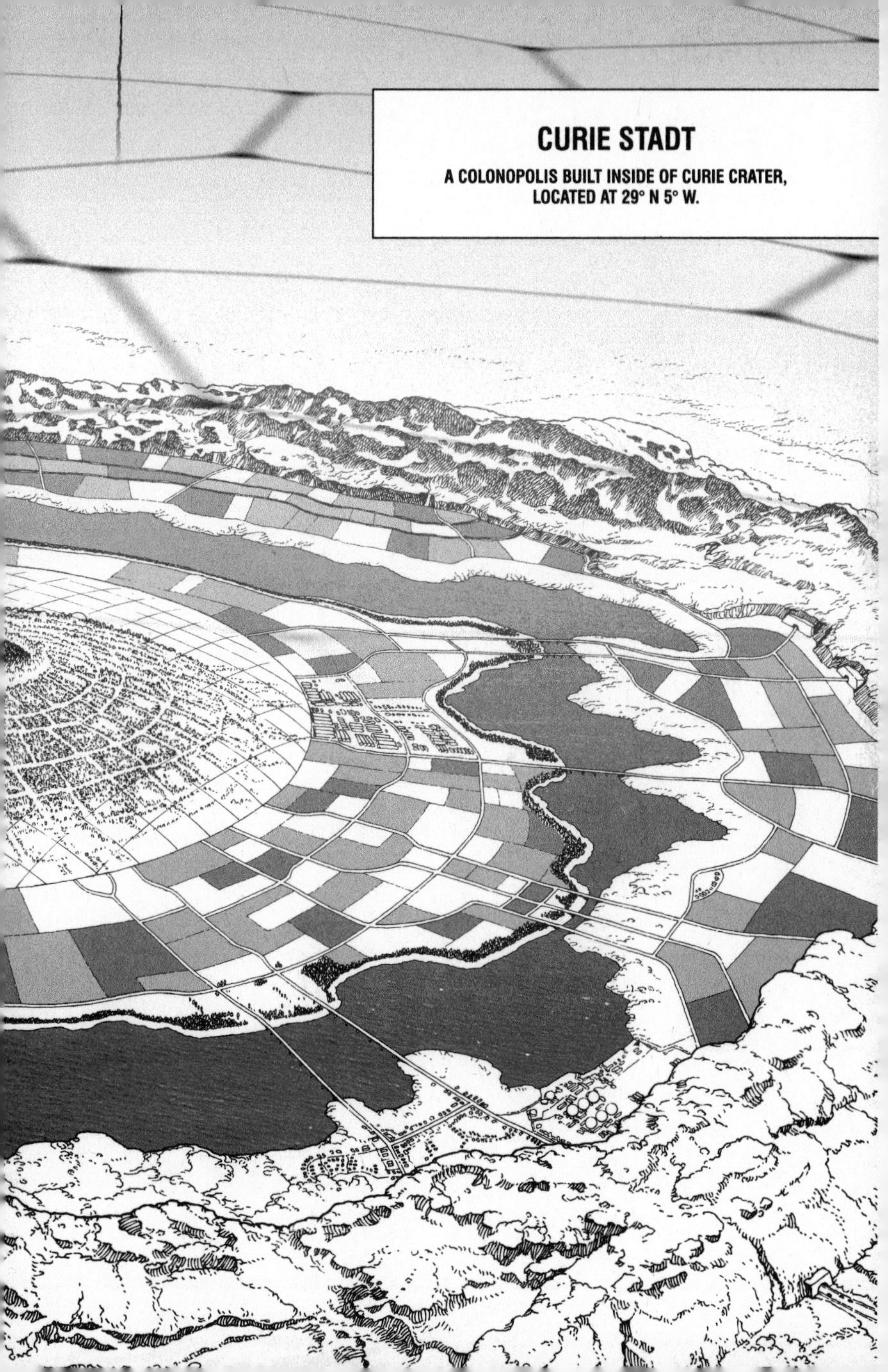
CURIE STADT
A COLONOPOLIS BUILT INSIDE OF CURIE CRATER, LOCATED AT 29° N 5° W.

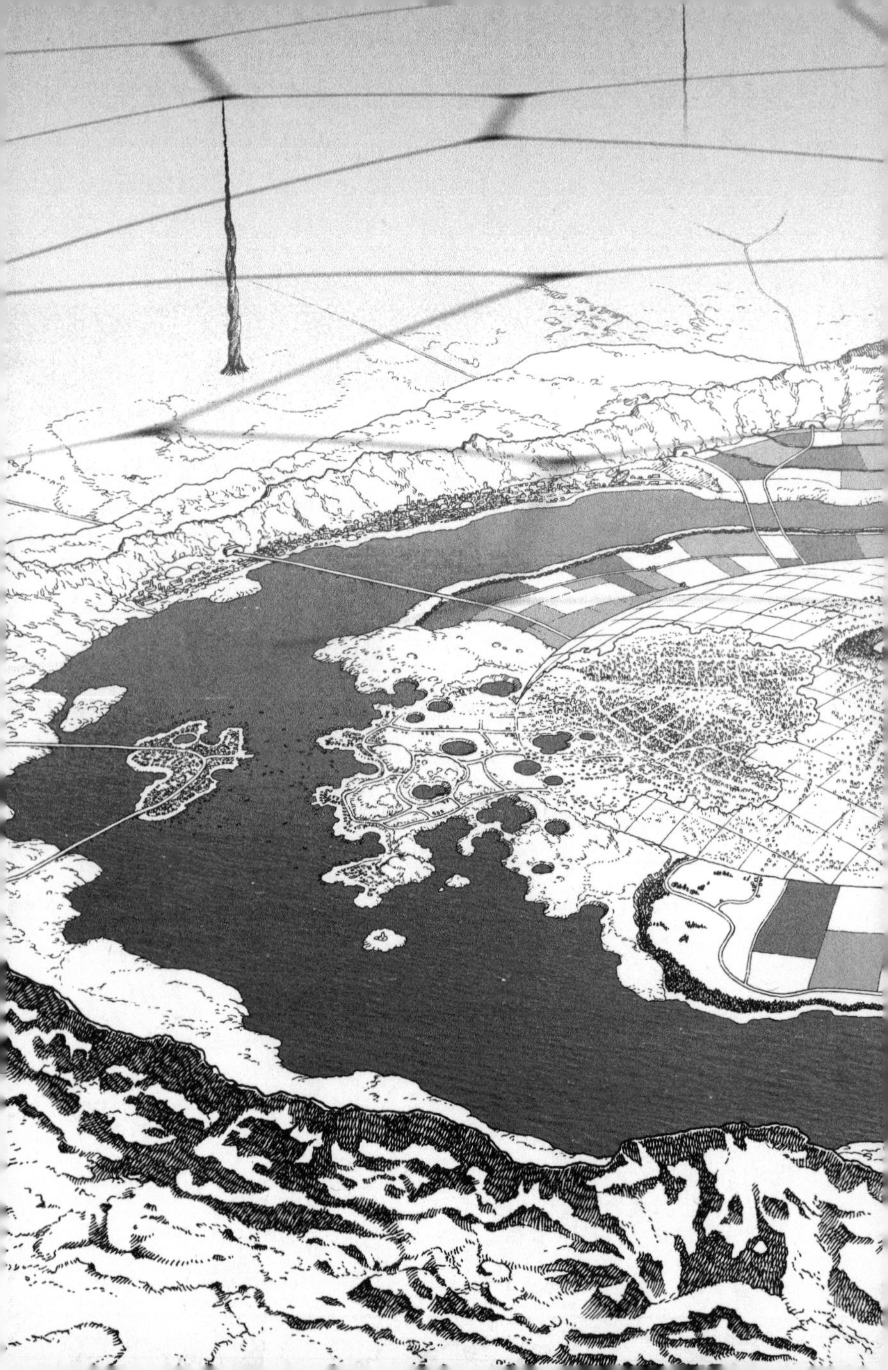

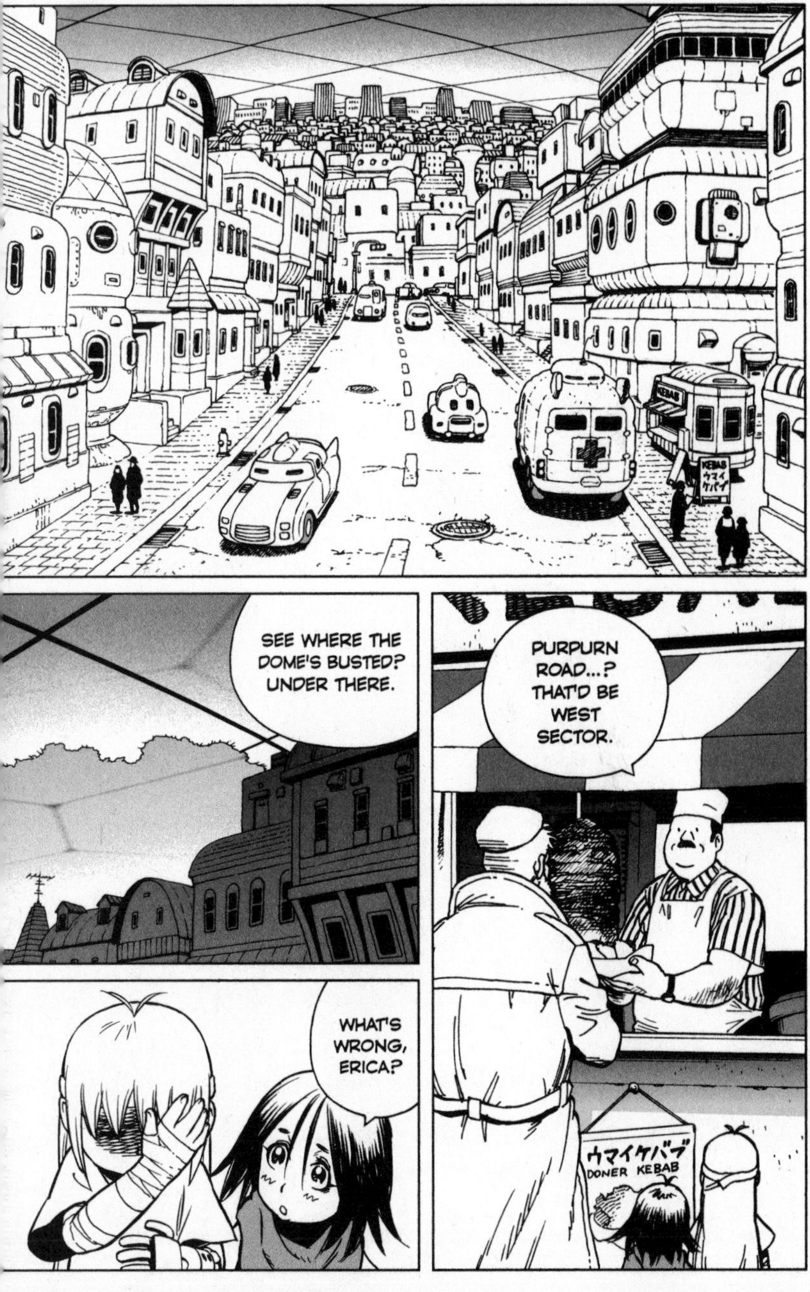
PURPURN ROAD...? THAT'D BE WEST SECTOR.
ウマイケバブ
DONER KEBAB
SEE WHERE THE DOME'S BUSTED? UNDER THERE.
WHAT'S WRONG, ERICA?

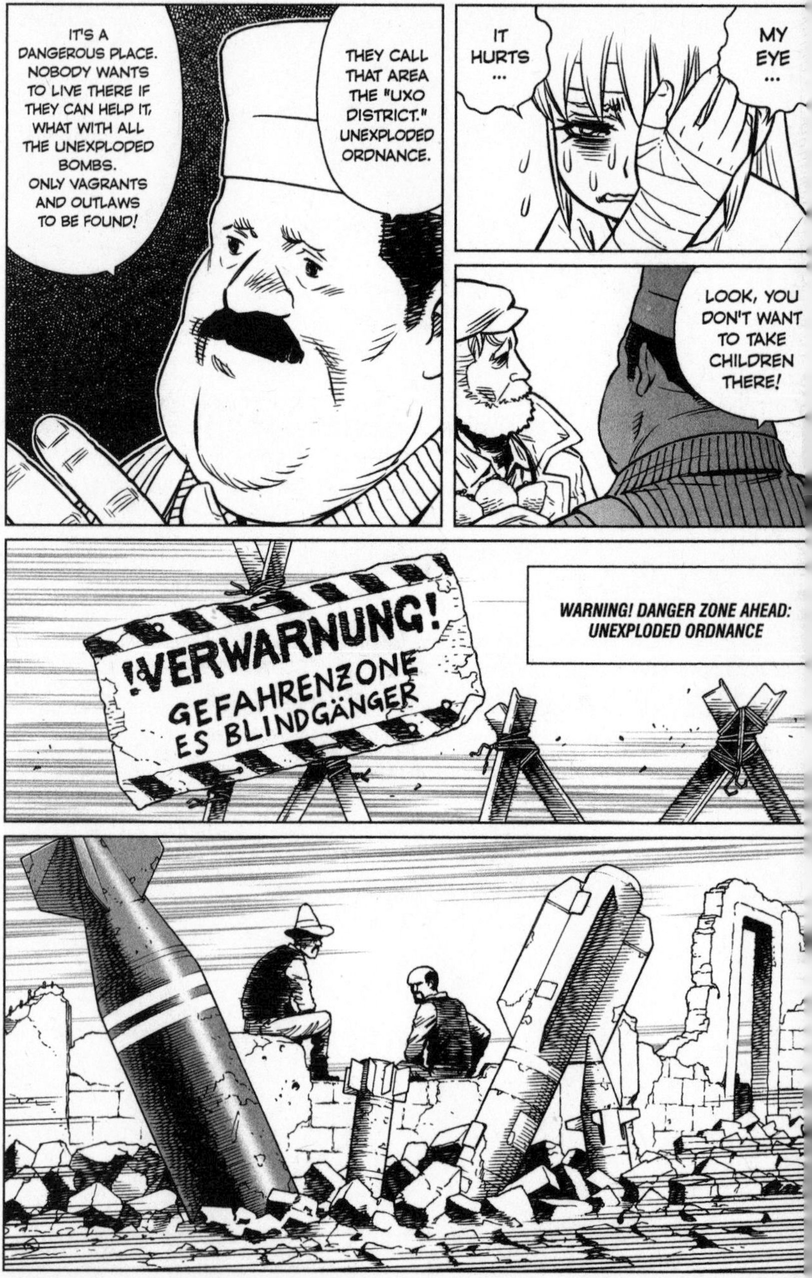
MY EYE ...
IT HURTS ...
LOOK, YOU DON'T WANT TO TAKE CHILDREN THERE!
THEY CALL THAT AREA THE "UXO DISTRICT." UNEXPLODED ORDNANCE.
IT'S A DANGEROUS PLACE. NOBODY WANTS TO LIVE THERE IF THEY CAN HELP IT, WHAT WITH ALL THE UNEXPLODED BOMBS. ONLY VAGRANTS AND OUTLAWS TO BE FOUND!
WARNING! DANGER ZONE AHEAD: UNEXPLODED ORDNANCE
!VERWARNUNG!
GEFAHRENZONE
ES BLINDGÄNGER

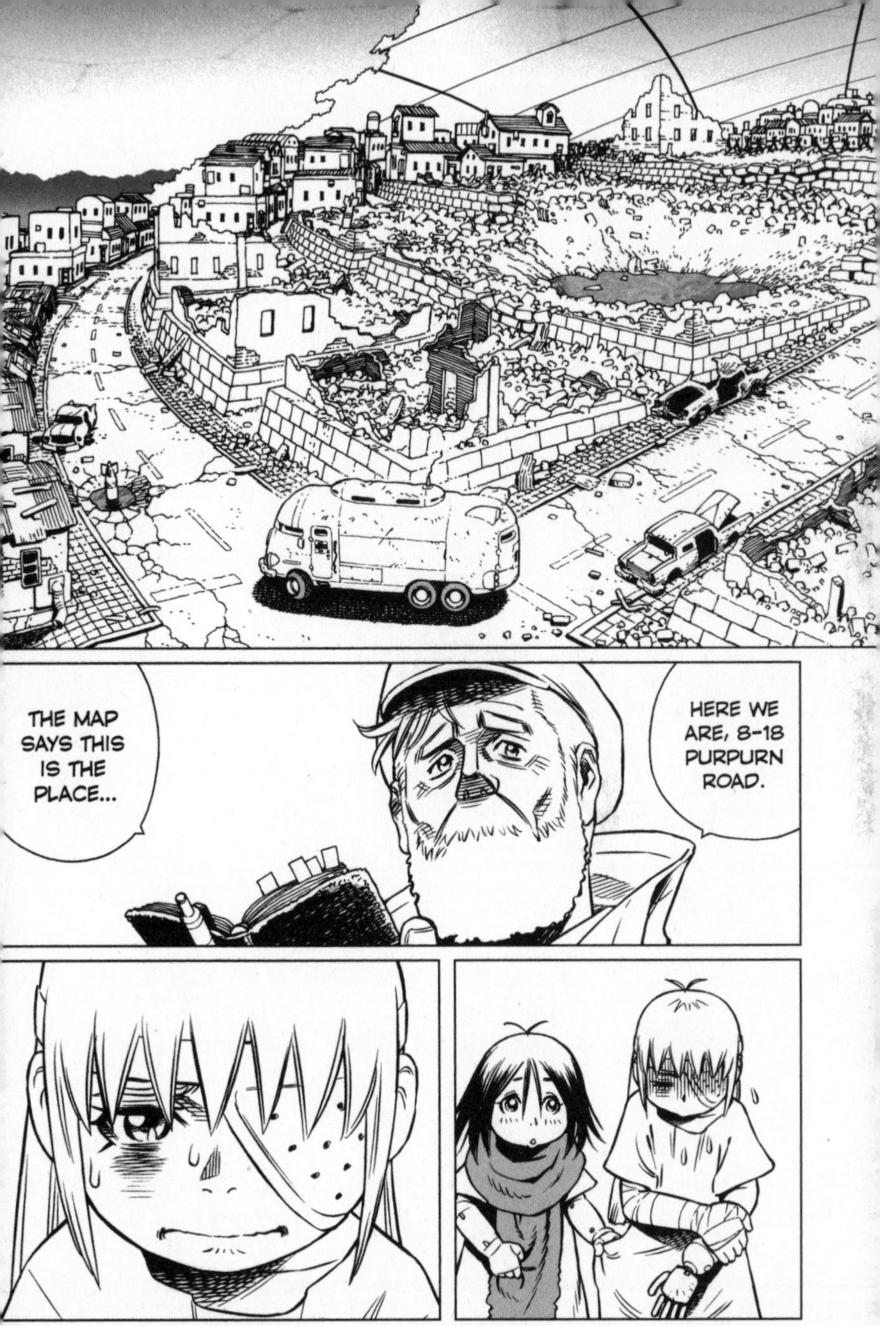
HERE WE ARE, 8-18 PURPURN ROAD.
THE MAP SAYS THIS IS THE PLACE...

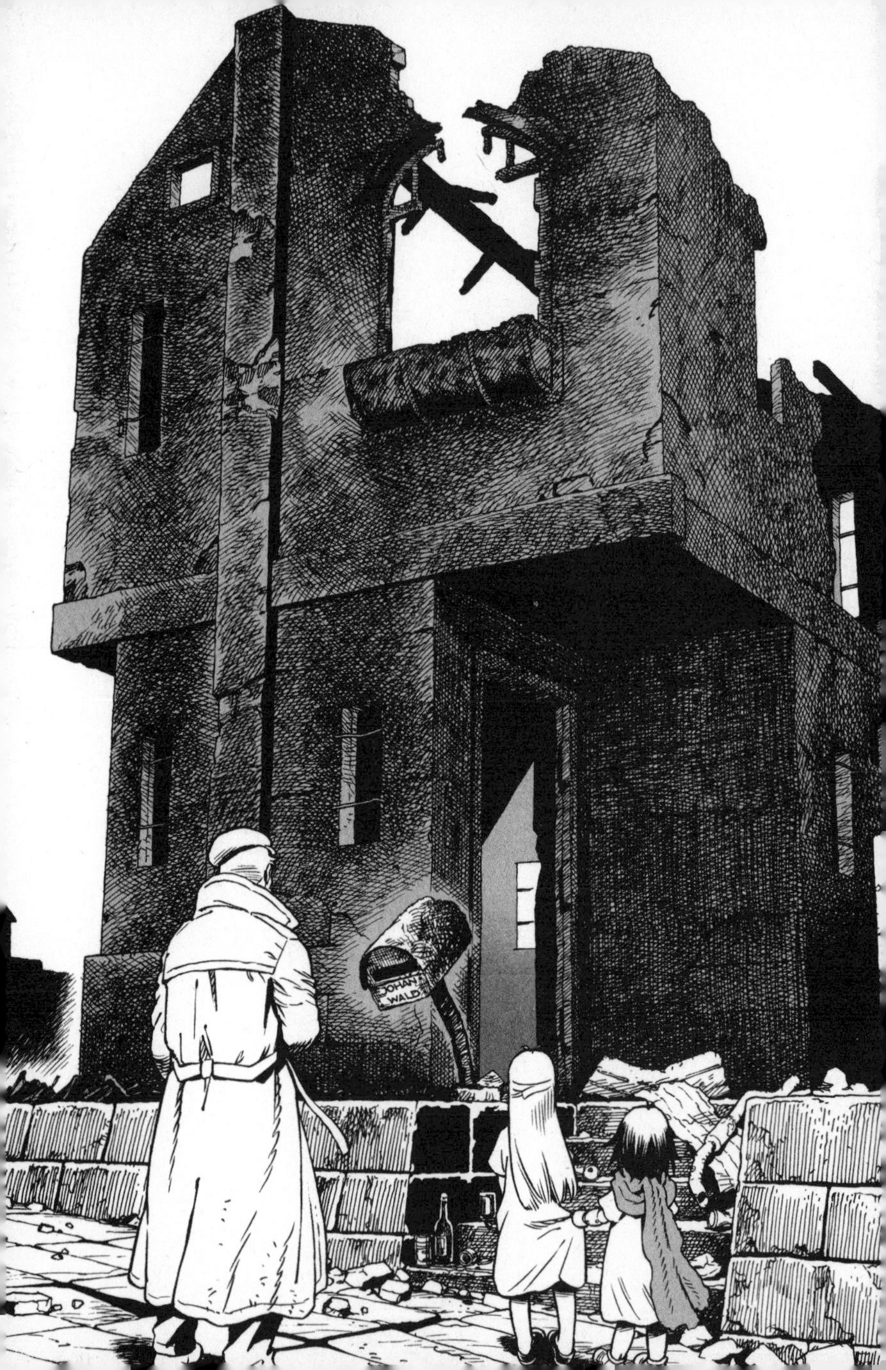
JOHAN
WALD

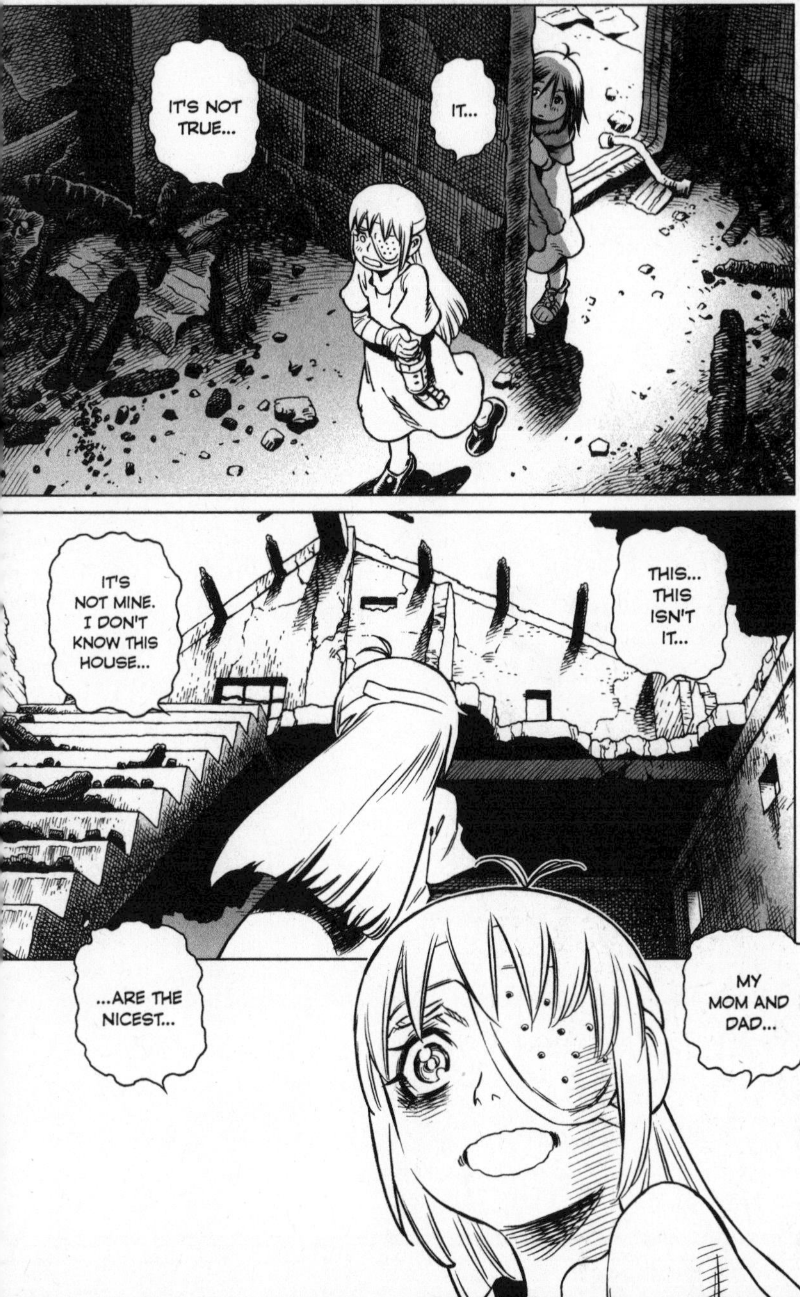
IT...
IT'S NOT TRUE...
THIS... THIS ISN'T IT...
IT'S NOT MINE. I DON'T KNOW THIS HOUSE...
MY MOM AND DAD...
...ARE THE NICEST...

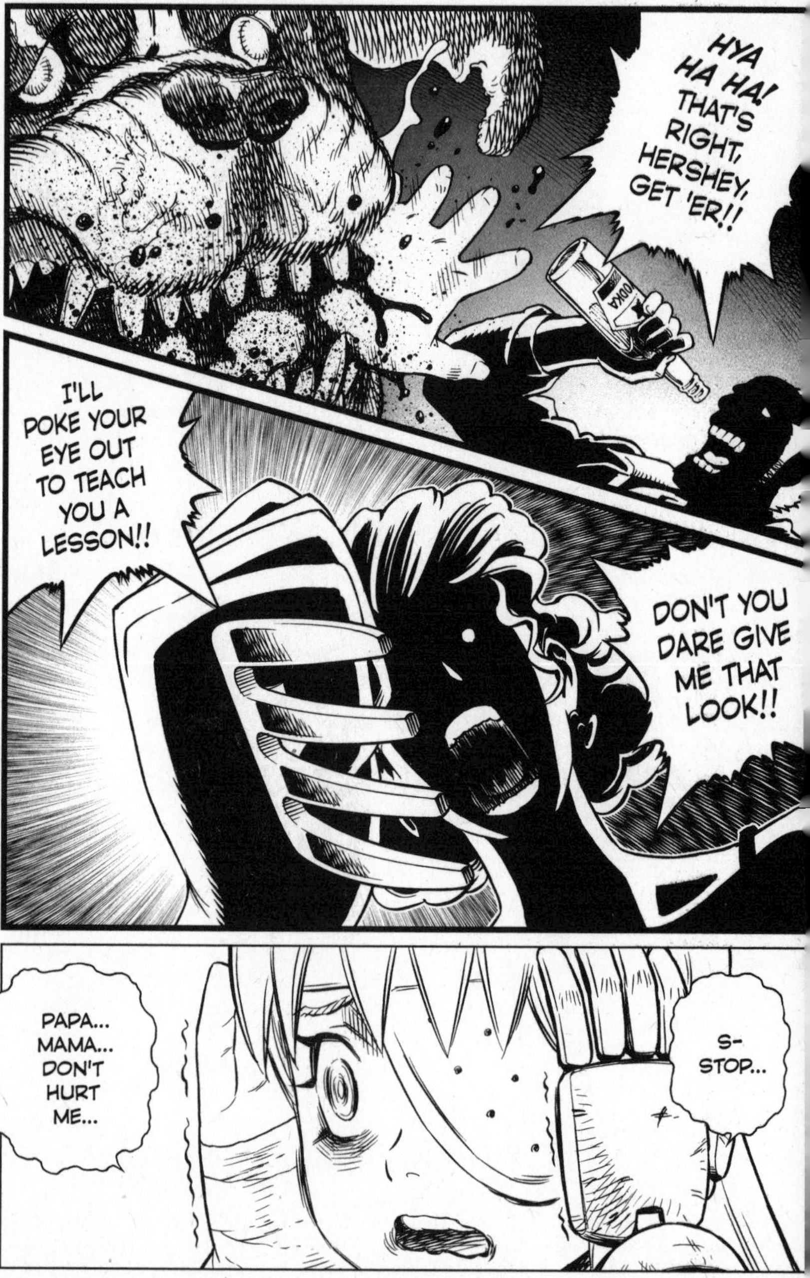
HYA HA HA! THAT'S RIGHT, HERSHEY, GET 'ER!!
DON'T YOU DARE GIVE ME THAT LOOK!!
I'LL POKE YOUR EYE OUT TO TEACH YOU A LESSON!!
S-STOP...
PAPA... MAMA... DON'T HURT ME...

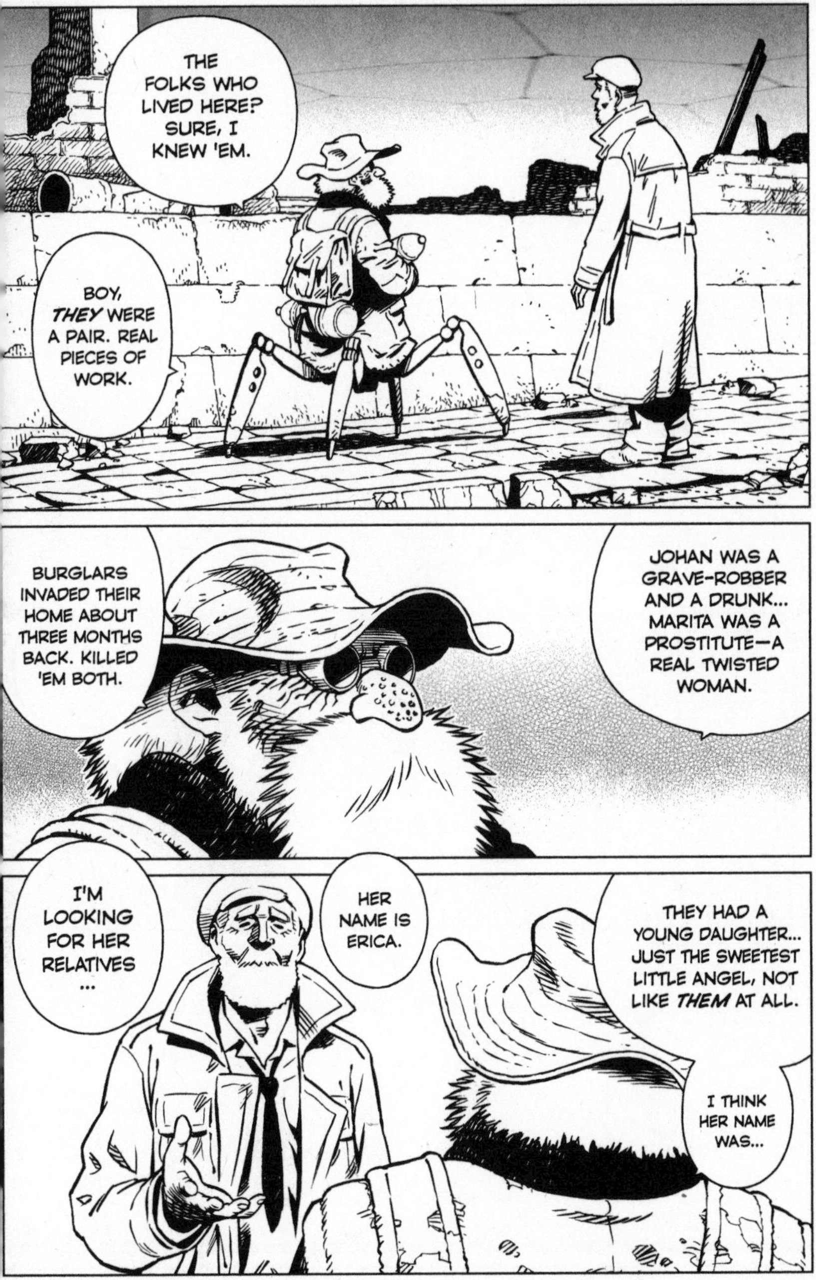
THE FOLKS WHO LIVED HERE? SURE, I KNEW 'EM.
BOY, THEY WERE A PAIR. REAL PIECES OF WORK.
JOHAN WAS A GRAVE-ROBBER AND A DRUNK... MARITA WAS A PROSTITUTE—A REAL TWISTED WOMAN.
BURGLARS INVADED THEIR HOME ABOUT THREE MONTHS BACK. KILLED 'EM BOTH.
THEY HAD A YOUNG DAUGHTER... JUST THE SWEETEST LITTLE ANGEL, NOT LIKE THEM AT ALL.
I THINK HER NAME WAS...
HER NAME IS ERICA.
I'M LOOKING FOR HER RELATIVES ...

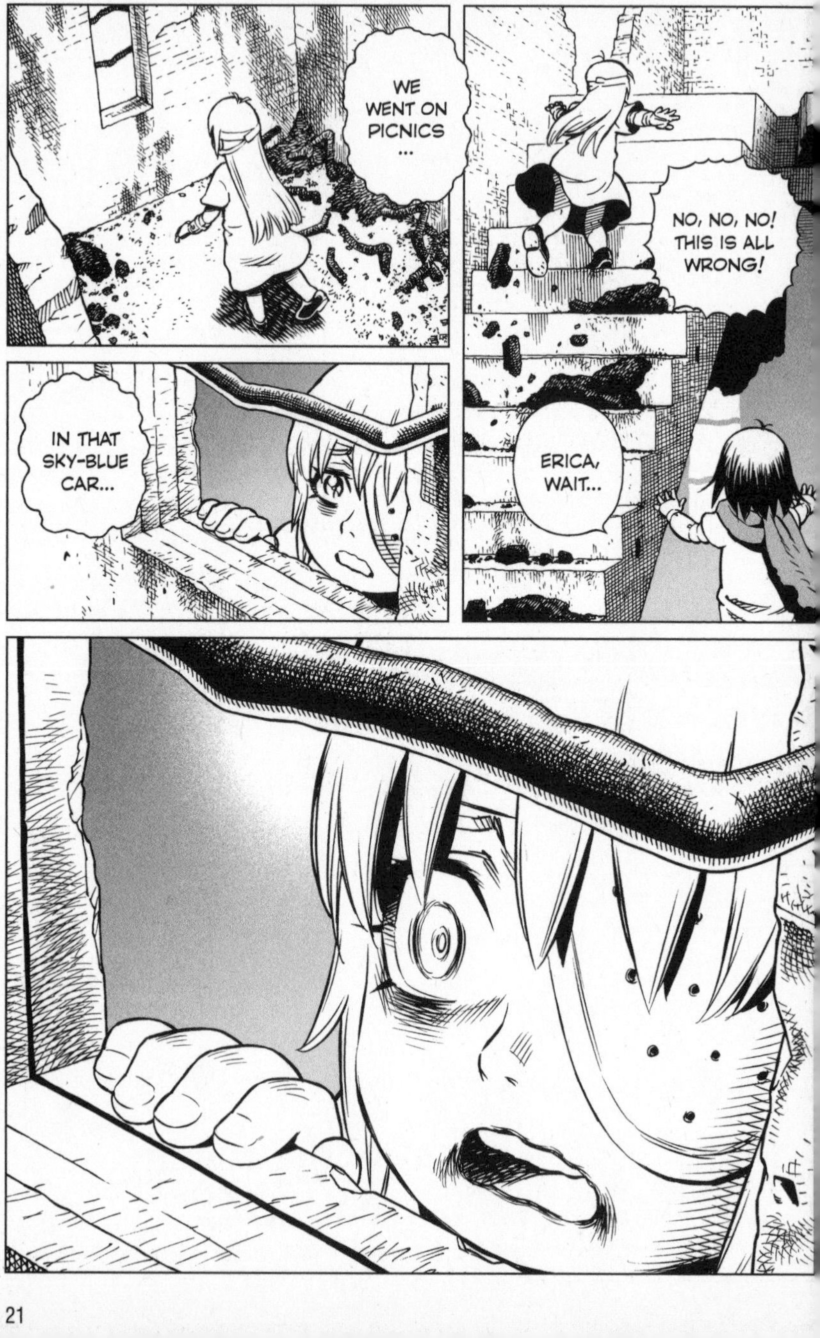
NO, NO, NO! THIS IS ALL WRONG!
ERICA, WAIT...
WE WENT ON PICNICS ...
IN THAT SKY-BLUE CAR...

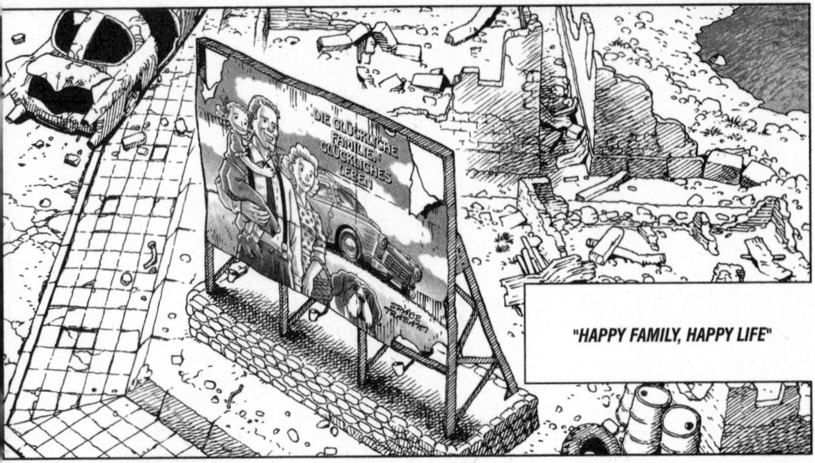
DIE GLÜCKLICHE FAMILIE, GLÜCKLICHES LEBEN
"HAPPY FAMILY, HAPPY LIFE"

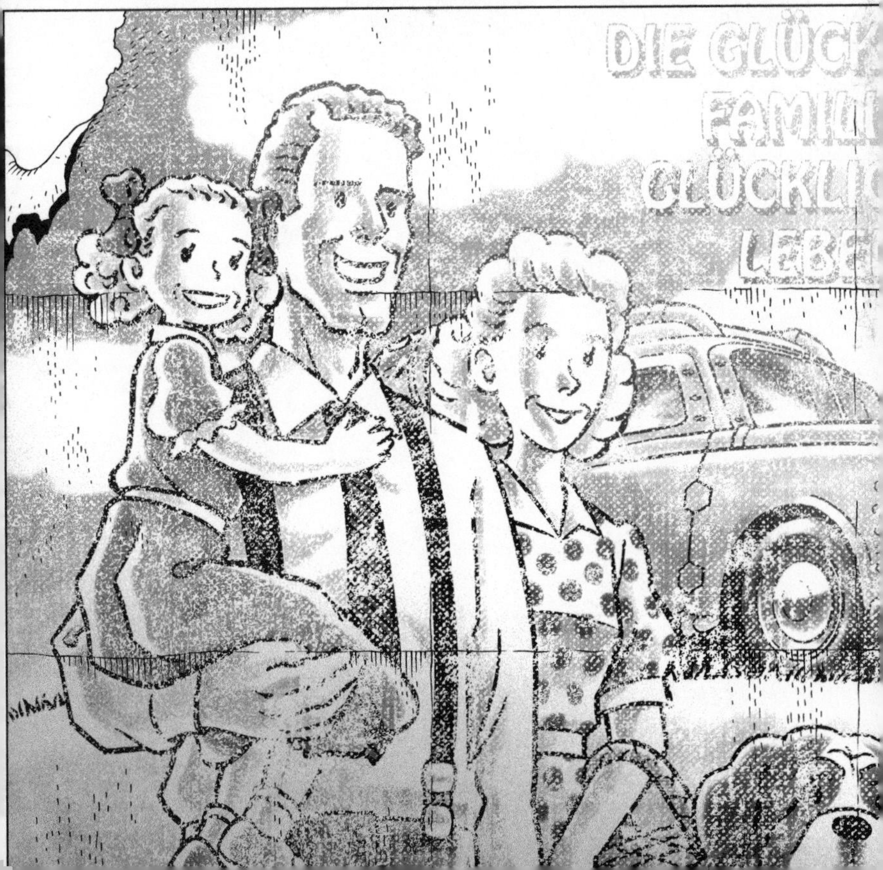
DIE GLÜCK
FAMILI
GLÜCKLIC
LEBE

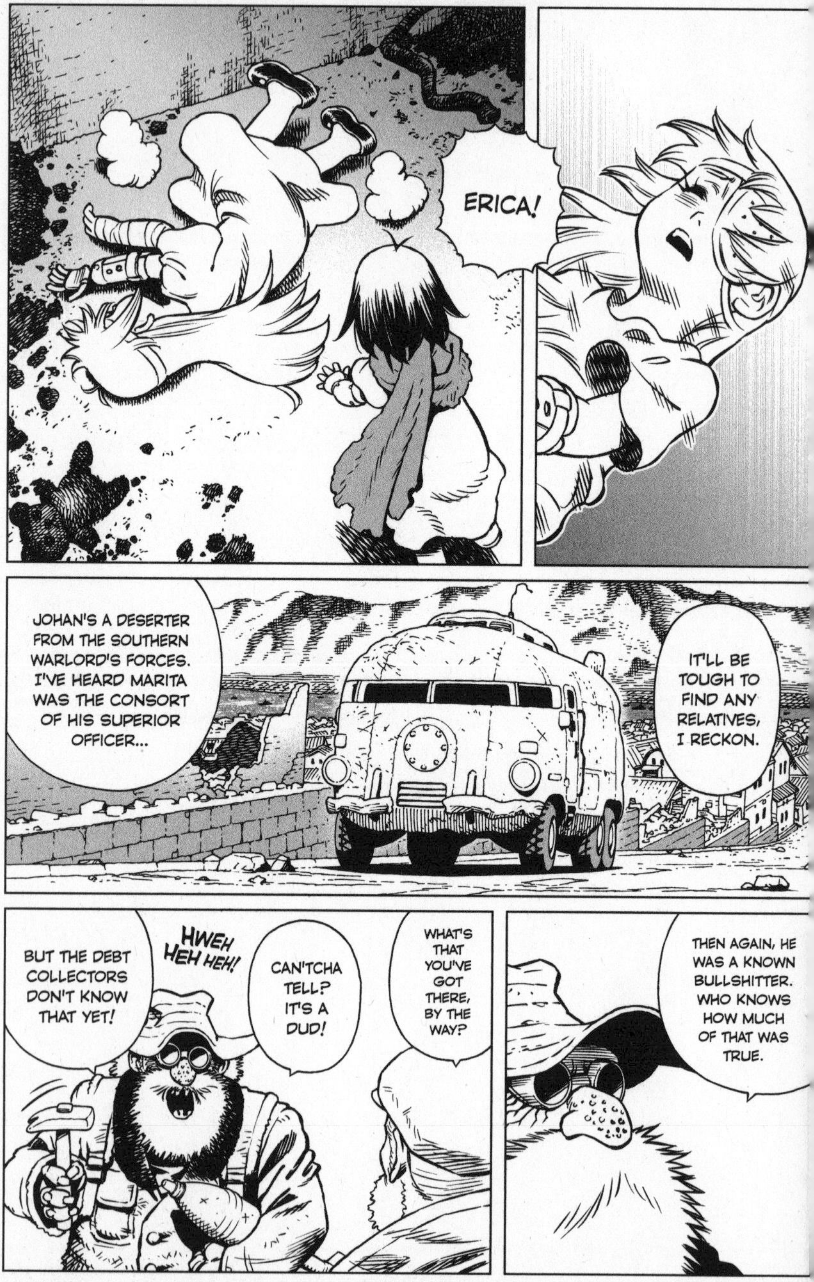
ERICA!
IT'LL BE TOUGH TO FIND ANY RELATIVES, I RECKON.
JOHAN'S A DESERTER FROM THE SOUTHERN WARLORD'S FORCES. I'VE HEARD MARITA WAS THE CONSORT OF HIS SUPERIOR OFFICER...
THEN AGAIN, HE WAS A KNOWN BULLSHITTER. WHO KNOWS HOW MUCH OF THAT WAS TRUE.
WHAT'S THAT YOU'VE GOT THERE, BY THE WAY?
CAN'TCHA TELL? IT'S A DUD!
HWEH HEH HEH!
BUT THE DEBT COLLECTORS DON'T KNOW THAT YET!

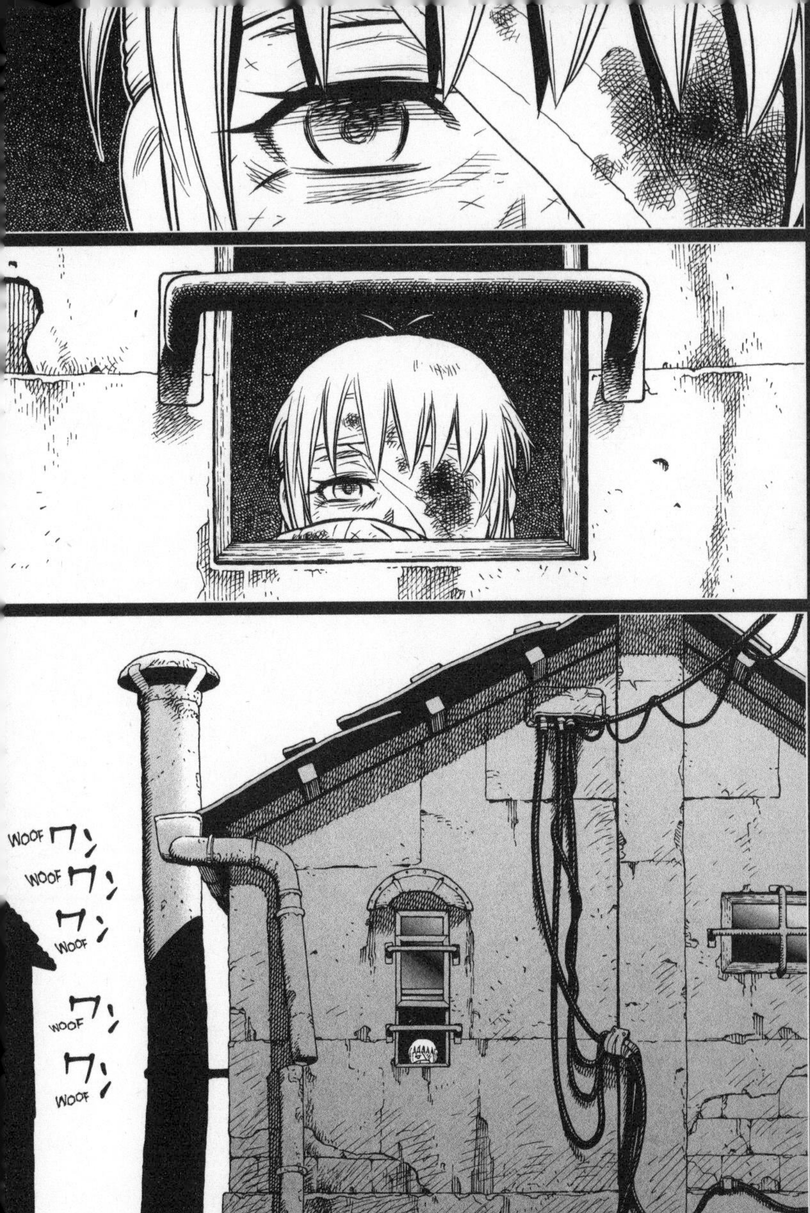
WOOF ワン
WOOF ワン
ワン WOOF
ワン WOOF
ワン WOOF

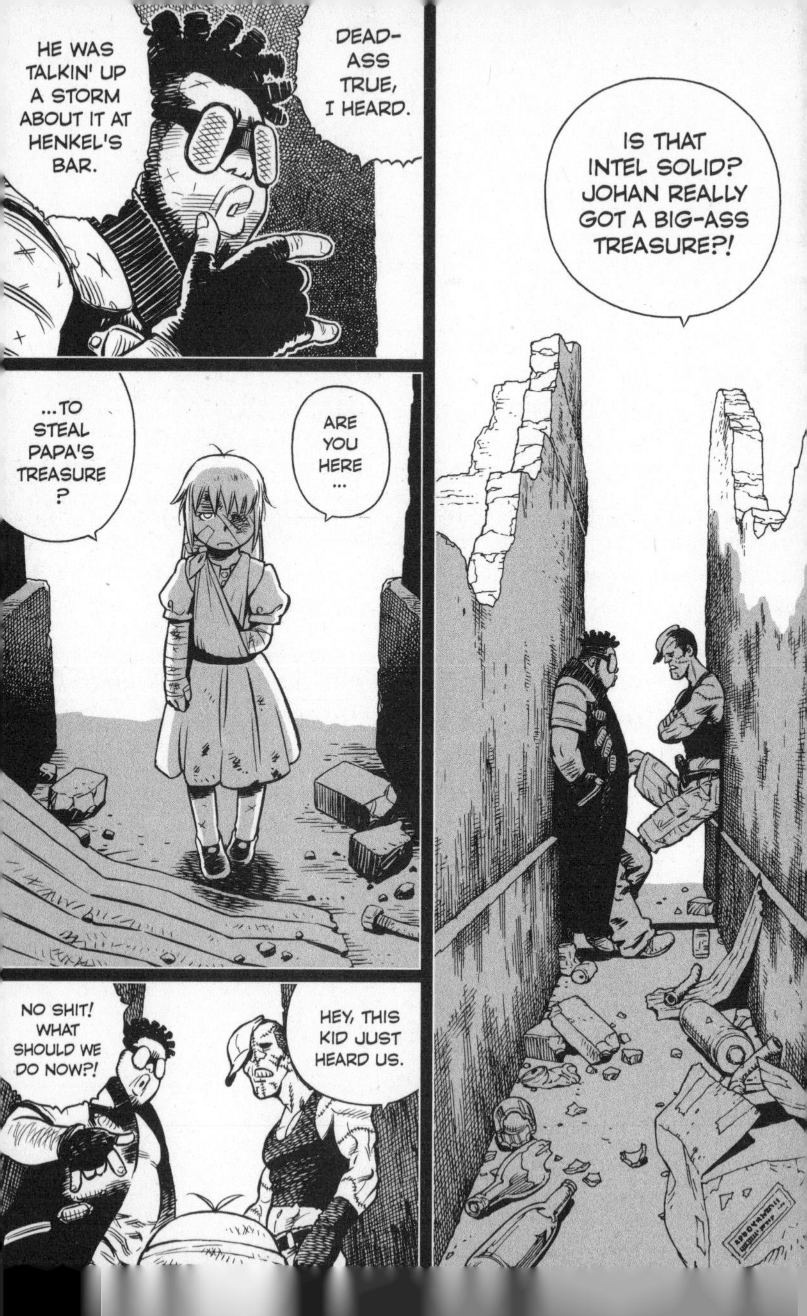
IS THAT INTEL SOLID? JOHAN REALLY GOT A BIG-ASS TREASURE?!
DEAD-ASS TRUE, I HEARD.
HE WAS TALKIN' UP A STORM ABOUT IT AT HENKEL'S BAR.
ARE YOU HERE ...
...TO STEAL PAPA'S TREASURE ?
HEY, THIS KID JUST HEARD US.
NO SHIT! WHAT SHOULD WE DO NOW?!

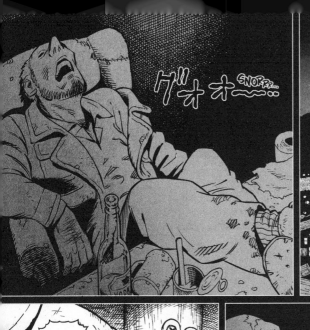

SNORRR...

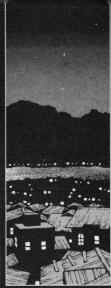

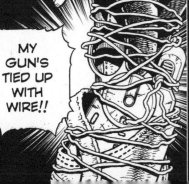

WHA ...?!

MY GUN'S TIED UP WITH WIRE!!

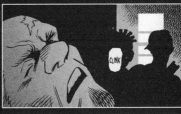

CLINK

WHO'S THERE ?!

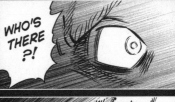

SWISH

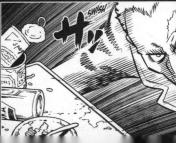

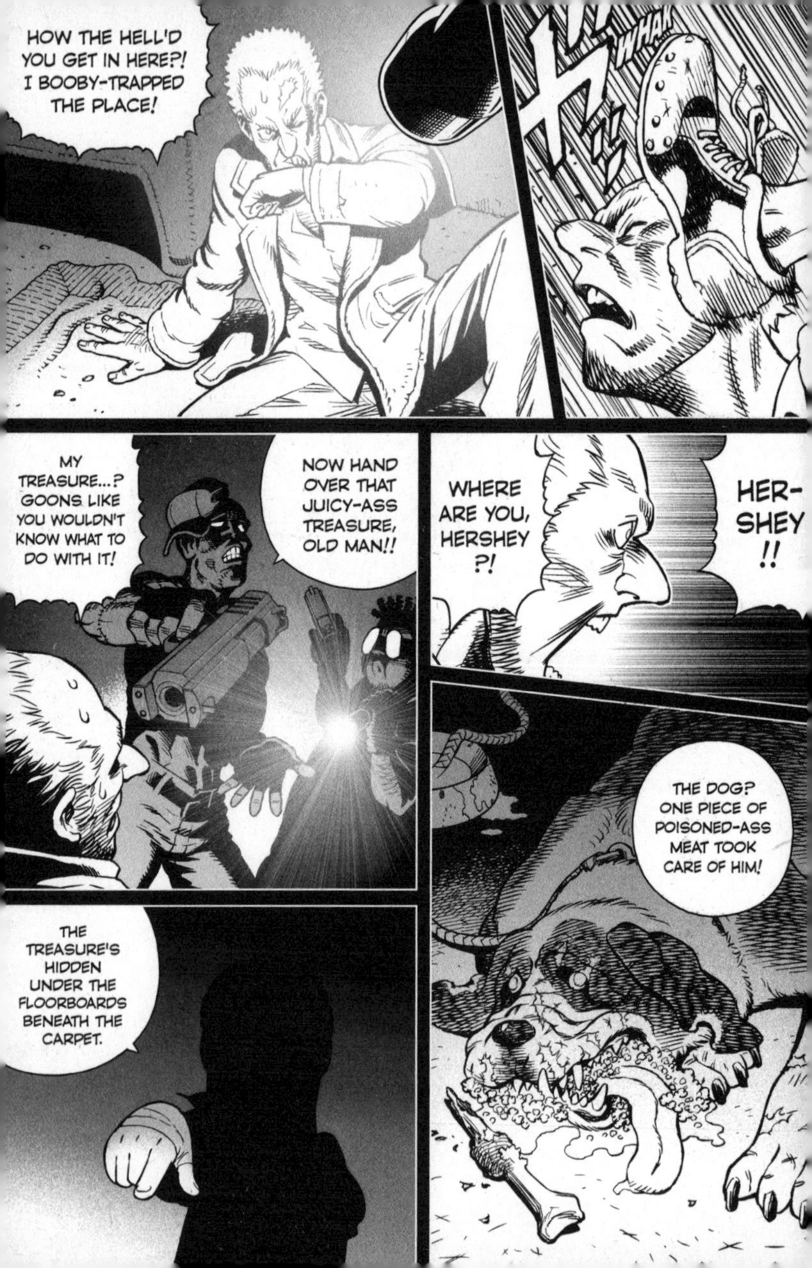
WHAK
HOW THE HELL'D YOU GET IN HERE?! I BOOBY-TRAPPED THE PLACE!
HER-SHEY !!
WHERE ARE YOU, HERSHEY ?!
NOW HAND OVER THAT JUICY-ASS TREASURE, OLD MAN!!
MY TREASURE...? GOONS LIKE YOU WOULDN'T KNOW WHAT TO DO WITH IT!
THE DOG? ONE PIECE OF POISONED-ASS MEAT TOOK CARE OF HIM!
THE TREASURE'S HIDDEN UNDER THE FLOORBOARDS BENEATH THE CARPET.

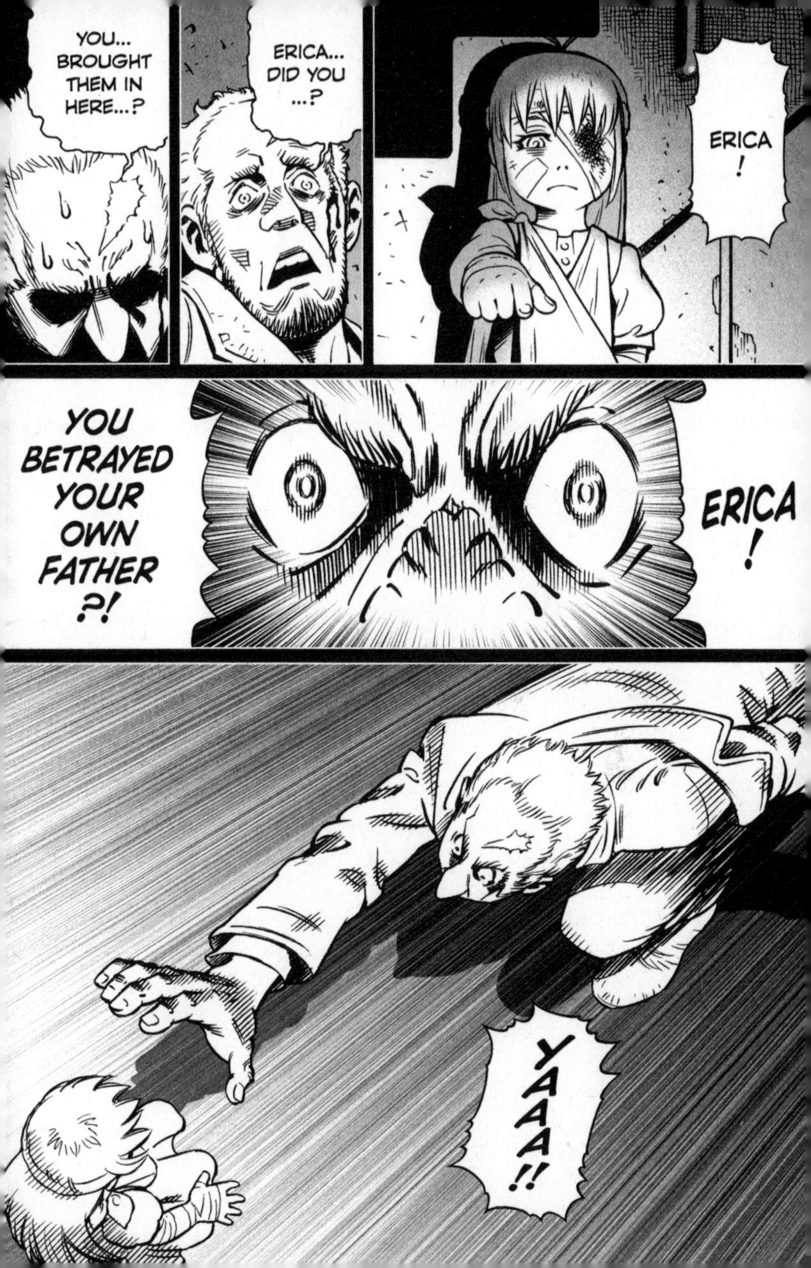
ERICA!
ERICA... DID YOU ...?
YOU... BROUGHT THEM IN HERE...?
ERICA!
YOU BETRAYED YOUR OWN FATHER ?!
YAAAA!!

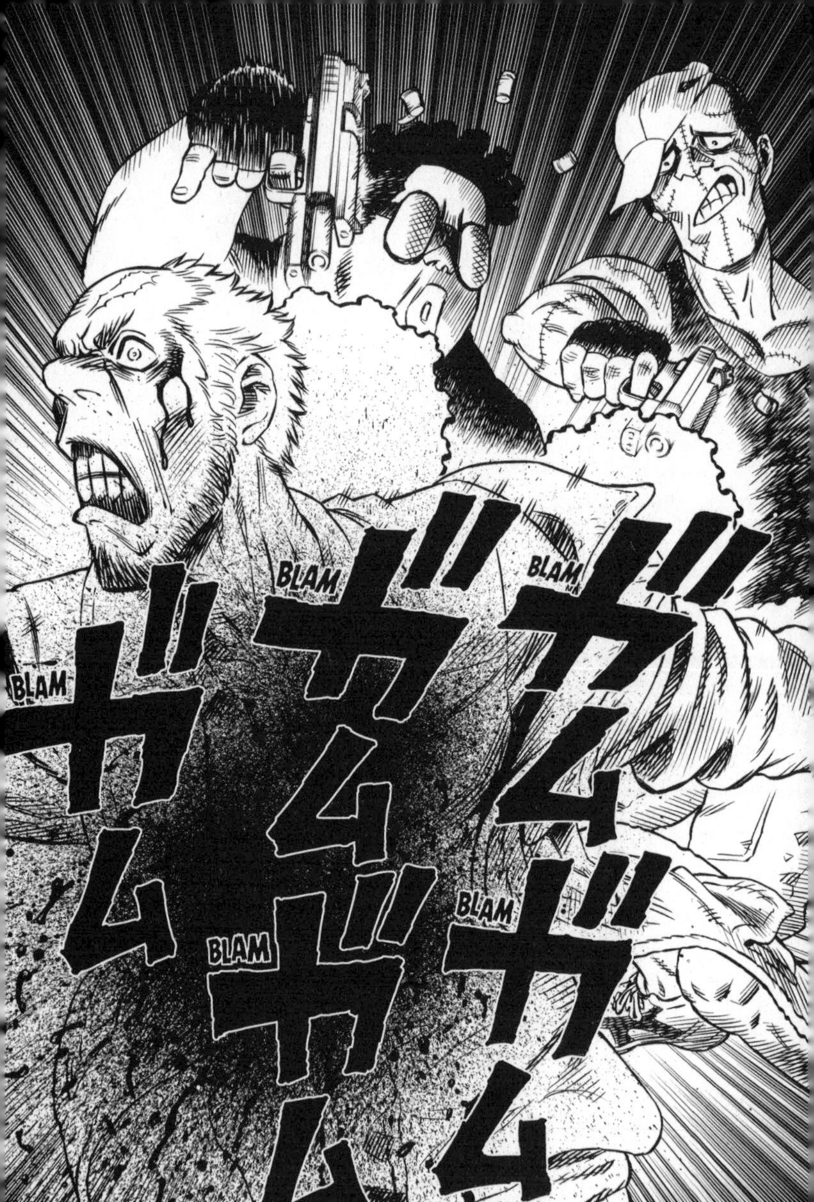
BLAM
BLAM
BLAM
BLAM
BLAM

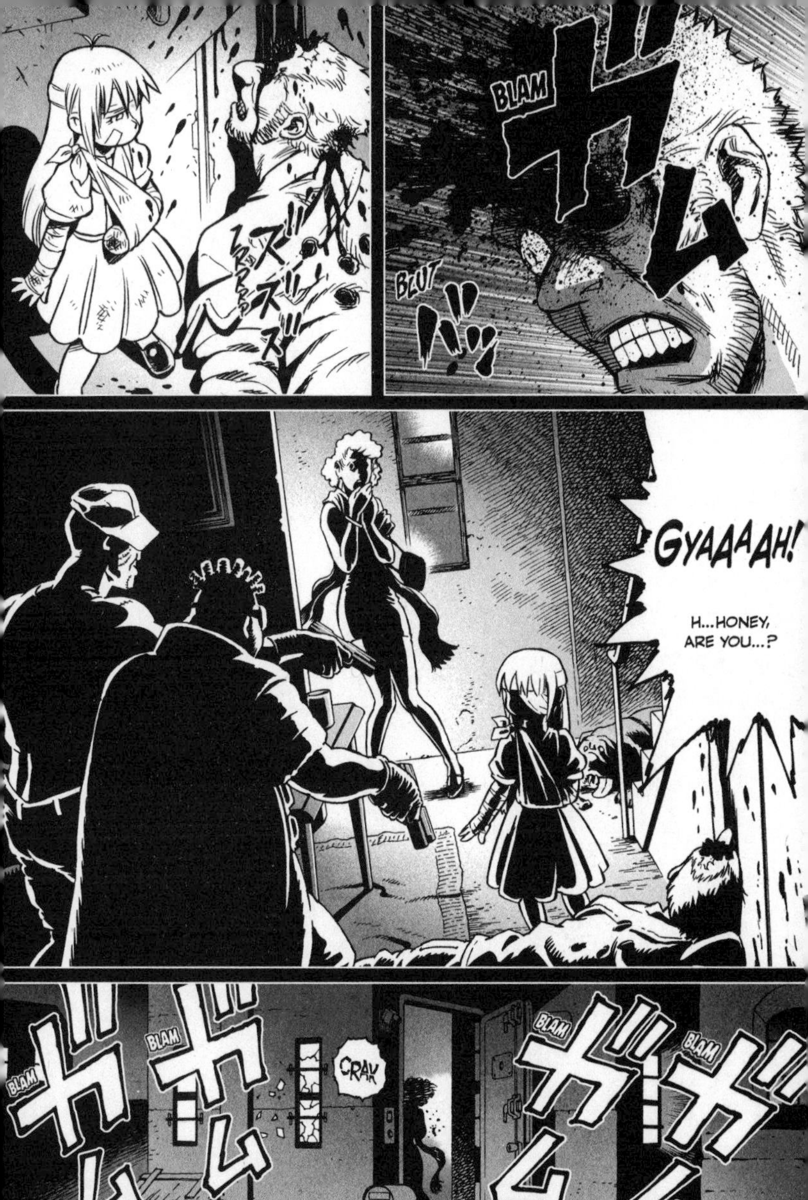
BLAM
BLUT
GYAAAAH!
H...HONEY, ARE YOU...?
BLAM
BLAM
CRAK
BLAM
BLAM

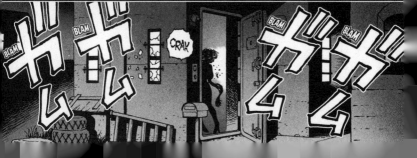

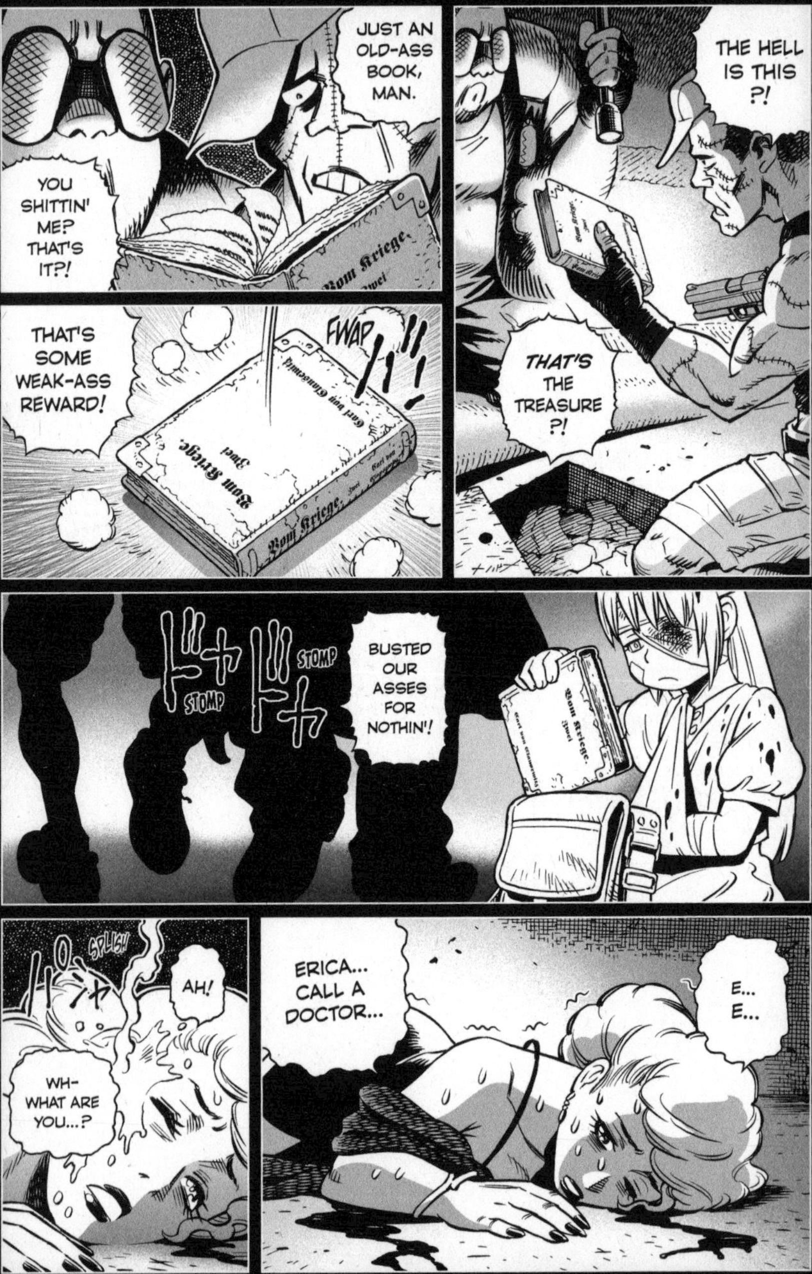
THE HELL IS THIS?!
THAT'S THE TREASURE?!
JUST AN OLD-ASS BOOK, MAN.
YOU SHITTIN' ME? THAT'S IT?!
FWAP
THAT'S SOME WEAK-ASS REWARD!
BUSTED OUR ASSES FOR NOTHIN'!
ドッ STOMP
ドッ STOMP
E... E...
ERICA... CALL A DOCTOR...
パシャ SPLISH
AH!
WH- WHAT ARE YOU...?

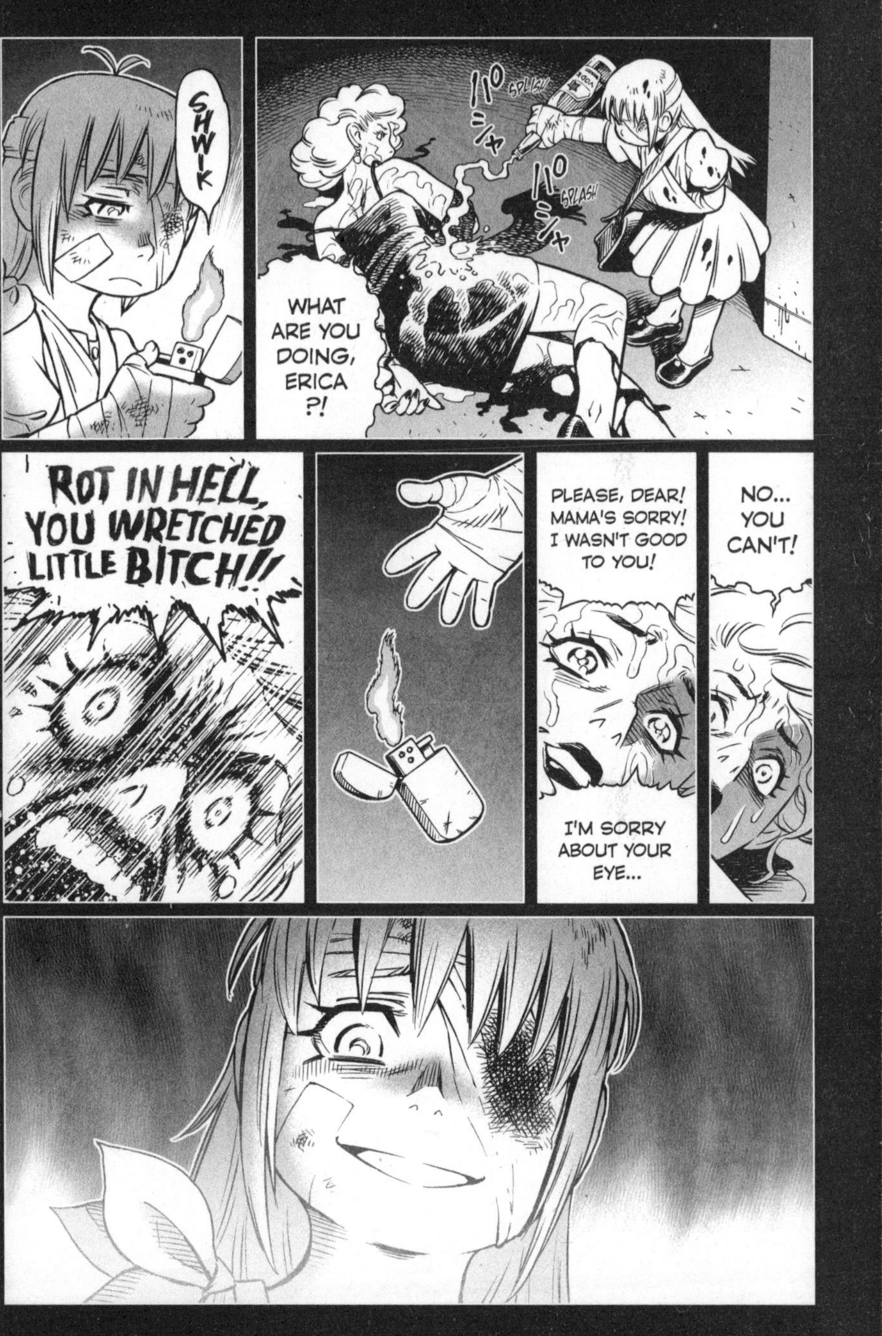
パシャ
SPLISH
パシャ
SPLASH
WHAT ARE YOU DOING, ERICA ?!
SHWIK
NO... YOU CAN'T!
PLEASE, DEAR! MAMA'S SORRY! I WASN'T GOOD TO YOU!
I'M SORRY ABOUT YOUR EYE...
ROT IN HELL, YOU WRETCHED LITTLE BITCH!!

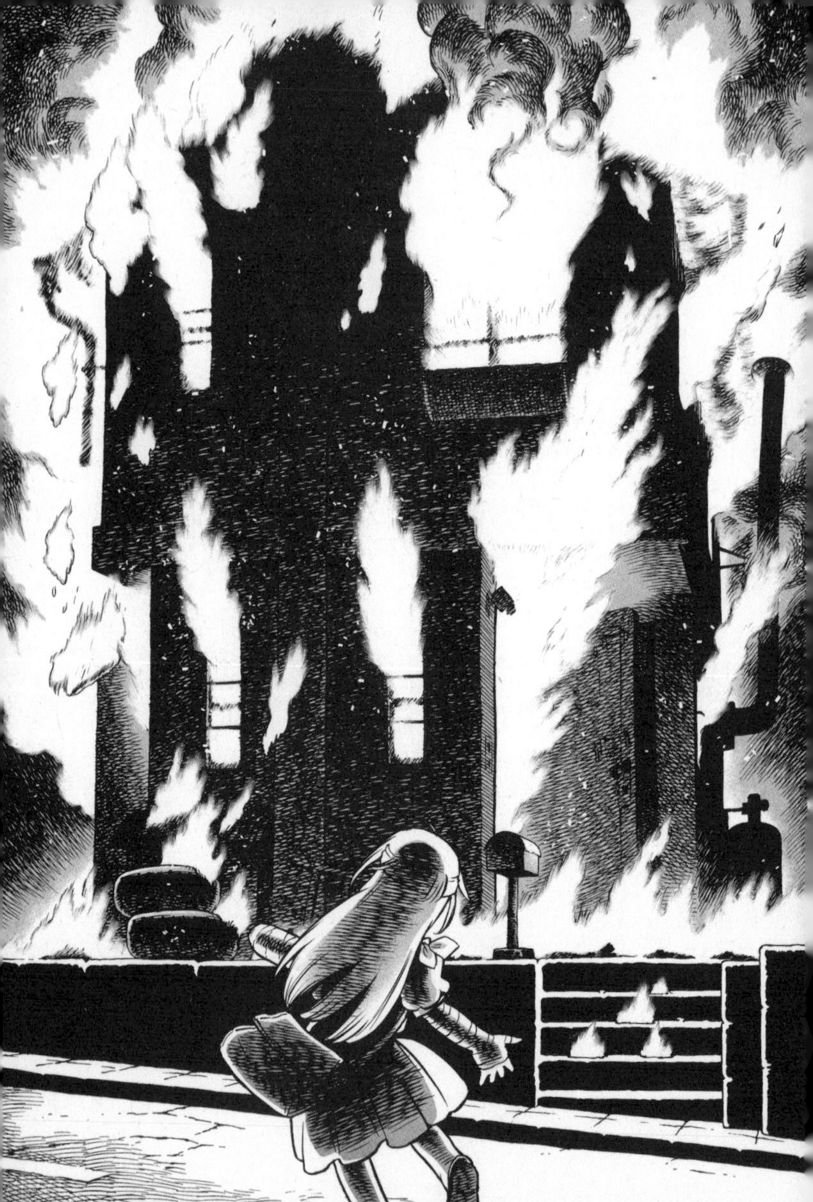

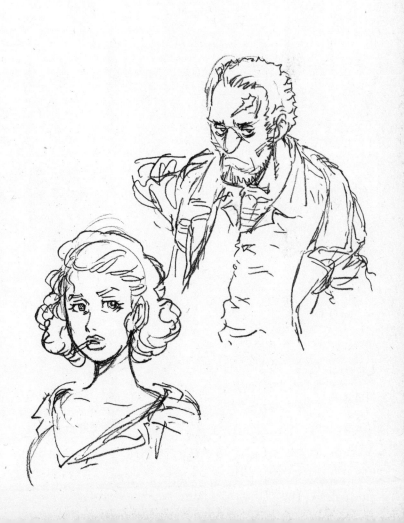

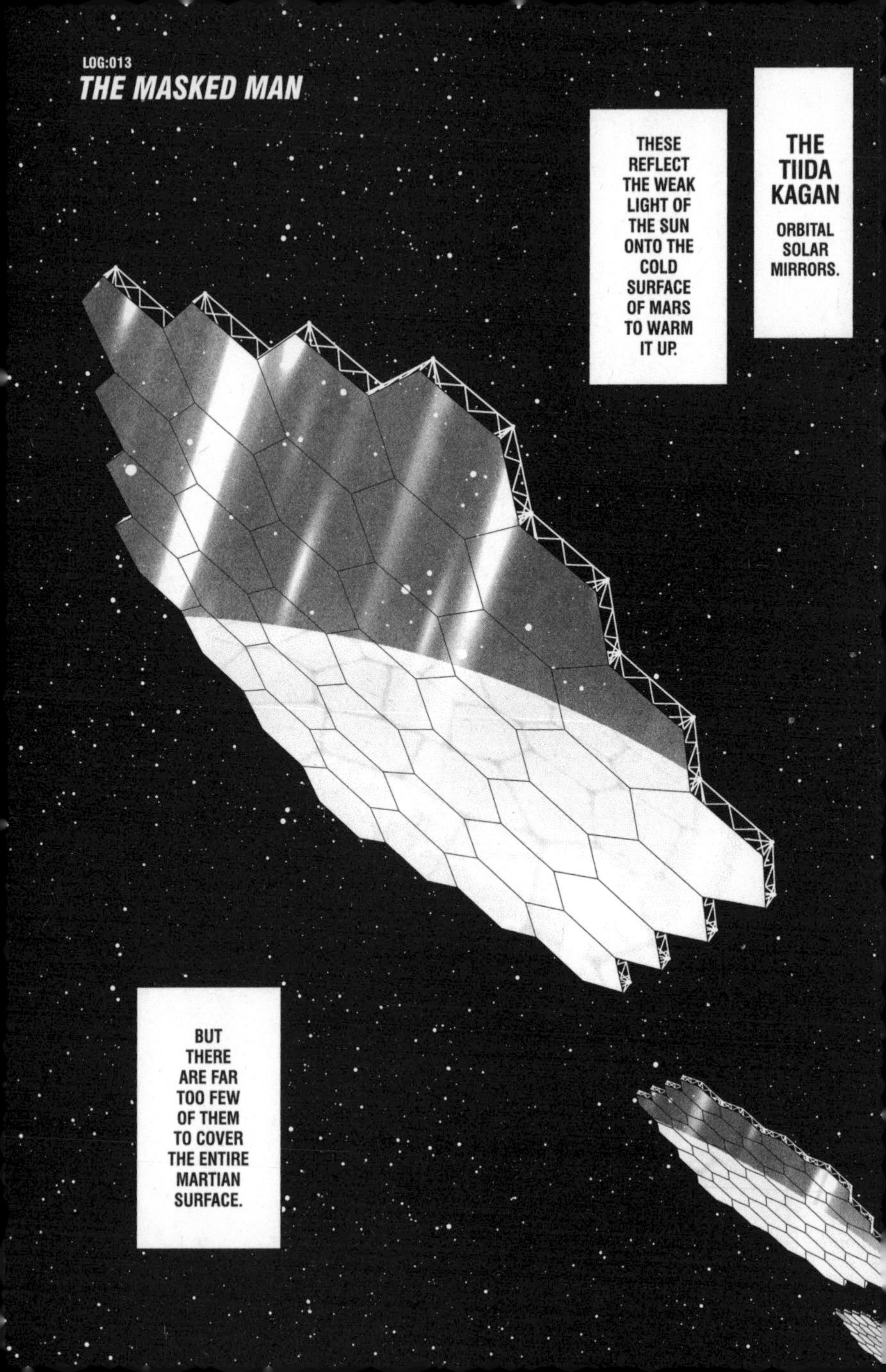
LOG:013
THE MASKED MAN
THE TIIDA KAGAN ORBITAL SOLAR MIRRORS.
THESE REFLECT THE WEAK LIGHT OF THE SUN ONTO THE COLD SURFACE OF MARS TO WARM IT UP.
BUT THERE ARE FAR TOO FEW OF THEM TO COVER THE ENTIRE MARTIAN SURFACE.

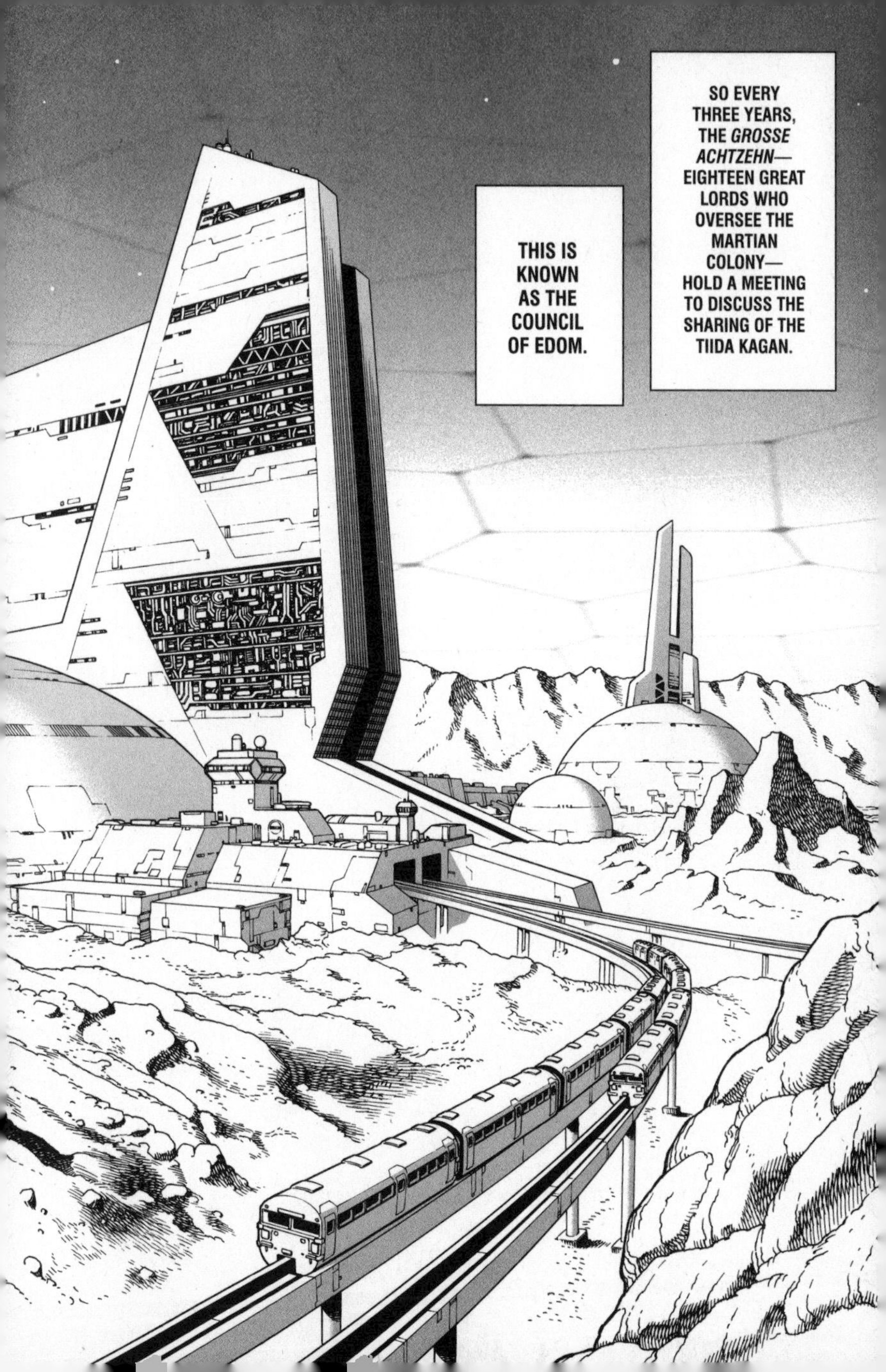
SO EVERY THREE YEARS, THE *GROSSE ACHTZEHN*—EIGHTEEN GREAT LORDS WHO OVERSEE THE MARTIAN COLONY—HOLD A MEETING TO DISCUSS THE SHARING OF THE TIIDA KAGAN.
THIS IS KNOWN AS THE COUNCIL OF EDOM.

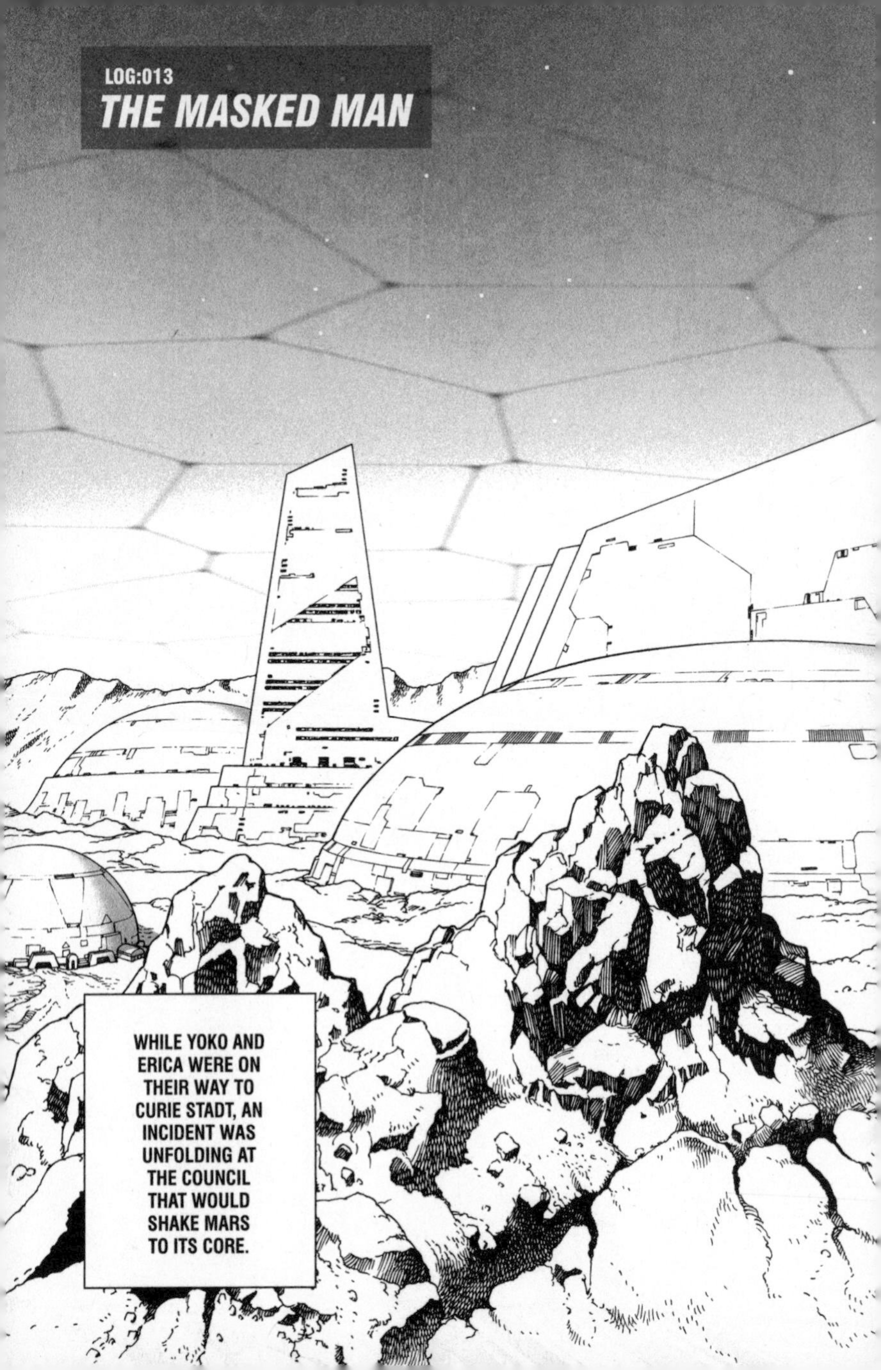
LOG:013
THE MASKED MAN
WHILE YOKO AND ERICA WERE ON THEIR WAY TO CURIE STADT, AN INCIDENT WAS UNFOLDING AT THE COUNCIL THAT WOULD SHAKE MARS TO ITS CORE.

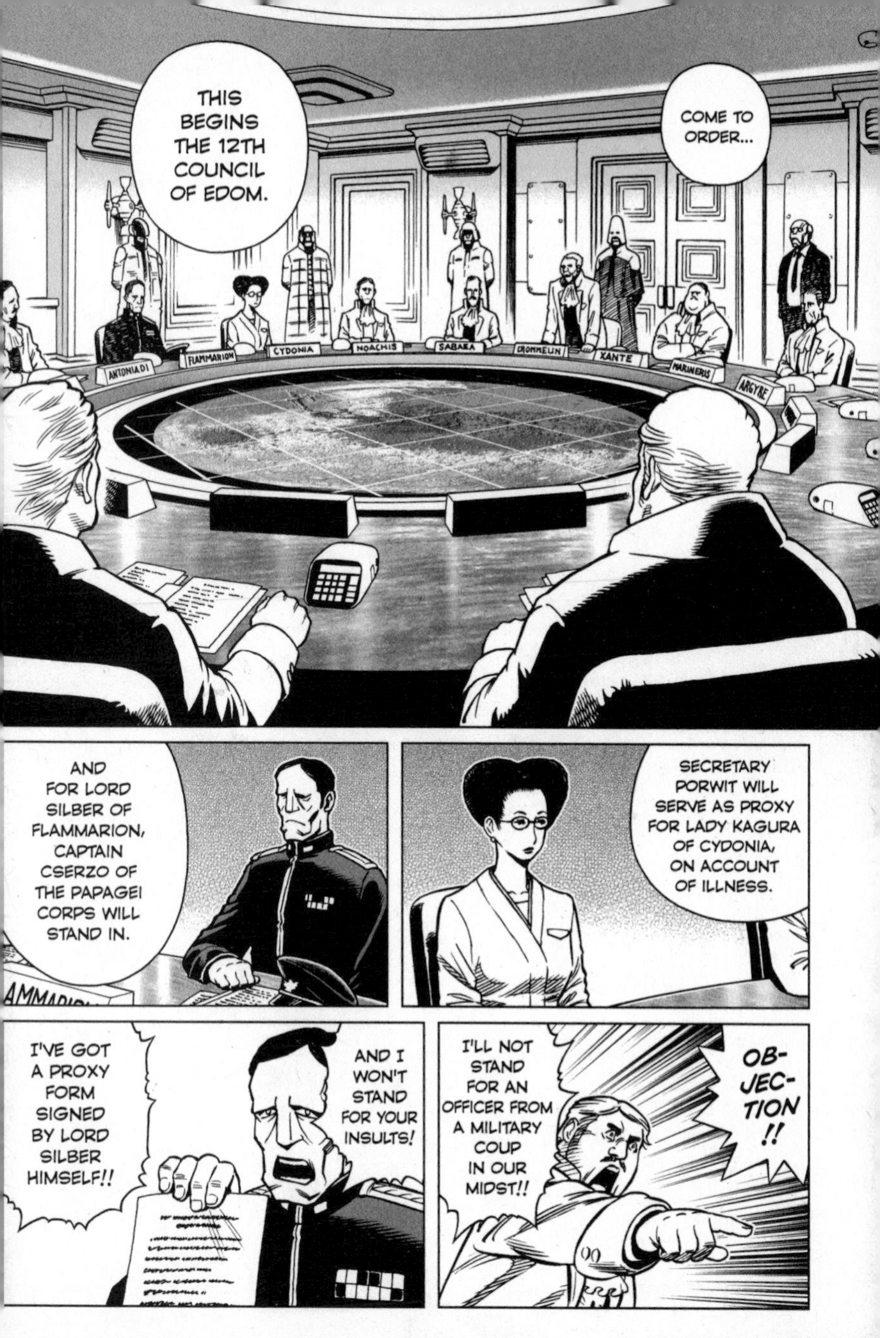
COME TO ORDER...
THIS BEGINS THE 12TH COUNCIL OF EDOM.
ARGYRE
MARINERIS
XANTE
SABAEA
NOACHIS
CYDONIA
FLAMMARION
ANTONIADI
SECRETARY PORWIT WILL SERVE AS PROXY FOR LADY KAGURA OF CYDONIA, ON ACCOUNT OF ILLNESS.
AND FOR LORD SILBER OF FLAMMARION, CAPTAIN CSERZO OF THE PAPAGEI CORPS WILL STAND IN.
OB-JEC-TION!!
I'LL NOT STAND FOR AN OFFICER FROM A MILITARY COUP IN OUR MIDST!!
AND I WON'T STAND FOR YOUR INSULTS!
I'VE GOT A PROXY FORM SIGNED BY LORD SILBER HIMSELF!!

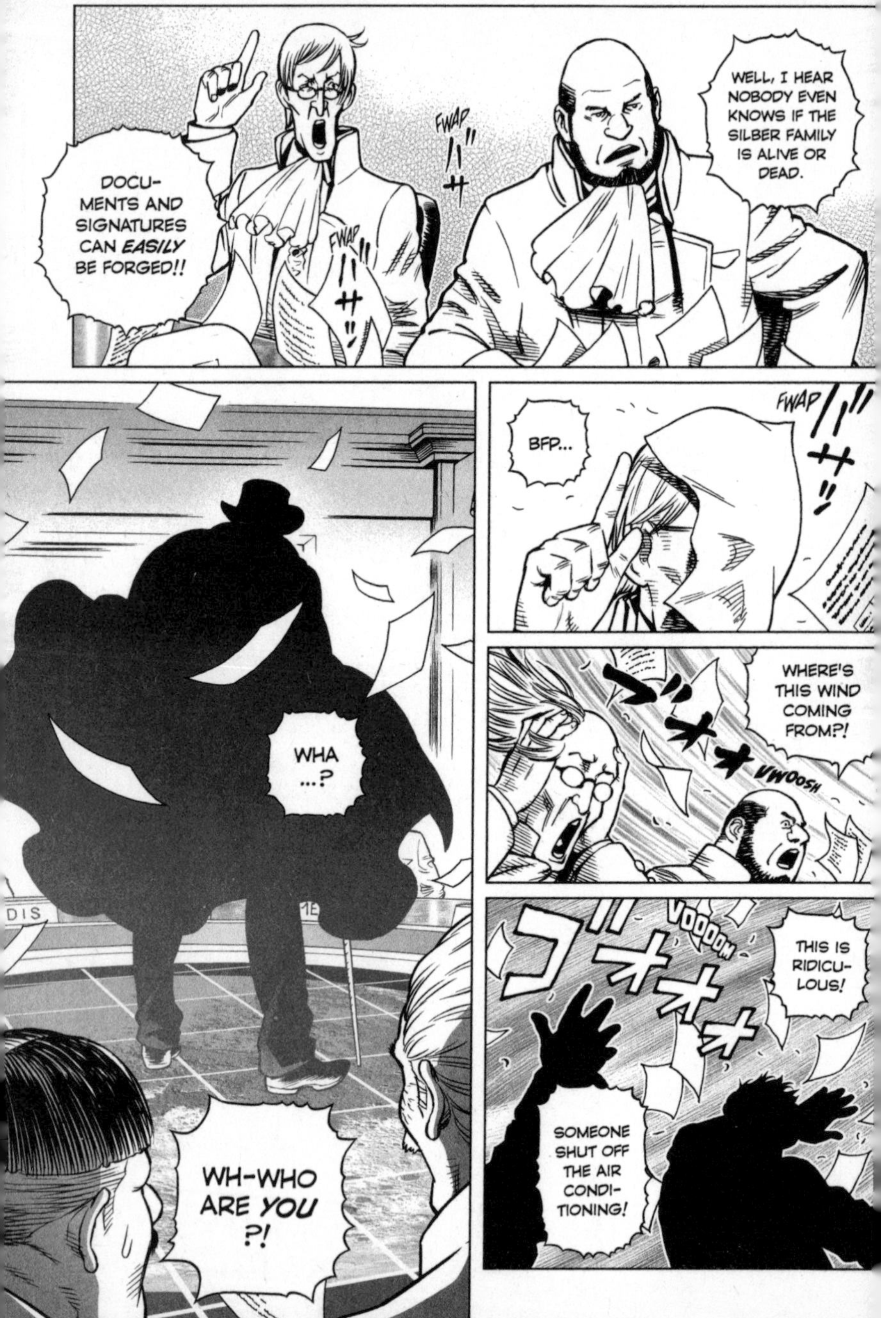
WELL, I HEAR NOBODY EVEN KNOWS IF THE SILBER FAMILY IS ALIVE OR DEAD.
FWAP
DOCU-MENTS AND SIGNATURES CAN *EASILY* BE FORGED!!
FWAP
FWAP
BFP...
WHERE'S THIS WIND COMING FROM?!
VWOOSH
THIS IS RIDICU-LOUS!
VOOOOM
SOMEONE SHUT OFF THE AIR CONDI-TIONING!
WHA ...?
DIS
WH-WHO ARE *YOU* ?!

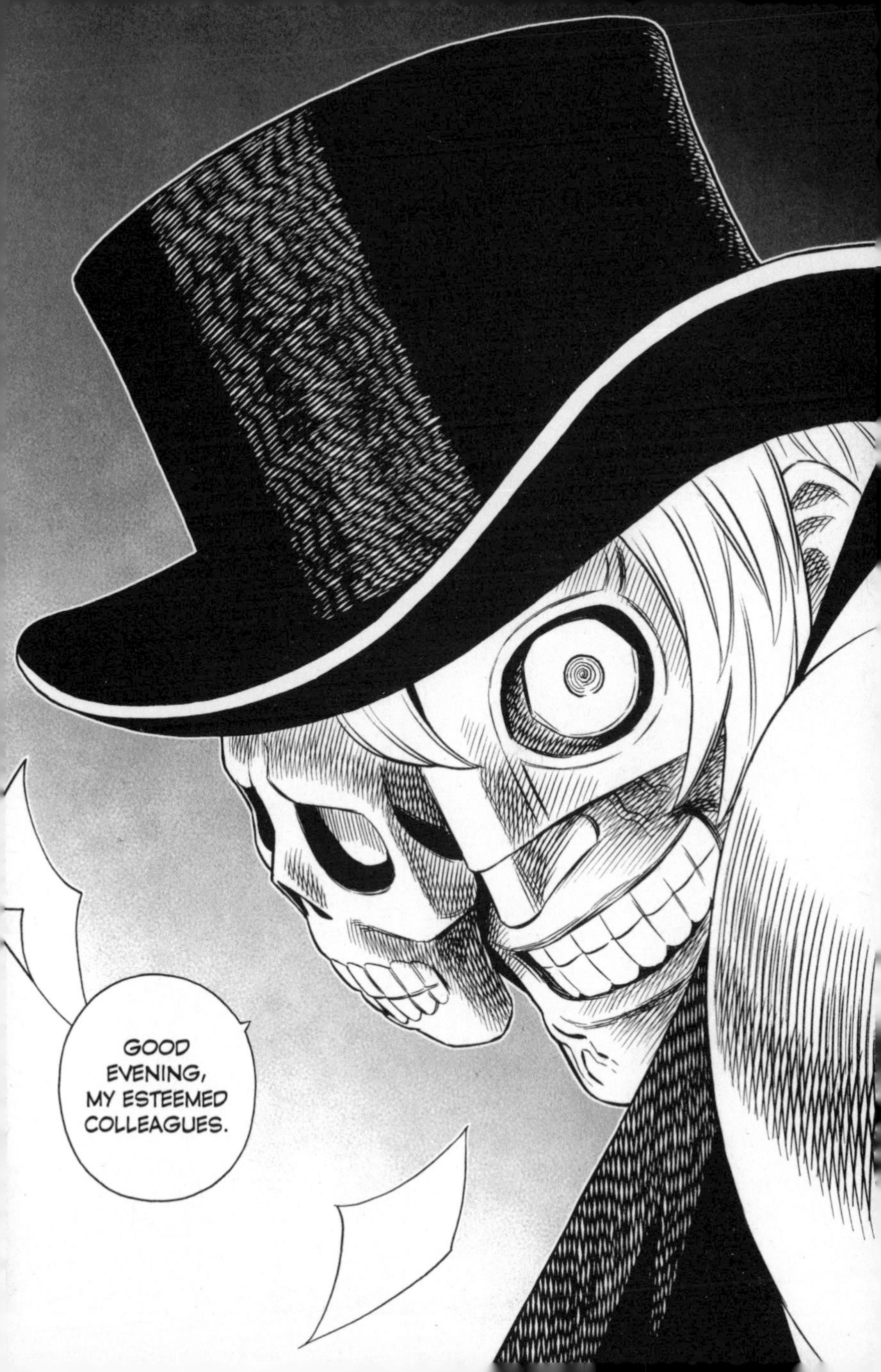
GOOD EVENING, MY ESTEEMED COLLEAGUES.

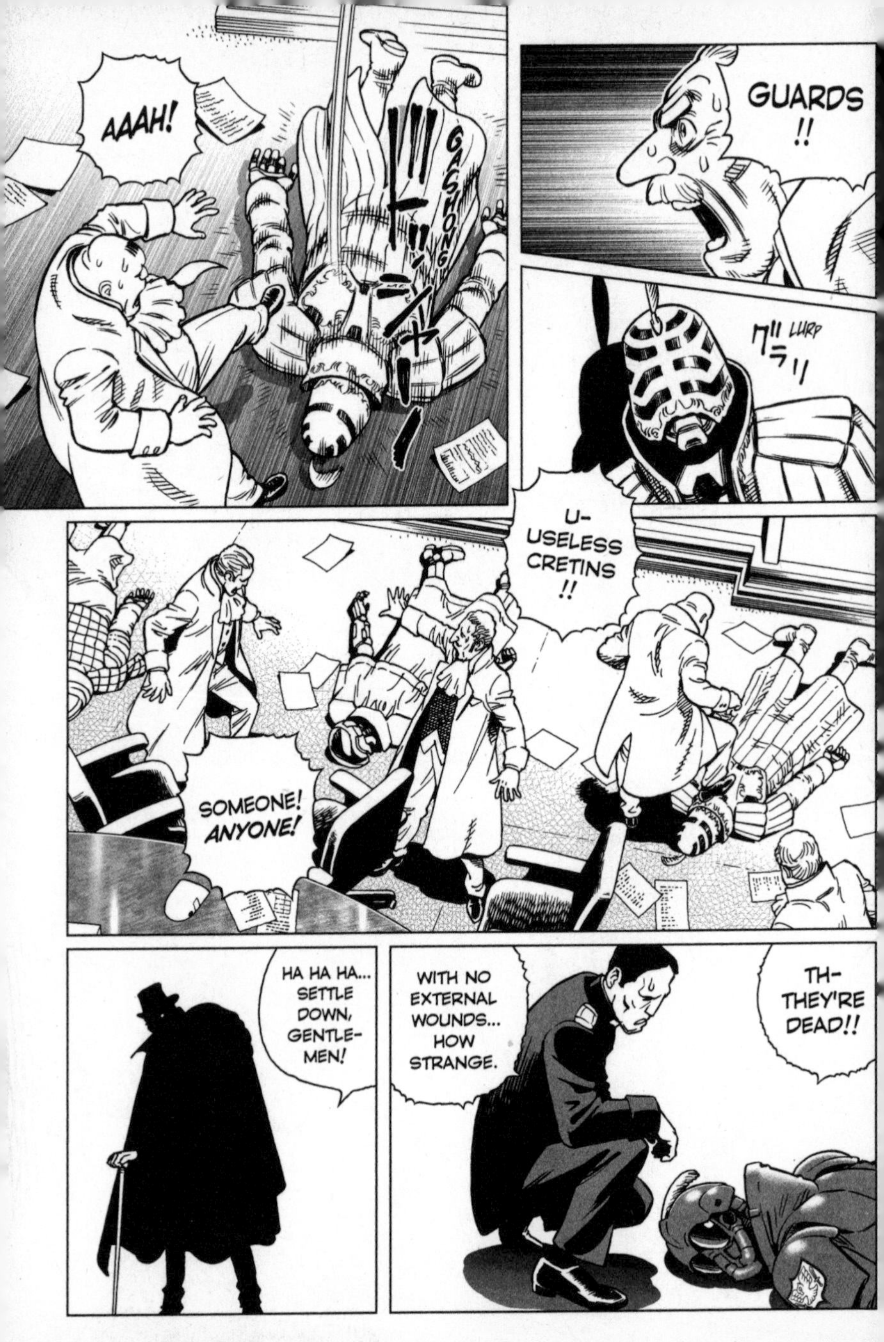

GUARDS!!
グラッ
LURP
GASHONG
AAAH!
U-USELESS CRETINS!!
SOMEONE! ANYONE!
TH-THEY'RE DEAD!!
WITH NO EXTERNAL WOUNDS... HOW STRANGE.
HA HA HA... SETTLE DOWN, GENTLE-MEN!

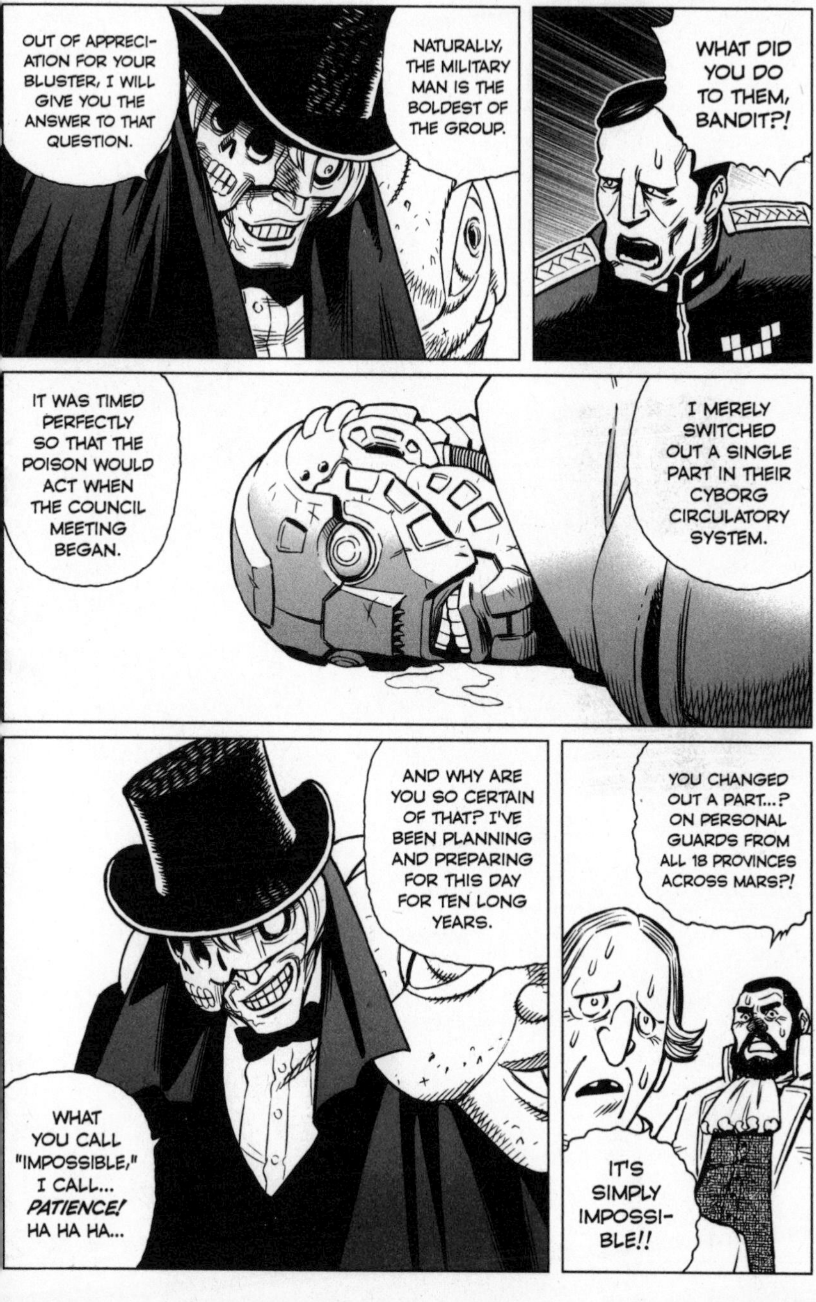
WHAT DID YOU DO TO THEM, BANDIT?!
NATURALLY, THE MILITARY MAN IS THE BOLDEST OF THE GROUP.
OUT OF APPRECIATION FOR YOUR BLUSTER, I WILL GIVE YOU THE ANSWER TO THAT QUESTION.
I MERELY SWITCHED OUT A SINGLE PART IN THEIR CYBORG CIRCULATORY SYSTEM.
IT WAS TIMED PERFECTLY SO THAT THE POISON WOULD ACT WHEN THE COUNCIL MEETING BEGAN.
YOU CHANGED OUT A PART...? ON PERSONAL GUARDS FROM ALL 18 PROVINCES ACROSS MARS?!
IT'S SIMPLY IMPOSSIBLE!!
AND WHY ARE YOU SO CERTAIN OF THAT? I'VE BEEN PLANNING AND PREPARING FOR THIS DAY FOR TEN LONG YEARS.
WHAT YOU CALL "IMPOSSIBLE," I CALL... *PATIENCE!* HA HA HA...

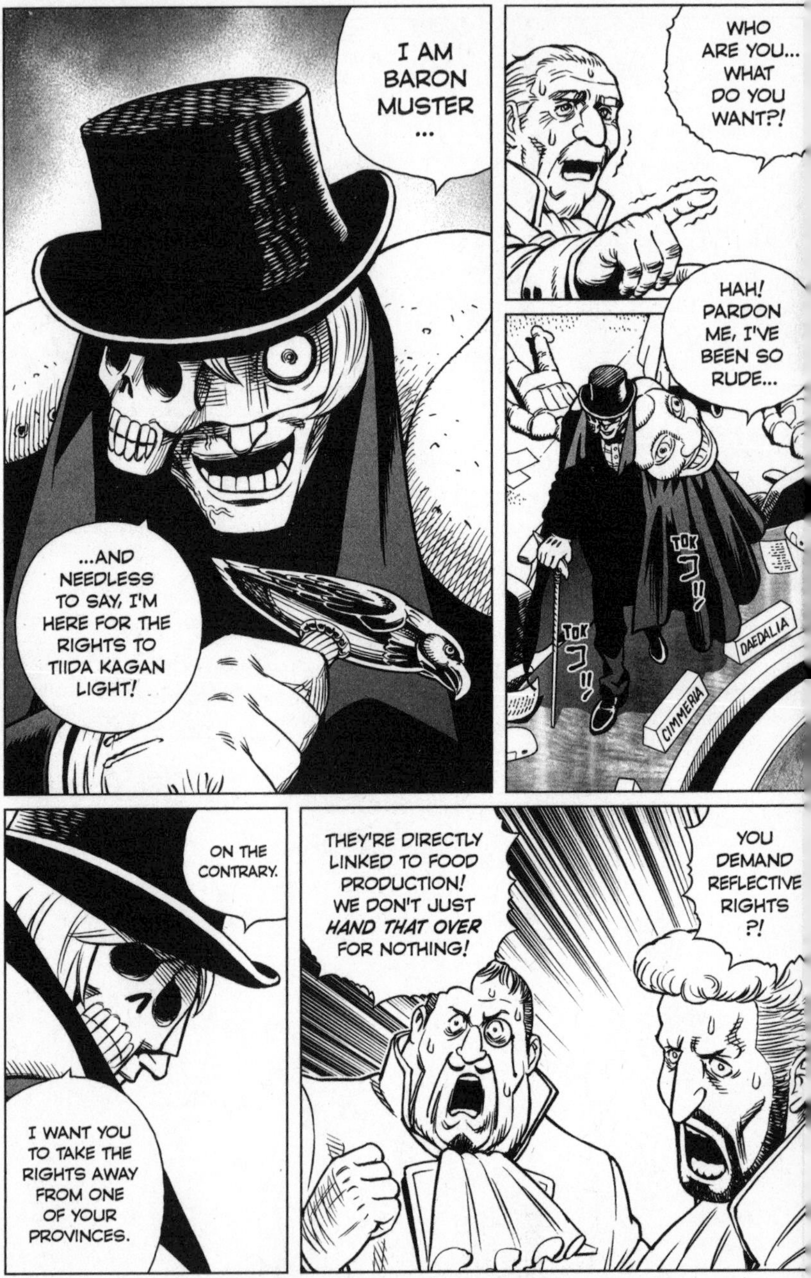
WHO ARE YOU... WHAT DO YOU WANT?!
HAH! PARDON ME, I'VE BEEN SO RUDE...
TOK
TOK
DAEDALIA
CIMMERIA
I AM BARON MUSTER ...
...AND NEEDLESS TO SAY, I'M HERE FOR THE RIGHTS TO TIIDA KAGAN LIGHT!
YOU DEMAND REFLECTIVE RIGHTS ?!
THEY'RE DIRECTLY LINKED TO FOOD PRODUCTION! WE DON'T JUST *HAND THAT OVER* FOR NOTHING!
ON THE CONTRARY.
I WANT YOU TO TAKE THE RIGHTS AWAY FROM ONE OF YOUR PROVINCES.

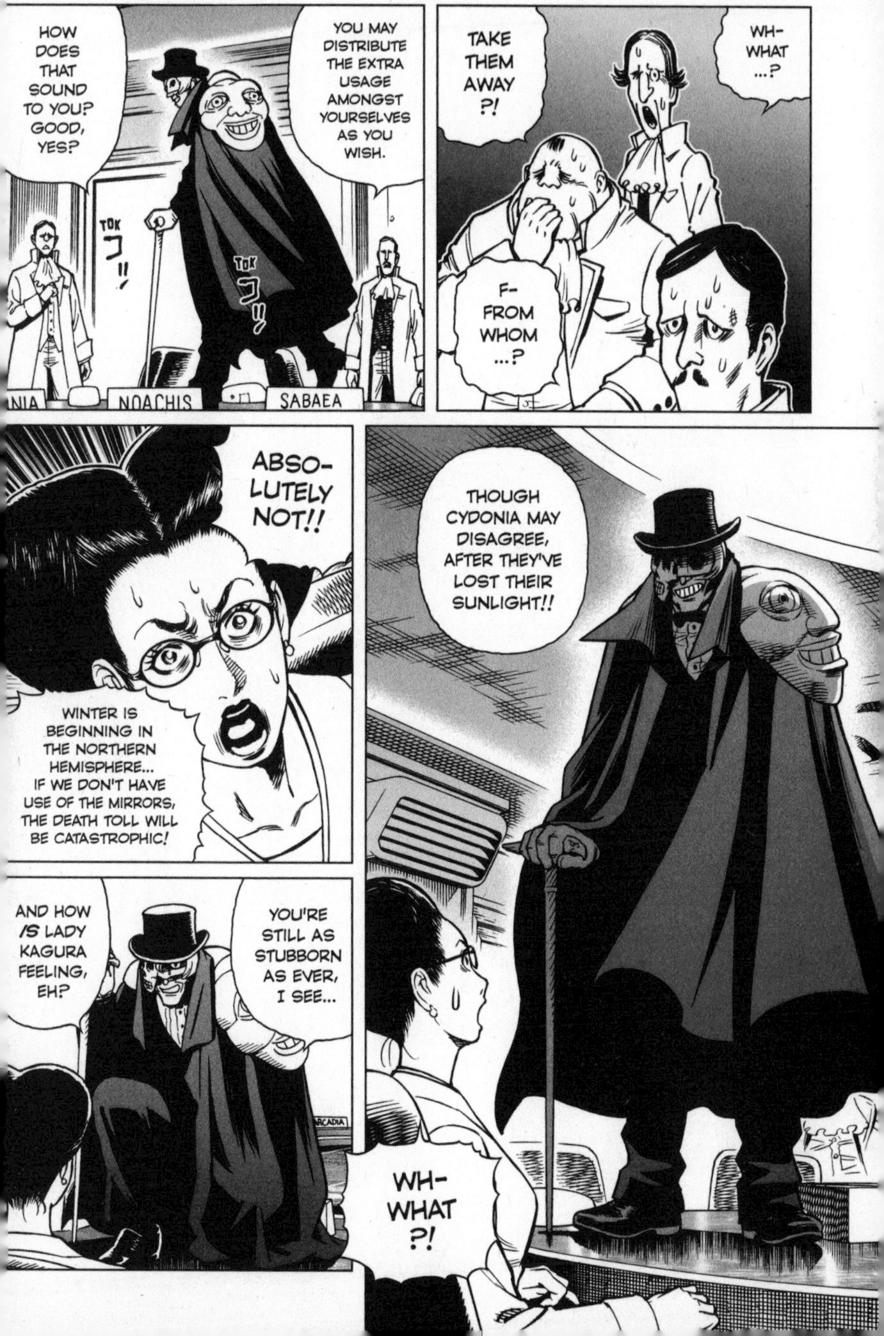
WH-WHAT ...?
TAKE THEM AWAY ?!
F-FROM WHOM ...?
YOU MAY DISTRIBUTE THE EXTRA USAGE AMONGST YOURSELVES AS YOU WISH.
HOW DOES THAT SOUND TO YOU? GOOD, YES?
TOK
TOK
NIA
NOACHIS
SABAEA
THOUGH CYDONIA MAY DISAGREE, AFTER THEY'VE LOST THEIR SUNLIGHT!!
ABSO-LUTELY NOT!!
WINTER IS BEGINNING IN THE NORTHERN HEMISPHERE... IF WE DON'T HAVE USE OF THE MIRRORS, THE DEATH TOLL WILL BE CATASTROPHIC!
YOU'RE STILL AS STUBBORN AS EVER, I SEE...
AND HOW *IS* LADY KAGURA FEELING, EH?
ARCADIA
WH-WHAT ?!

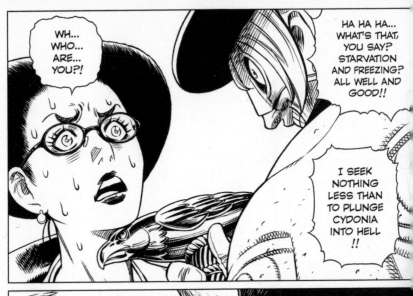

WH... WHO... ARE... YOU?!

HA HA HA... WHAT'S THAT, YOU SAY? STARVATION AND FREEZING? ALL WELL AND GOOD!!

I SEEK NOTHING LESS THAN TO PLUNGE CYDONIA INTO HELL !!

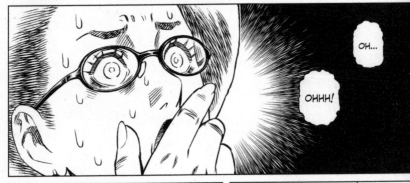

OH...

OHHH!

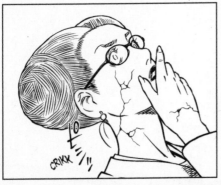

CRIKK

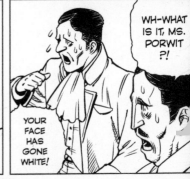

WH-WHAT IS IT, MS. PORWIT?!

YOUR FACE HAS GONE WHITE!

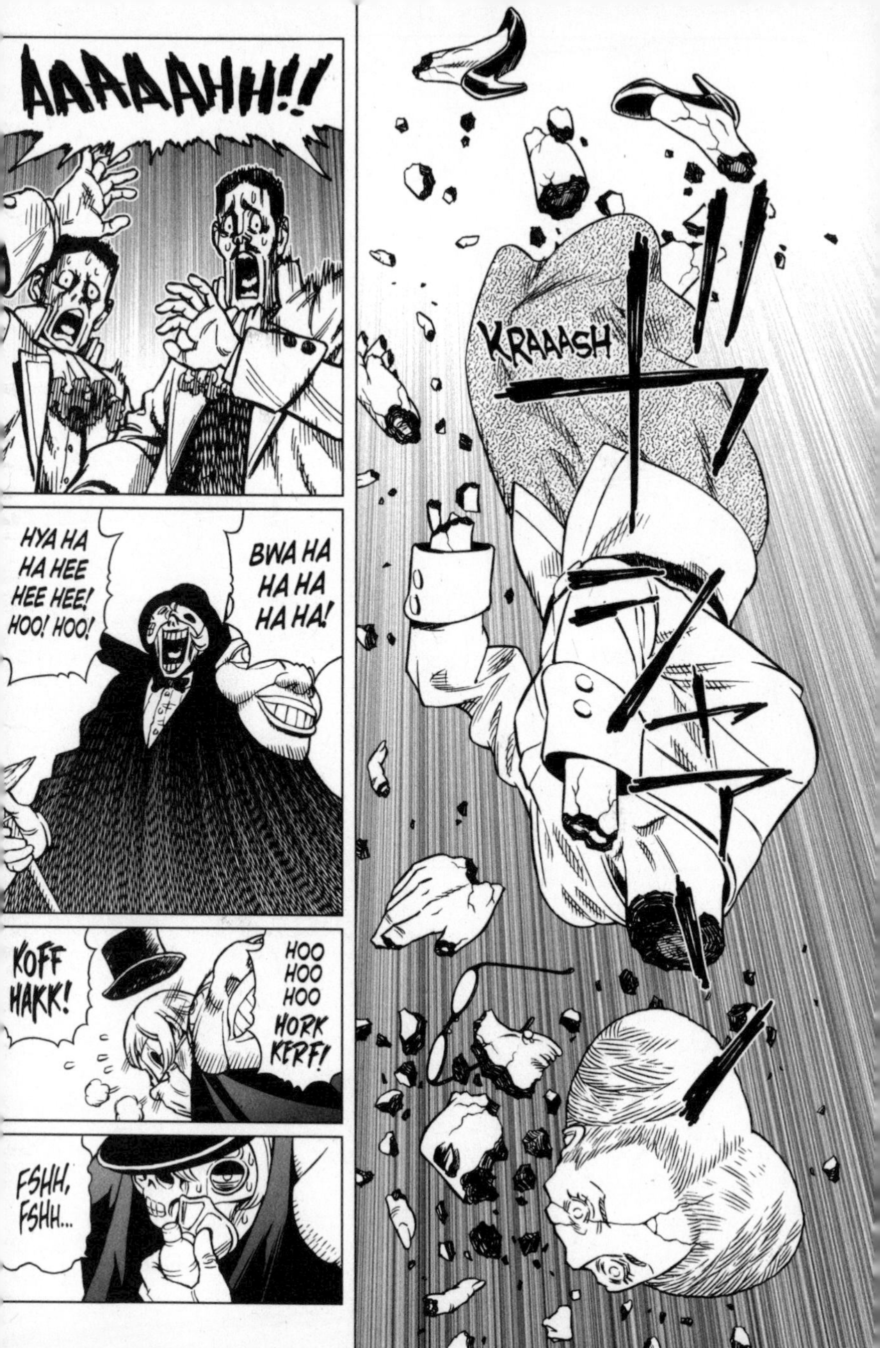
KRAAASH
AAAAAHH!!
BWA HA HA HA HA HA!
HYA HA HA HEE HEE HEE! HOO! HOO!
HOO HOO HOO HORK KERF!
KOFF HAKK!
FSHH, FSHH...

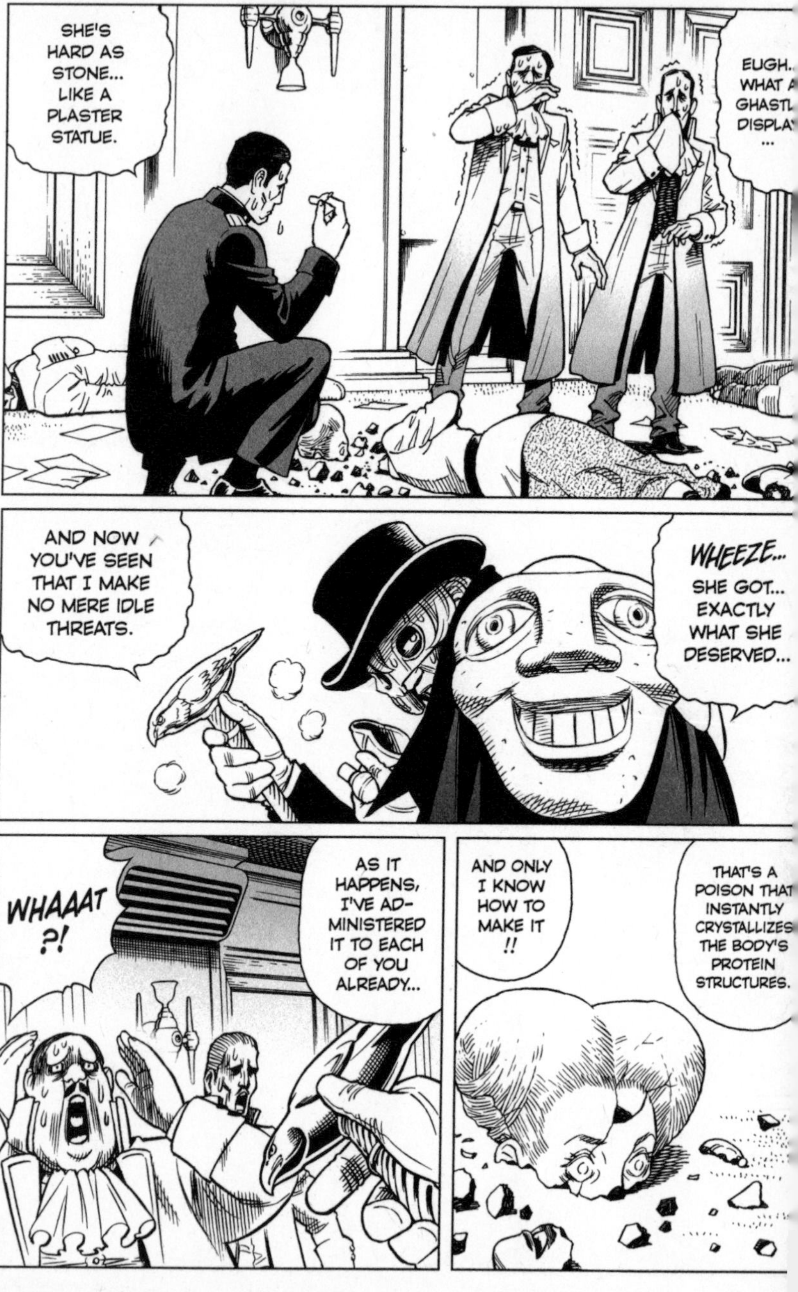
EUGH.. WHAT A GHASTL DISPLA ...
SHE'S HARD AS STONE... LIKE A PLASTER STATUE.
WHEEZE... SHE GOT... EXACTLY WHAT SHE DESERVED...
AND NOW YOU'VE SEEN THAT I MAKE NO MERE IDLE THREATS.
THAT'S A POISON THAT INSTANTLY CRYSTALLIZES THE BODY'S PROTEIN STRUCTURES.
AND ONLY I KNOW HOW TO MAKE IT !!
AS IT HAPPENS, I'VE AD-MINISTERED IT TO EACH OF YOU ALREADY...
WHAAAT ?!

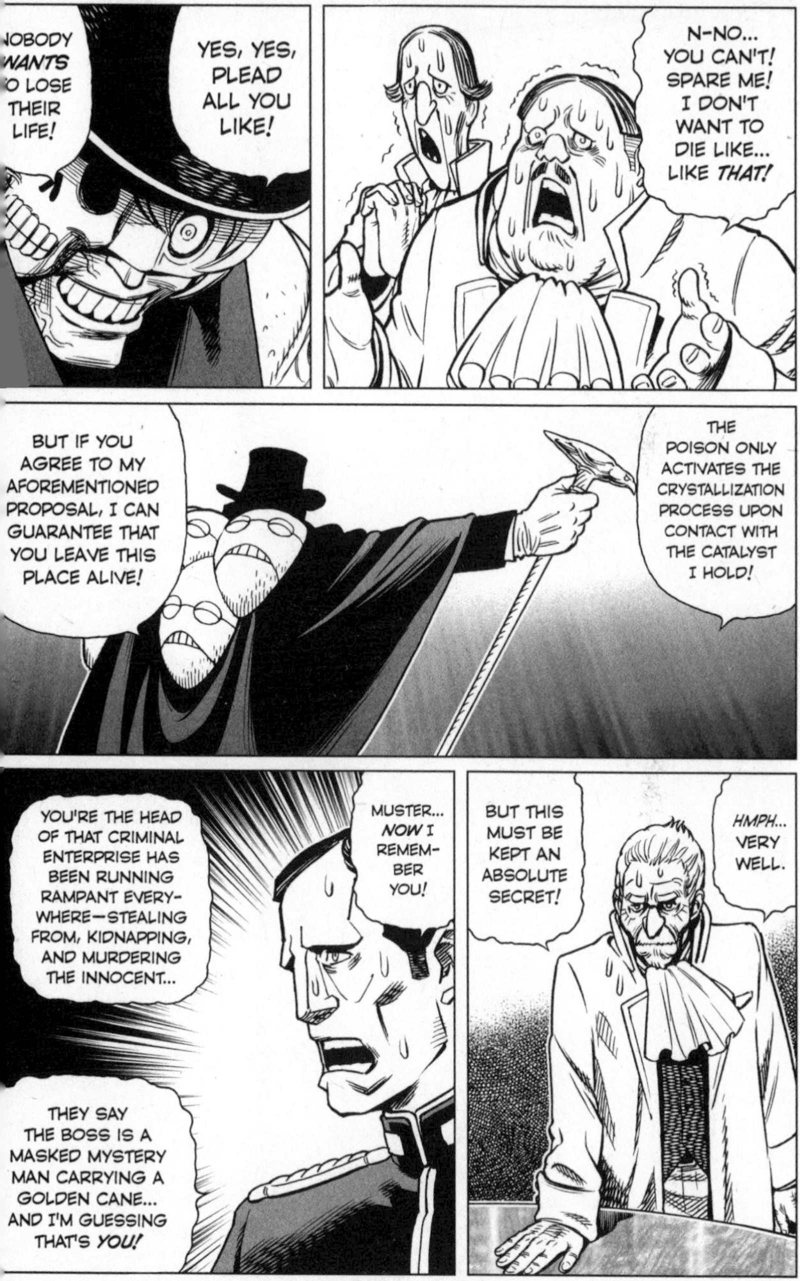
N-NO... YOU CAN'T! SPARE ME! I DON'T WANT TO DIE LIKE... LIKE *THAT!*
YES, YES, PLEAD ALL YOU LIKE!
NOBODY *WANTS* O LOSE THEIR LIFE!
THE POISON ONLY ACTIVATES THE CRYSTALLIZATION PROCESS UPON CONTACT WITH THE CATALYST I HOLD!
BUT IF YOU AGREE TO MY AFOREMENTIONED PROPOSAL, I CAN GUARANTEE THAT YOU LEAVE THIS PLACE ALIVE!
HMPH... VERY WELL.
BUT THIS MUST BE KEPT AN ABSOLUTE SECRET!
MUSTER... *NOW* I REMEMBER YOU!
YOU'RE THE HEAD OF THAT CRIMINAL ENTERPRISE HAS BEEN RUNNING RAMPANT EVERYWHERE—STEALING FROM, KIDNAPPING, AND MURDERING THE INNOCENT...
THEY SAY THE BOSS IS A MASKED MYSTERY MAN CARRYING A GOLDEN CANE... AND I'M GUESSING THAT'S *YOU!*

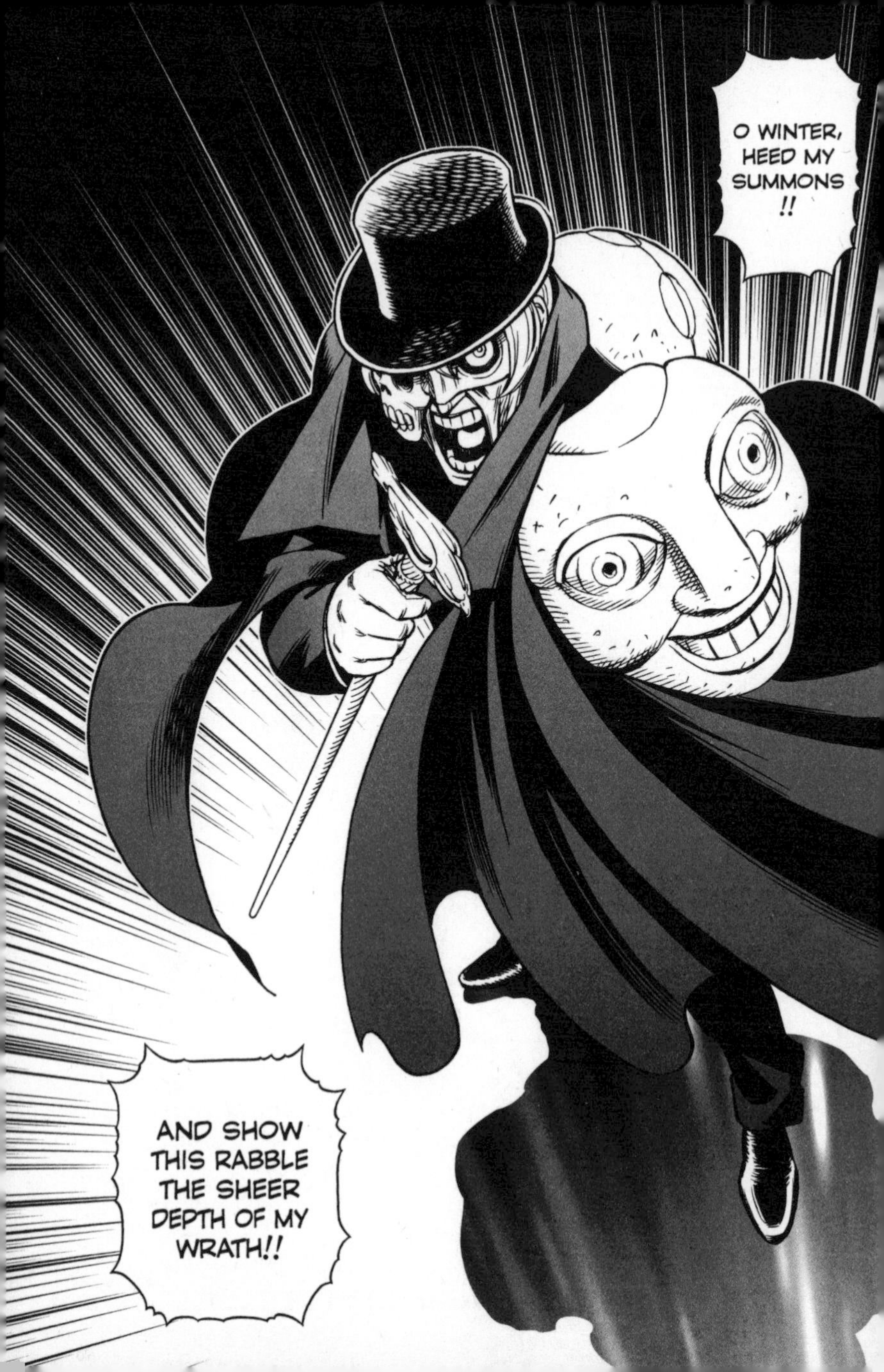
O WINTER, HEED MY SUMMONS !!
AND SHOW THIS RABBLE THE SHEER DEPTH OF MY WRATH!!

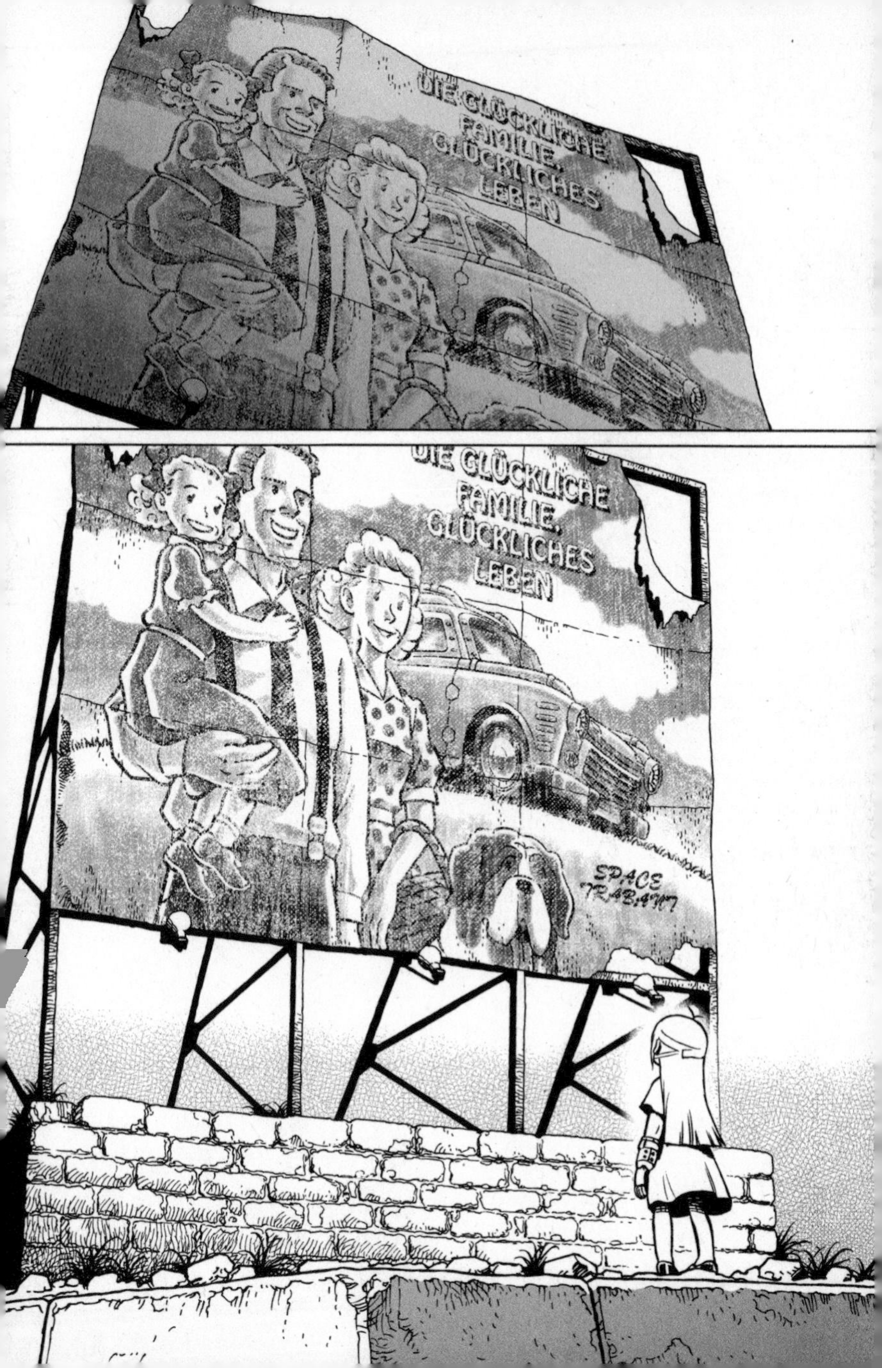
DIE GLÜCKLICHE FAMILIE, GLÜCKLICHES LEBEN
DIE GLÜCKLICHE FAMILIE, GLÜCKLICHES LEBEN
SPACE TRABANT

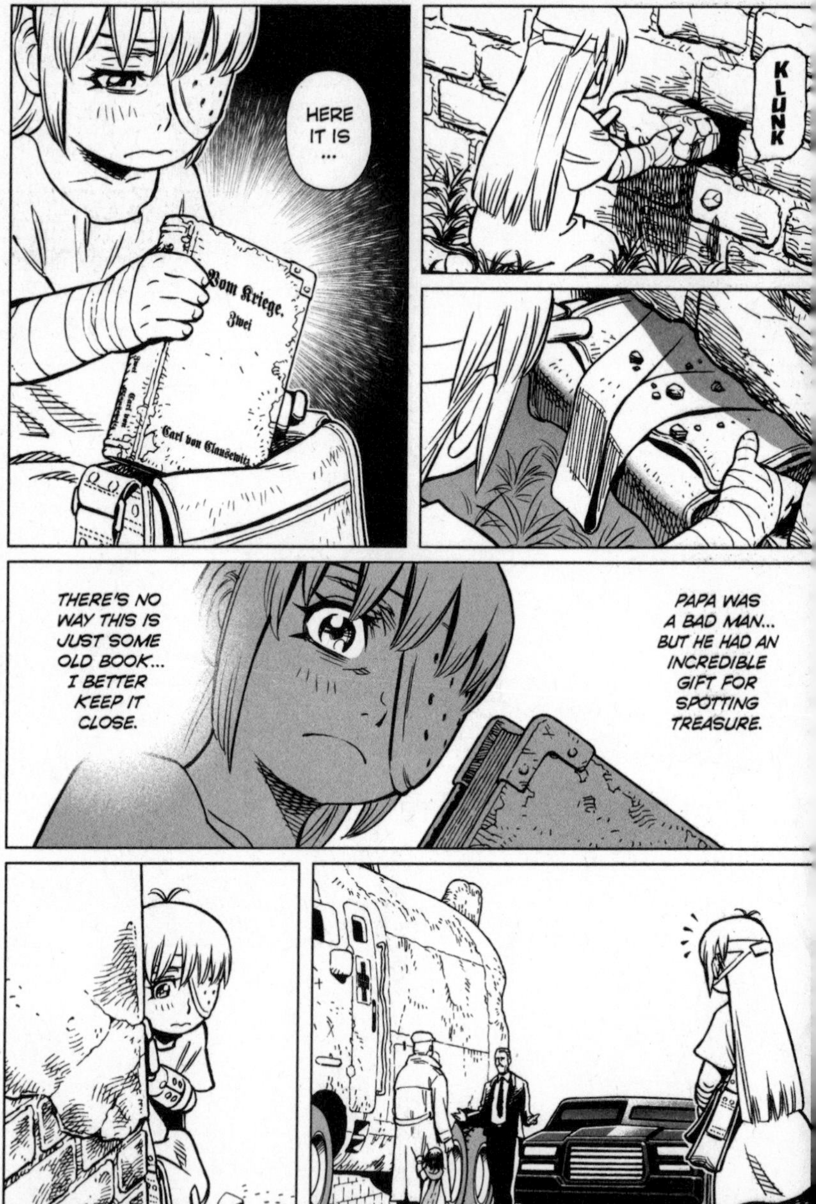
KLUNK
HERE IT IS ...
Vom Kriege. Zwei
Carl von Clausewitz
PAPA WAS A BAD MAN... BUT HE HAD AN INCREDIBLE GIFT FOR SPOTTING TREASURE.
THERE'S NO WAY THIS IS JUST SOME OLD BOOK... I BETTER KEEP IT CLOSE.

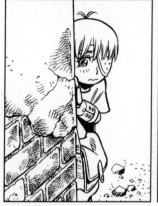

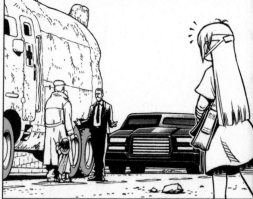

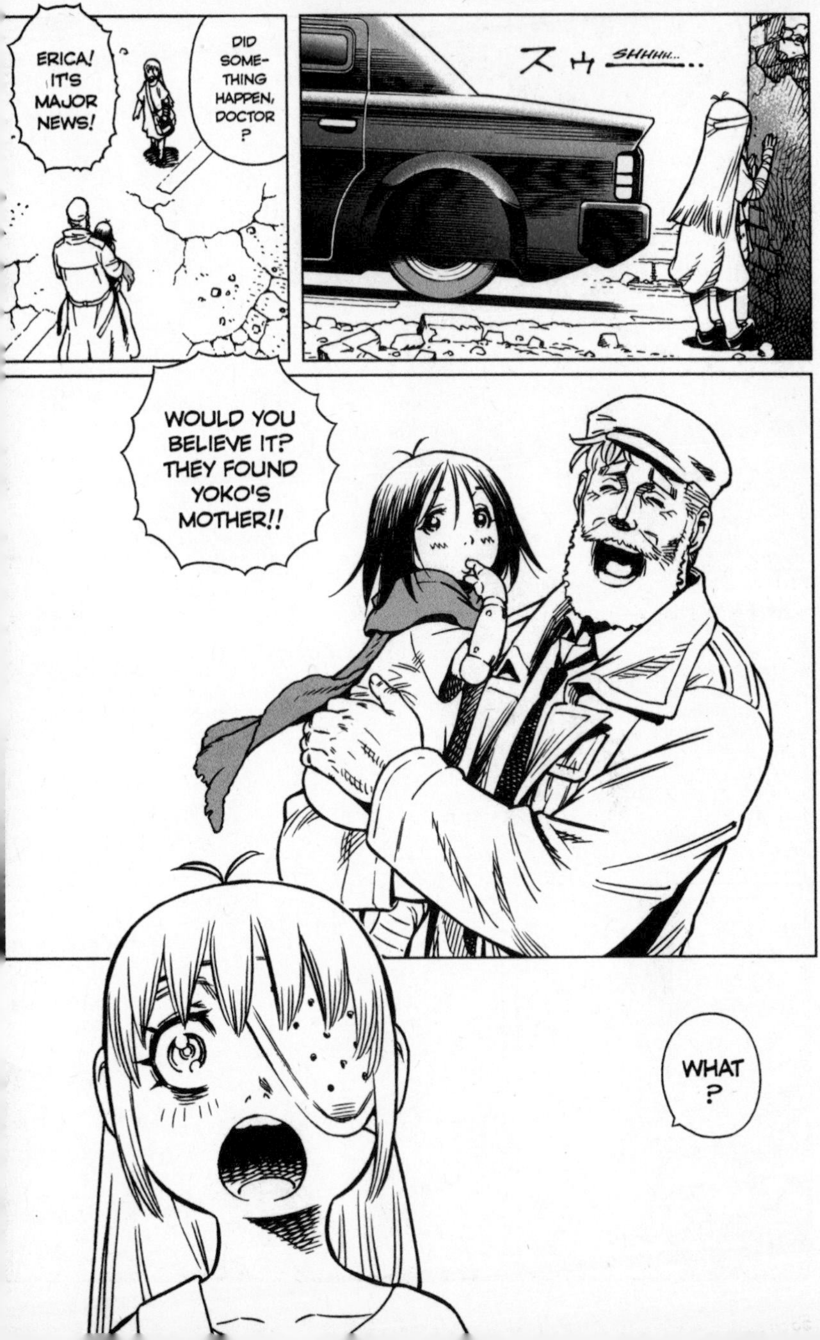
スゥ SHHHH...
DID SOMETHING HAPPEN, DOCTOR?
ERICA! IT'S MAJOR NEWS!
WOULD YOU BELIEVE IT? THEY FOUND YOKO'S MOTHER!!
WHAT?

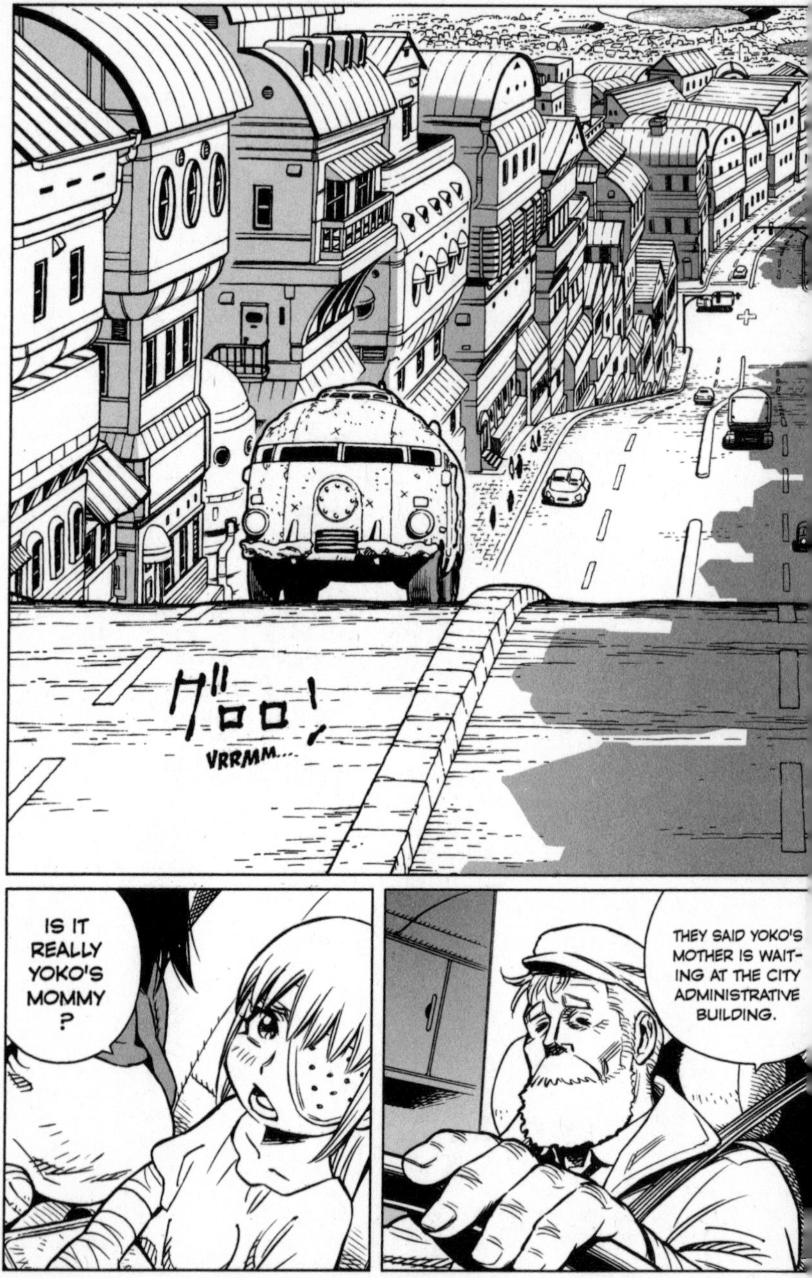
ゴロロ
VRRMM...
THEY SAID YOKO'S MOTHER IS WAIT-ING AT THE CITY ADMINISTRATIVE BUILDING.
IS IT REALLY YOKO'S MOMMY ?

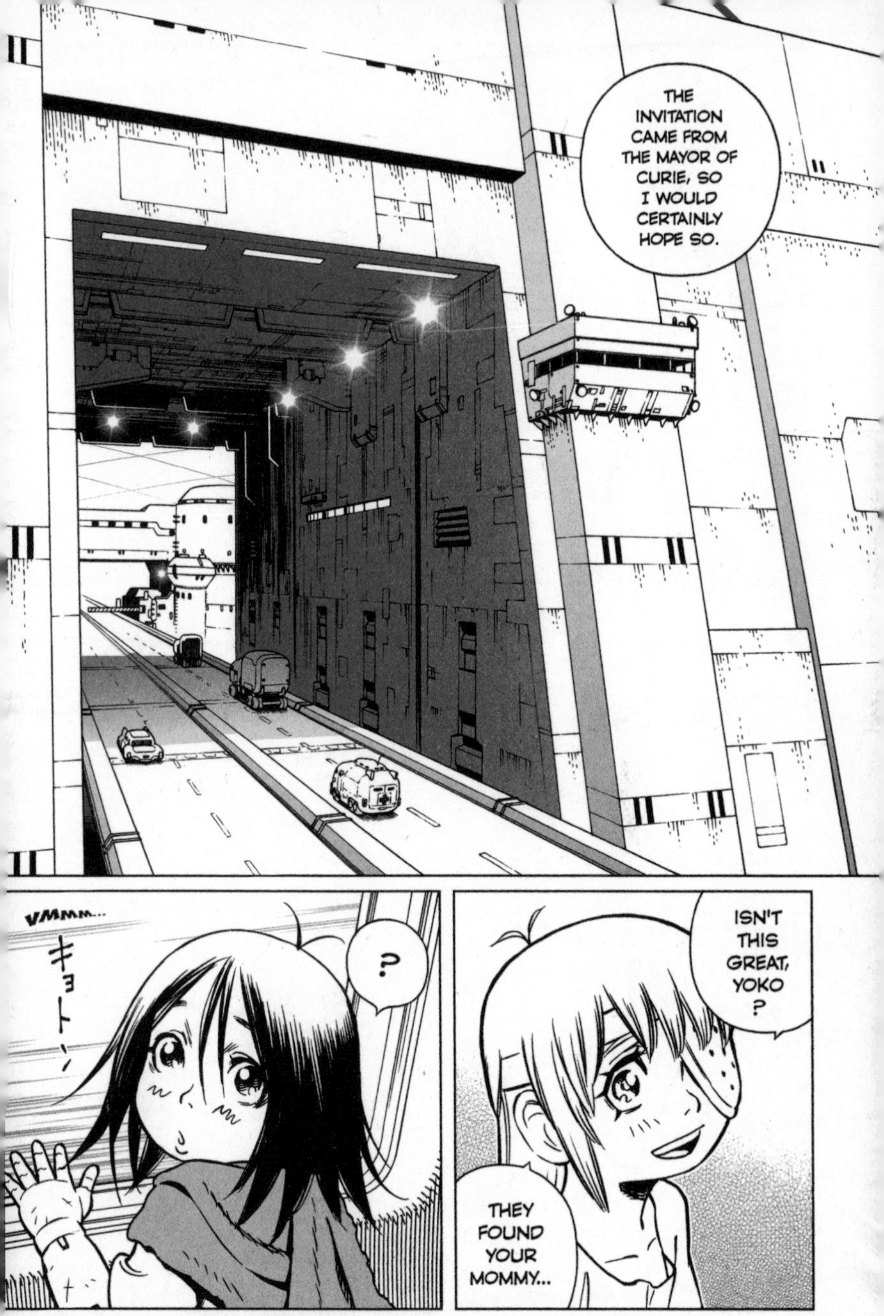
THE INVITATION CAME FROM THE MAYOR OF CURIE, SO I WOULD CERTAINLY HOPE SO.
ISN'T THIS GREAT, YOKO?
THEY FOUND YOUR MOMMY...
VMMM...
キョトン
?

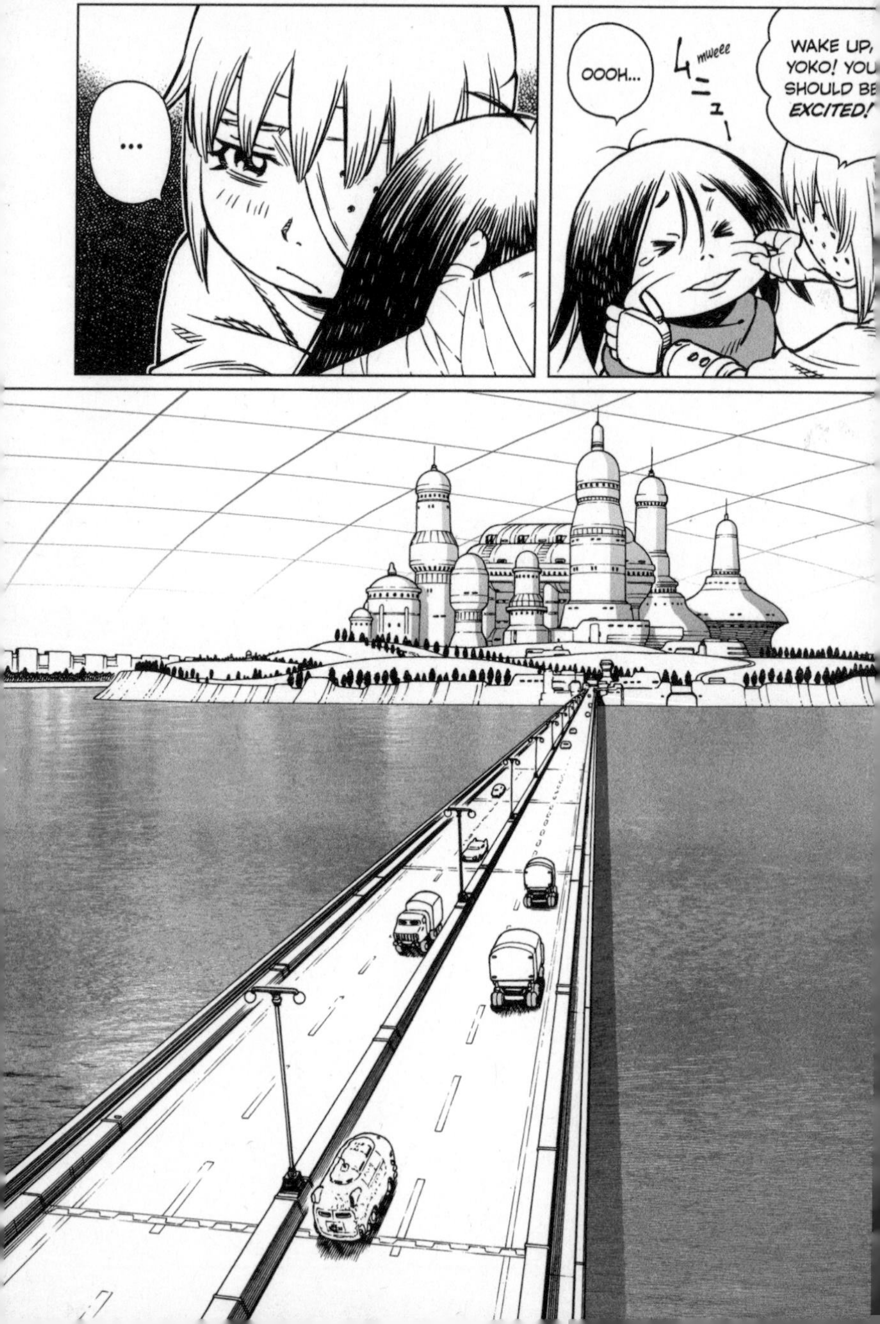
WAKE UP, YOKO! YOU SHOULD BE EXCITED!
mweee
OOOH...
...

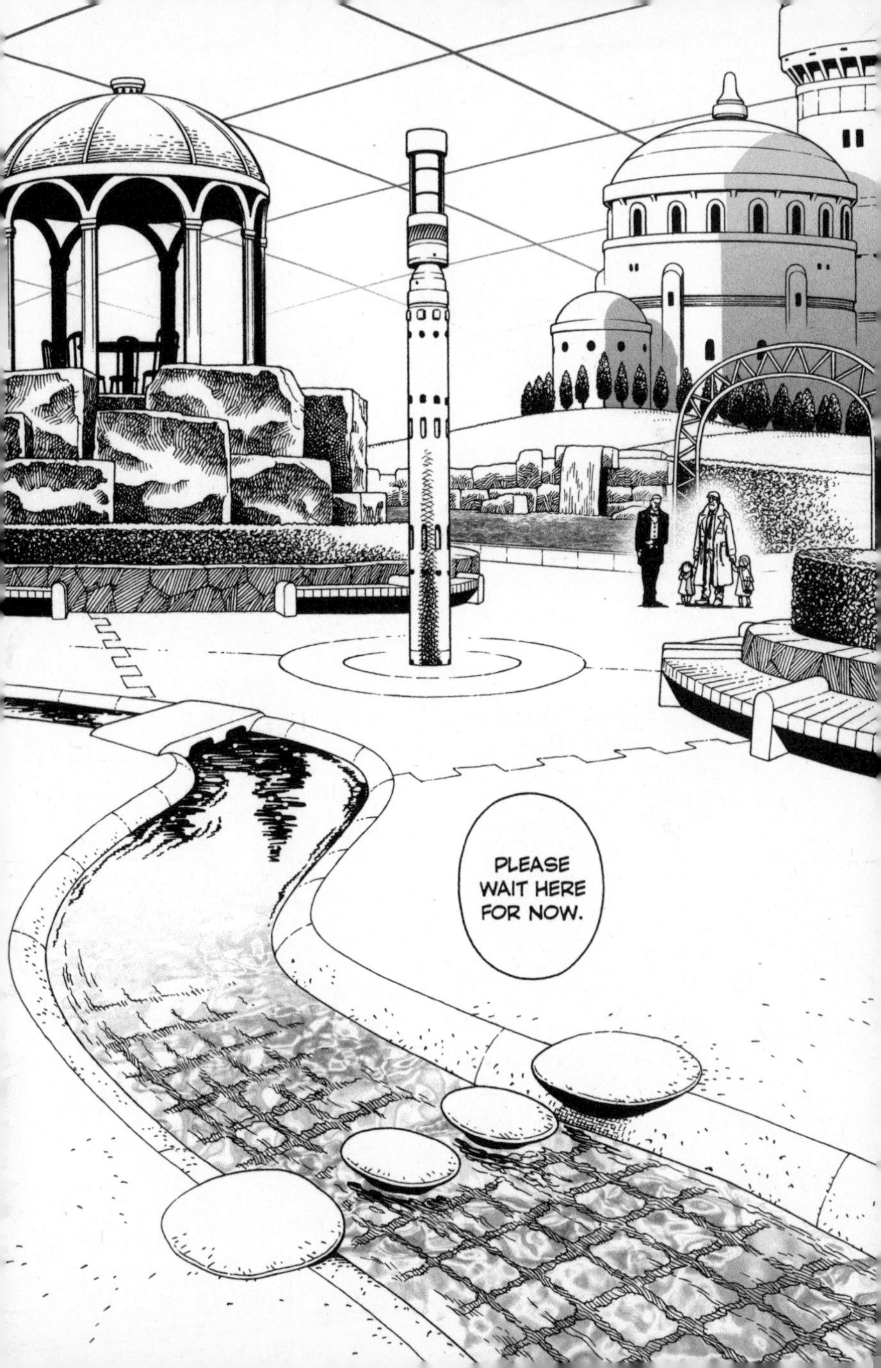
PLEASE WAIT HERE FOR NOW.

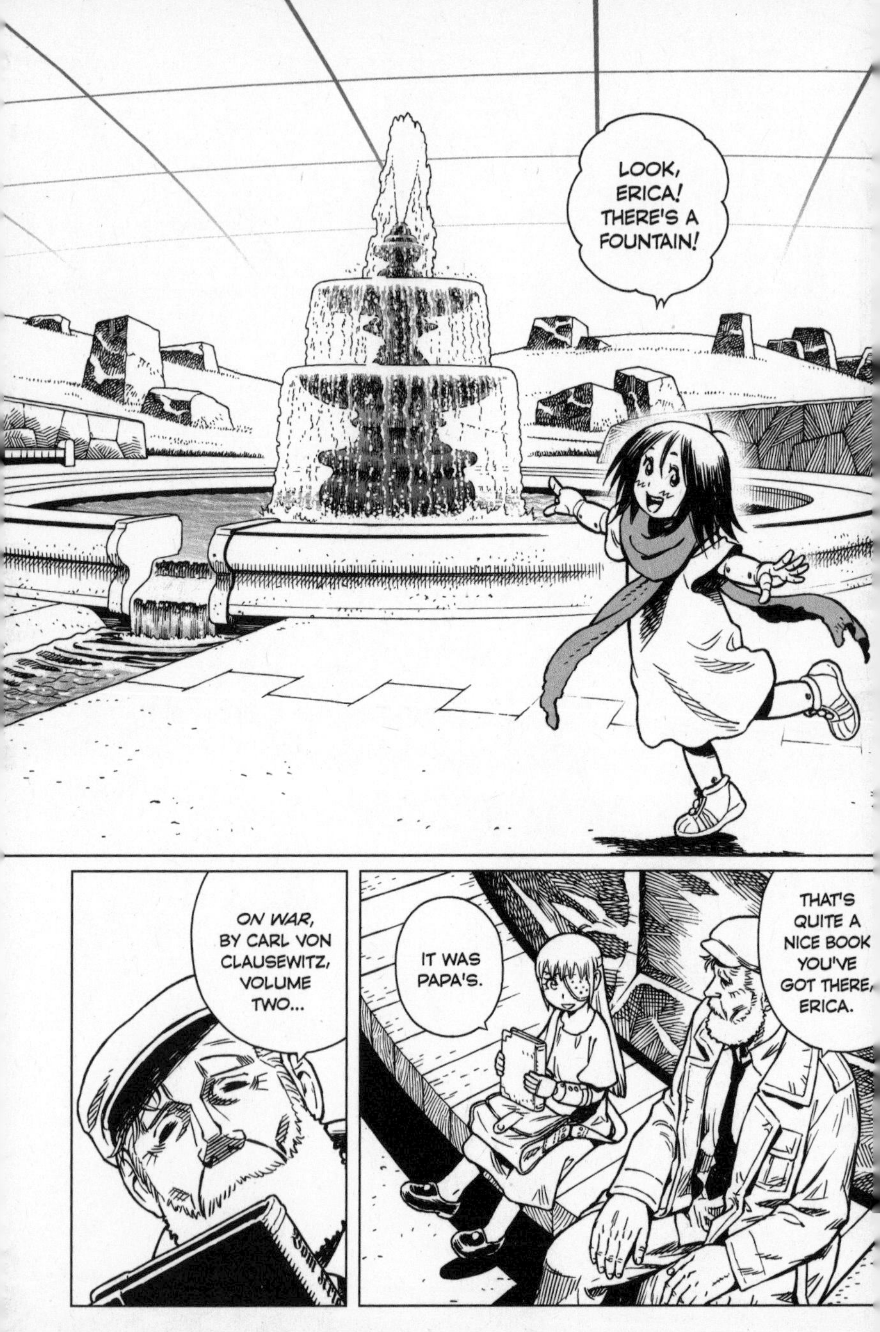
LOOK, ERICA! THERE'S A FOUNTAIN!
THAT'S QUITE A NICE BOOK YOU'VE GOT THERE, ERICA.
IT WAS PAPA'S.
ON WAR, BY CARL VON CLAUSEWITZ, VOLUME TWO...

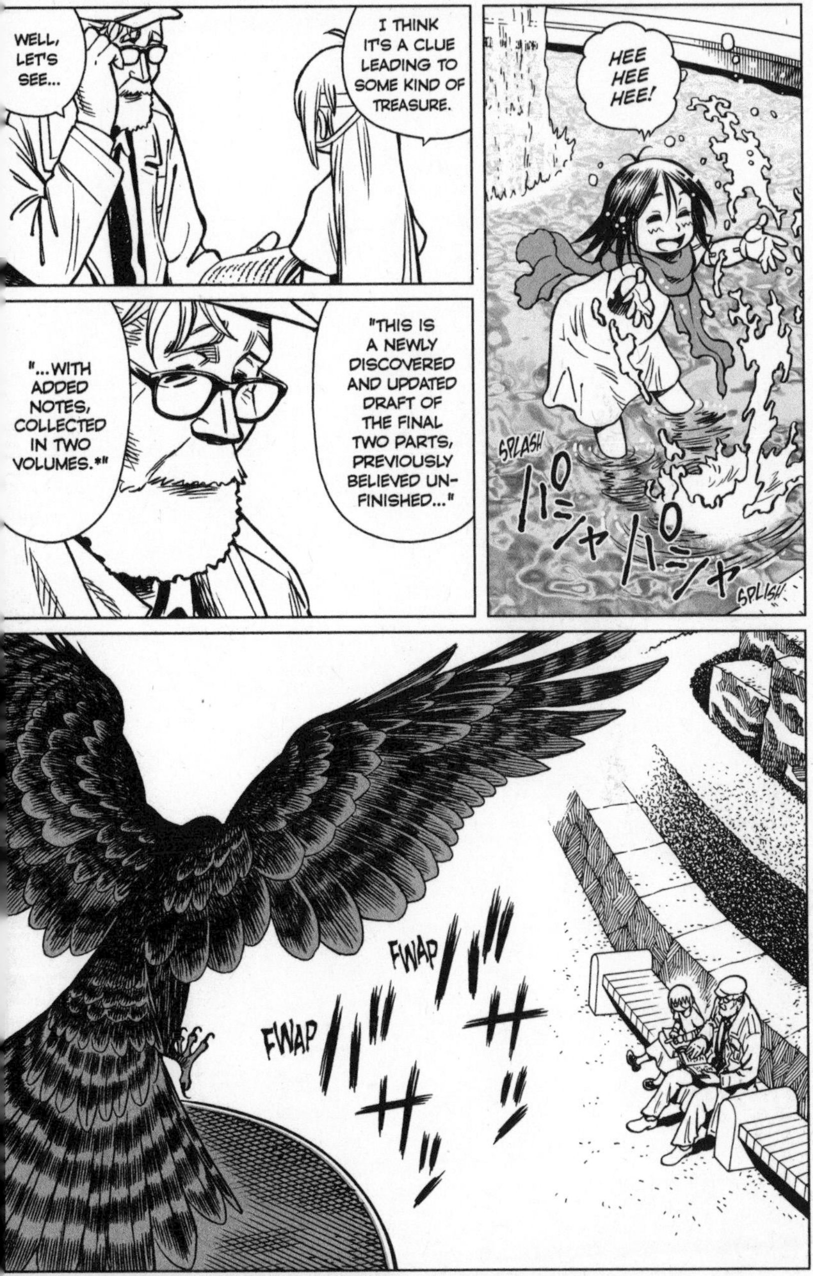
HEE HEE HEE!
SPLASH
パシャ
パシャ
SPLISH
I THINK IT'S A CLUE LEADING TO SOME KIND OF TREASURE.
WELL, LET'S SEE...
"THIS IS A NEWLY DISCOVERED AND UPDATED DRAFT OF THE FINAL TWO PARTS, PREVIOUSLY BELIEVED UN-FINISHED..."
"...WITH ADDED NOTES, COLLECTED IN TWO VOLUMES.*"
FWAP
FWAP

*CLAUSEWITZ'S *ON WAR*: A book on military strategy by Prussian general Carl von Clausewitz (1780-1831). His widow Marie compiled his unfinished script and published it after his death.

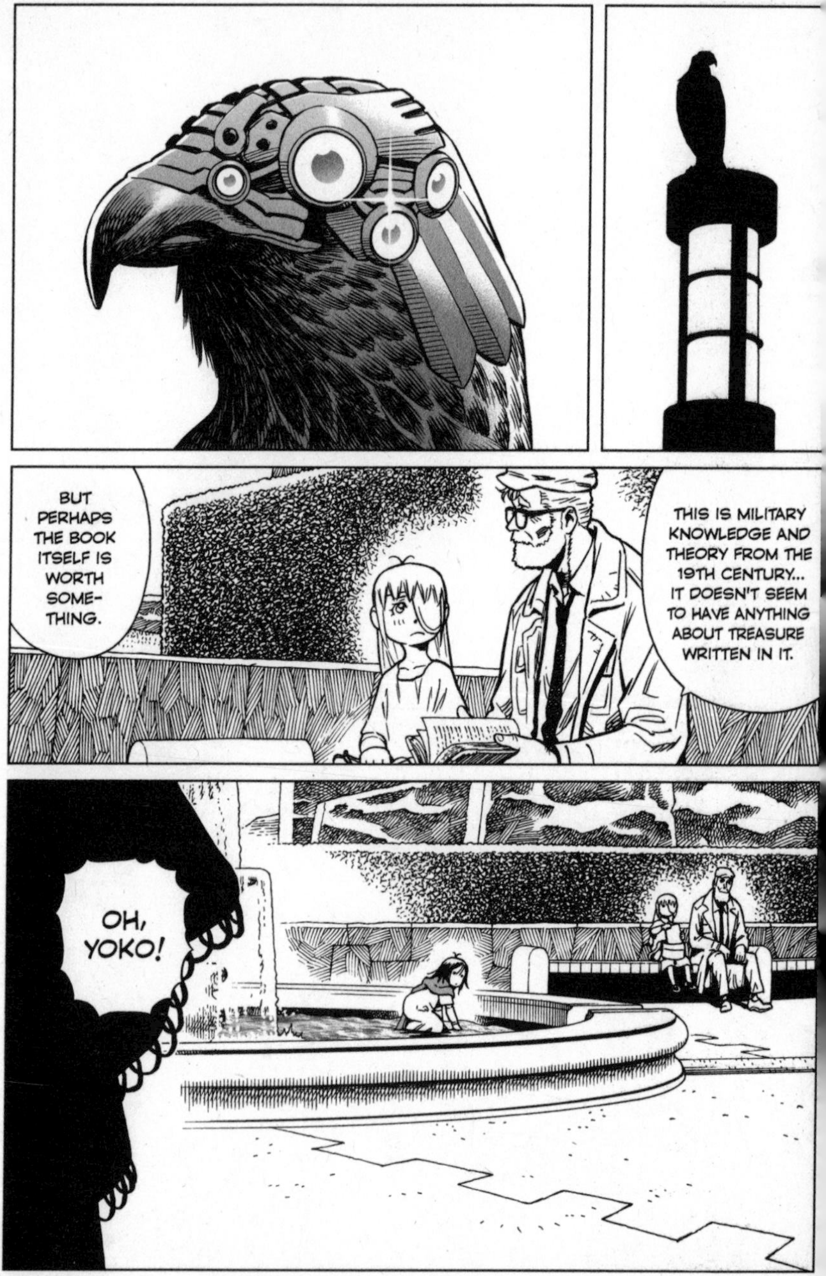
THIS IS MILITARY KNOWLEDGE AND THEORY FROM THE 19TH CENTURY... IT DOESN'T SEEM TO HAVE ANYTHING ABOUT TREASURE WRITTEN IN IT.
BUT PERHAPS THE BOOK ITSELF IS WORTH SOME-THING.
OH, YOKO!

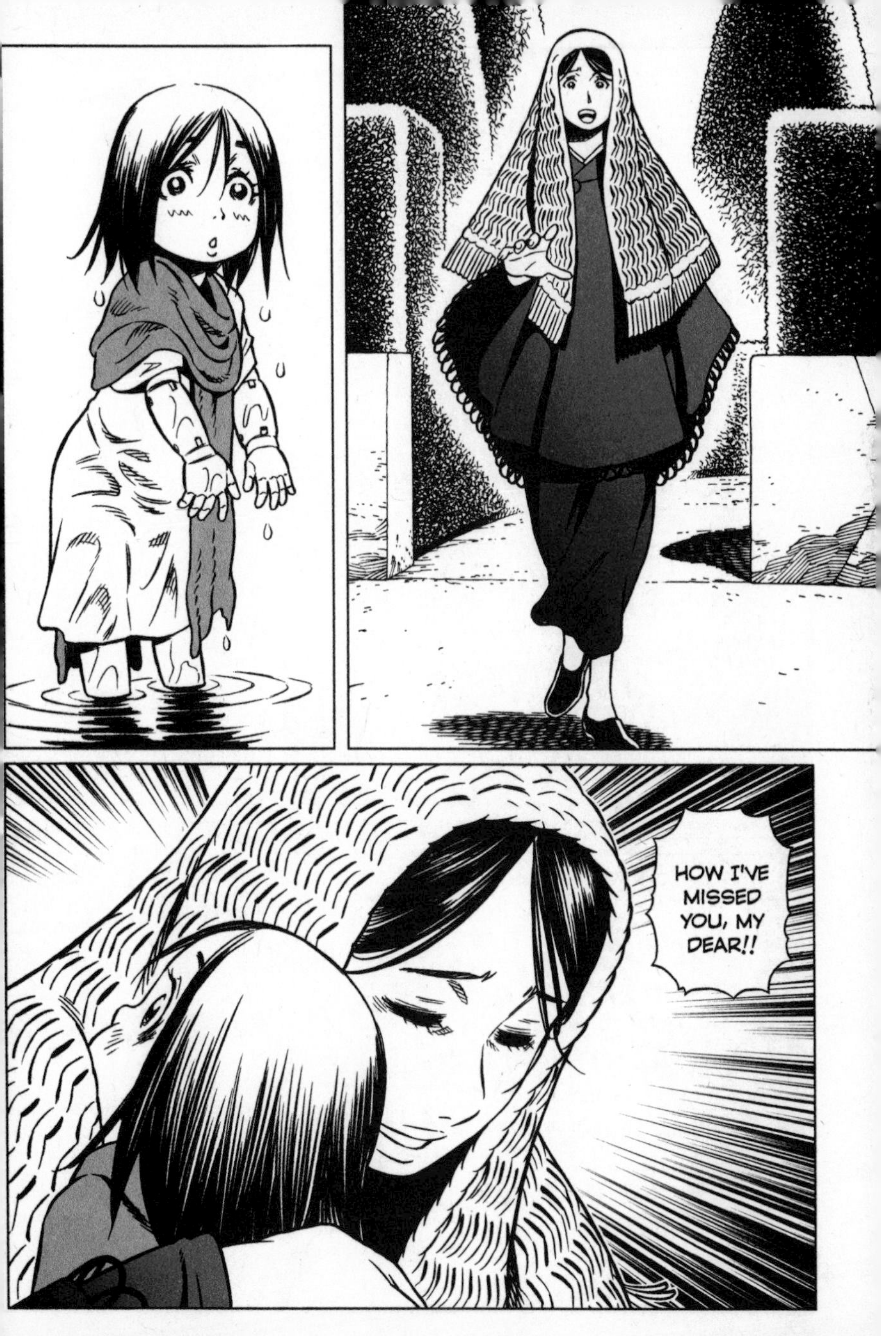
HOW I'VE MISSED YOU, MY DEAR!!

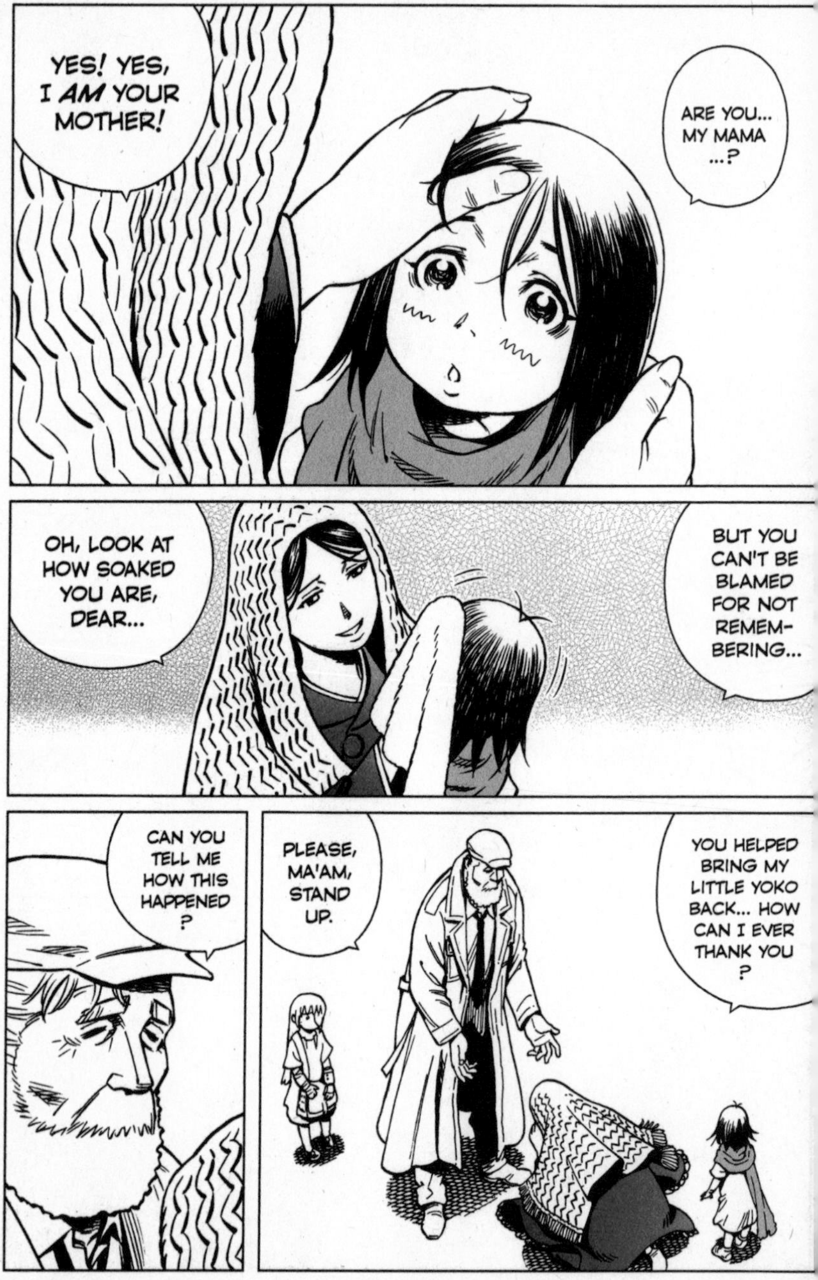
ARE YOU... MY MAMA ...?
YES! YES, I *AM* YOUR MOTHER!
BUT YOU CAN'T BE BLAMED FOR NOT REMEMBERING...
OH, LOOK AT HOW SOAKED YOU ARE, DEAR...
YOU HELPED BRING MY LITTLE YOKO BACK... HOW CAN I EVER THANK YOU?
PLEASE, MA'AM, STAND UP.
CAN YOU TELL ME HOW THIS HAPPENED?

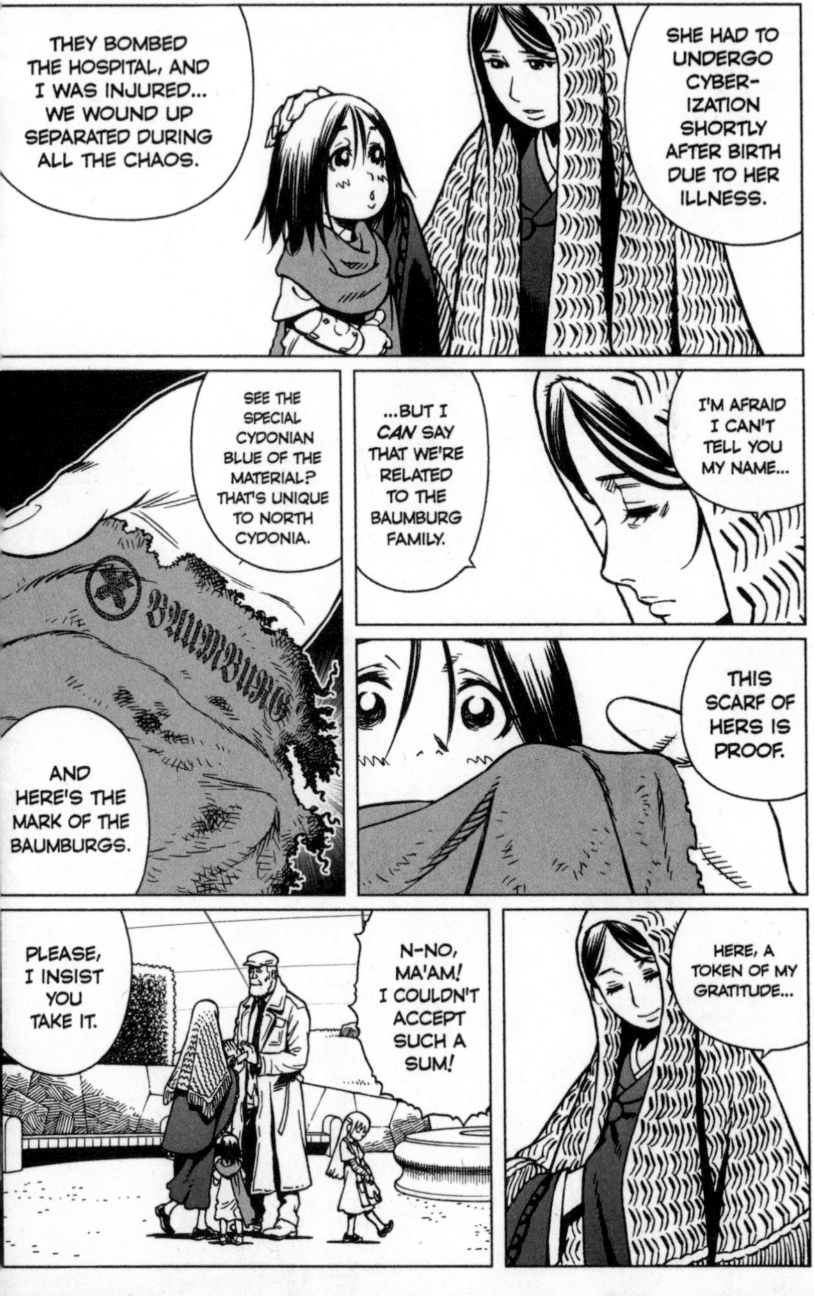
SHE HAD TO UNDERGO CYBER-IZATION SHORTLY AFTER BIRTH DUE TO HER ILLNESS.
THEY BOMBED THE HOSPITAL, AND I WAS INJURED... WE WOUND UP SEPARATED DURING ALL THE CHAOS.
I'M AFRAID I CAN'T TELL YOU MY NAME...
...BUT I *CAN* SAY THAT WE'RE RELATED TO THE BAUMBURG FAMILY.
THIS SCARF OF HERS IS PROOF.
SEE THE SPECIAL CYDONIAN BLUE OF THE MATERIAL? THAT'S UNIQUE TO NORTH CYDONIA.
BAUMBURG
AND HERE'S THE MARK OF THE BAUMBURGS.
HERE, A TOKEN OF MY GRATITUDE...
N-NO, MA'AM! I COULDN'T ACCEPT SUCH A SUM!
PLEASE, I INSIST YOU TAKE IT.

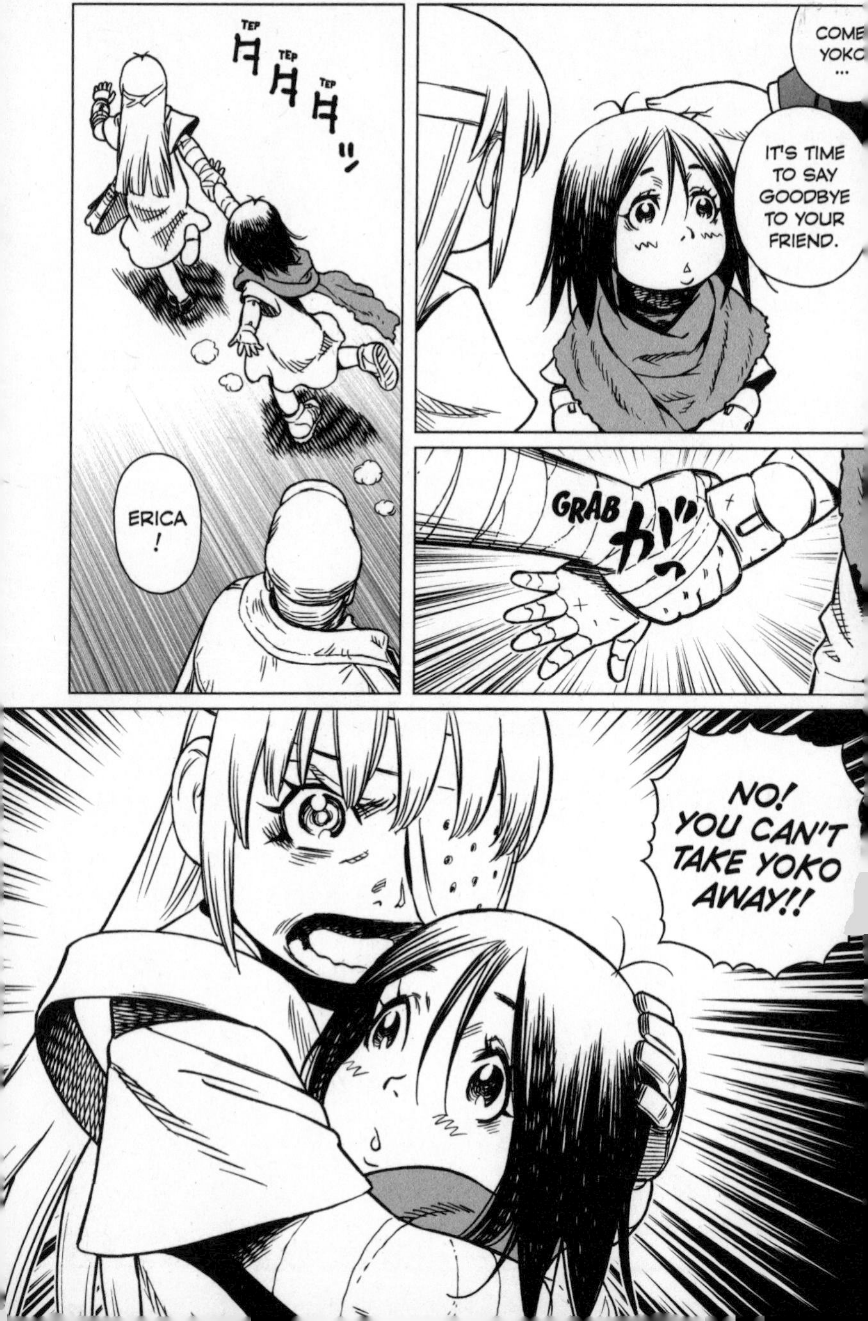
COME YOKO ...
IT'S TIME TO SAY GOODBYE TO YOUR FRIEND.
GRAB
ガッ
TEP TEP TEP
ERICA !
NO! YOU CAN'T TAKE YOKO AWAY!!

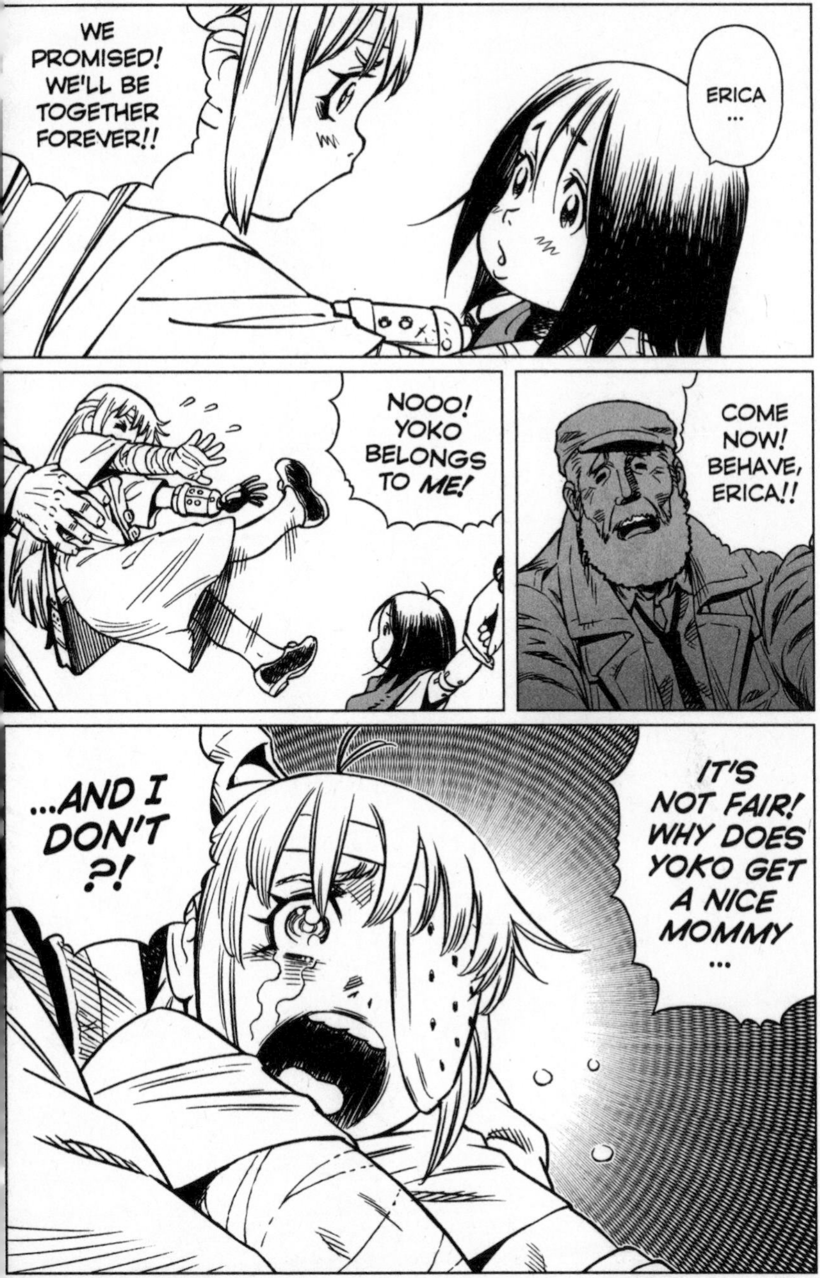
ERICA ...
WE PROMISED! WE'LL BE TOGETHER FOREVER!!
COME NOW! BEHAVE, ERICA!!
NOOO! YOKO BELONGS TO *ME!*
IT'S NOT FAIR! WHY DOES YOKO GET A NICE MOMMY ...
...AND I DON'T ?!

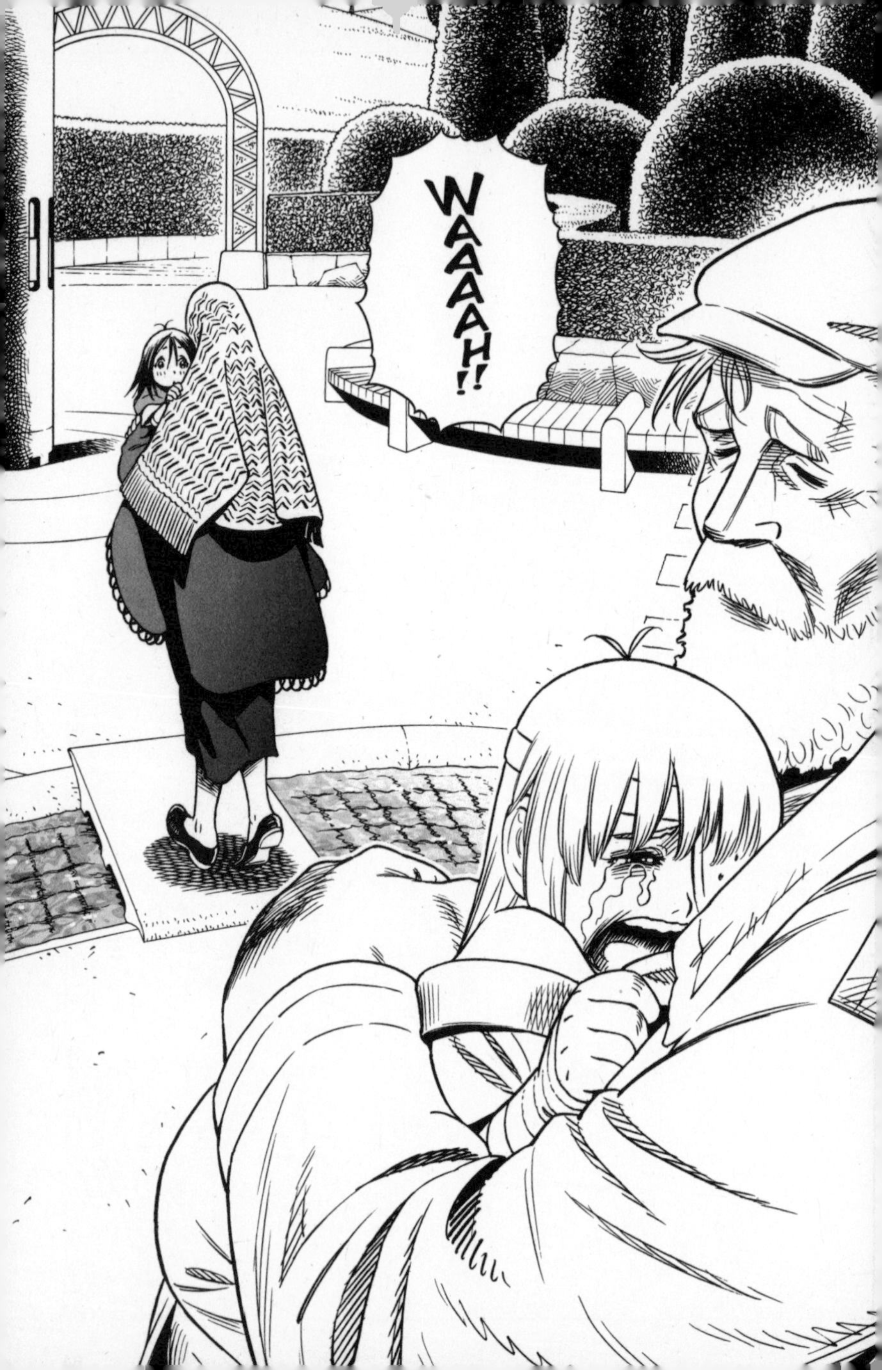
WAAAAH!!

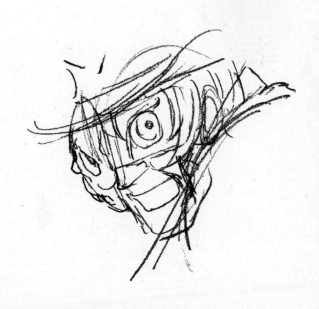

LOG:014
THE ROAR OF THE GUILLOTINE BELT

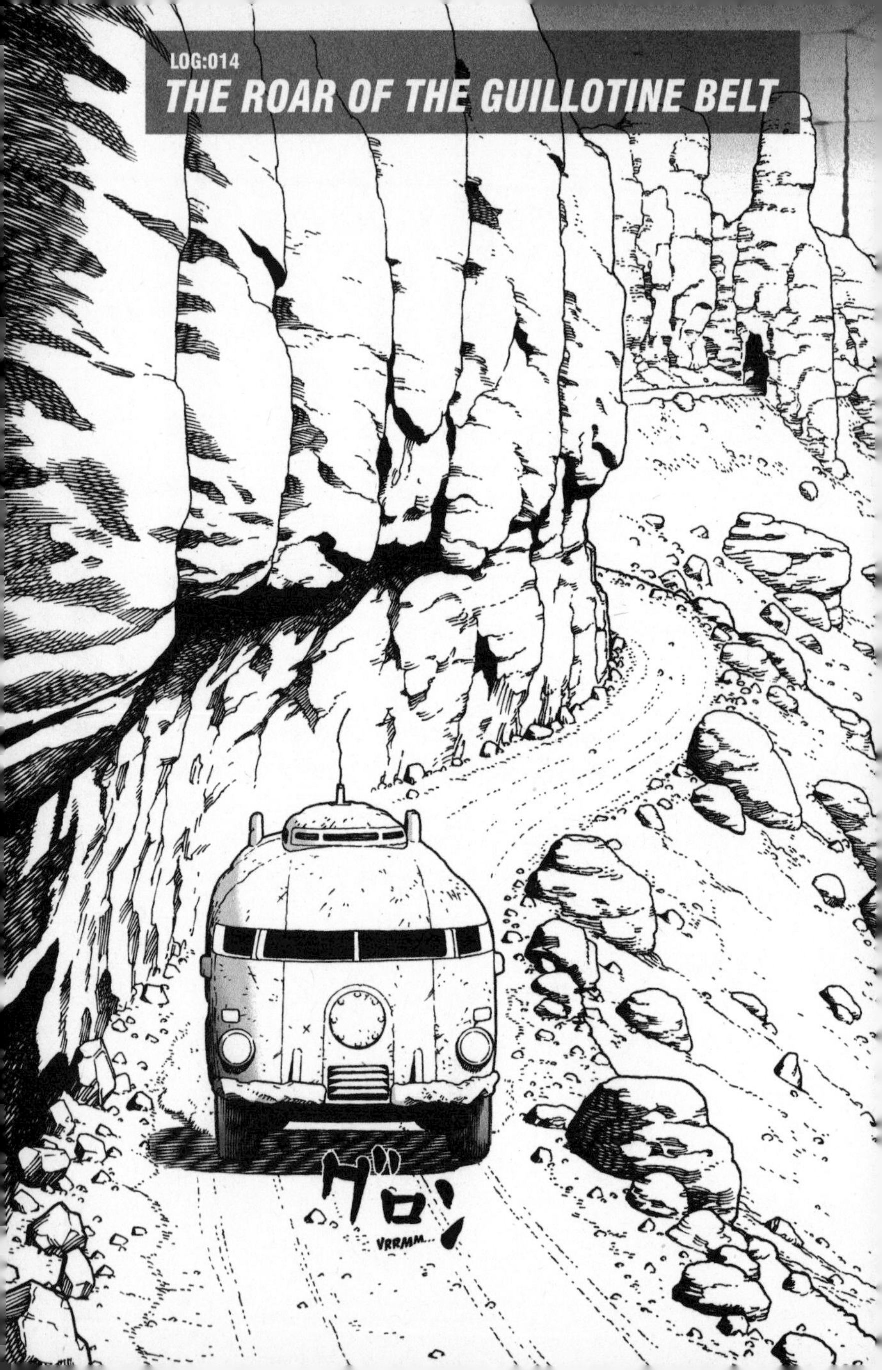
VRRMM...

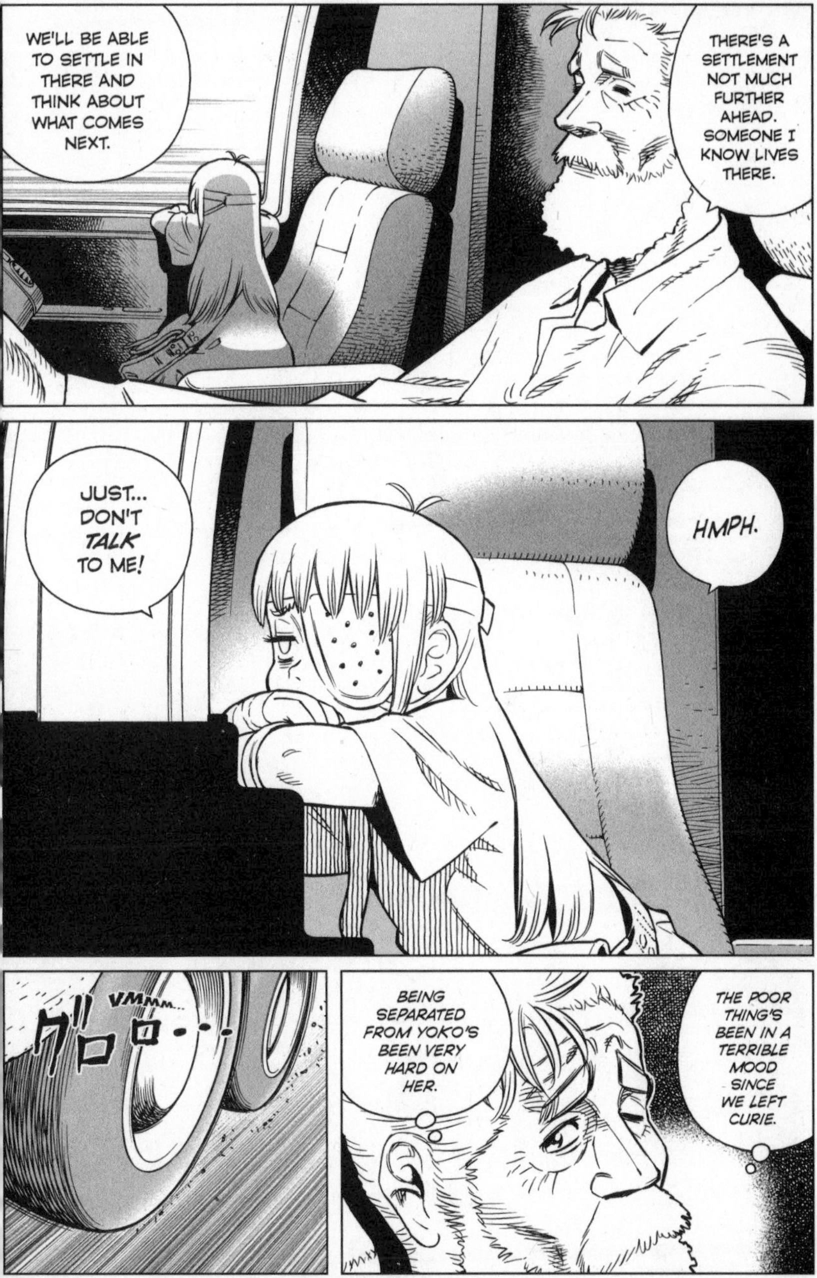
THERE'S A SETTLEMENT NOT MUCH FURTHER AHEAD. SOMEONE I KNOW LIVES THERE.
WE'LL BE ABLE TO SETTLE IN THERE AND THINK ABOUT WHAT COMES NEXT.
HMPH.
JUST... DON'T *TALK* TO ME!
THE POOR THING'S BEEN IN A TERRIBLE MOOD SINCE WE LEFT CURIE.
BEING SEPARATED FROM YOKO'S BEEN VERY HARD ON HER.
VMMM...

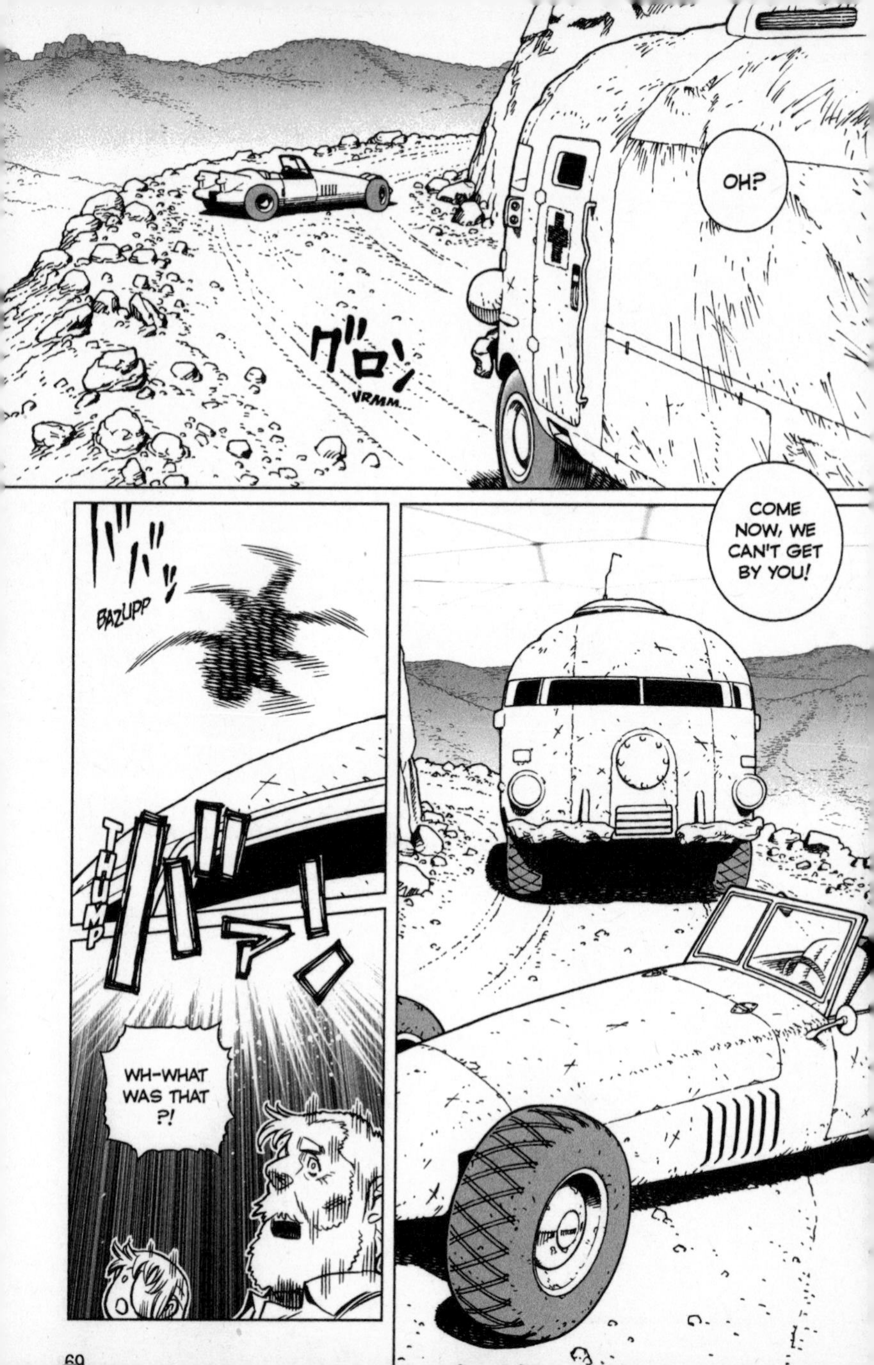
OH?
VRMM
COME NOW, WE CAN'T GET BY YOU!
BAZUPP
THUMP
WH-WHAT WAS THAT ?!

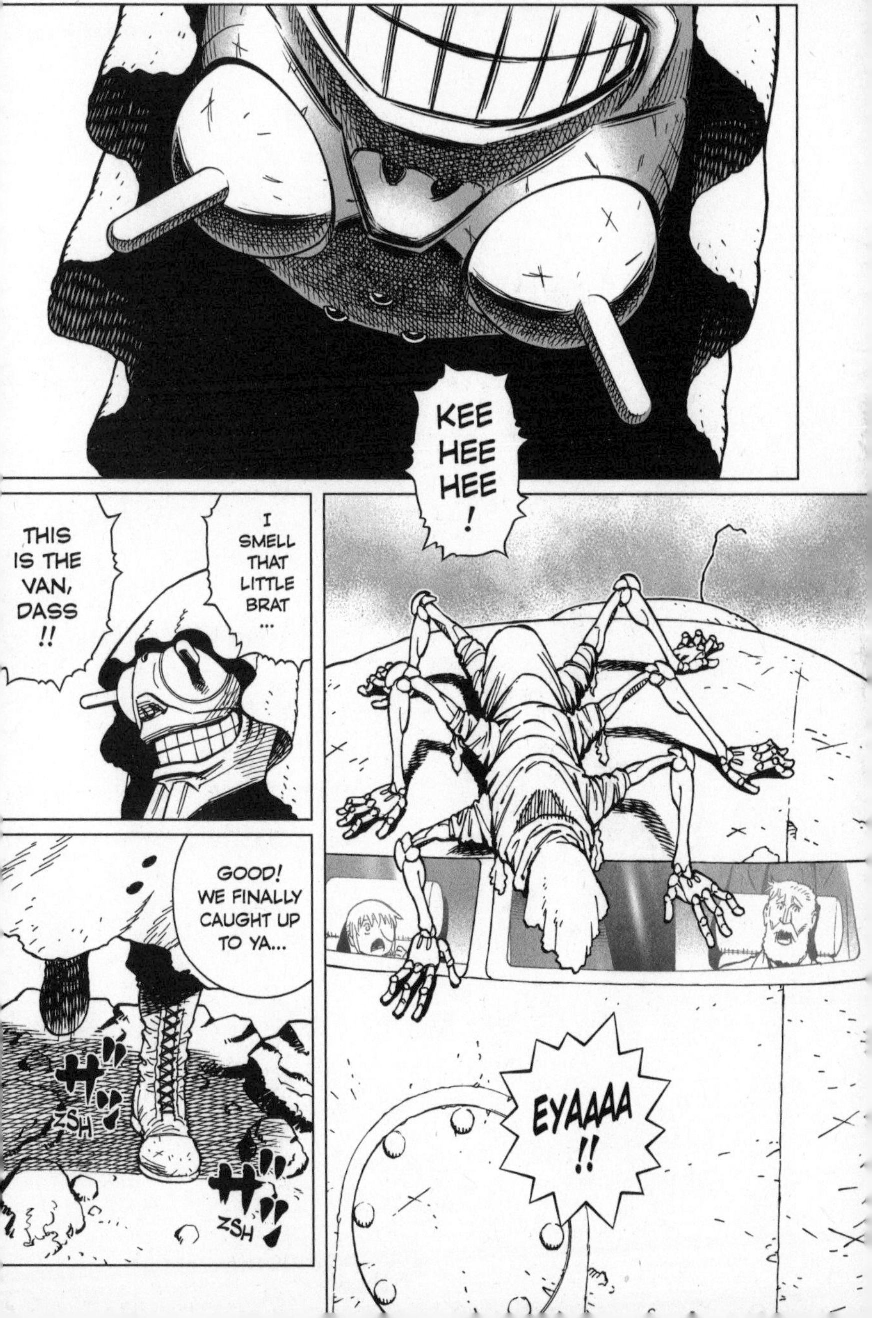
KEE HEE HEE!
EYAAAA!!
I SMELL THAT LITTLE BRAT...
THIS IS THE VAN, DASS!!
GOOD! WE FINALLY CAUGHT UP TO YA...
ZSH
ZSH

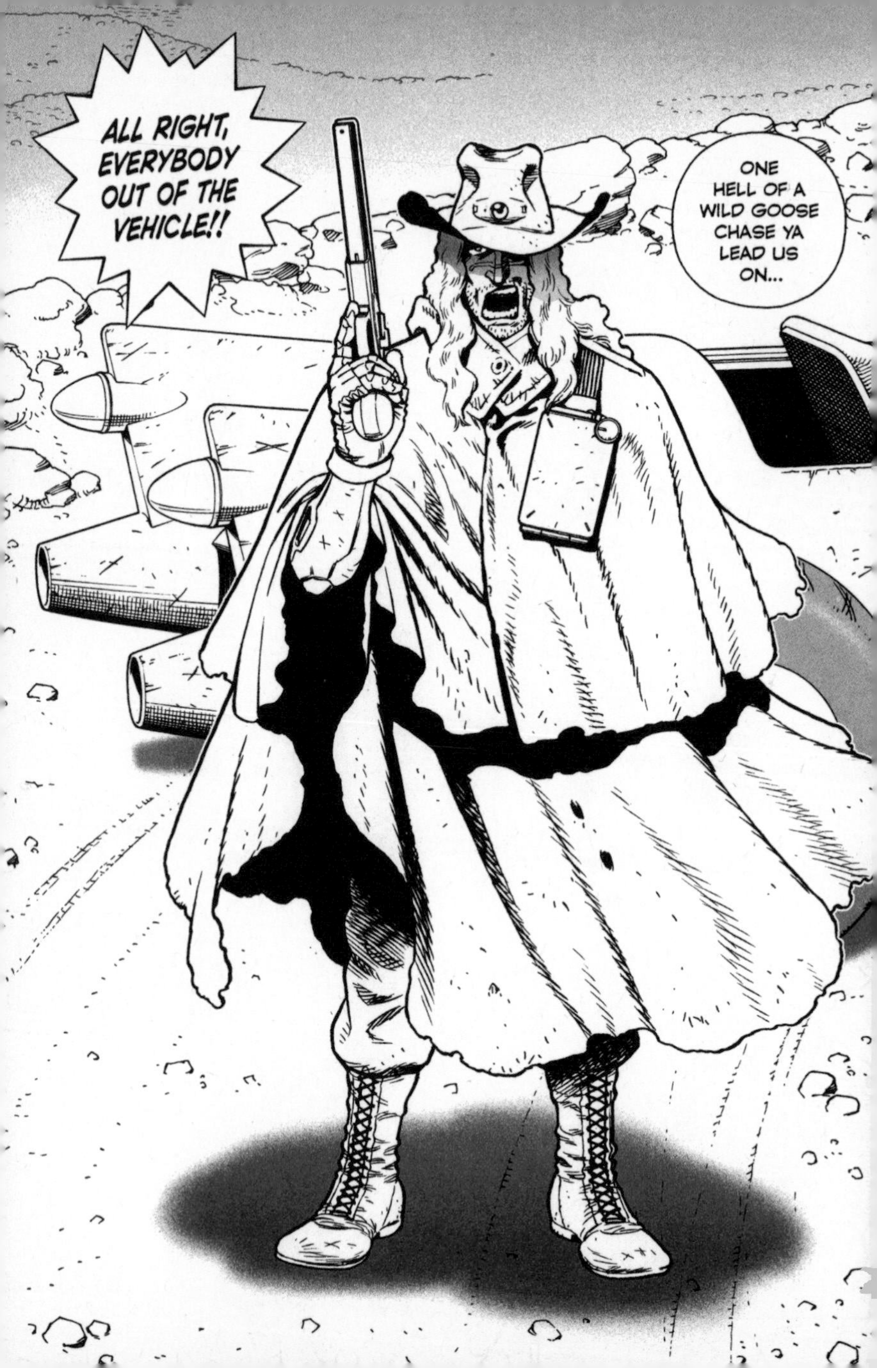
ONE HELL OF A WILD GOOSE CHASE YA LEAD US ON...
ALL RIGHT, EVERYBODY OUT OF THE VEHICLE!!

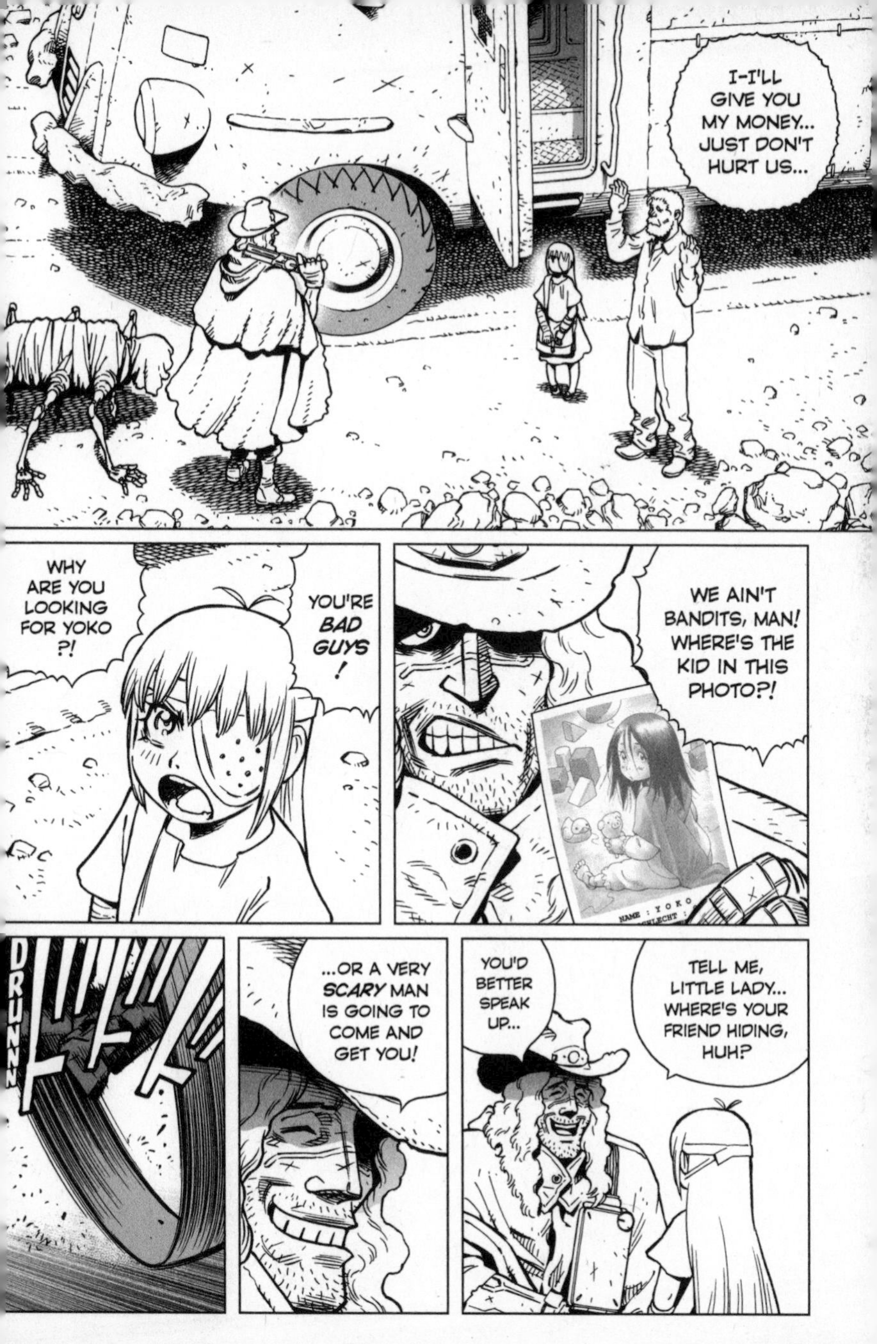
I-I'LL GIVE YOU MY MONEY... JUST DON'T HURT US...
WE AIN'T BANDITS, MAN! WHERE'S THE KID IN THIS PHOTO?!
WHY ARE YOU LOOKING FOR YOKO?!
YOU'RE *BAD GUYS*!
TELL ME, LITTLE LADY... WHERE'S YOUR FRIEND HIDING, HUH?
YOU'D BETTER SPEAK UP...
...OR A VERY *SCARY* MAN IS GOING TO COME AND GET YOU!
DRUNNN

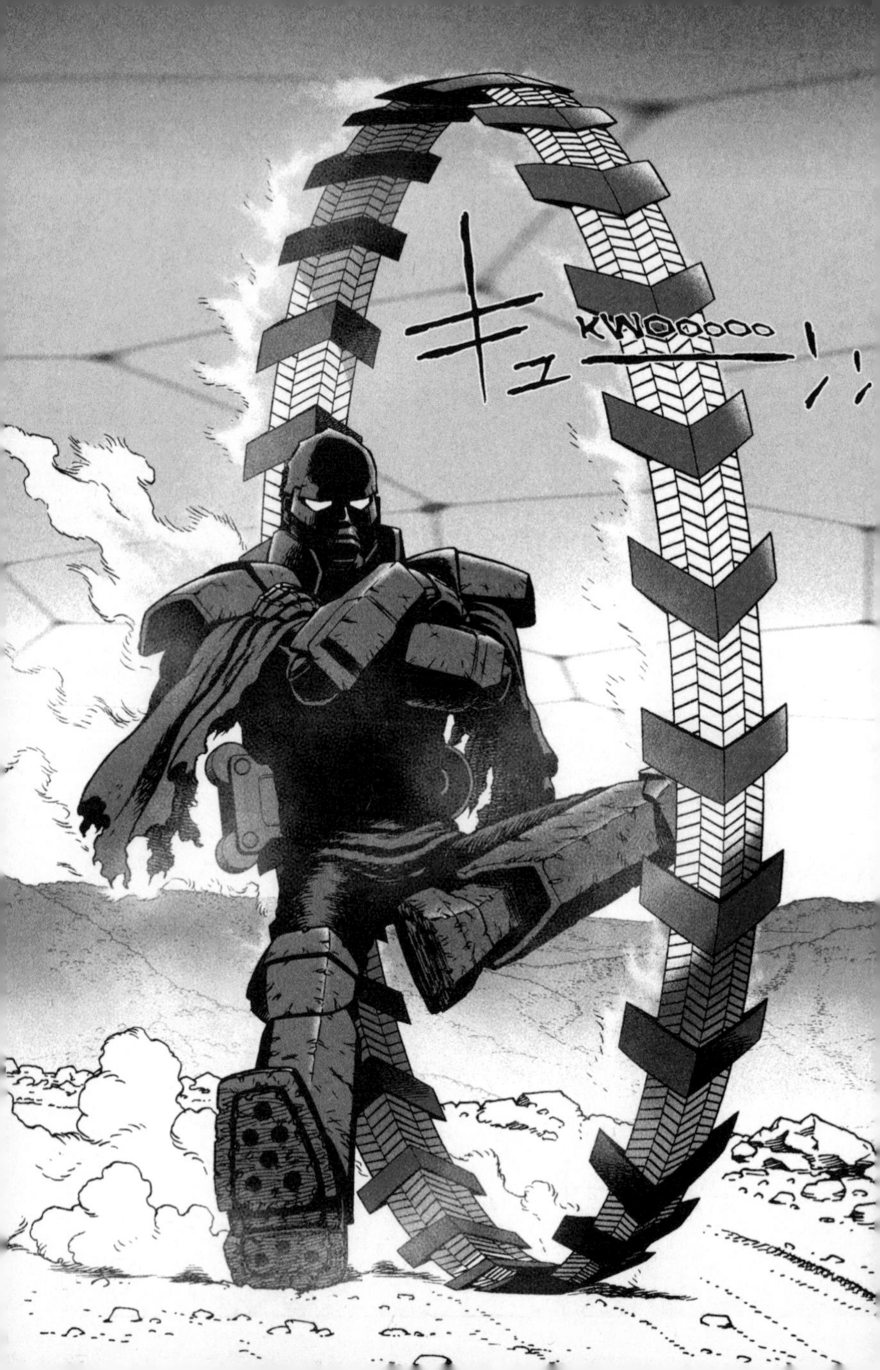
キュ—!!
KWOOOOOO

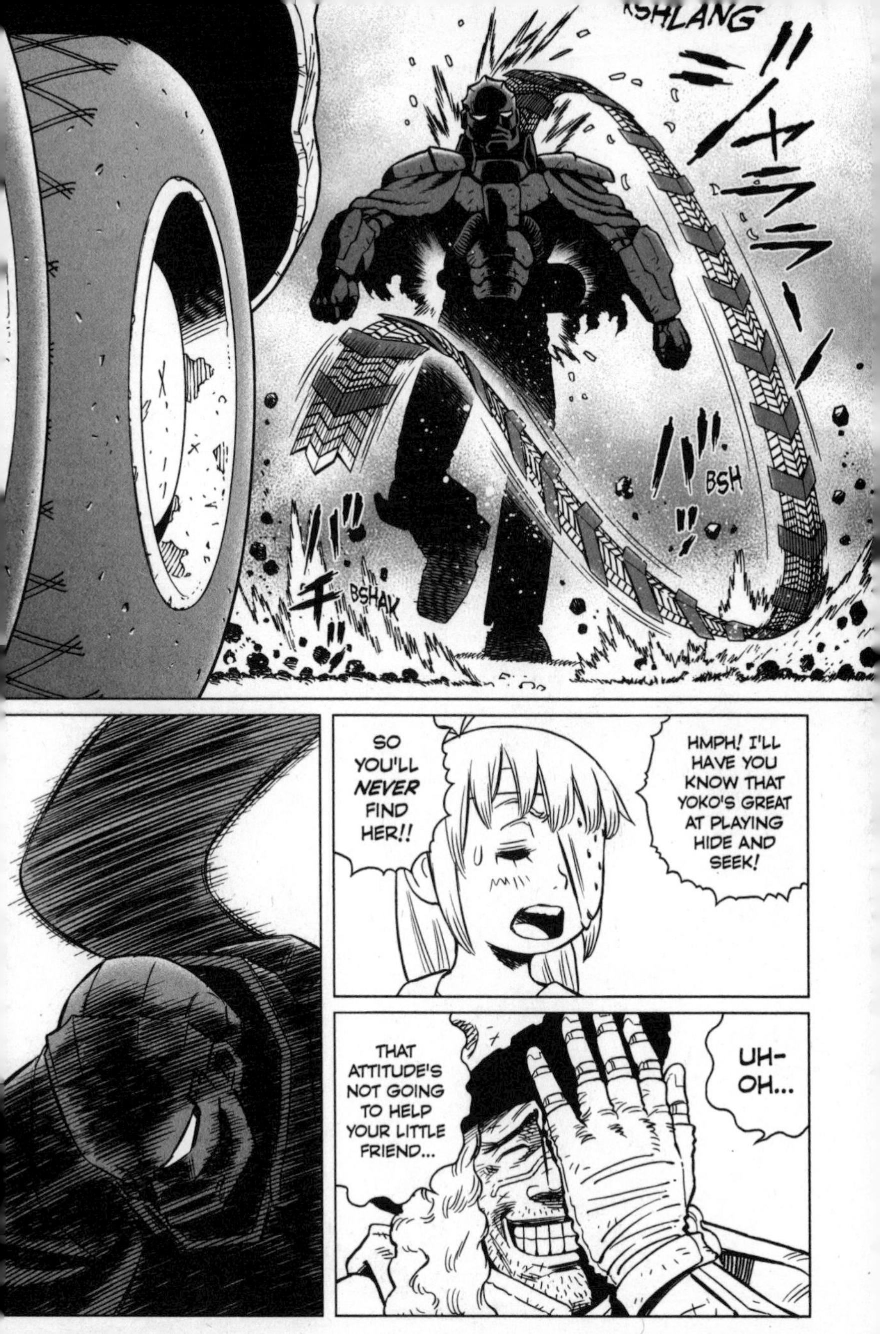
KSHLANG
BSH
BSHAK
HMPH! I'LL HAVE YOU KNOW THAT YOKO'S GREAT AT PLAYING HIDE AND SEEK!
SO YOU'LL *NEVER* FIND HER!!
UH-OH...
THAT ATTITUDE'S NOT GOING TO HELP YOUR LITTLE FRIEND...

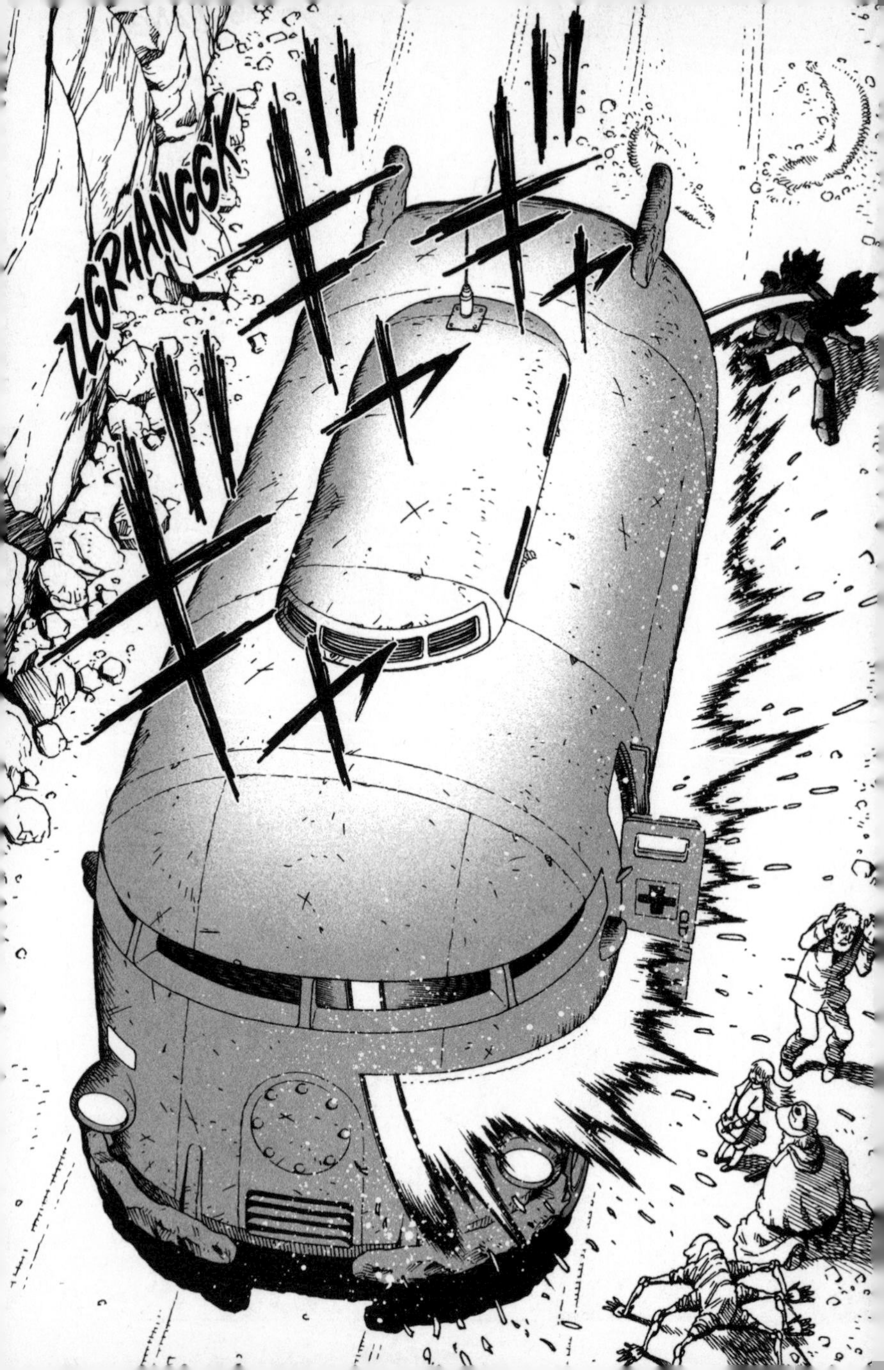
ZZGRAANGGK

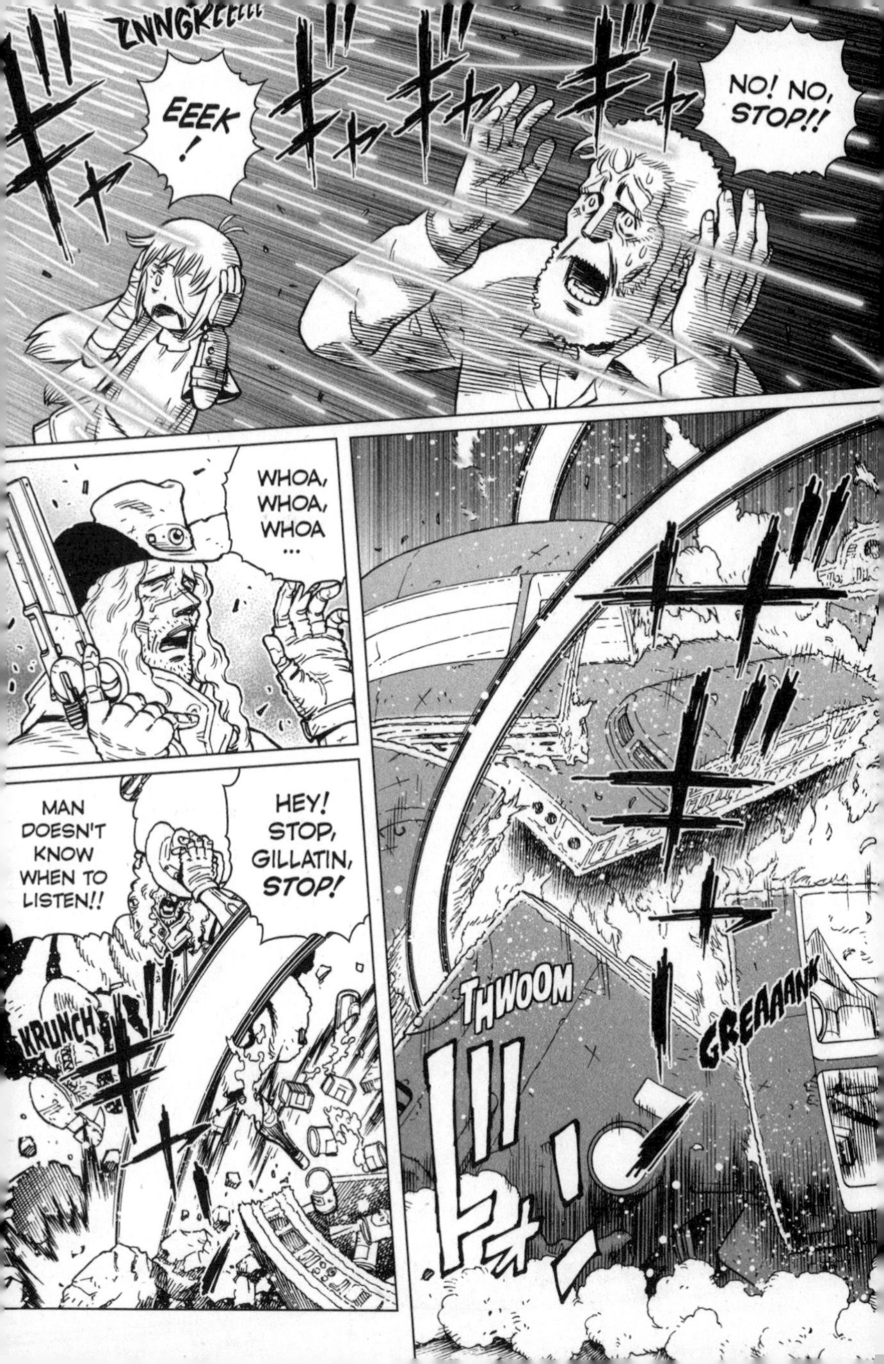
NO! NO, STOP!!
EEEK!
ZNNGKEEEEE
GREAAANK
THWOOM
WHOA, WHOA, WHOA ...
HEY! STOP, GILLATIN, STOP!
MAN DOESN'T KNOW WHEN TO LISTEN!!
KRUNCH

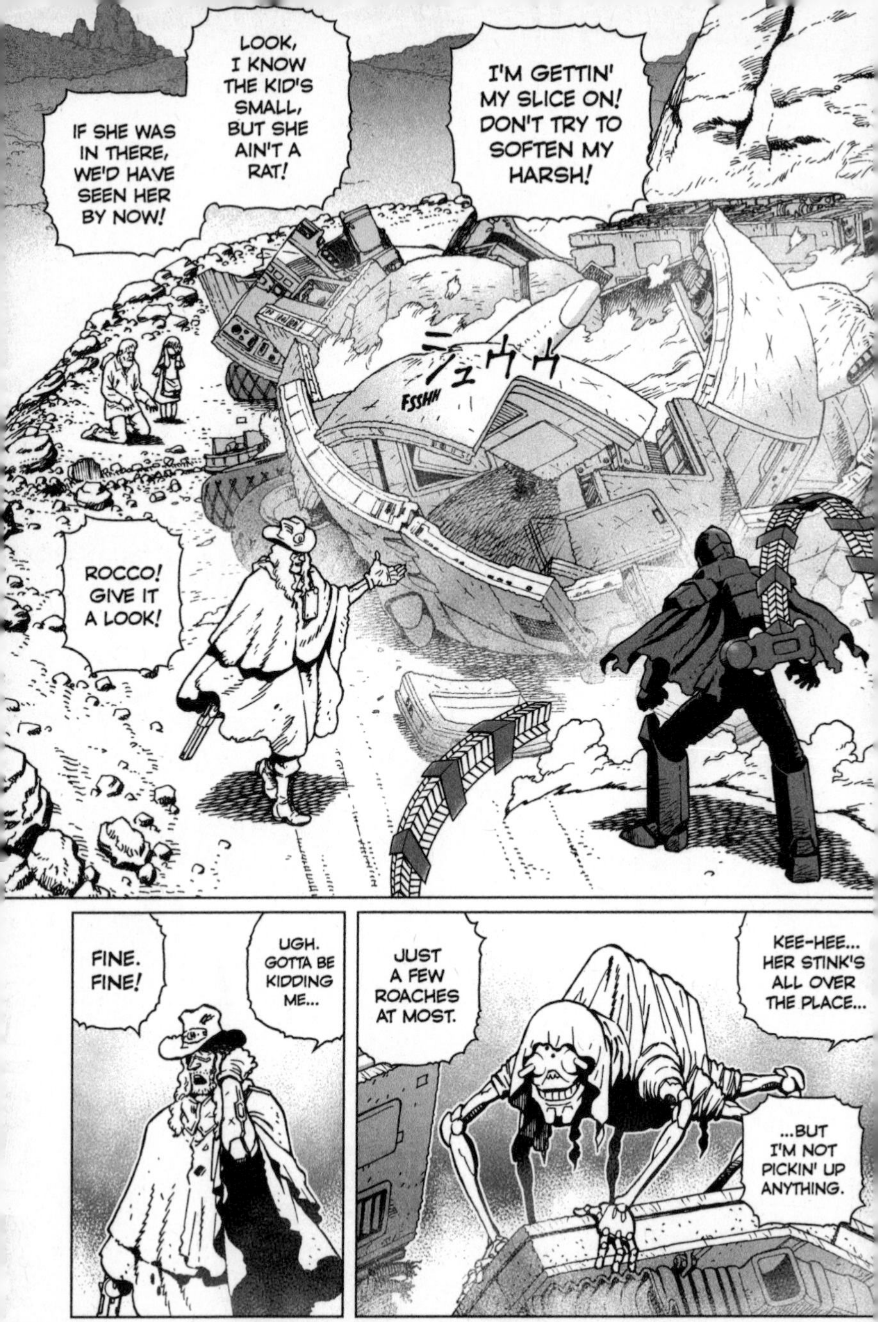
I'M GETTIN' MY SLICE ON! DON'T TRY TO SOFTEN MY HARSH!
LOOK, I KNOW THE KID'S SMALL, BUT SHE AIN'T A RAT!
IF SHE WAS IN THERE, WE'D HAVE SEEN HER BY NOW!
シュウウ
FSSHH
ROCCO! GIVE IT A LOOK!
KEE-HEE... HER STINK'S ALL OVER THE PLACE...
JUST A FEW ROACHES AT MOST.
...BUT I'M NOT PICKIN' UP ANYTHING.
UGH. GOTTA BE KIDDING ME...
FINE. FINE!

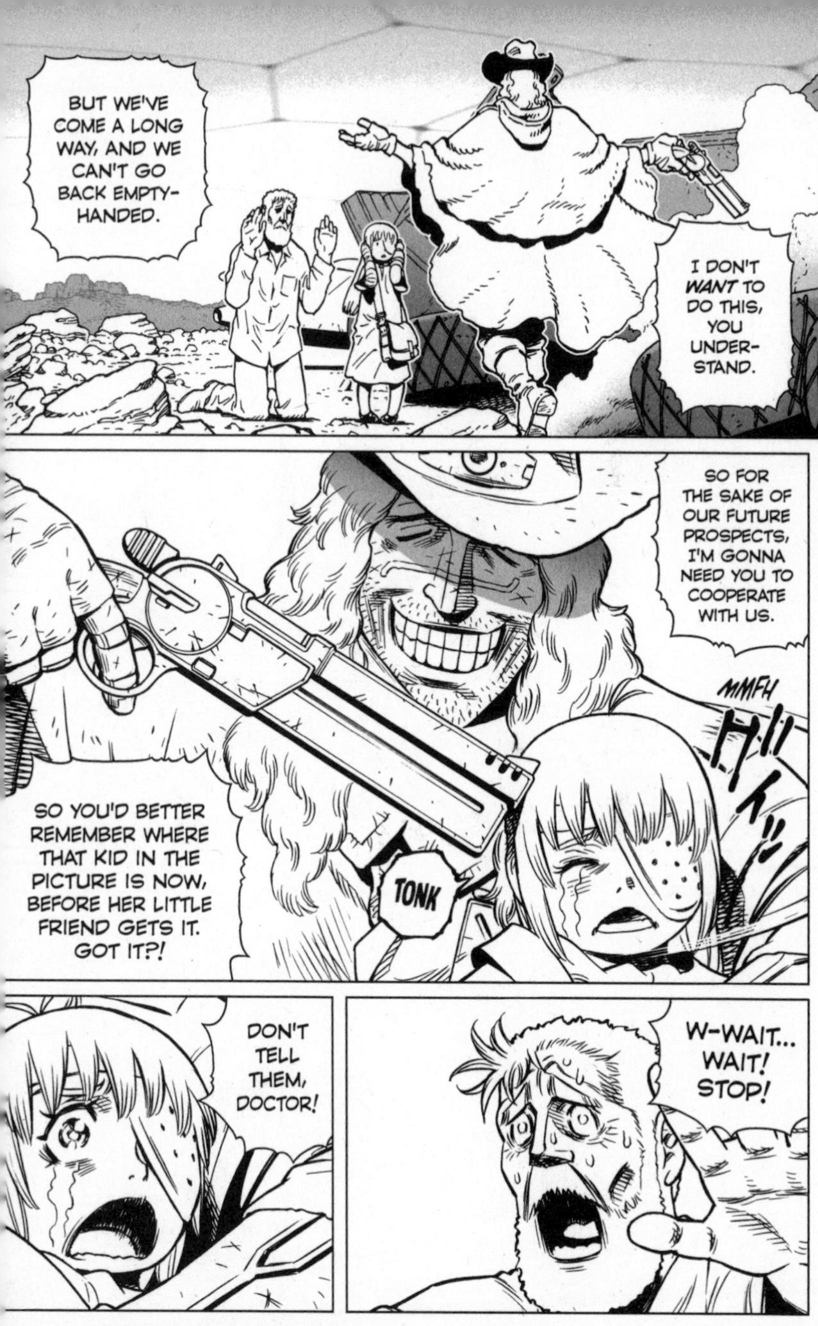
I DON'T WANT TO DO THIS, YOU UNDERSTAND.
BUT WE'VE COME A LONG WAY, AND WE CAN'T GO BACK EMPTY-HANDED.
SO FOR THE SAKE OF OUR FUTURE PROSPECTS, I'M GONNA NEED YOU TO COOPERATE WITH US.
MMFH
TONK
SO YOU'D BETTER REMEMBER WHERE THAT KID IN THE PICTURE IS NOW, BEFORE HER LITTLE FRIEND GETS IT. GOT IT?!
W-WAIT... WAIT! STOP!
DON'T TELL THEM, DOCTOR!

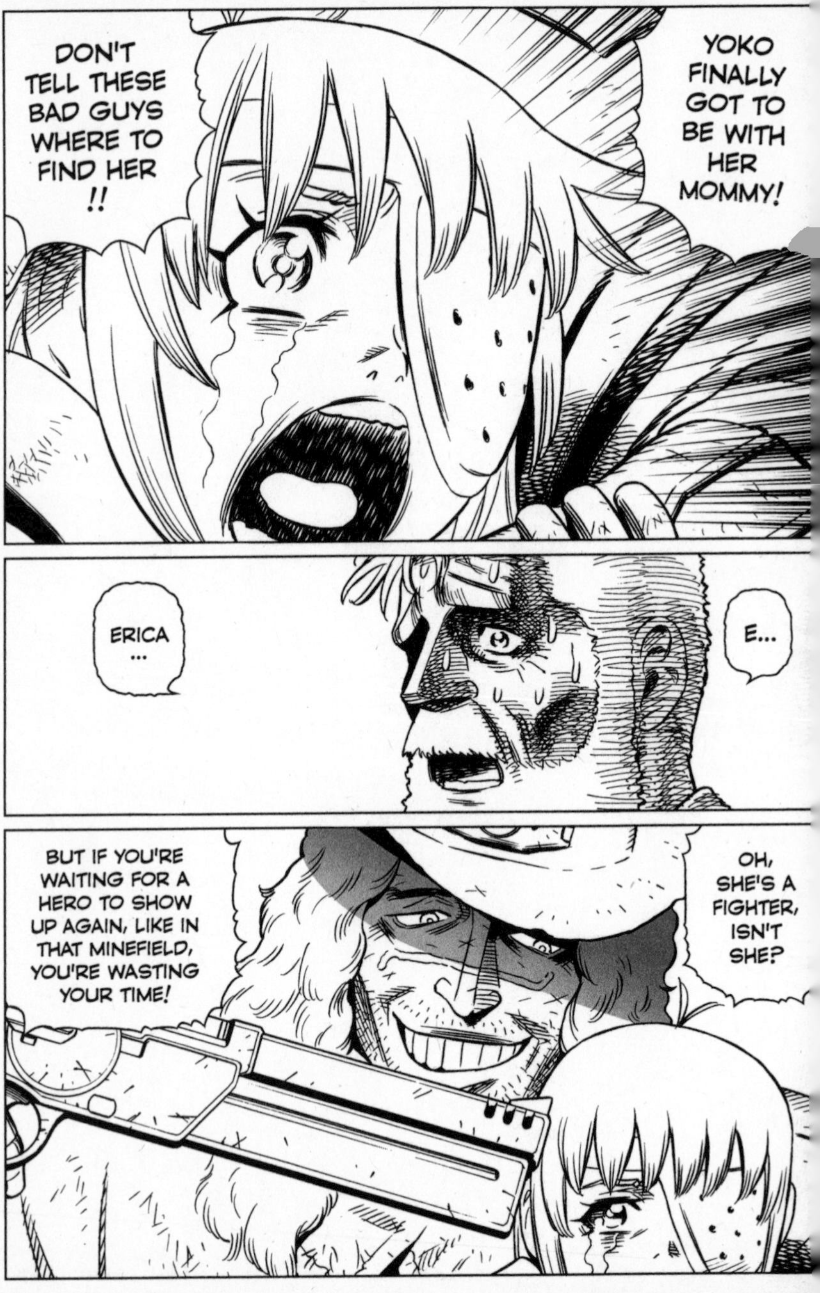
YOKO FINALLY GOT TO BE WITH HER MOMMY!
DON'T TELL THESE BAD GUYS WHERE TO FIND HER !!
E...
ERICA ...
OH, SHE'S A FIGHTER, ISN'T SHE?
BUT IF YOU'RE WAITING FOR A HERO TO SHOW UP AGAIN, LIKE IN THAT MINEFIELD, YOU'RE WASTING YOUR TIME!

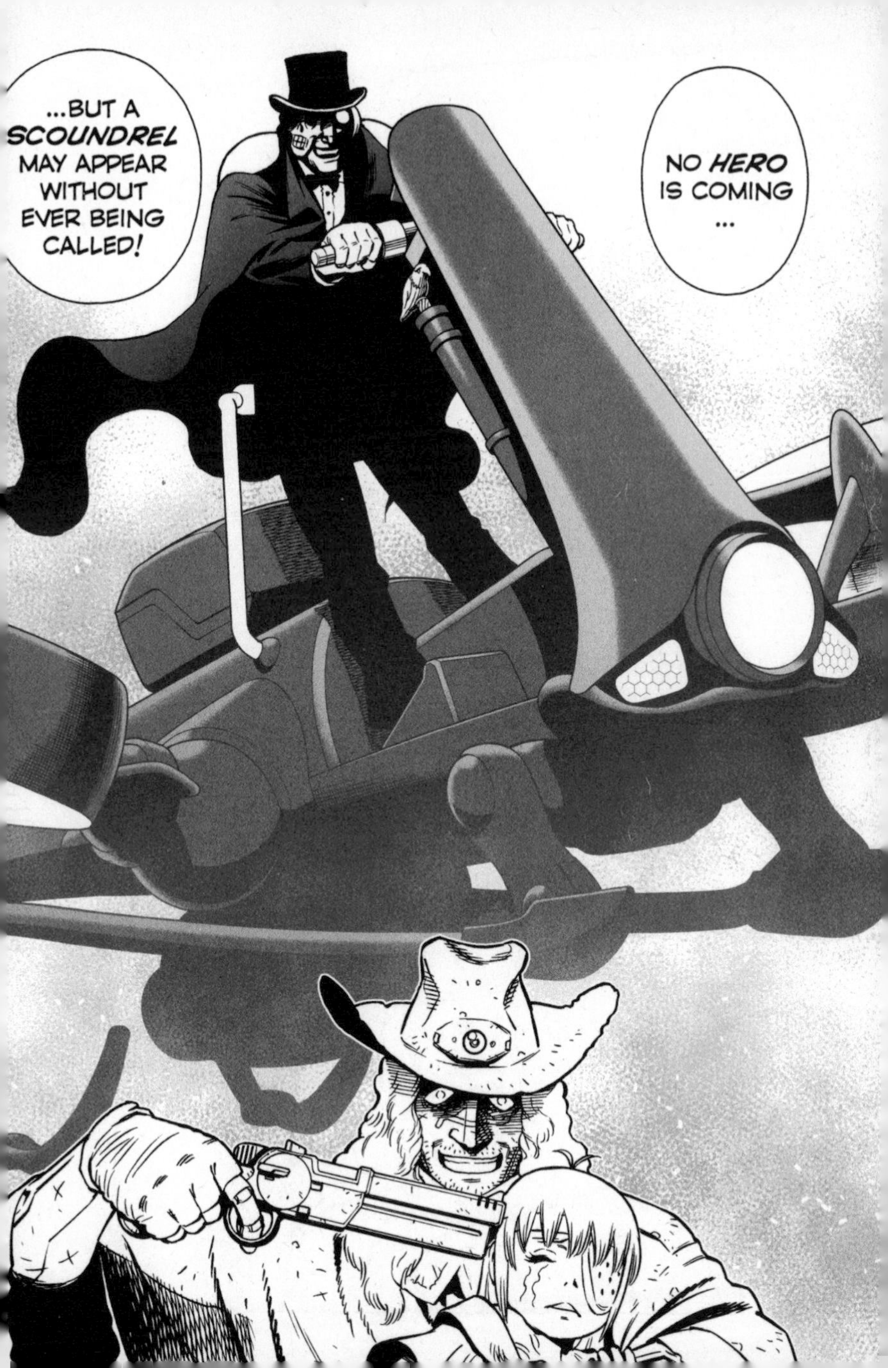
NO HERO IS COMING ...
...BUT A SCOUNDREL MAY APPEAR WITHOUT EVER BEING CALLED!

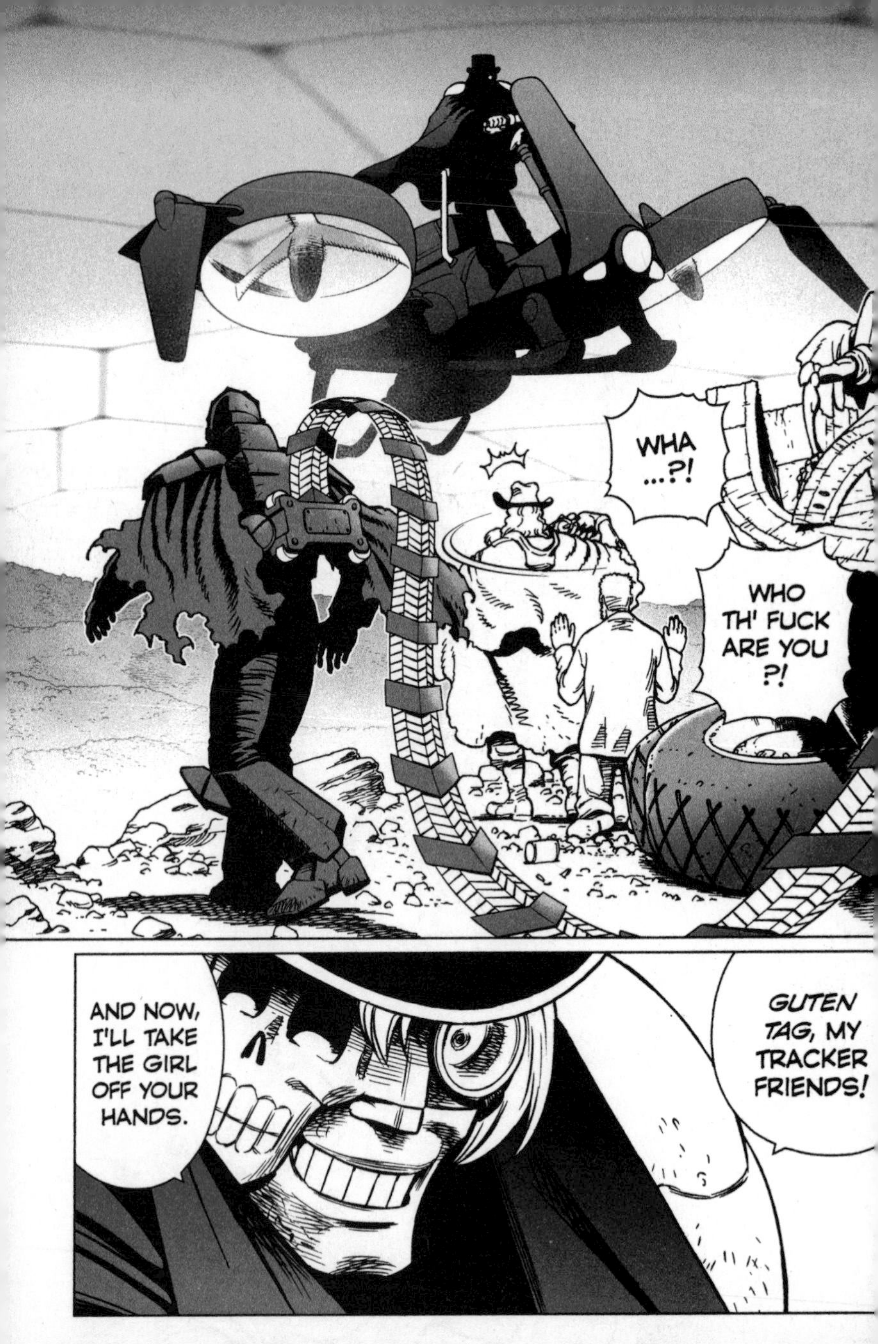
WHA ...?!
WHO TH' FUCK ARE YOU ?!
GUTEN TAG, MY TRACKER FRIENDS!
AND NOW, I'LL TAKE THE GIRL OFF YOUR HANDS.

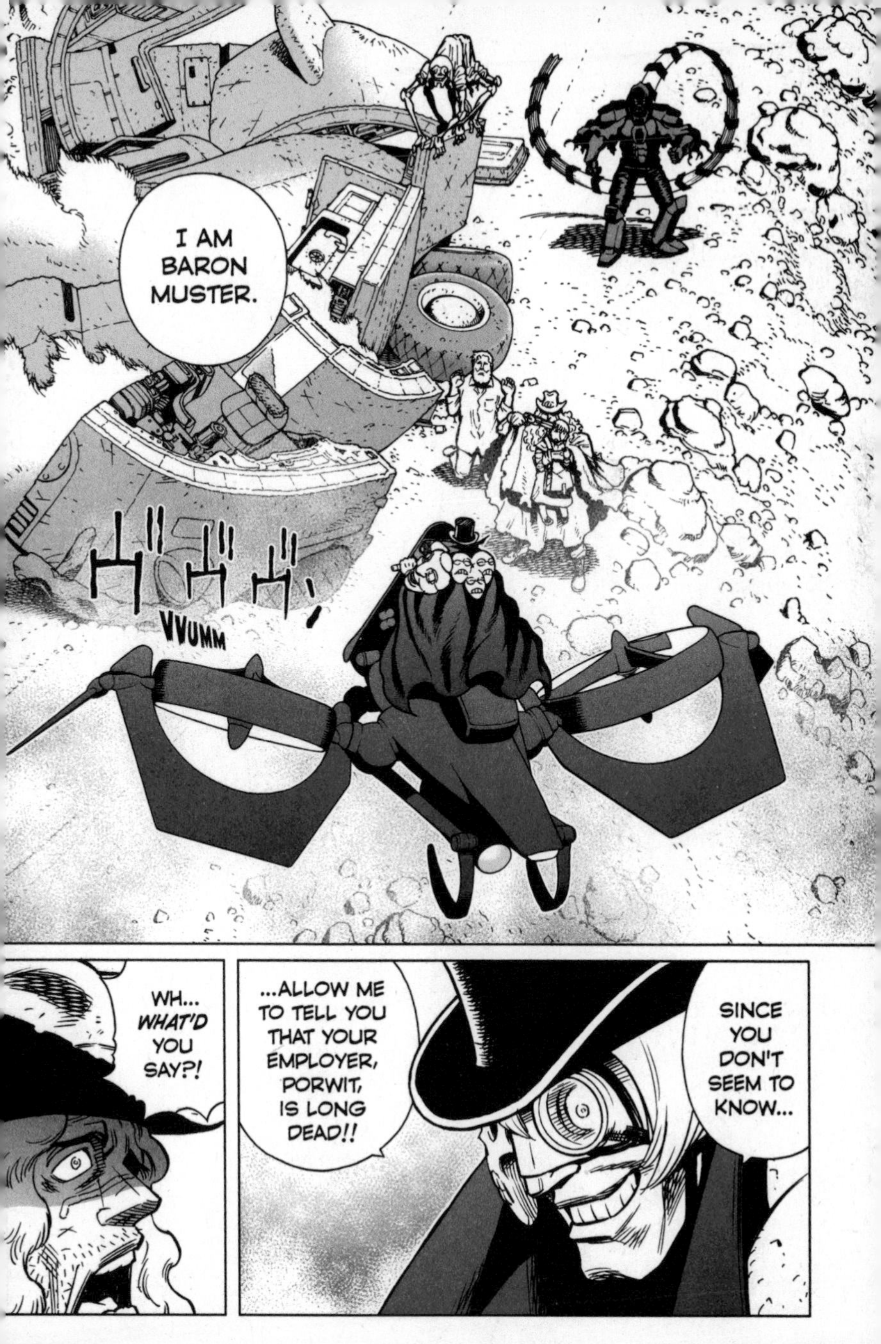
I AM BARON MUSTER.
VVUMM
SINCE YOU DON'T SEEM TO KNOW...
...ALLOW ME TO TELL YOU THAT YOUR EMPLOYER, PORWIT, IS LONG DEAD!!
WH... *WHAT'D* YOU SAY?!

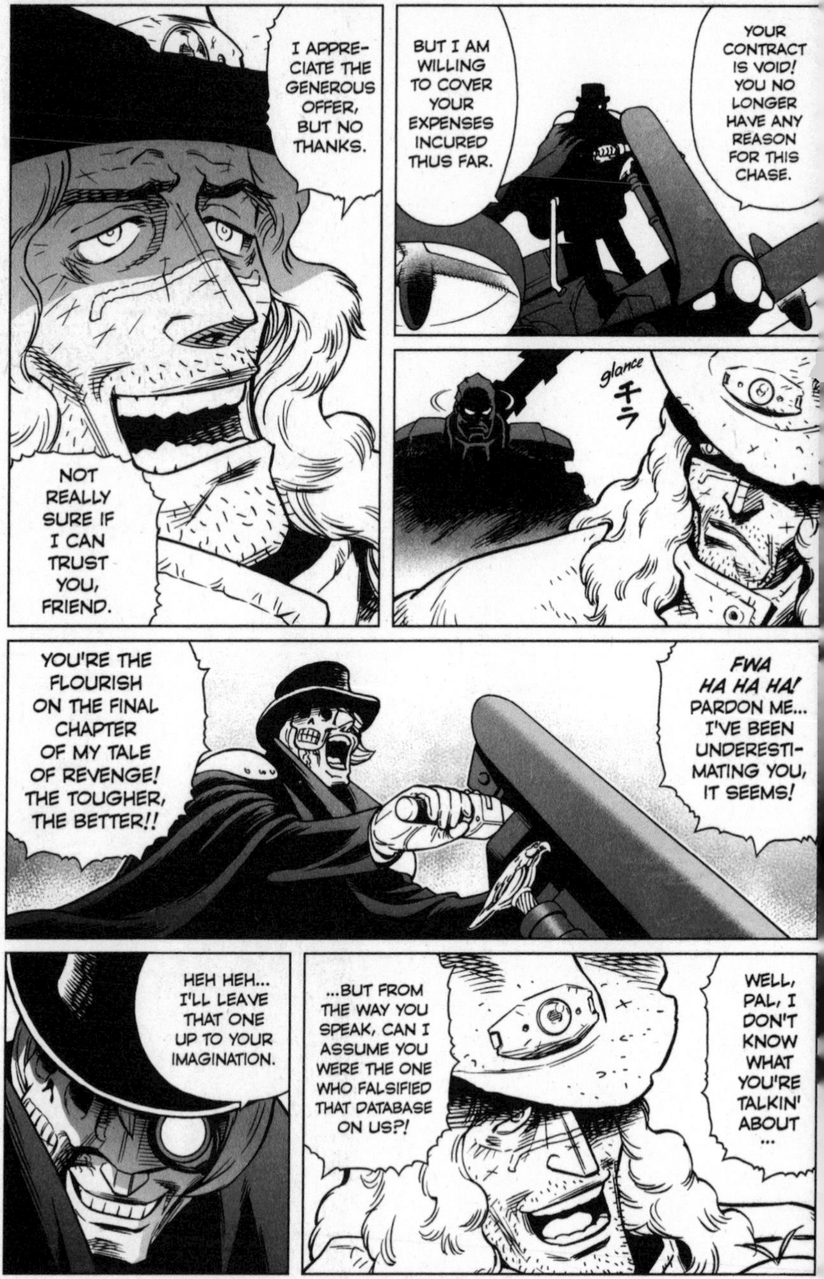
YOUR CONTRACT IS VOID! YOU NO LONGER HAVE ANY REASON FOR THIS CHASE.
BUT I AM WILLING TO COVER YOUR EXPENSES INCURED THUS FAR.
glance チラ
I APPRE-CIATE THE GENEROUS OFFER, BUT NO THANKS.
NOT REALLY SURE IF I CAN TRUST YOU, FRIEND.
FWA HA HA HA! PARDON ME... I'VE BEEN UNDERESTI-MATING YOU, IT SEEMS!
YOU'RE THE FLOURISH ON THE FINAL CHAPTER OF MY TALE OF REVENGE! THE TOUGHER, THE BETTER!!
WELL, PAL, I DON'T KNOW WHAT YOU'RE TALKIN' ABOUT ...
...BUT FROM THE WAY YOU SPEAK, CAN I ASSUME YOU WERE THE ONE WHO FALSIFIED THAT DATABASE ON US?!
HEH HEH... I'LL LEAVE THAT ONE UP TO YOUR IMAGINATION.

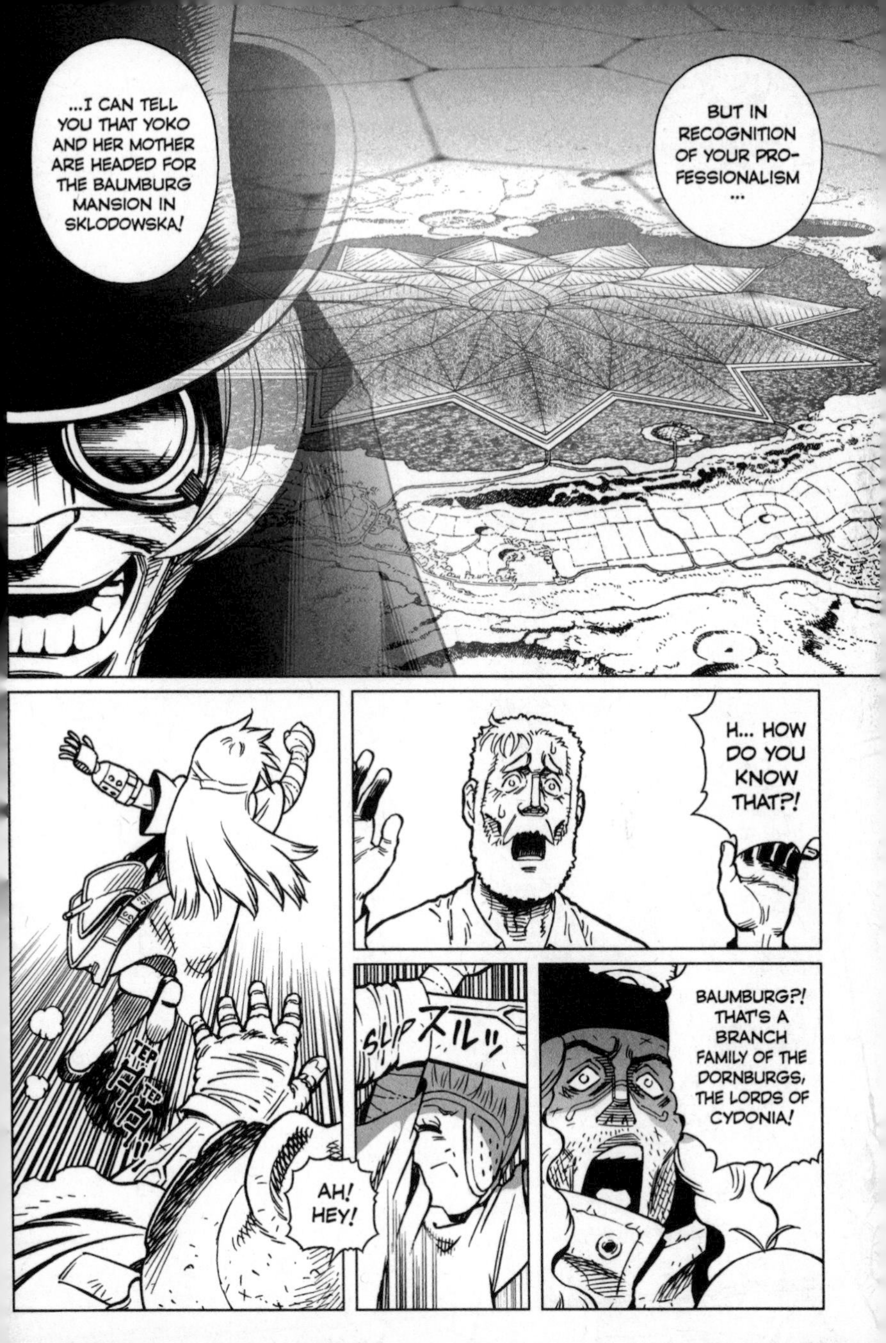
BUT IN RECOGNITION OF YOUR PRO-FESSIONALISM ...
...I CAN TELL YOU THAT YOKO AND HER MOTHER ARE HEADED FOR THE BAUMBURG MANSION IN SKLODOWSKA!
H... HOW DO YOU KNOW THAT?!
BAUMBURG?! THAT'S A BRANCH FAMILY OF THE DORNBURGS, THE LORDS OF CYDONIA!
SLIP スル!!
AH! HEY!
TEP
TEP

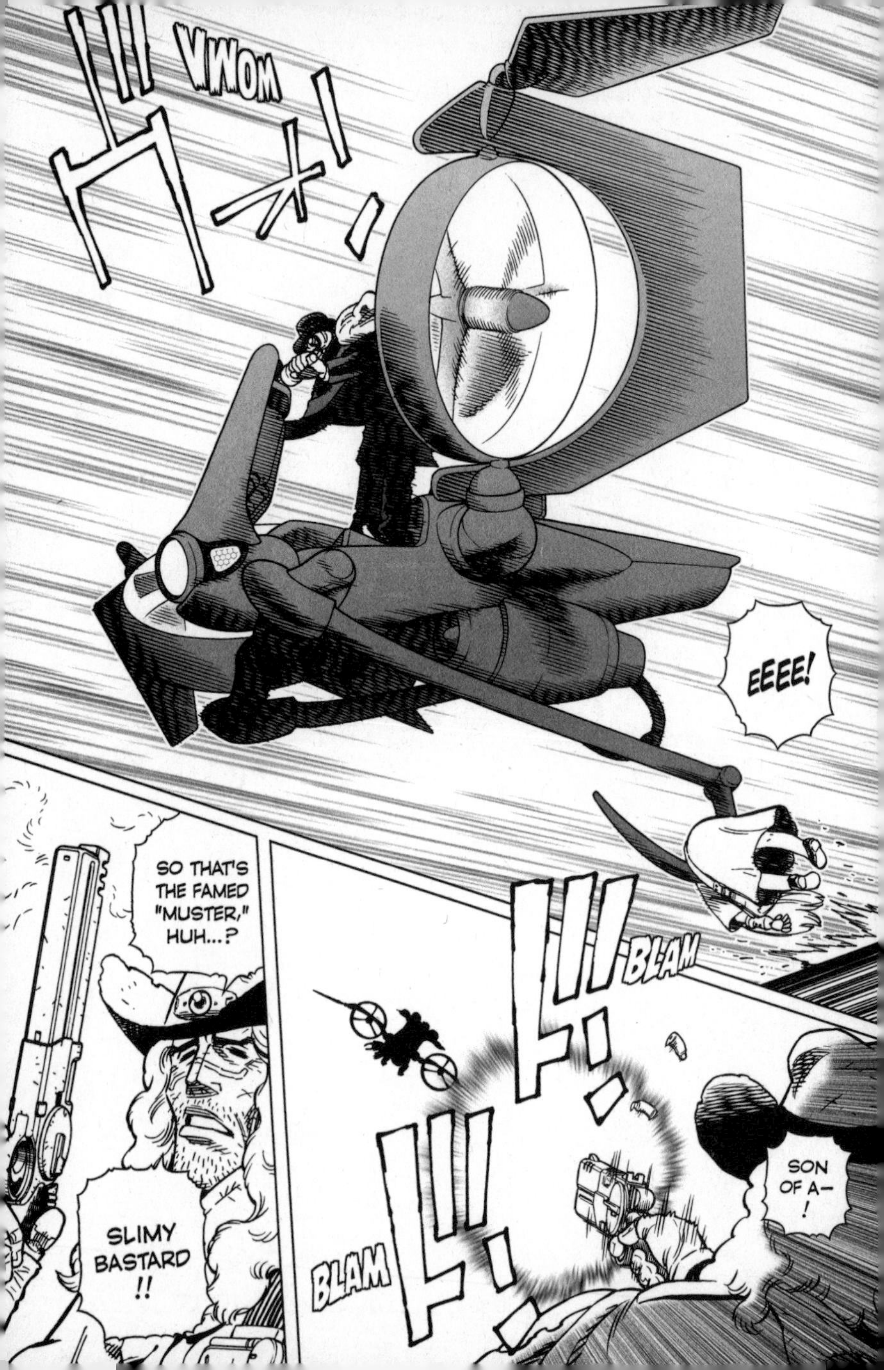
VWOM
EEEE!
BLAM
SON OF A—!
BLAM
SO THAT'S THE FAMED "MUSTER," HUH...?
SLIMY BASTARD!!

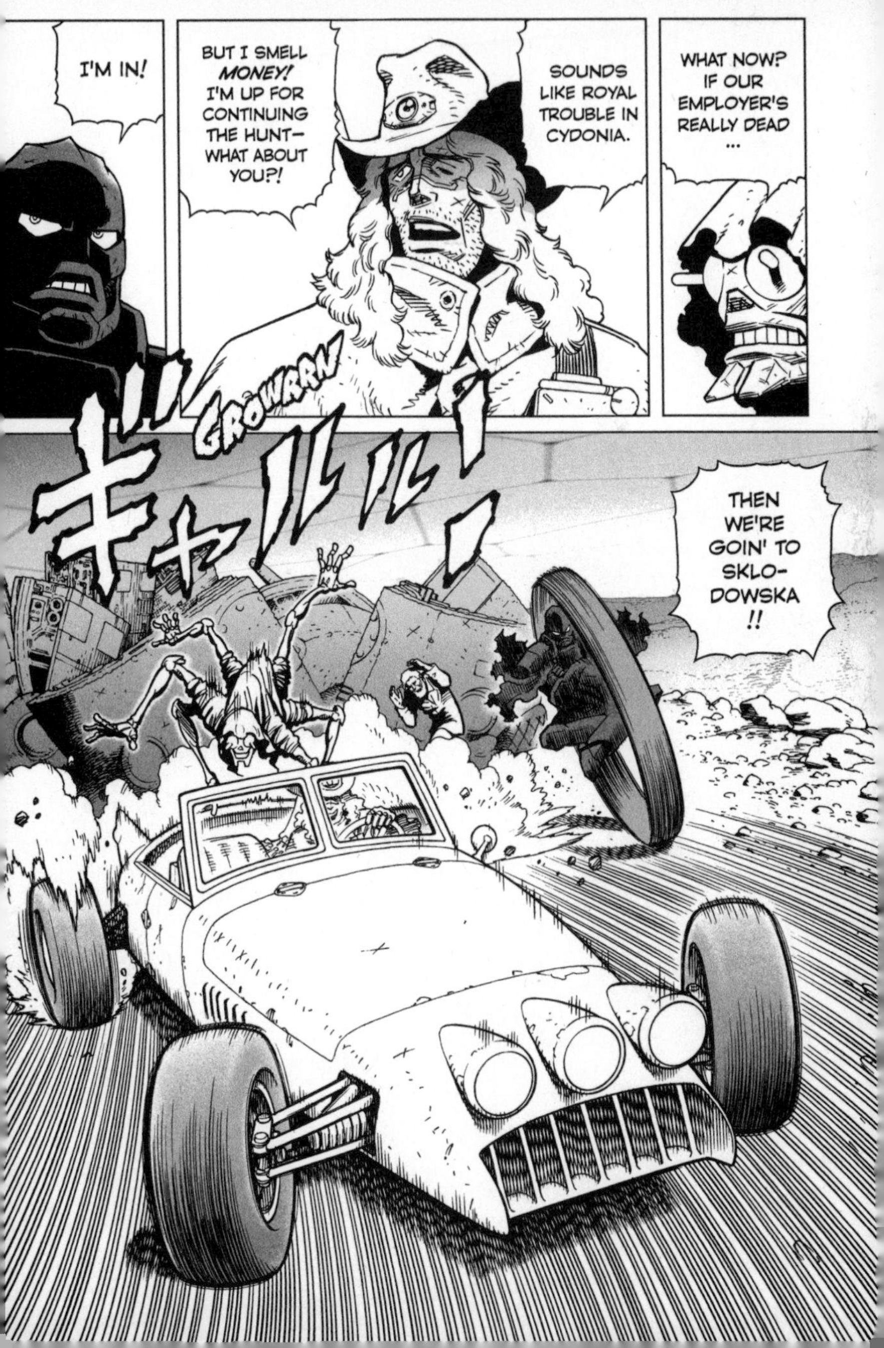
WHAT NOW? IF OUR EMPLOYER'S REALLY DEAD ...
SOUNDS LIKE ROYAL TROUBLE IN CYDONIA.
BUT I SMELL *MONEY!* I'M UP FOR CONTINUING THE HUNT—WHAT ABOUT YOU?!
I'M IN!
GROWRRN
ギャルル
THEN WE'RE GOIN' TO SKLO-DOWSKA!!

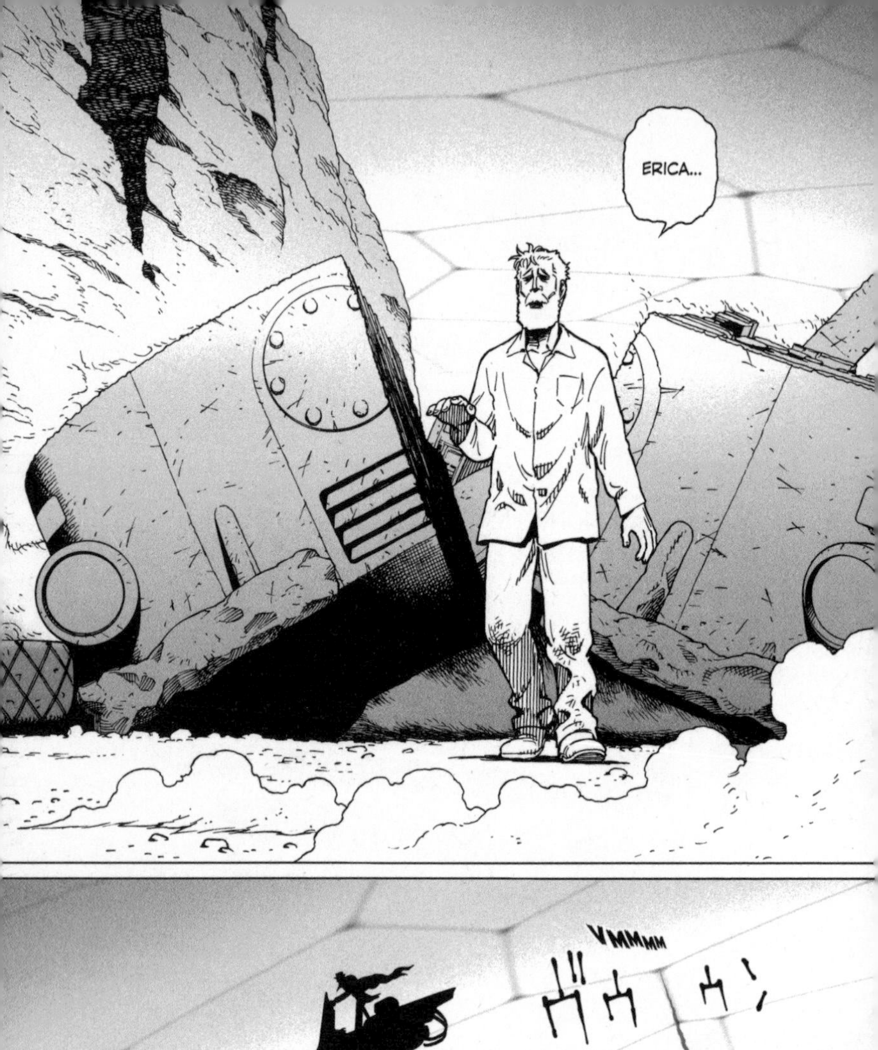
ERICA...
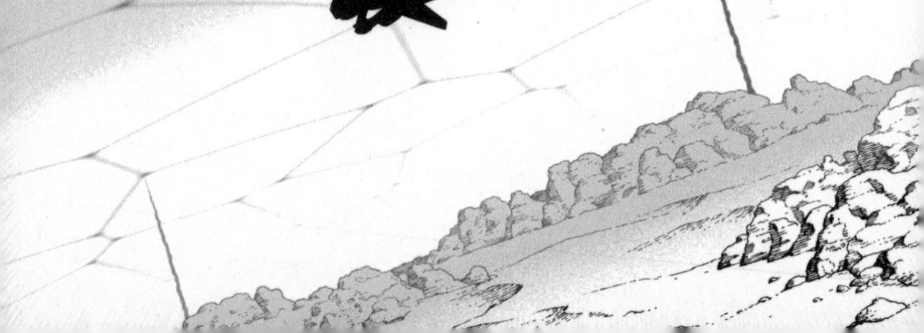
VMMMM

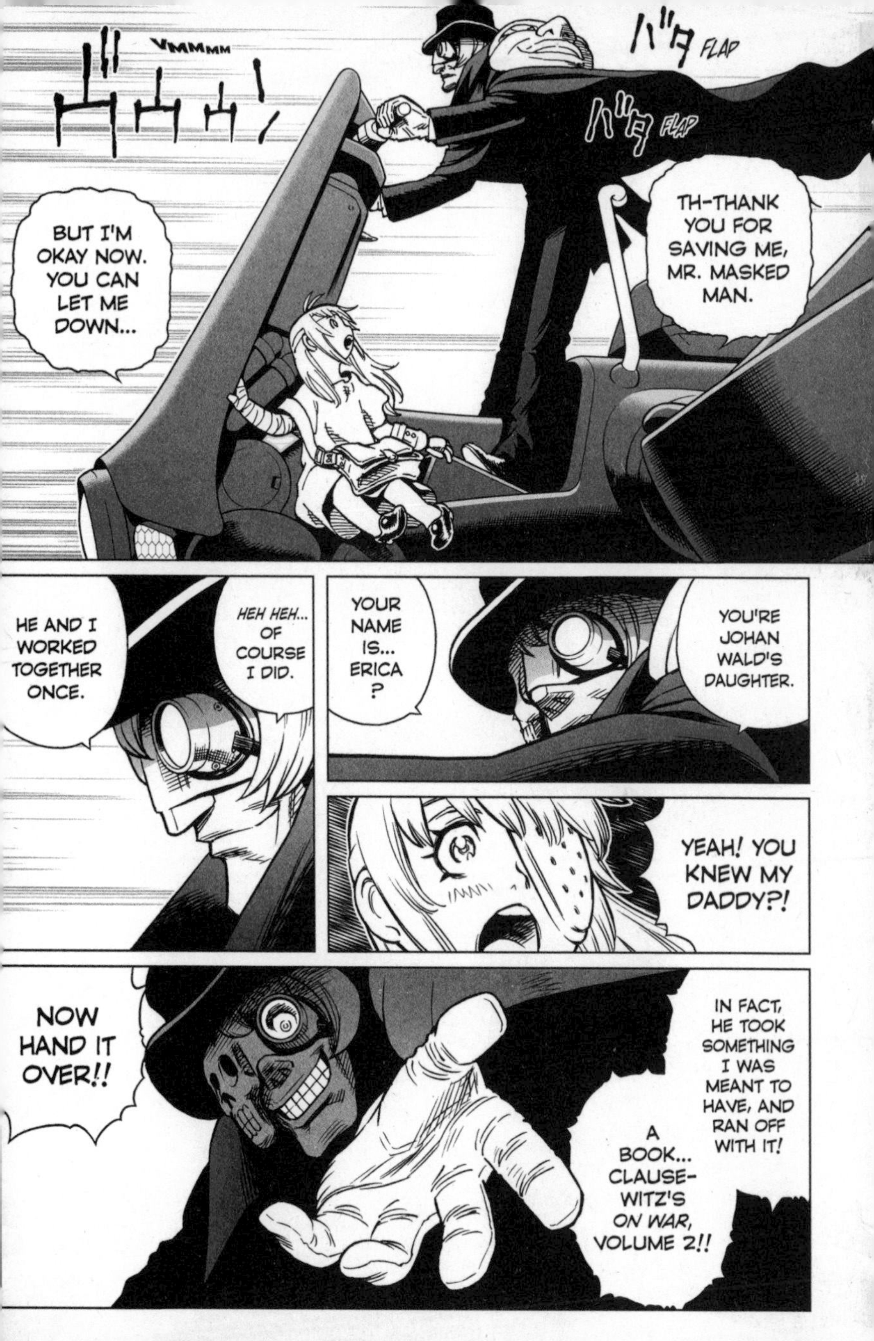
バタ FLAP
VMMMM
バタ FLAP
TH-THANK YOU FOR SAVING ME, MR. MASKED MAN.
BUT I'M OKAY NOW. YOU CAN LET ME DOWN...
YOU'RE JOHAN WALD'S DAUGHTER.
YOUR NAME IS... ERICA?
YEAH! YOU KNEW MY DADDY?!
HEH HEH... OF COURSE I DID.
HE AND I WORKED TOGETHER ONCE.
IN FACT, HE TOOK SOMETHING I WAS MEANT TO HAVE, AND RAN OFF WITH IT!
A BOOK... CLAUSE-WITZ'S ON WAR, VOLUME 2!!
NOW HAND IT OVER!!

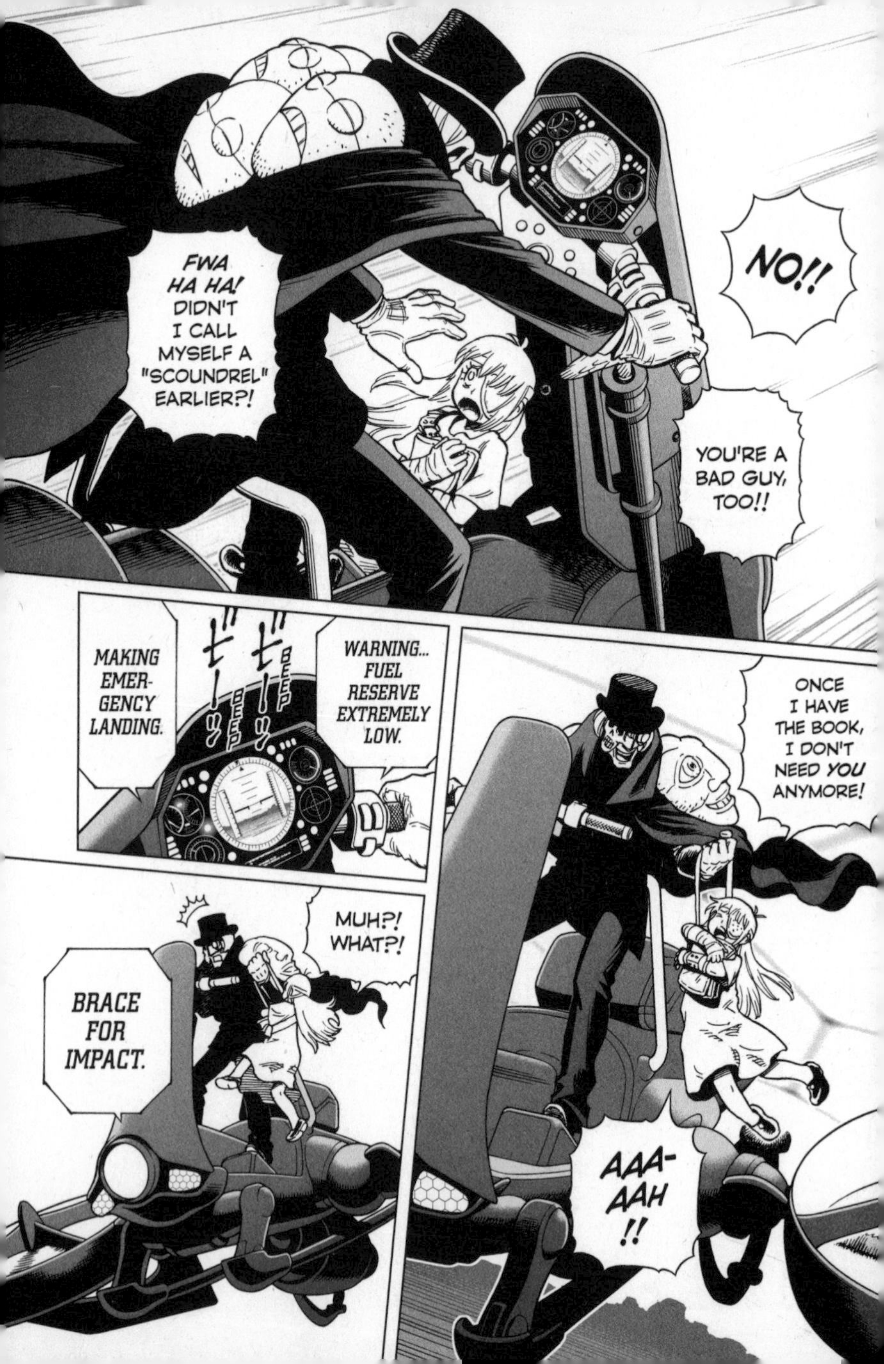

NO!!
FWA HA HA! DIDN'T I CALL MYSELF A "SCOUNDREL" EARLIER?!
YOU'RE A BAD GUY, TOO!!
ONCE I HAVE THE BOOK, I DON'T NEED *YOU* ANYMORE!
AAA-AAH!!
WARNING... FUEL RESERVE EXTREMELY LOW.
BEEP
BEEP
MAKING EMERGENCY LANDING.
MUH?! WHAT?!
BRACE FOR IMPACT.

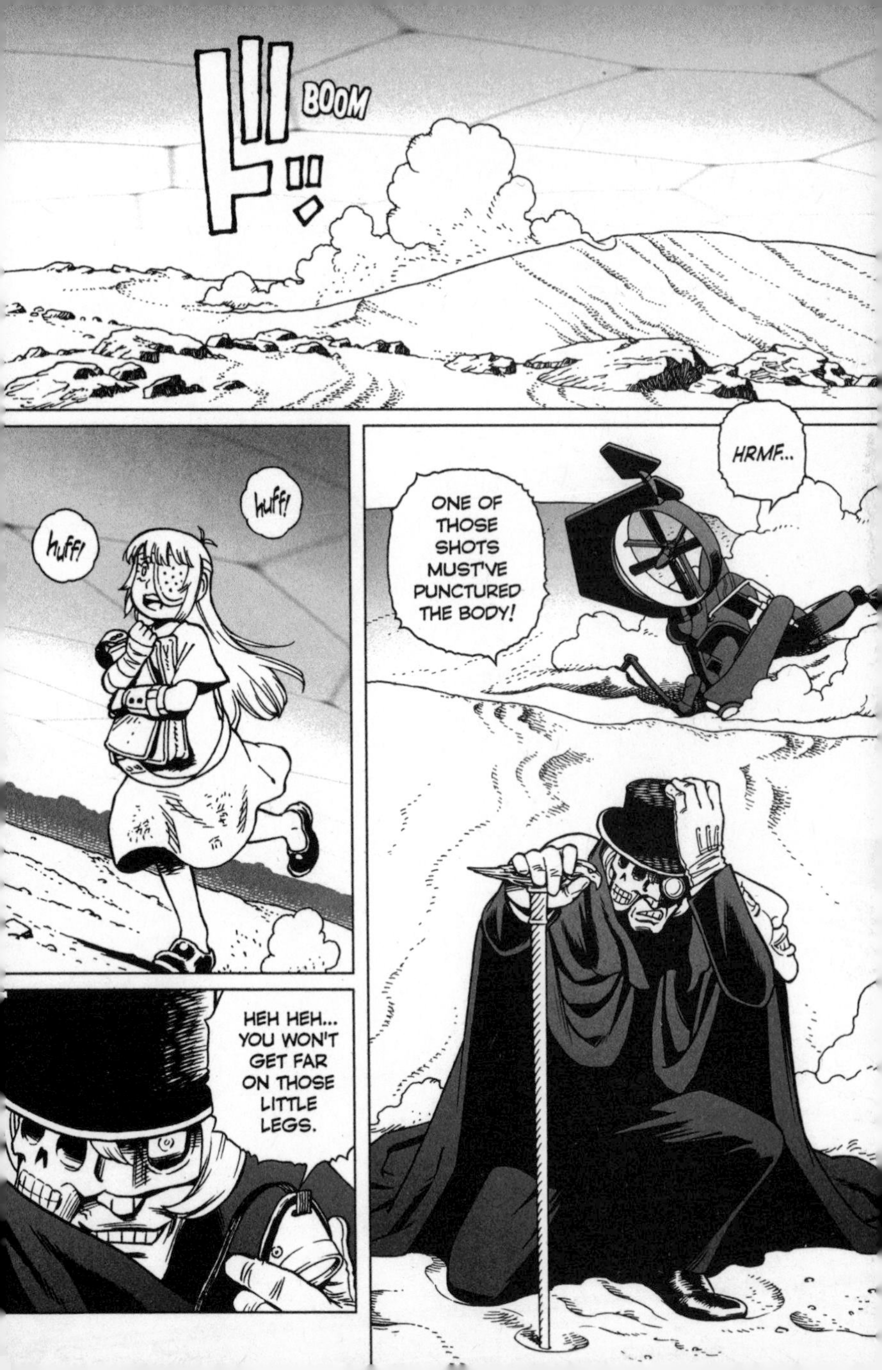
BOOM
HRMF...
ONE OF THOSE SHOTS MUST'VE PUNCTURED THE BODY!
huff!
huff!
HEH HEH... YOU WON'T GET FAR ON THOSE LITTLE LEGS.

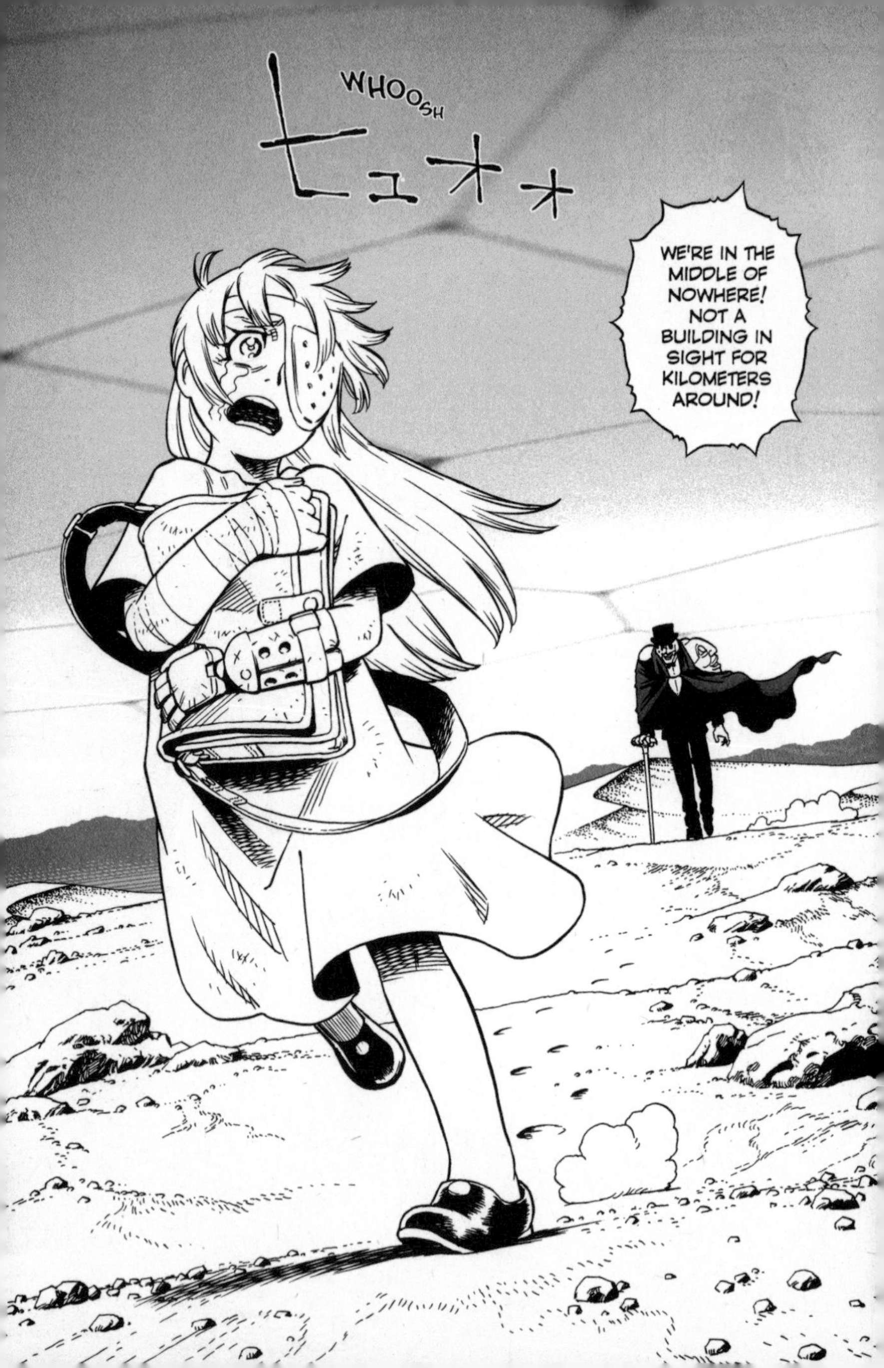
WHOOSH
ヒュオオ
WE'RE IN THE MIDDLE OF NOWHERE! NOT A BUILDING IN SIGHT FOR KILOMETERS AROUND!

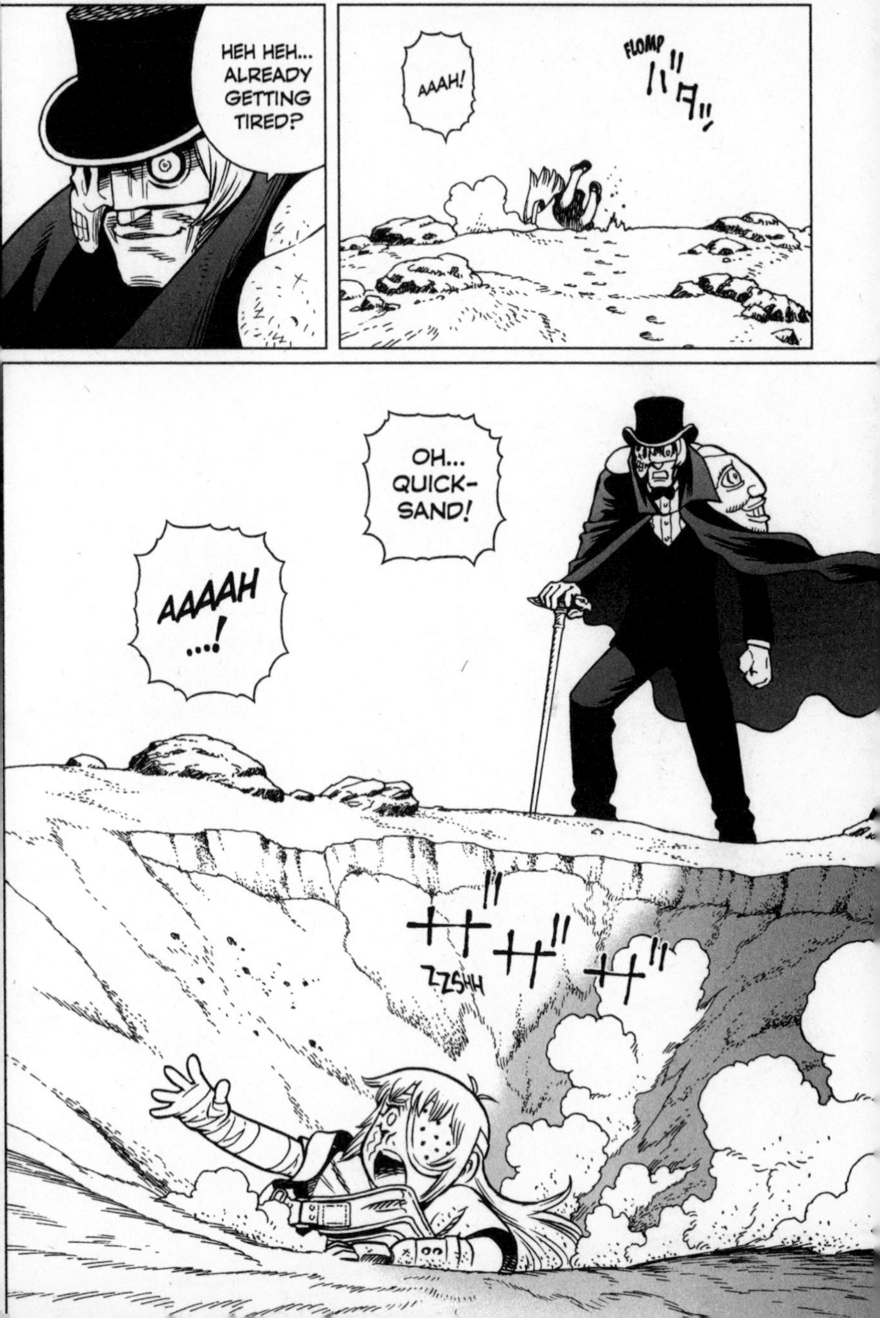
AAAH!
FLOMP
バタッ
HEH HEH... ALREADY GETTING TIRED?
OH... QUICK-SAND!
AAAAH ...!
ZZSHH

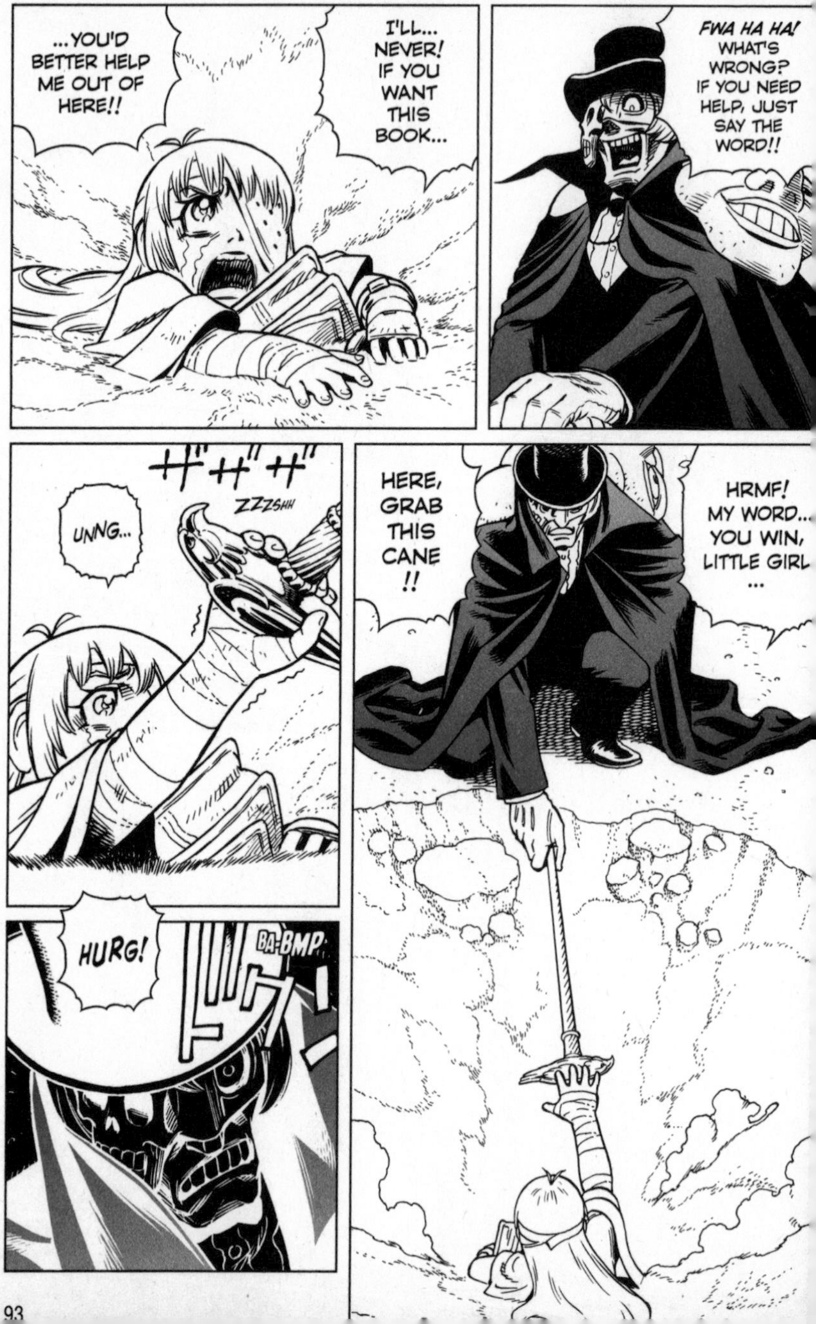
FWA HA HA! WHAT'S WRONG? IF YOU NEED HELP, JUST SAY THE WORD!!
I'LL... NEVER! IF YOU WANT THIS BOOK...
...YOU'D BETTER HELP ME OUT OF HERE!!
HRMF! MY WORD... YOU WIN, LITTLE GIRL...
HERE, GRAB THIS CANE!!
ザザザ
ZZZSHH
UNNG...
HURG!
BA-BMP

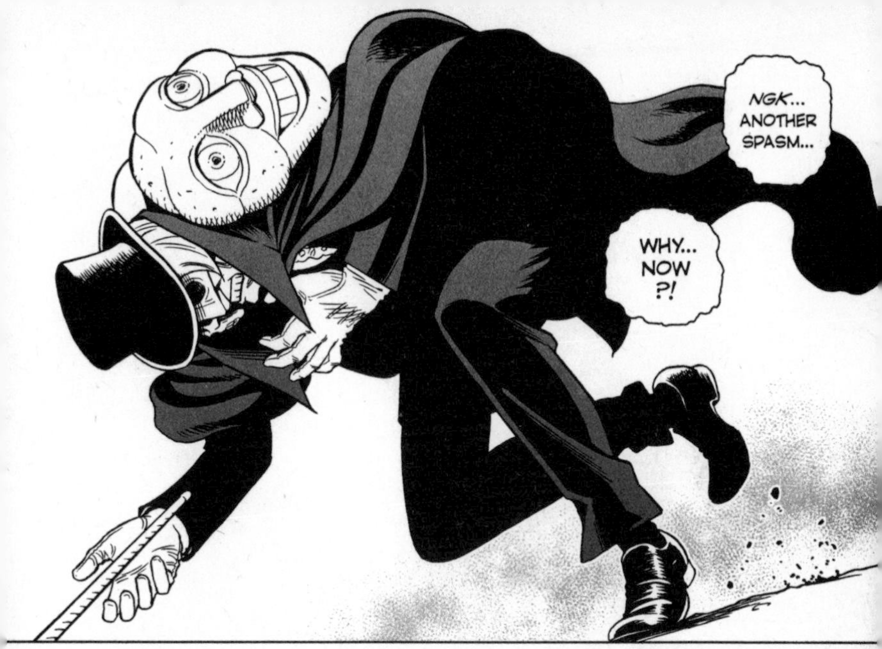
NGK... ANOTHER SPASM...
WHY... NOW ?!

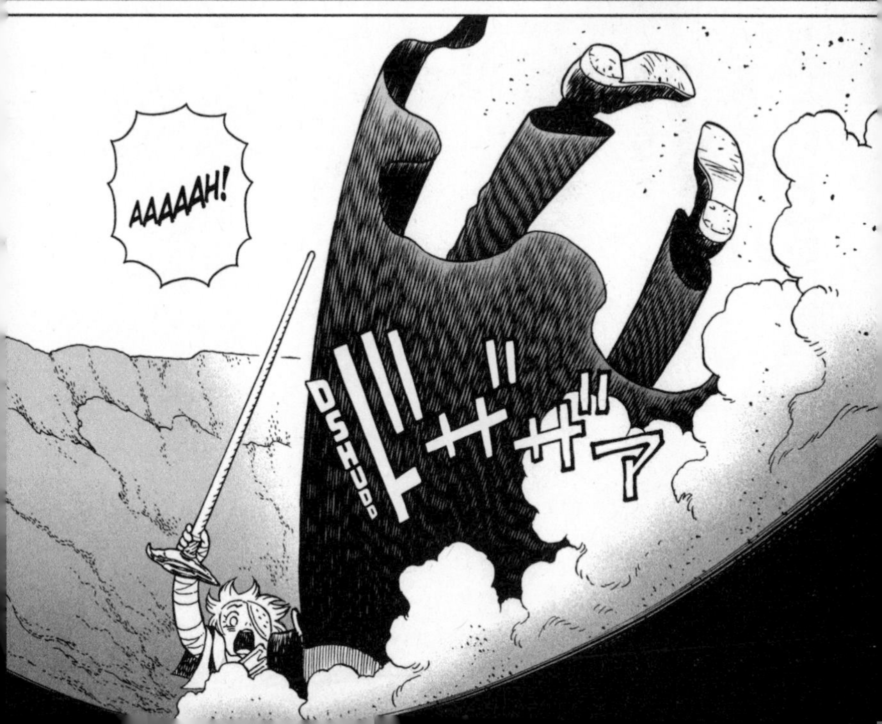
AAAAAH!
ドザザァ
DSHUDDD

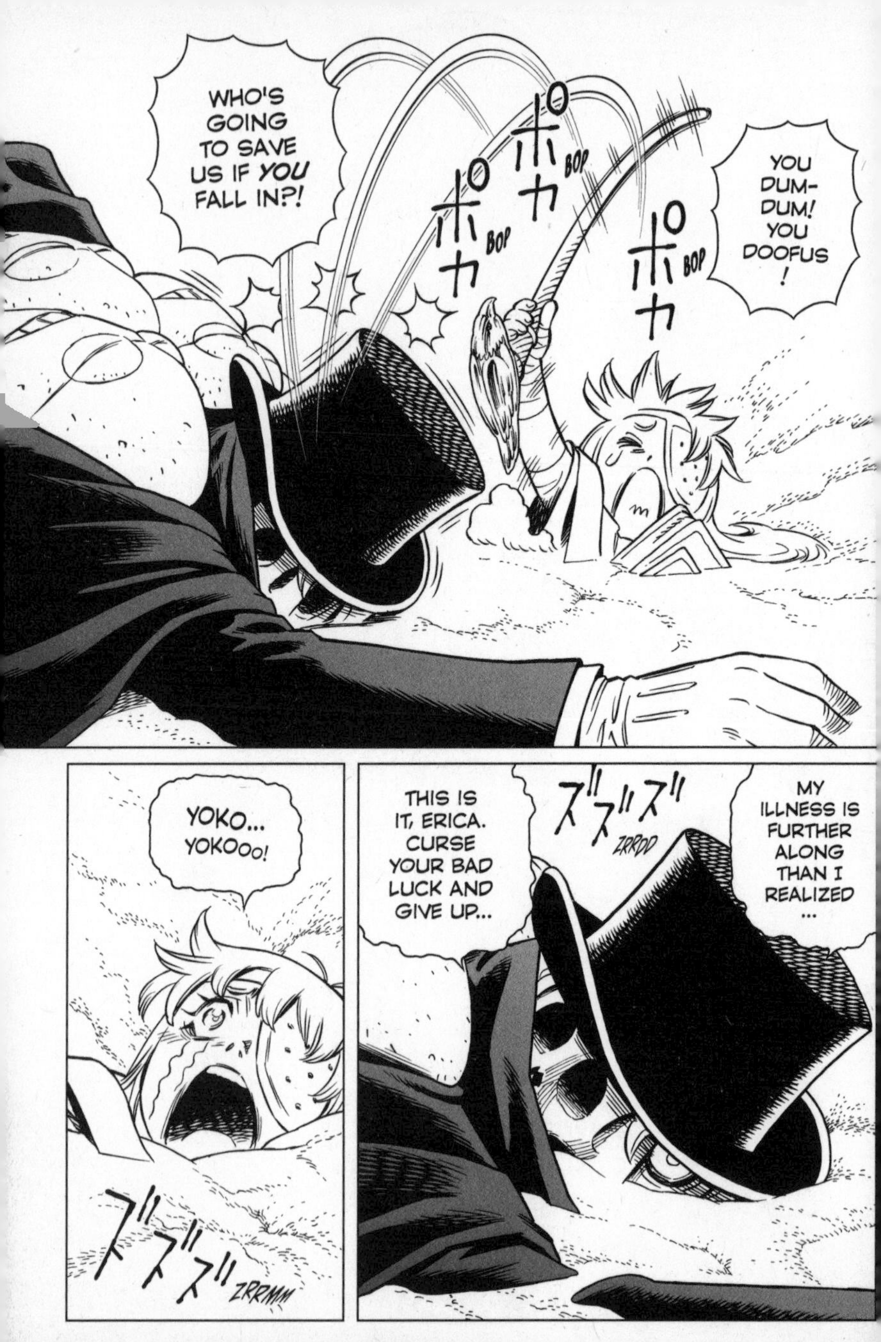
YOU DUM-DUM! YOU DOOFUS!
ポカ BOP
ポカ BOP
ポカ BOP
WHO'S GOING TO SAVE US IF *YOU* FALL IN?!
MY ILLNESS IS FURTHER ALONG THAN I REALIZED...
ズズズ ZRRDD
THIS IS IT, ERICA. CURSE YOUR BAD LUCK AND GIVE UP...
YOKO... YOKOooo!
ズズズ ZRRMM

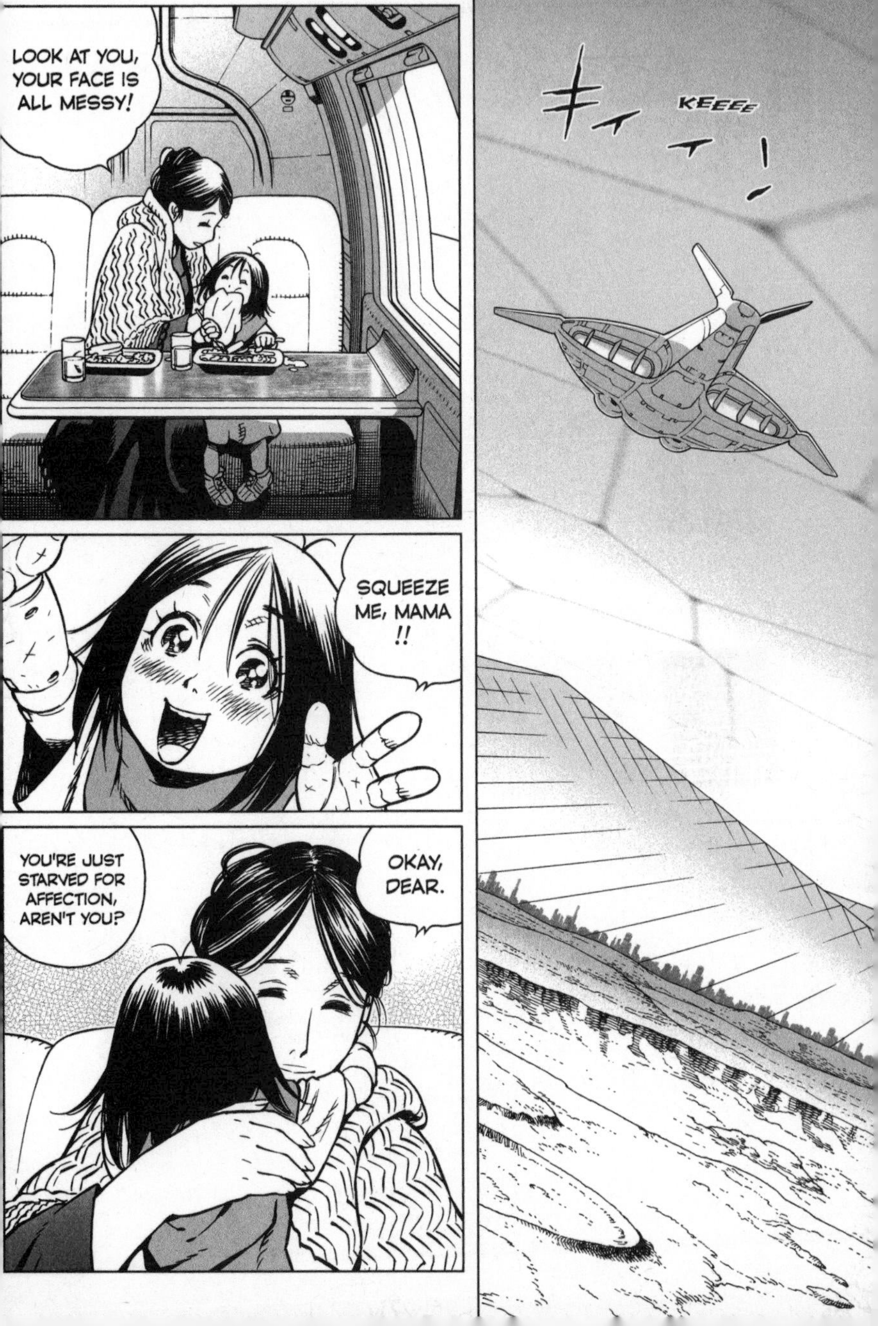
KEEEE
LOOK AT YOU, YOUR FACE IS ALL MESSY!
SQUEEZE ME, MAMA !!
OKAY, DEAR.
YOU'RE JUST STARVED FOR AFFECTION, AREN'T YOU?

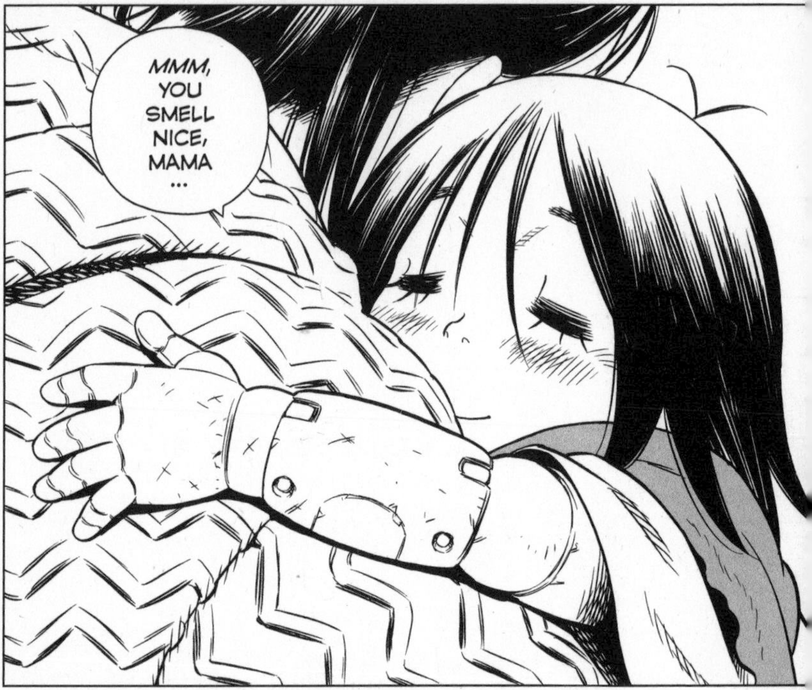
MMM, YOU SMELL NICE, MAMA ...

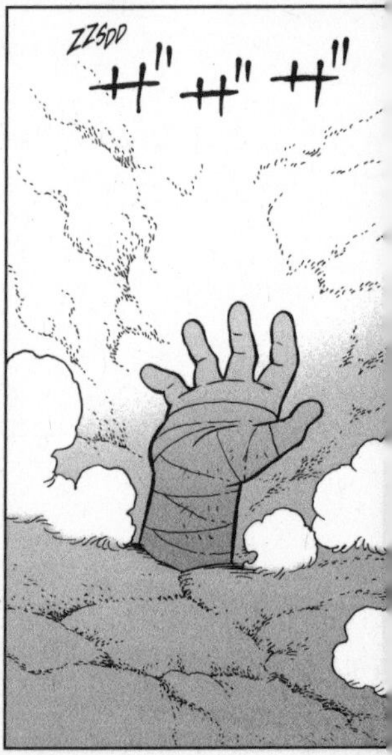
ZZSDD
ザザザ

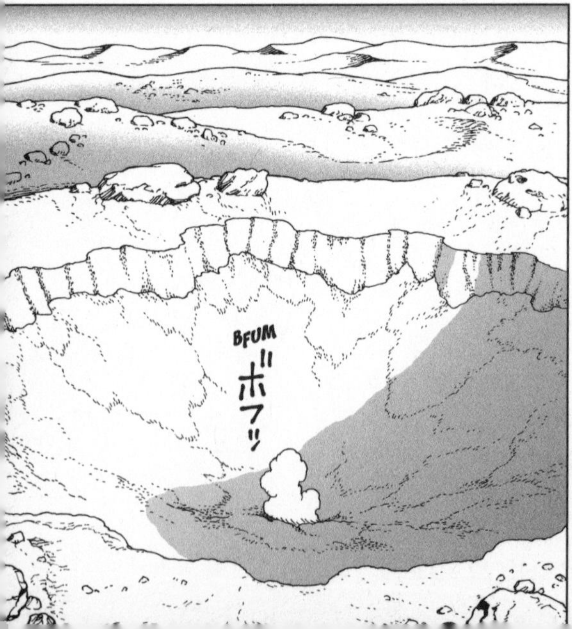
BFUM
ボフッ

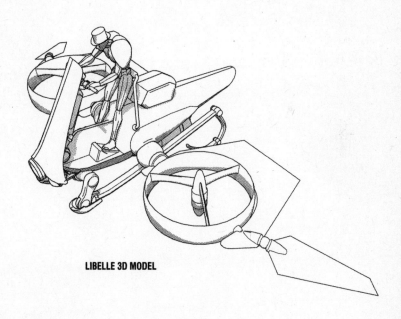

LIBELLE 3D MODEL

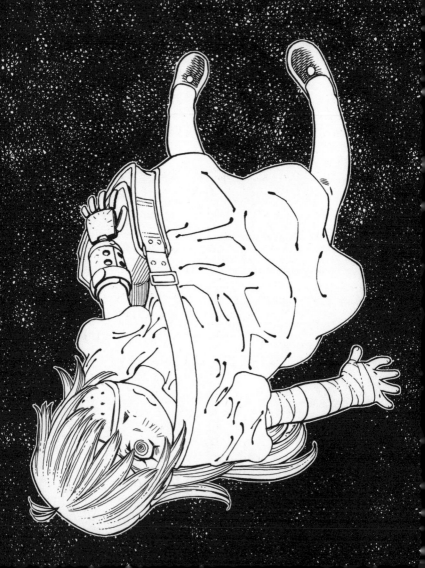

LOG:015
ALONE TOGETHER

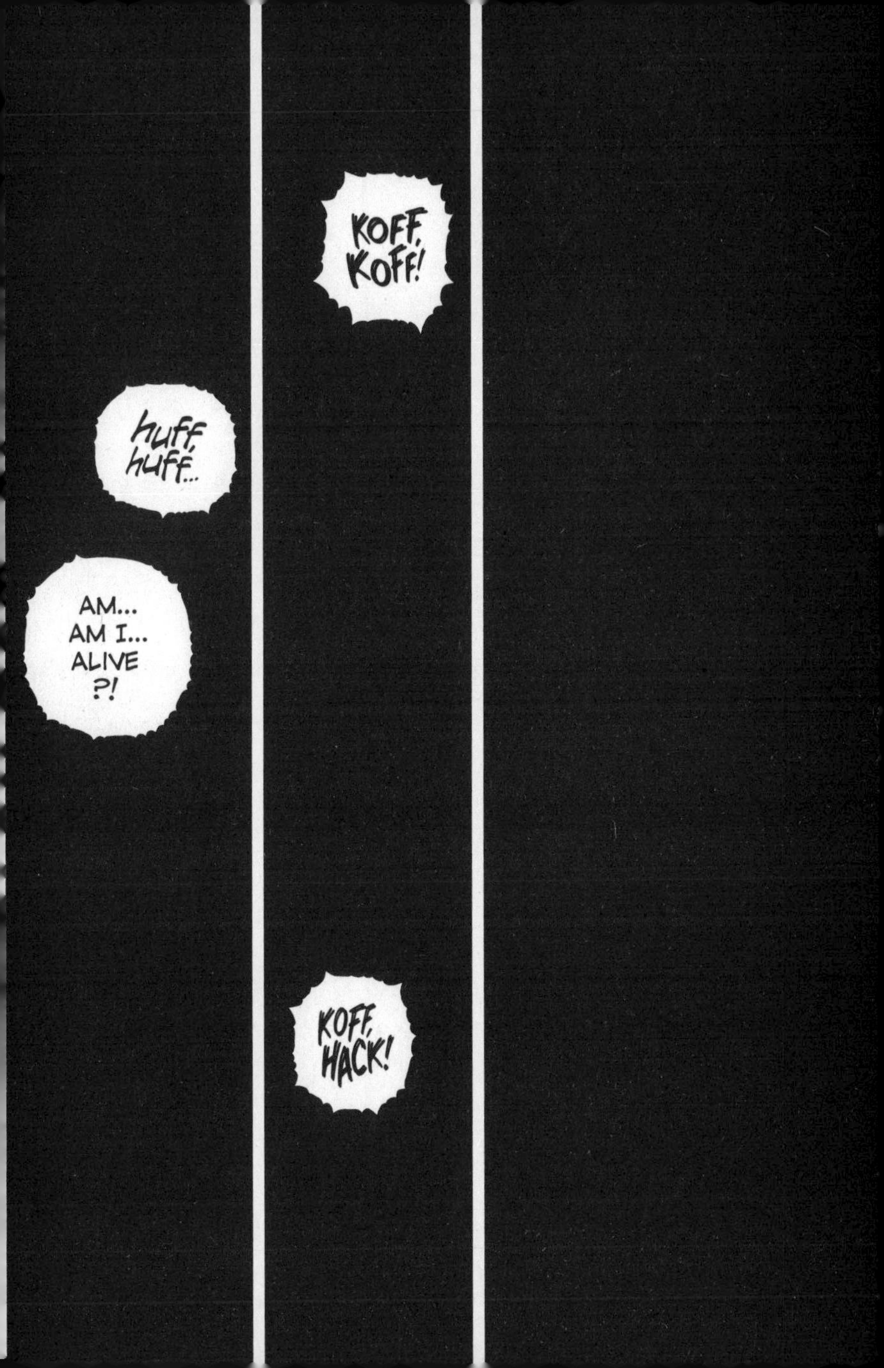
KOFF, KOFF!
KOFF, HACK!
huff, huff...
AM... AM I... ALIVE ?!

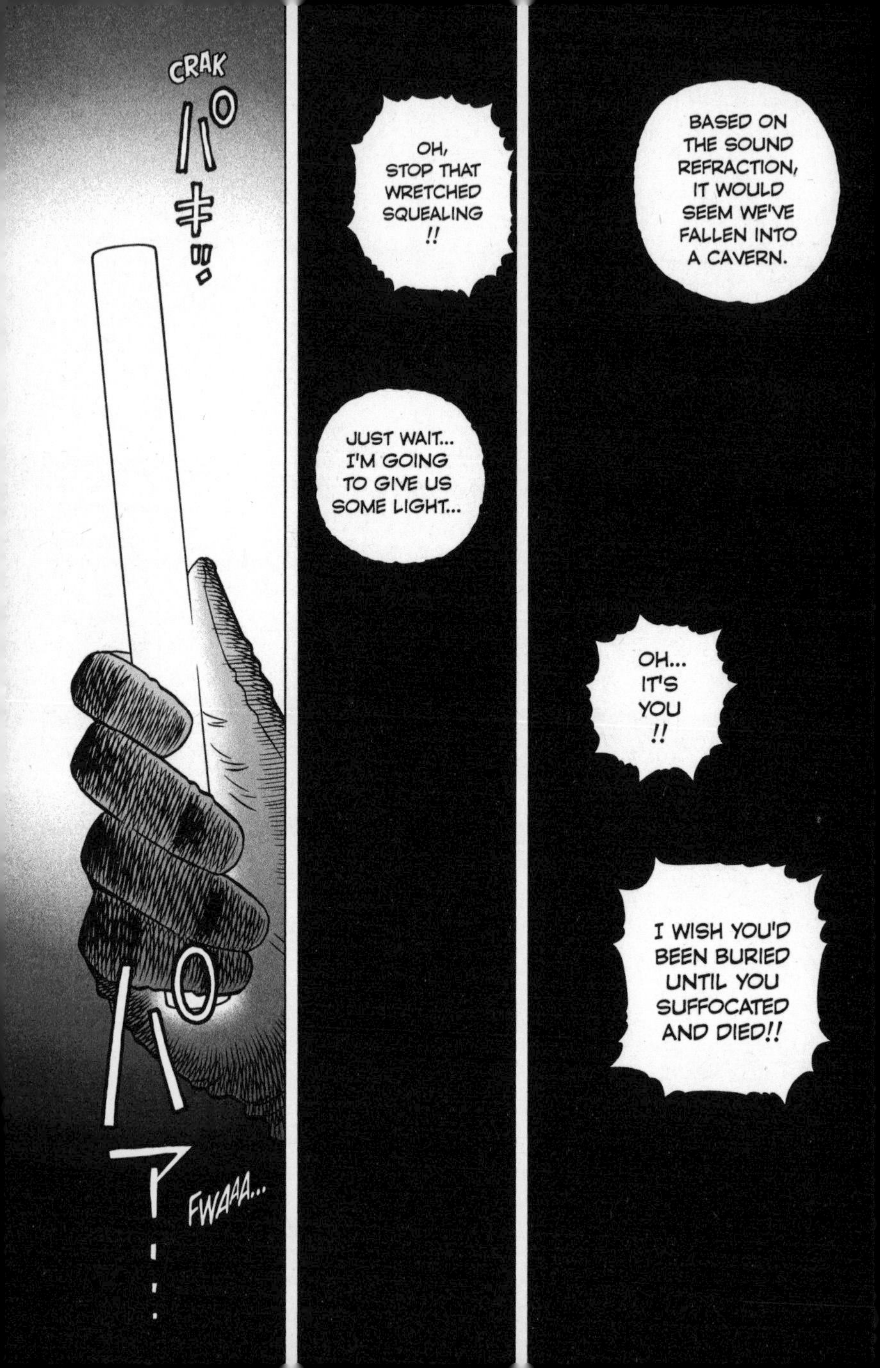
BASED ON THE SOUND REFRACTION, IT WOULD SEEM WE'VE FALLEN INTO A CAVERN.
OH... IT'S YOU!!
I WISH YOU'D BEEN BURIED UNTIL YOU SUFFOCATED AND DIED!!
OH, STOP THAT WRETCHED SQUEALING!!
JUST WAIT... I'M GOING TO GIVE US SOME LIGHT...
CRAK
FWAAA...

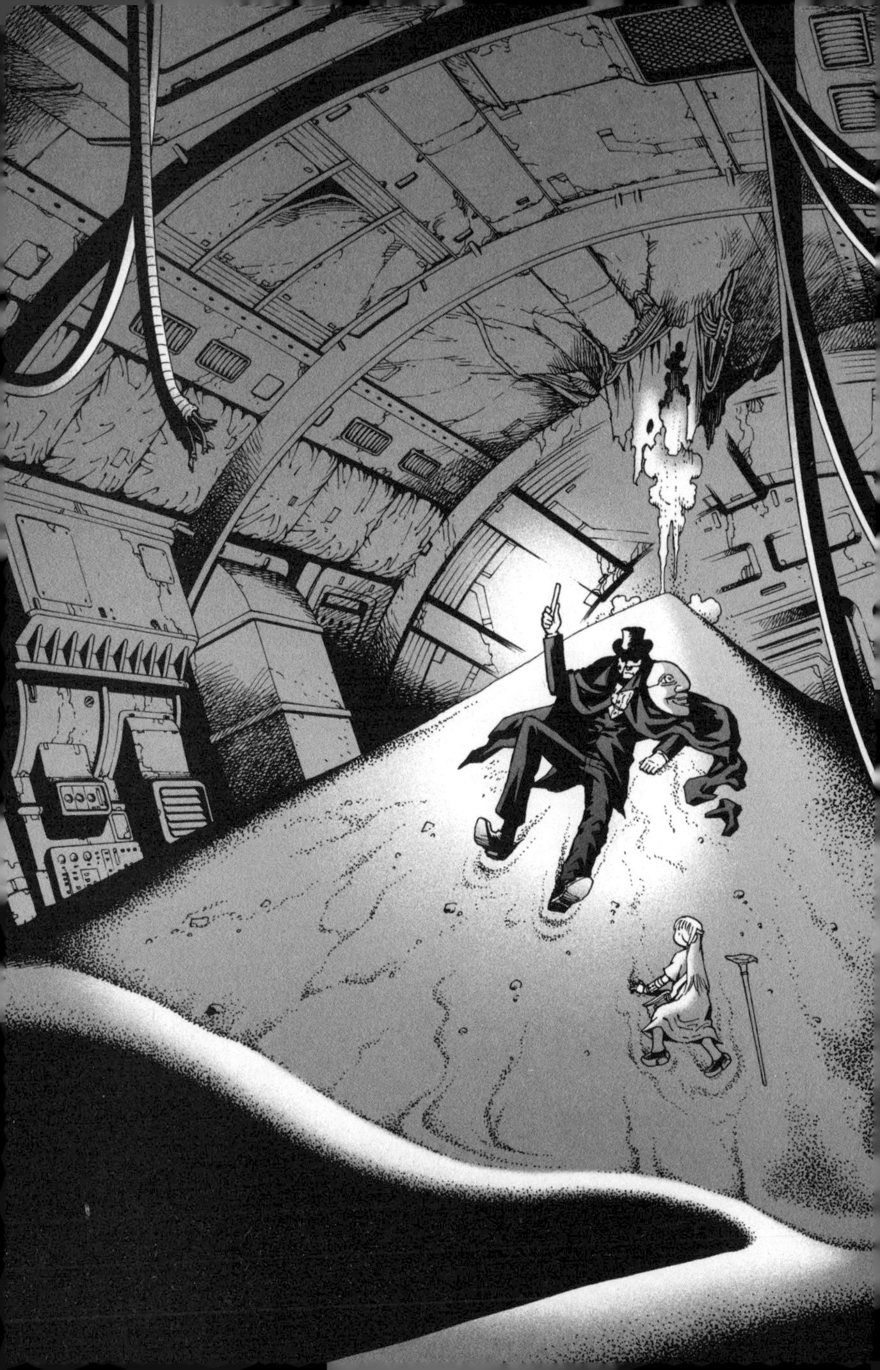

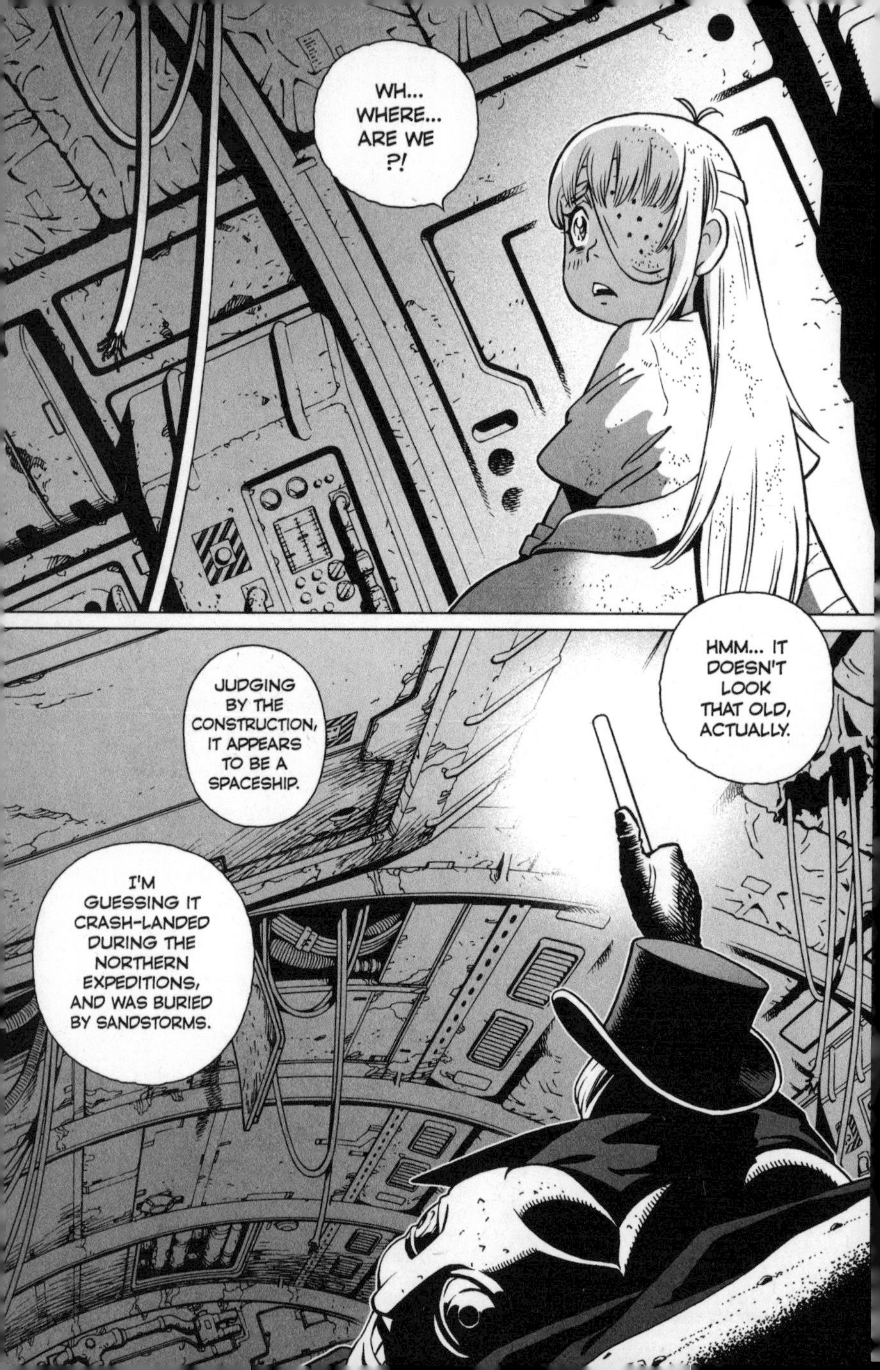
WH... WHERE... ARE WE ?!
HMM... IT DOESN'T LOOK THAT OLD, ACTUALLY.
JUDGING BY THE CONSTRUCTION, IT APPEARS TO BE A SPACESHIP.
I'M GUESSING IT CRASH-LANDED DURING THE NORTHERN EXPEDITIONS, AND WAS BURIED BY SANDSTORMS.

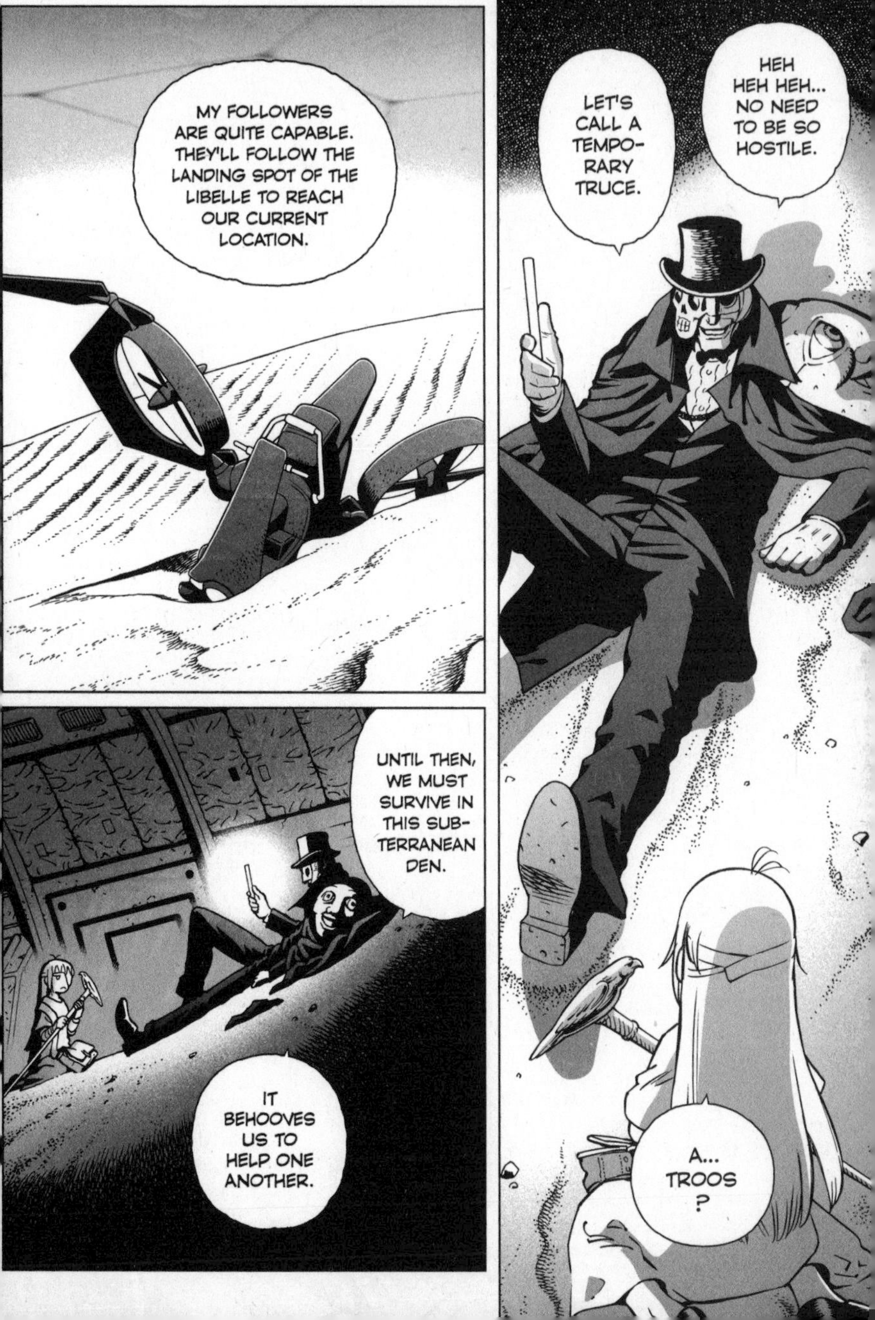
HEH HEH HEH... NO NEED TO BE SO HOSTILE.
LET'S CALL A TEMPO-RARY TRUCE.
A... TROOS ?
MY FOLLOWERS ARE QUITE CAPABLE. THEY'LL FOLLOW THE LANDING SPOT OF THE LIBELLE TO REACH OUR CURRENT LOCATION.
UNTIL THEN, WE MUST SURVIVE IN THIS SUB-TERRANEAN DEN.
IT BEHOOVES US TO HELP ONE ANOTHER.

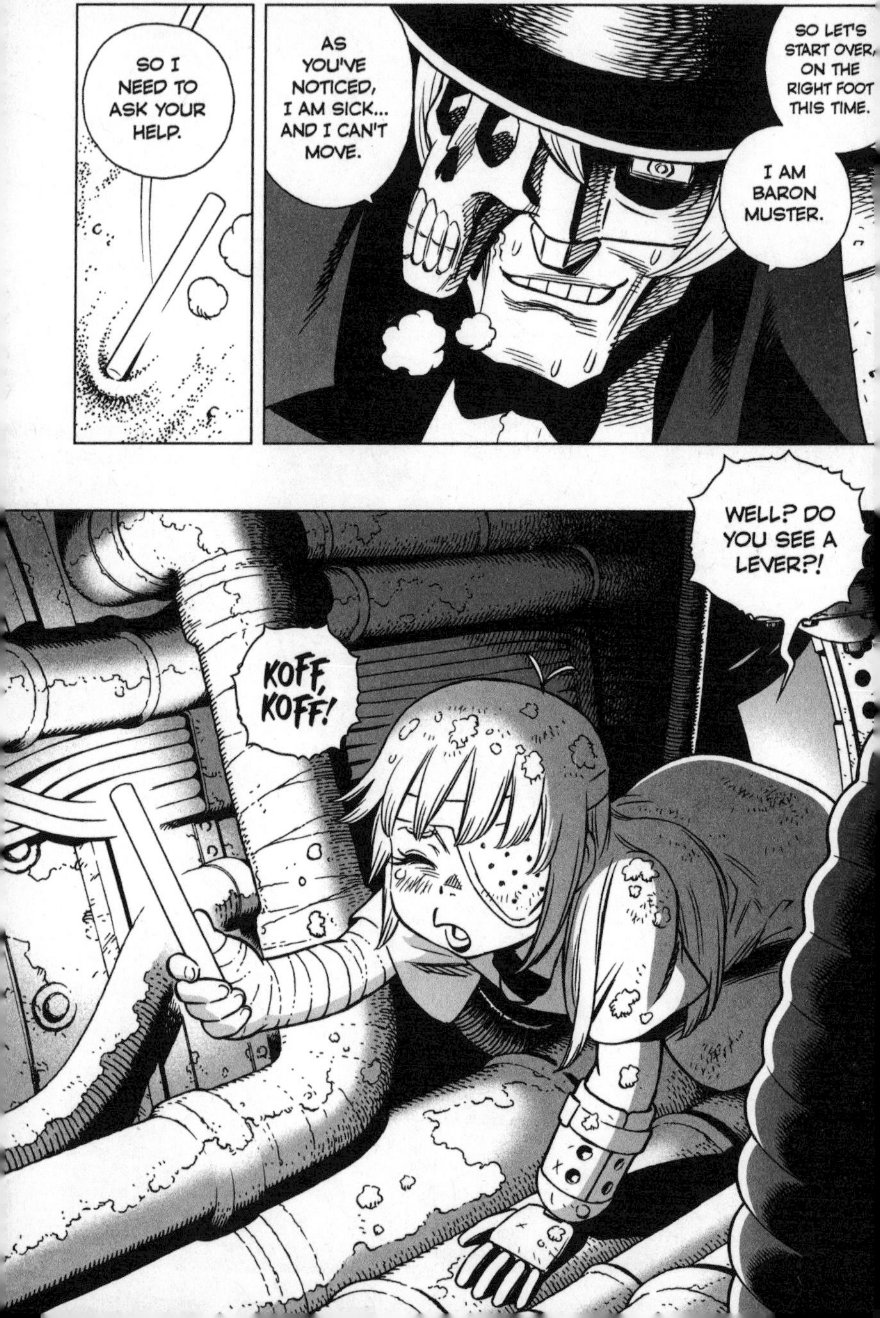
SO LET'S START OVER, ON THE RIGHT FOOT THIS TIME.
I AM BARON MUSTER.
AS YOU'VE NOTICED, I AM SICK... AND I CAN'T MOVE.
SO I NEED TO ASK YOUR HELP.
WELL? DO YOU SEE A LEVER?!
KOFF, KOFF!

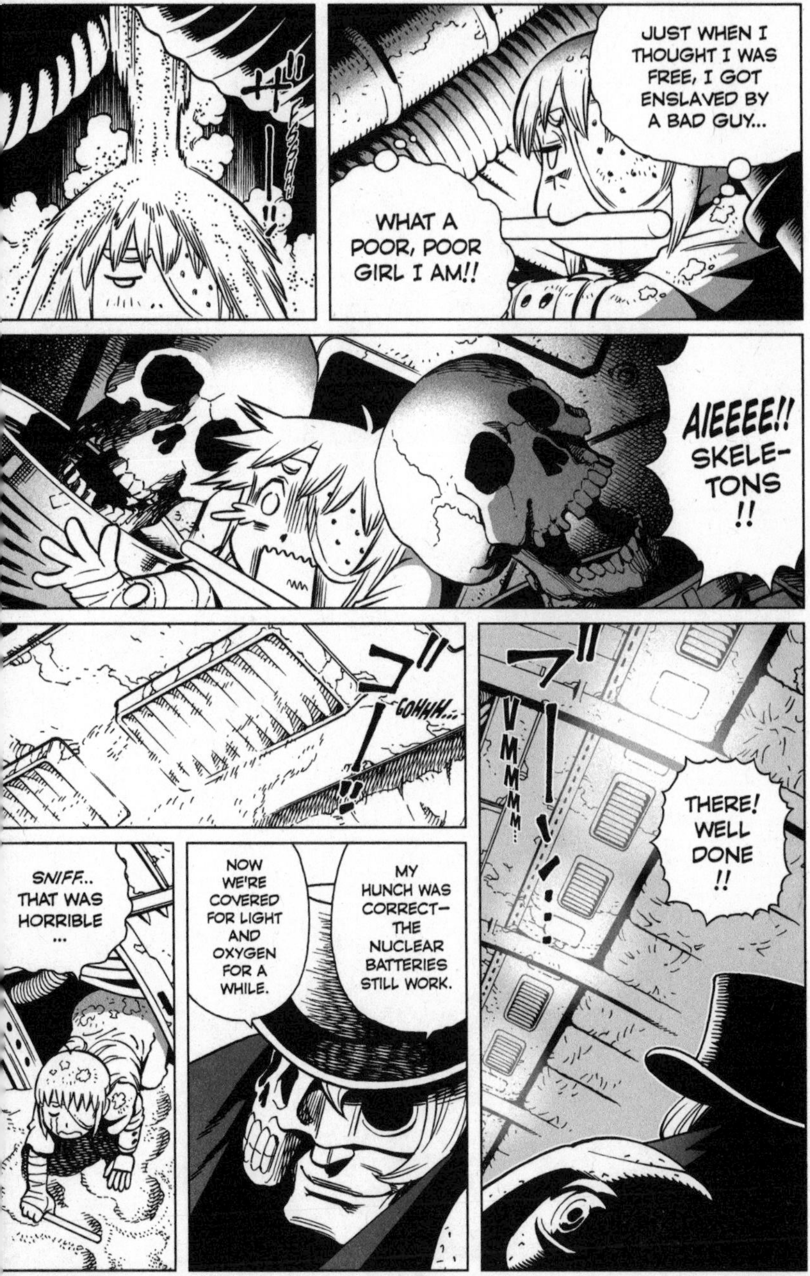
JUST WHEN I THOUGHT I WAS FREE, I GOT ENSLAVED BY A BAD GUY...
WHAT A POOR, POOR GIRL I AM!!
AIEEEEE!! SKELE-TONS!!
VMMMM...
THERE! WELL DONE!!
GOHHH...
MY HUNCH WAS CORRECT— THE NUCLEAR BATTERIES STILL WORK.
NOW WE'RE COVERED FOR LIGHT AND OXYGEN FOR A WHILE.
SNIFF... THAT WAS HORRIBLE...

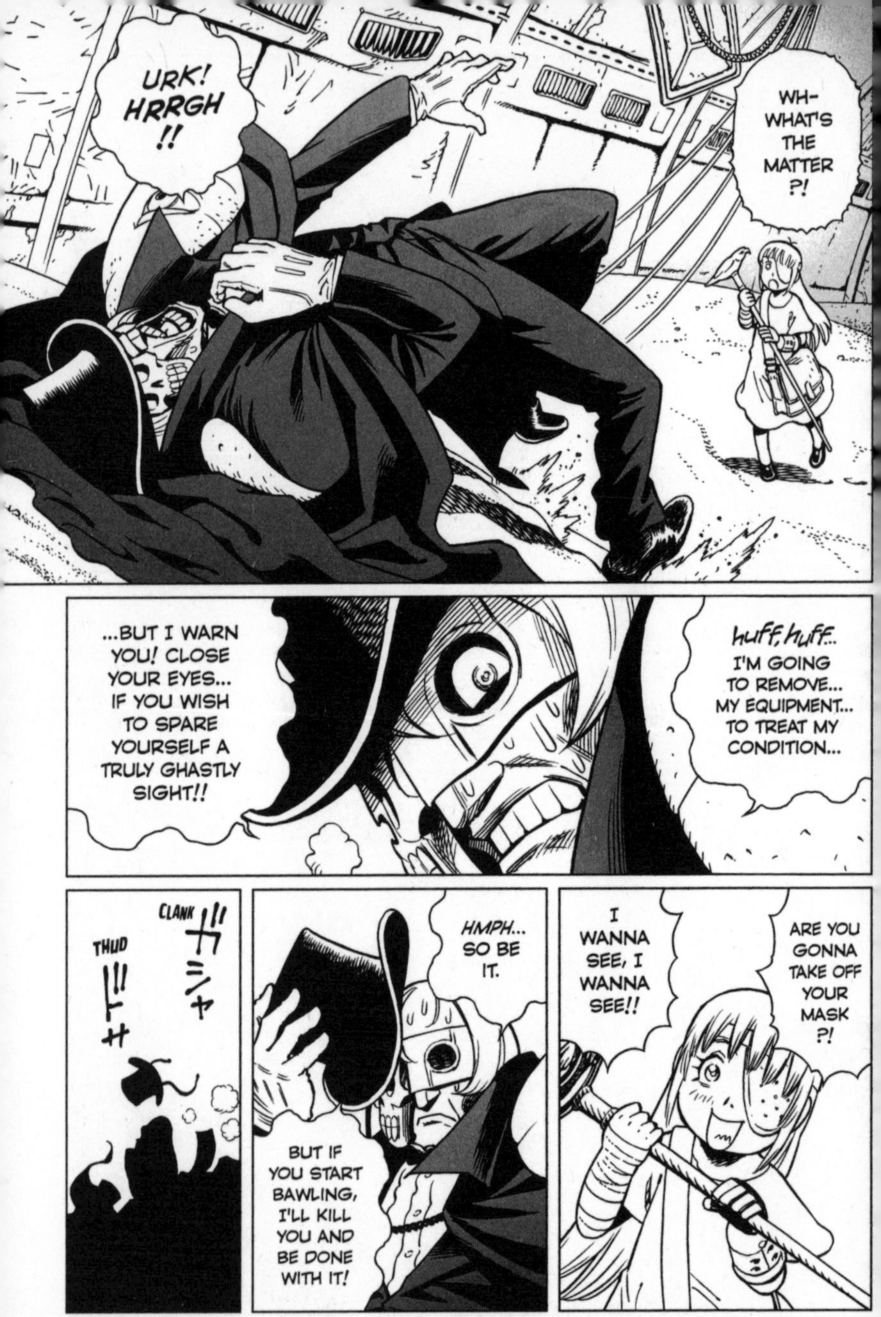
WH- WHAT'S THE MATTER ?!
URK! HRRGH !!
huff, huff... I'M GOING TO REMOVE... MY EQUIPMENT... TO TREAT MY CONDITION...
...BUT I WARN YOU! CLOSE YOUR EYES... IF YOU WISH TO SPARE YOURSELF A TRULY GHASTLY SIGHT!!
ARE YOU GONNA TAKE OFF YOUR MASK ?!
I WANNA SEE, I WANNA SEE!!
HMPH... SO BE IT.
BUT IF YOU START BAWLING, I'LL KILL YOU AND BE DONE WITH IT!
CLANK
ガシャ
THUD
ドサ

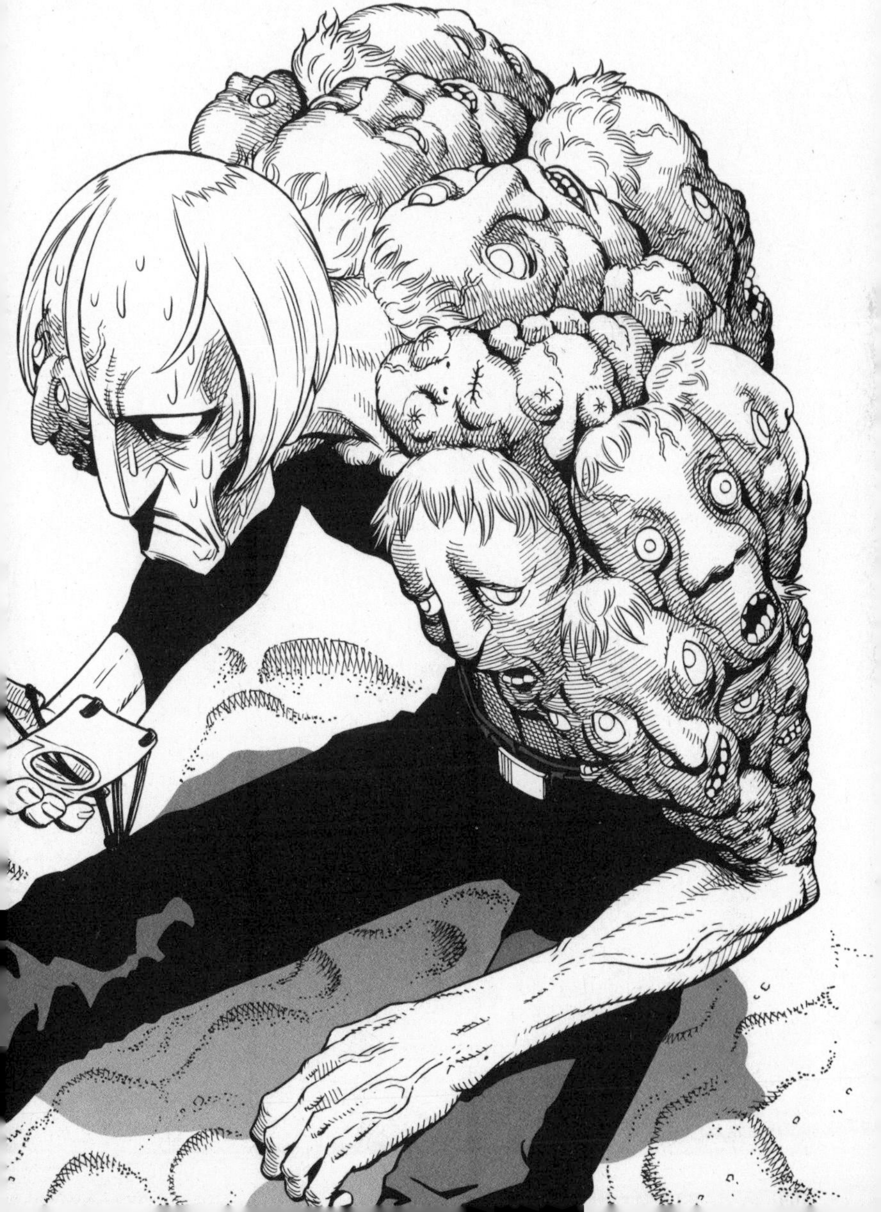

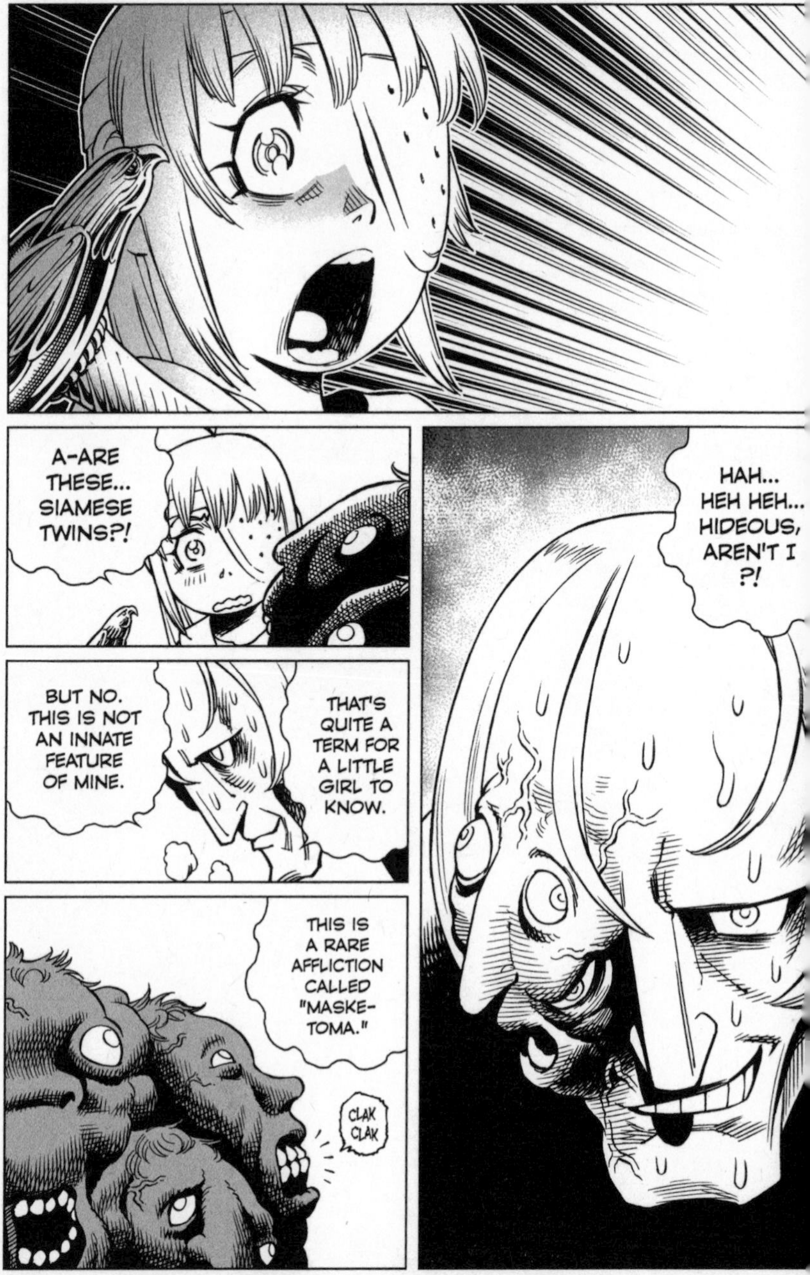
HAH... HEH HEH... HIDEOUS, AREN'T I ?!
A-ARE THESE... SIAMESE TWINS?!
THAT'S QUITE A TERM FOR A LITTLE GIRL TO KNOW.
BUT NO. THIS IS NOT AN INNATE FEATURE OF MINE.
THIS IS A RARE AFFLICTION CALLED "MASKE-TOMA."
CLAK CLAK

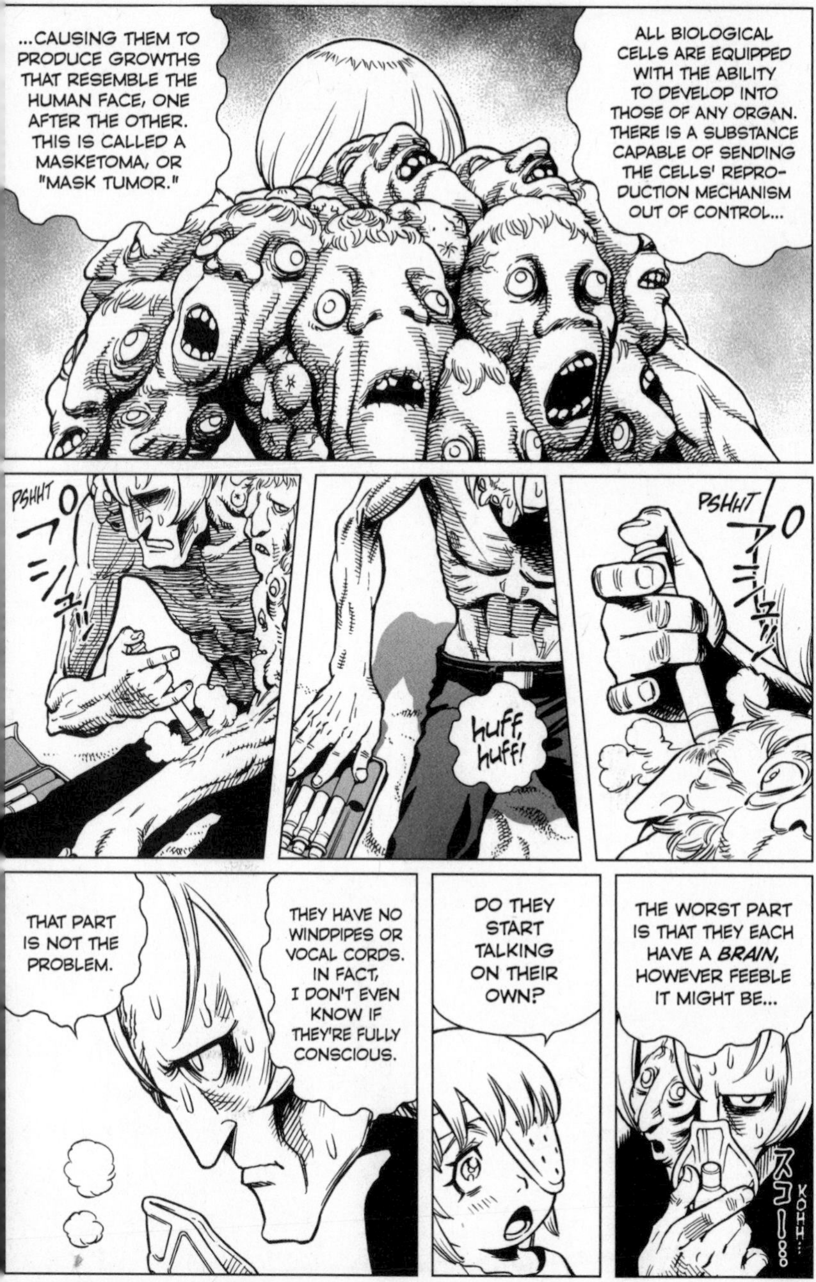
ALL BIOLOGICAL CELLS ARE EQUIPPED WITH THE ABILITY TO DEVELOP INTO THOSE OF ANY ORGAN. THERE IS A SUBSTANCE CAPABLE OF SENDING THE CELLS' REPRODUCTION MECHANISM OUT OF CONTROL...
...CAUSING THEM TO PRODUCE GROWTHS THAT RESEMBLE THE HUMAN FACE, ONE AFTER THE OTHER. THIS IS CALLED A MASKETOMA, OR "MASK TUMOR."
PSHHT
huff, huff!
PSHHT
THE WORST PART IS THAT THEY EACH HAVE A *BRAIN,* HOWEVER FEEBLE IT MIGHT BE...
KOHH...
DO THEY START TALKING ON THEIR OWN?
THEY HAVE NO WINDPIPES OR VOCAL CORDS. IN FACT, I DON'T EVEN KNOW IF THEY'RE FULLY CONSCIOUS.
THAT PART IS NOT THE PROBLEM.

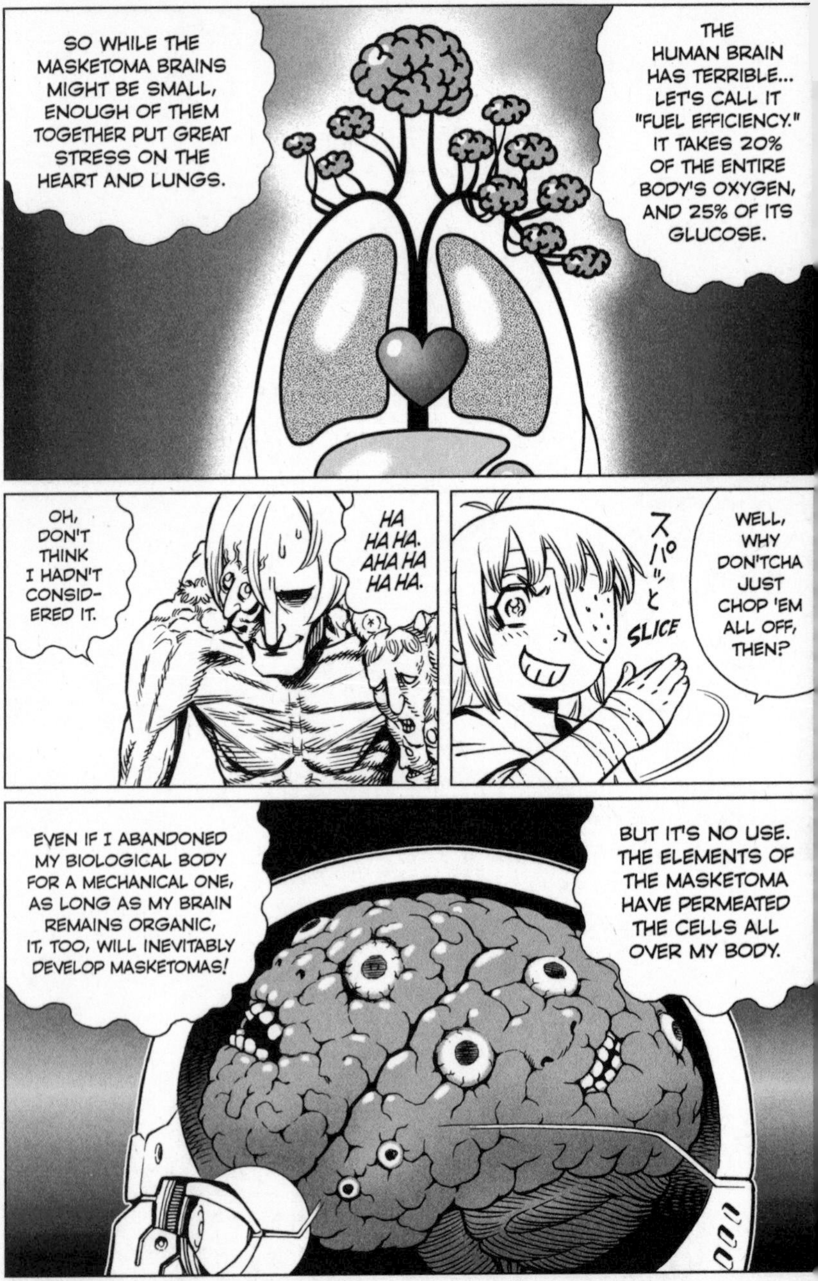
THE HUMAN BRAIN HAS TERRIBLE... LET'S CALL IT "FUEL EFFICIENCY." IT TAKES 20% OF THE ENTIRE BODY'S OXYGEN, AND 25% OF ITS GLUCOSE.
SO WHILE THE MASKETOMA BRAINS MIGHT BE SMALL, ENOUGH OF THEM TOGETHER PUT GREAT STRESS ON THE HEART AND LUNGS.
WELL, WHY DON'TCHA JUST CHOP 'EM ALL OFF, THEN?
スパッと
SLICE
HA HA HA. AHA HA HA HA.
OH, DON'T THINK I HADN'T CONSID-ERED IT.
BUT IT'S NO USE. THE ELEMENTS OF THE MASKETOMA HAVE PERMEATED THE CELLS ALL OVER MY BODY.
EVEN IF I ABANDONED MY BIOLOGICAL BODY FOR A MECHANICAL ONE, AS LONG AS MY BRAIN REMAINS ORGANIC, IT, TOO, WILL INEVITABLY DEVELOP MASKETOMAS!

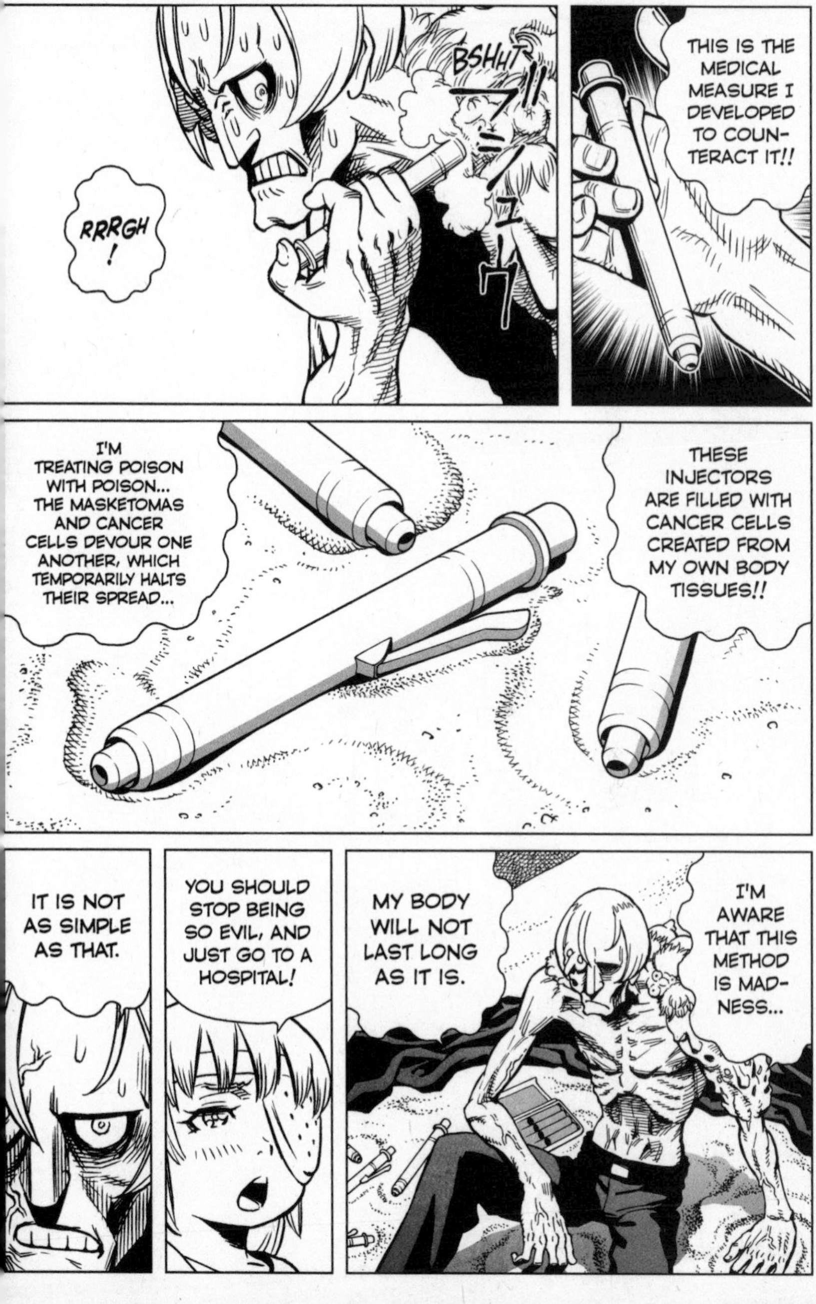
THIS IS THE MEDICAL MEASURE I DEVELOPED TO COUNTERACT IT!!
BSHHT
RRRGH!
THESE INJECTORS ARE FILLED WITH CANCER CELLS CREATED FROM MY OWN BODY TISSUES!!
I'M TREATING POISON WITH POISON... THE MASKETOMAS AND CANCER CELLS DEVOUR ONE ANOTHER, WHICH TEMPORARILY HALTS THEIR SPREAD...
I'M AWARE THAT THIS METHOD IS MADNESS...
MY BODY WILL NOT LAST LONG AS IT IS.
YOU SHOULD STOP BEING SO EVIL, AND JUST GO TO A HOSPITAL!
IT IS NOT AS SIMPLE AS THAT.

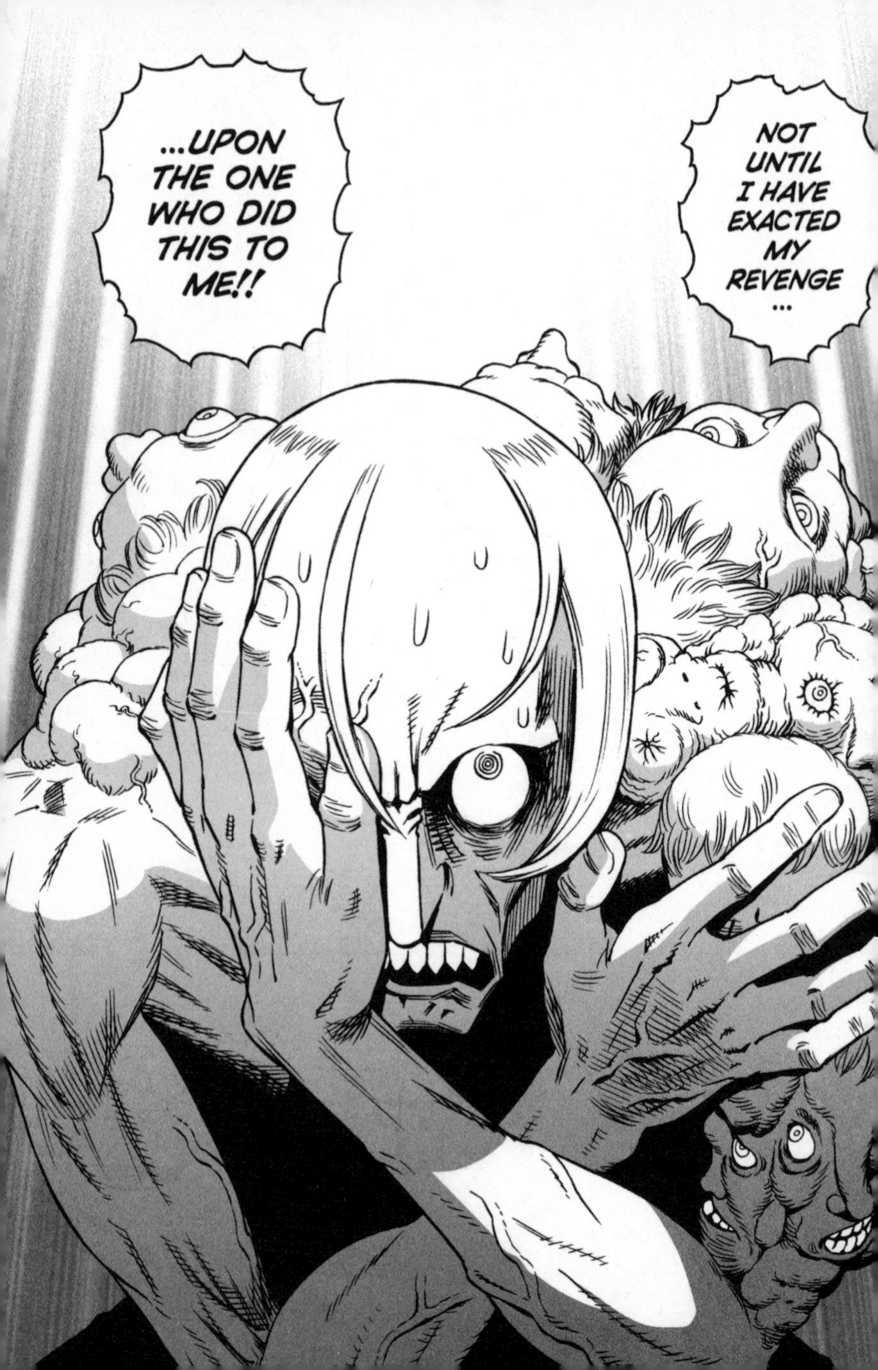
NOT UNTIL I HAVE EXACTED MY REVENGE...
...UPON THE ONE WHO DID THIS TO ME!!

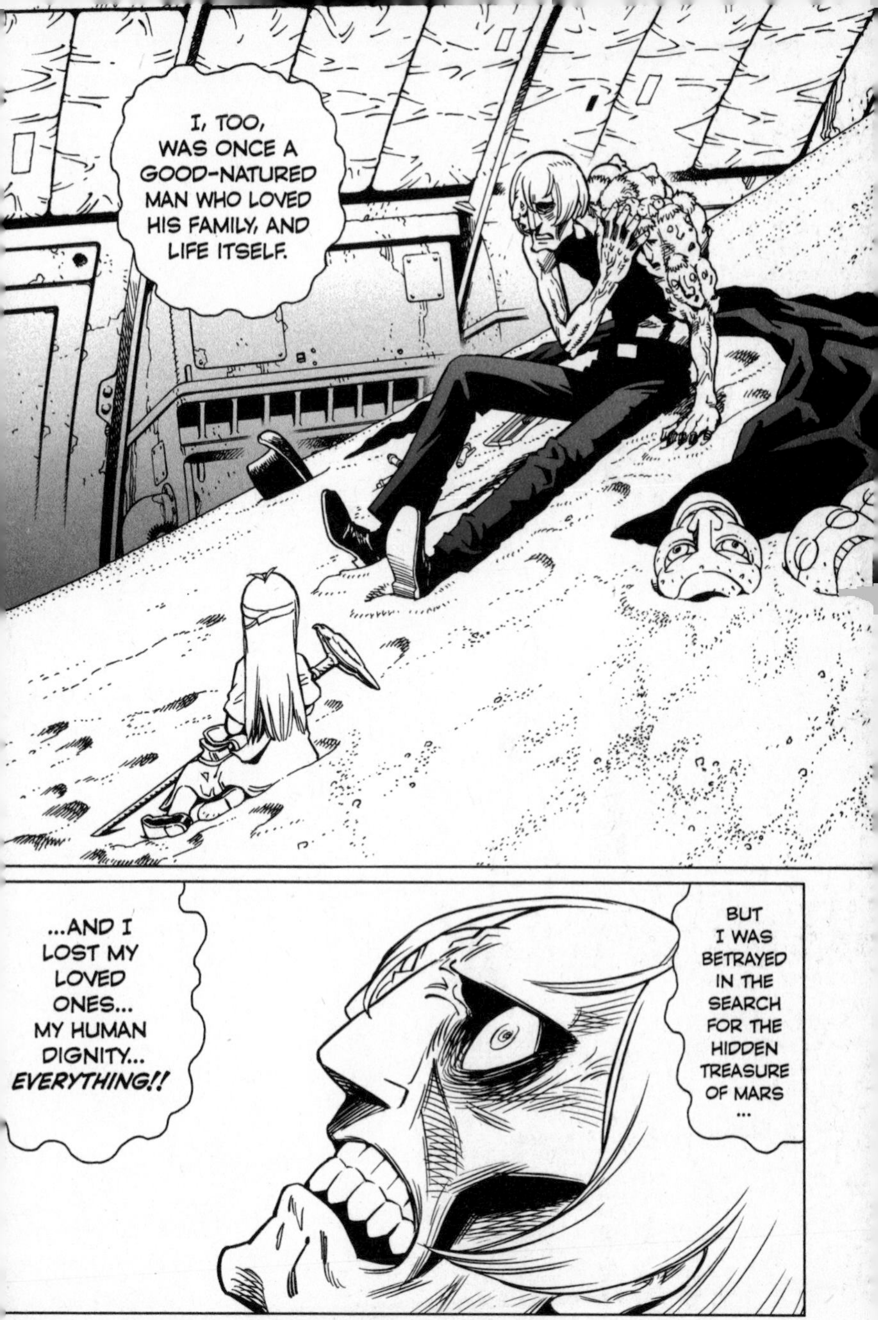
I, TOO, WAS ONCE A GOOD-NATURED MAN WHO LOVED HIS FAMILY, AND LIFE ITSELF.
BUT I WAS BETRAYED IN THE SEARCH FOR THE HIDDEN TREASURE OF MARS ...
...AND I LOST MY LOVED ONES... MY HUMAN DIGNITY... *EVERYTHING!!*

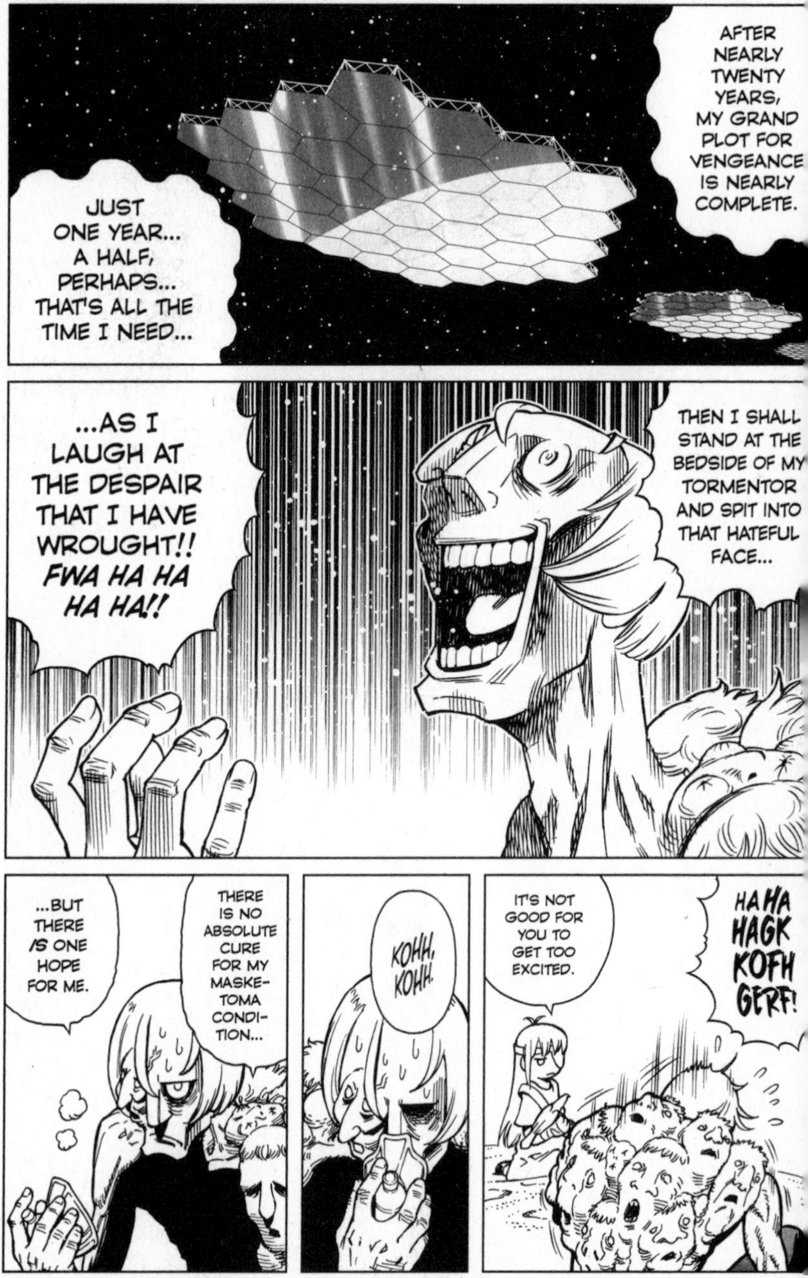
AFTER NEARLY TWENTY YEARS, MY GRAND PLOT FOR VENGEANCE IS NEARLY COMPLETE.
JUST ONE YEAR... A HALF, PERHAPS... THAT'S ALL THE TIME I NEED...
THEN I SHALL STAND AT THE BEDSIDE OF MY TORMENTOR AND SPIT INTO THAT HATEFUL FACE...
...AS I LAUGH AT THE DESPAIR THAT I HAVE WROUGHT!! *FWA HA HA HA HA!!*
HA HA HAGK KOFH GERF!
IT'S NOT GOOD FOR YOU TO GET TOO EXCITED.
KOHH, KOHH.
THERE IS NO ABSOLUTE CURE FOR MY MASKE-TOMA CONDI-TION...
...BUT THERE *IS* ONE HOPE FOR ME.

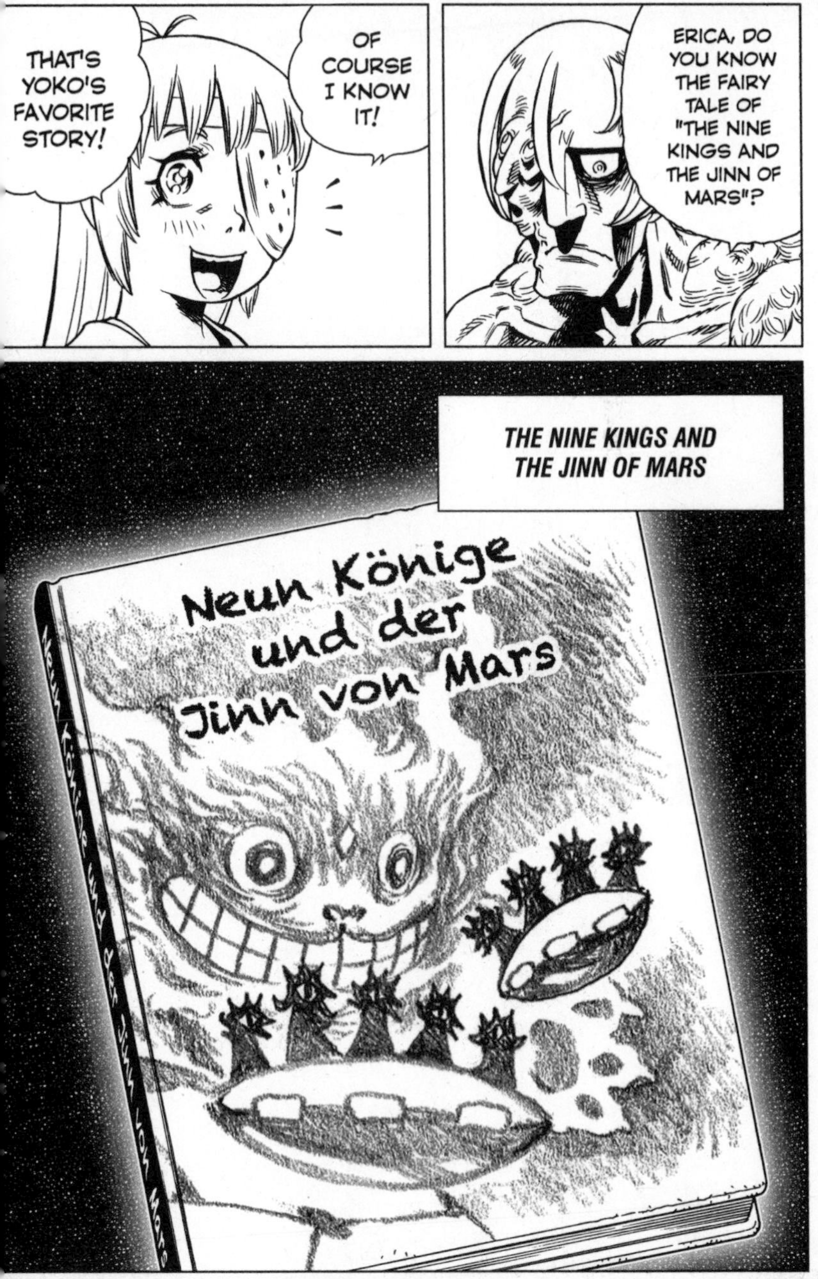
ERICA, DO YOU KNOW THE FAIRY TALE OF "THE NINE KINGS AND THE JINN OF MARS"?
OF COURSE I KNOW IT!
THAT'S YOKO'S FAVORITE STORY!
THE NINE KINGS AND THE JINN OF MARS
Neun Könige und der Jinn von Mars
Neun Könige und der Jinn von Mars

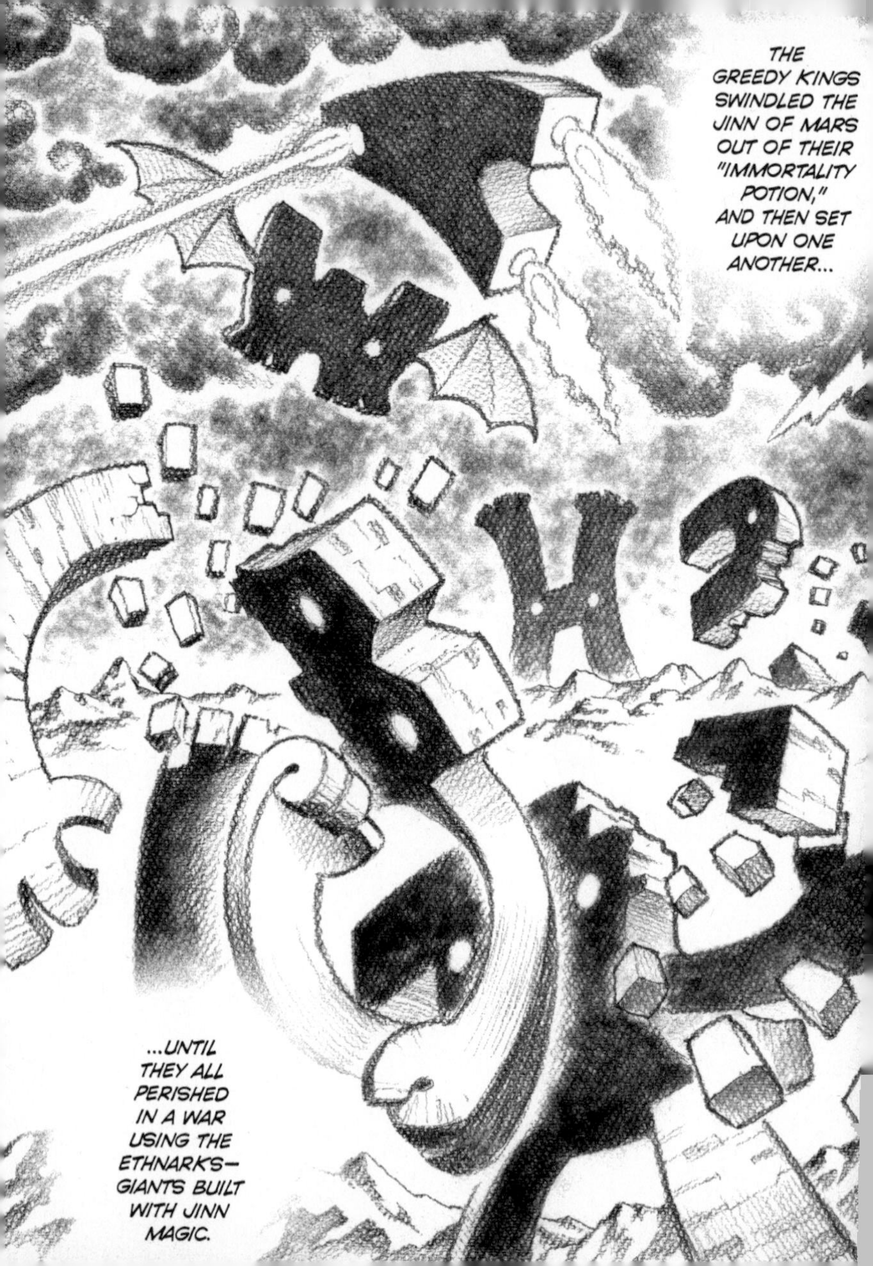
THE GREEDY KINGS SWINDLED THE JINN OF MARS OUT OF THEIR "IMMORTALITY POTION," AND THEN SET UPON ONE ANOTHER...
...UNTIL THEY ALL PERISHED IN A WAR USING THE ETHNARKS—GIANTS BUILT WITH JINN MAGIC.

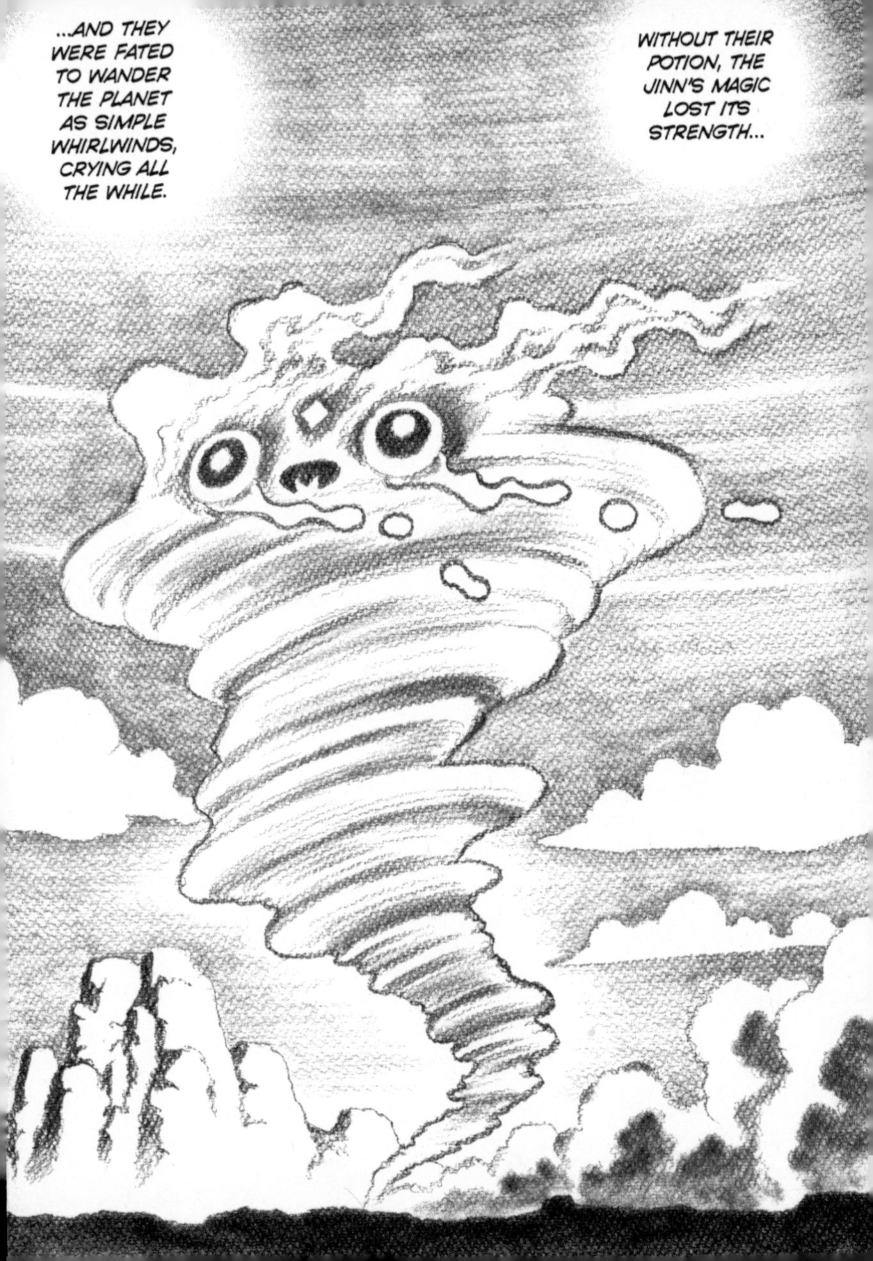
WITHOUT THEIR POTION, THE JINN'S MAGIC LOST ITS STRENGTH...
...AND THEY WERE FATED TO WANDER THE PLANET AS SIMPLE WHIRLWINDS, CRYING ALL THE WHILE.

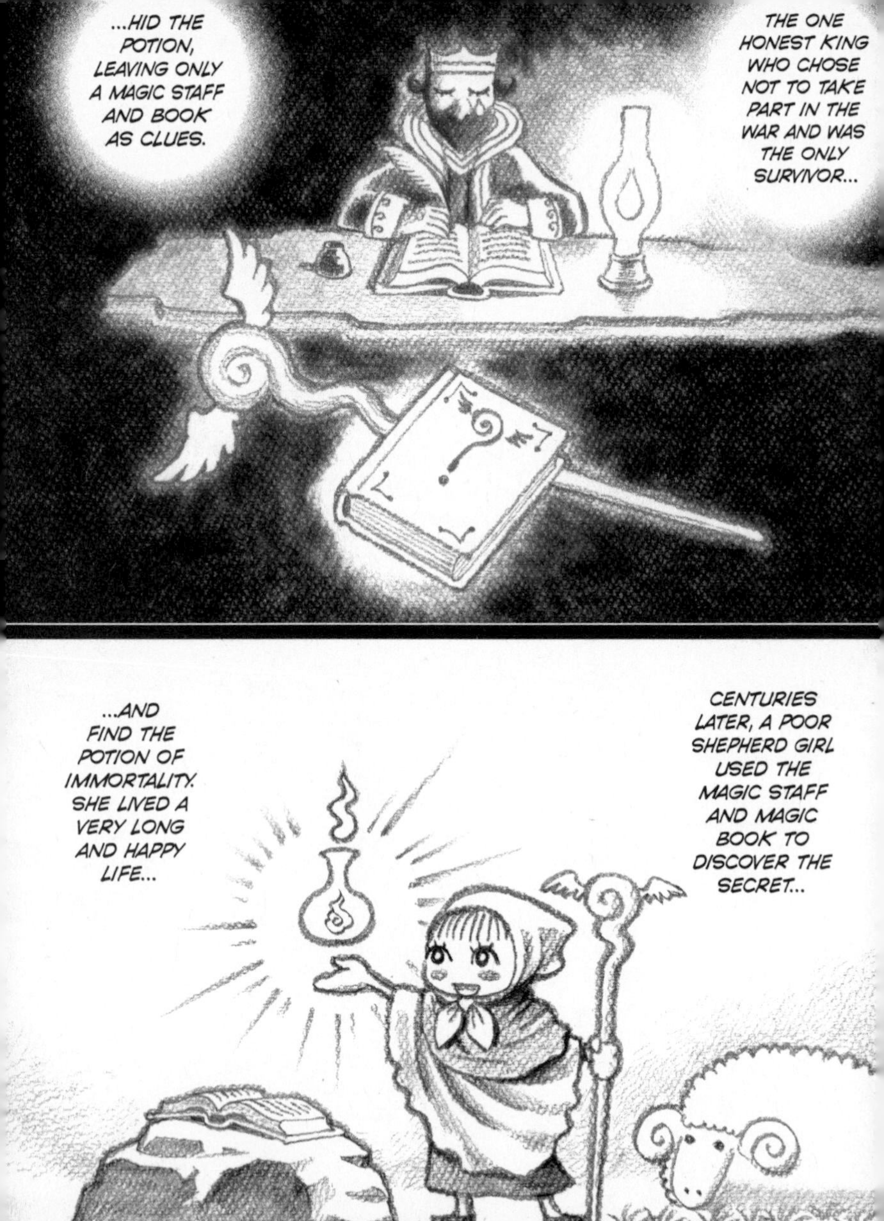
THE ONE HONEST KING WHO CHOSE NOT TO TAKE PART IN THE WAR AND WAS THE ONLY SURVIVOR...
...HID THE POTION, LEAVING ONLY A MAGIC STAFF AND BOOK AS CLUES.
CENTURIES LATER, A POOR SHEPHERD GIRL USED THE MAGIC STAFF AND MAGIC BOOK TO DISCOVER THE SECRET...
...AND FIND THE POTION OF IMMORTALITY. SHE LIVED A VERY LONG AND HAPPY LIFE...

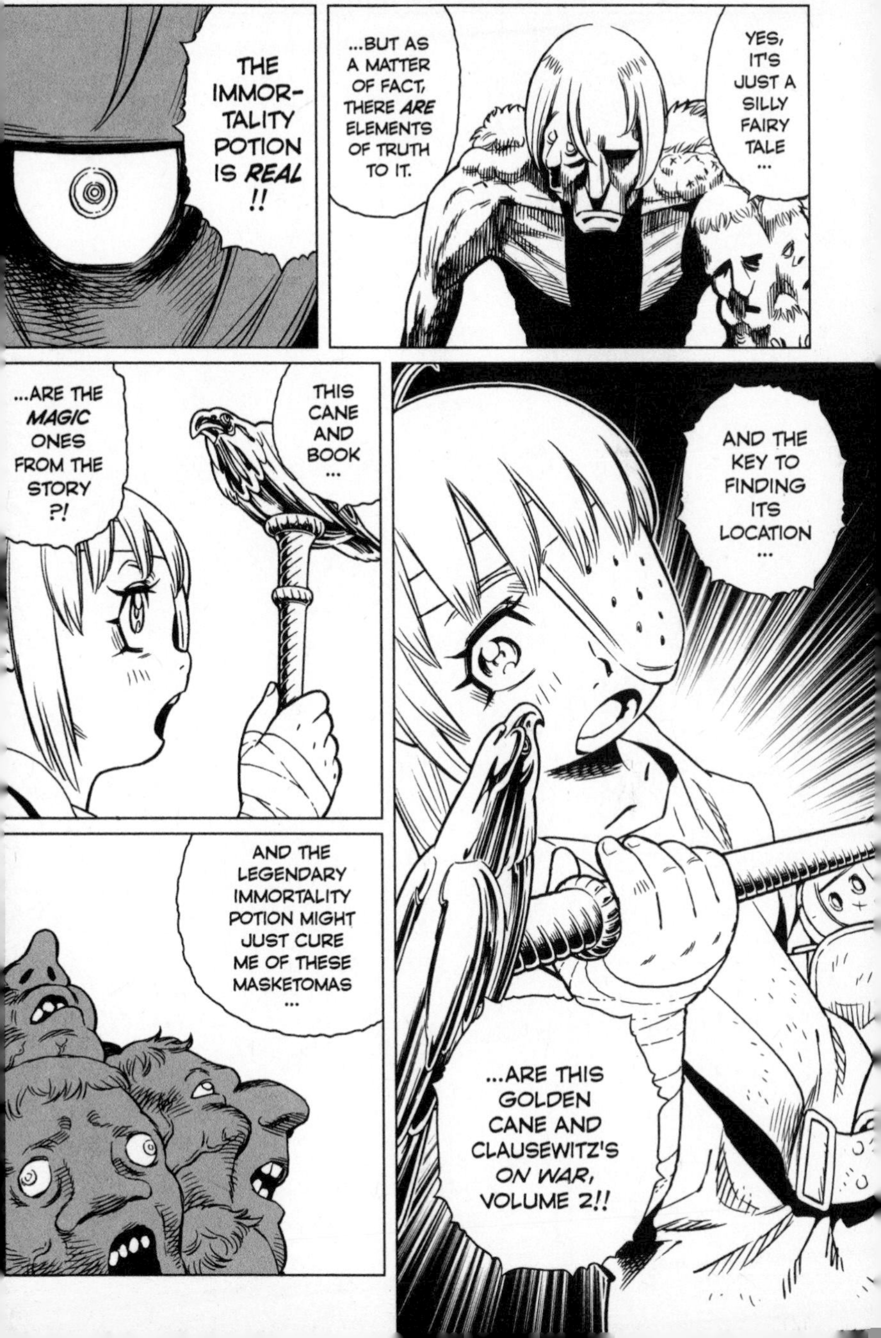
YES, IT'S JUST A SILLY FAIRY TALE ...
...BUT AS A MATTER OF FACT, THERE *ARE* ELEMENTS OF TRUTH TO IT.
THE IMMORTALITY POTION IS *REAL* !!
AND THE KEY TO FINDING ITS LOCATION ...
...ARE THIS GOLDEN CANE AND CLAUSEWITZ'S *ON WAR*, VOLUME 2!!
THIS CANE AND BOOK ...
...ARE THE *MAGIC* ONES FROM THE STORY ?!
AND THE LEGENDARY IMMORTALITY POTION MIGHT JUST CURE ME OF THESE MASKETOMAS ...

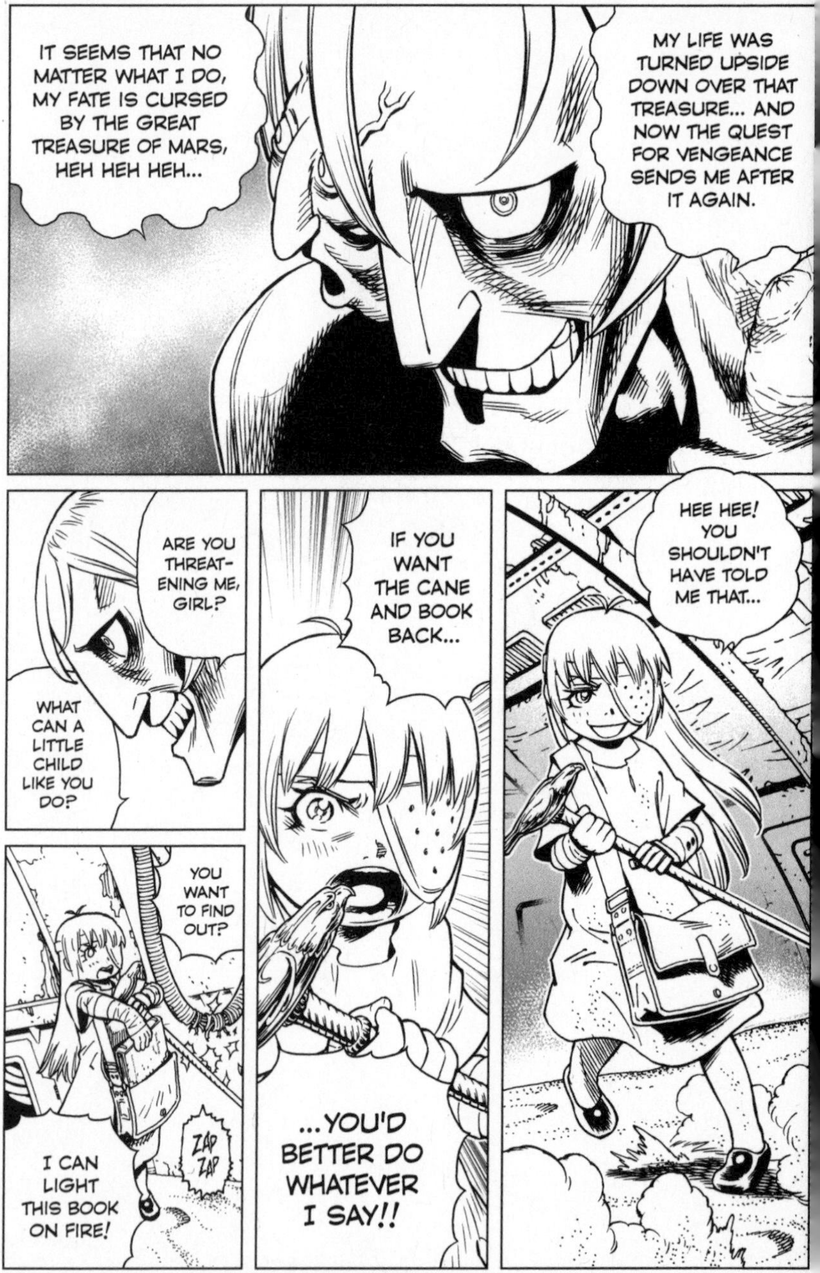
MY LIFE WAS TURNED UPSIDE DOWN OVER THAT TREASURE... AND NOW THE QUEST FOR VENGEANCE SENDS ME AFTER IT AGAIN.
IT SEEMS THAT NO MATTER WHAT I DO, MY FATE IS CURSED BY THE GREAT TREASURE OF MARS, HEH HEH HEH...
HEE HEE! YOU SHOULDN'T HAVE TOLD ME THAT...
IF YOU WANT THE CANE AND BOOK BACK...
...YOU'D BETTER DO WHATEVER I SAY!!
ARE YOU THREAT-ENING ME, GIRL?
WHAT CAN A LITTLE CHILD LIKE YOU DO?
YOU WANT TO FIND OUT?
ZAP ZAP
I CAN LIGHT THIS BOOK ON FIRE!

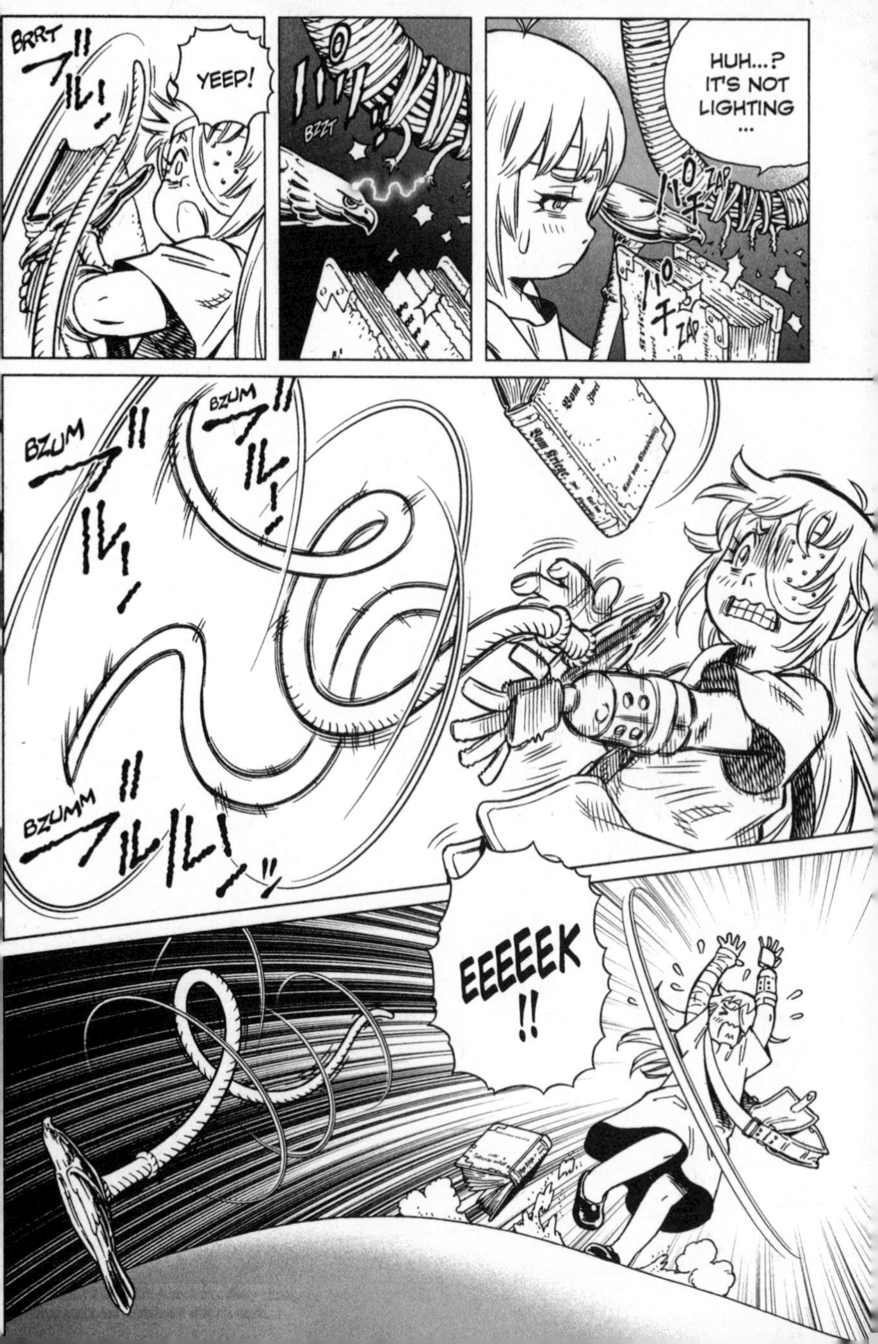
HUH...? IT'S NOT LIGHTING ...
ZAP
ZAP
BZZT
BRRT
YEEP!
BZUM
BZUM
BZUMM
EEEEEK !!

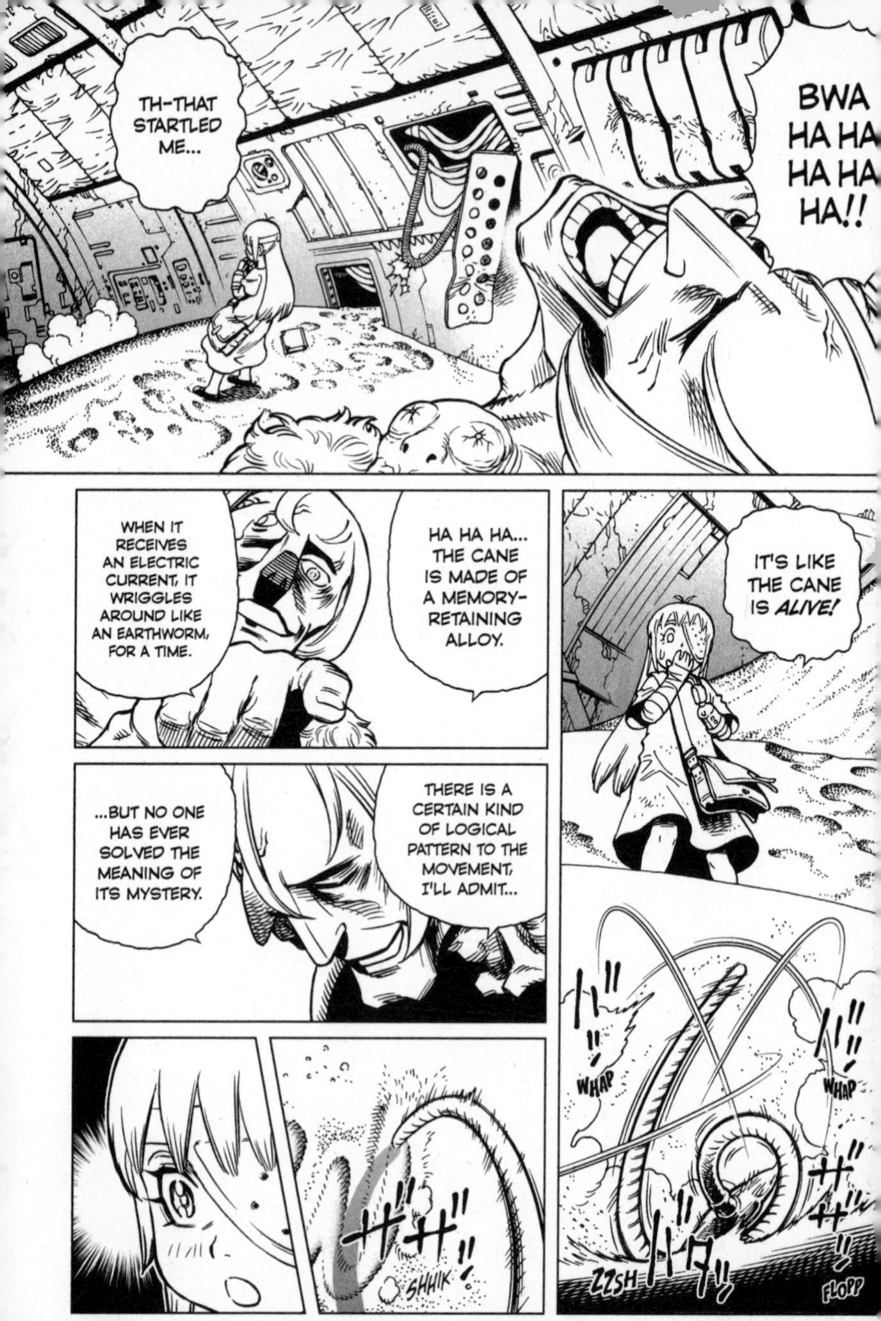

BWA HA HA HA HA HA!!
TH-THAT STARTLED ME...
IT'S LIKE THE CANE IS *ALIVE!*
WHAP
WHAP
ZZSH
FLOPP
HA HA HA... THE CANE IS MADE OF A MEMORY-RETAINING ALLOY.
WHEN IT RECEIVES AN ELECTRIC CURRENT, IT WRIGGLES AROUND LIKE AN EARTHWORM, FOR A TIME.
THERE IS A CERTAIN KIND OF LOGICAL PATTERN TO THE MOVEMENT, I'LL ADMIT...
...BUT NO ONE HAS EVER SOLVED THE MEANING OF ITS MYSTERY.
SHHIK

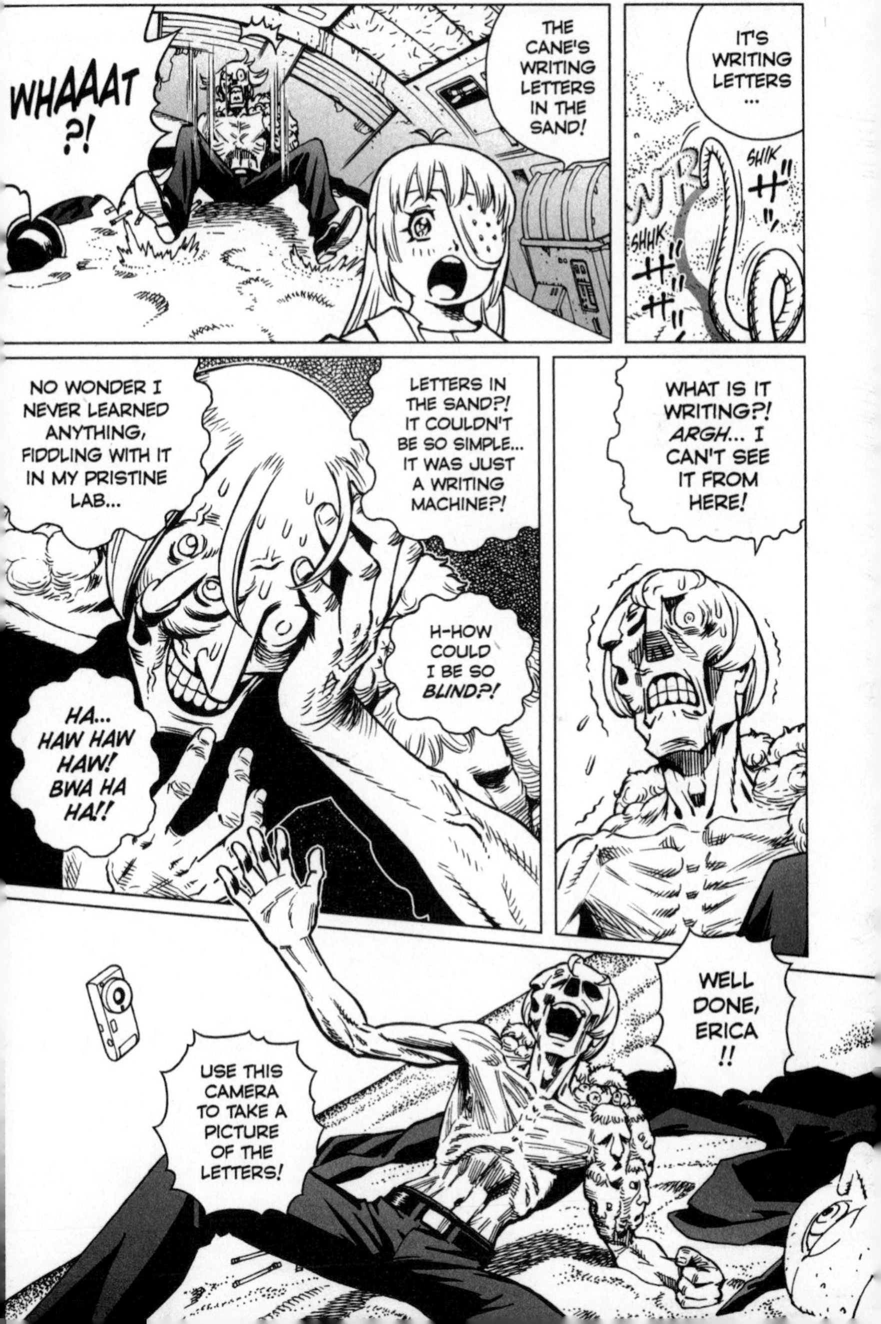
IT'S WRITING LETTERS ...
SHIK
SHHK
THE CANE'S WRITING LETTERS IN THE SAND!
WHAAAT ?!
WHAT IS IT WRITING?! ARGH... I CAN'T SEE IT FROM HERE!
LETTERS IN THE SAND?! IT COULDN'T BE SO SIMPLE... IT WAS JUST A WRITING MACHINE?!
NO WONDER I NEVER LEARNED ANYTHING, FIDDLING WITH IT IN MY PRISTINE LAB...
H-HOW COULD I BE SO BLIND?!
HA... HAW HAW HAW! BWA HA HA!!
WELL DONE, ERICA !!
USE THIS CAMERA TO TAKE A PICTURE OF THE LETTERS!

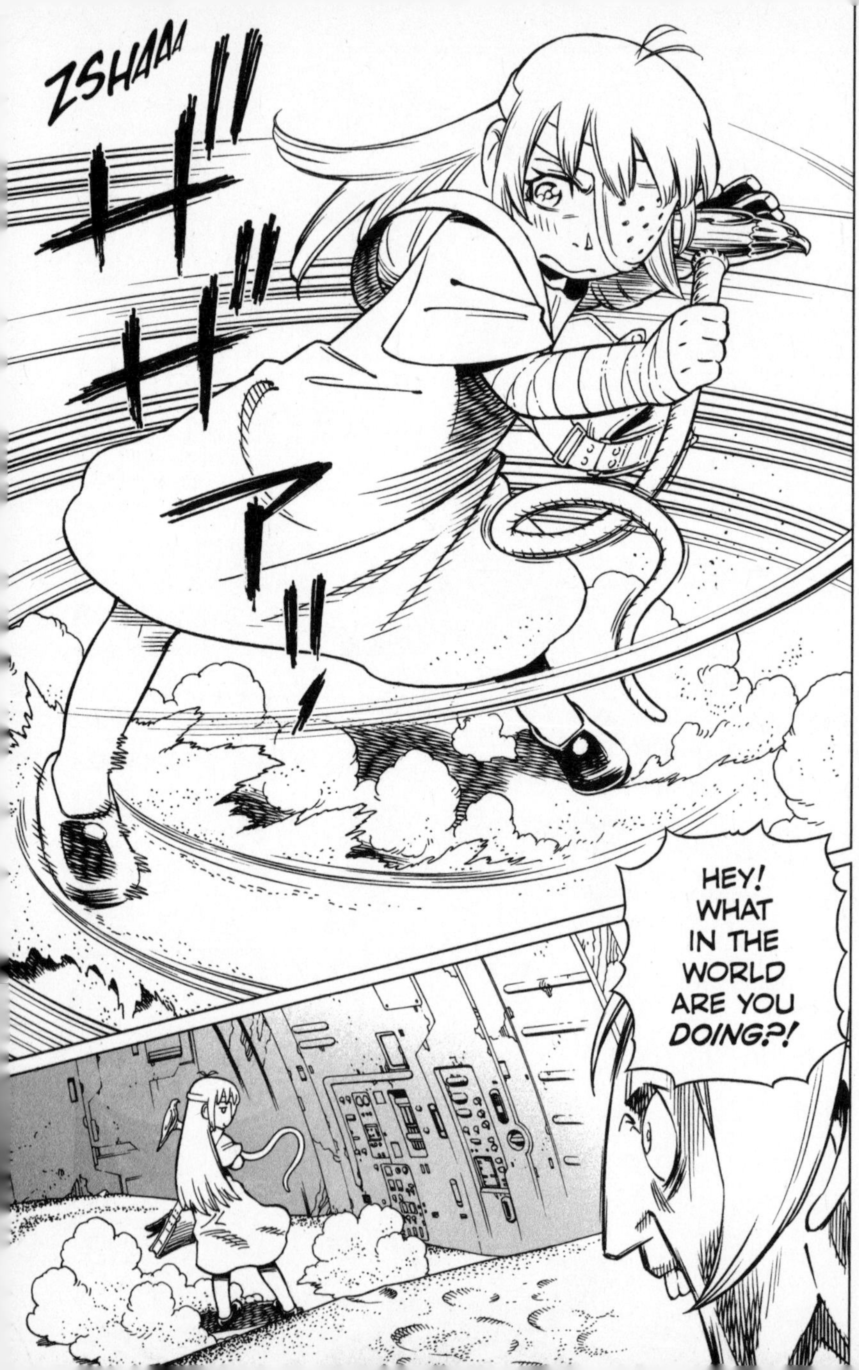
ZSHAAA
HEY! WHAT IN THE WORLD ARE YOU DOING?!

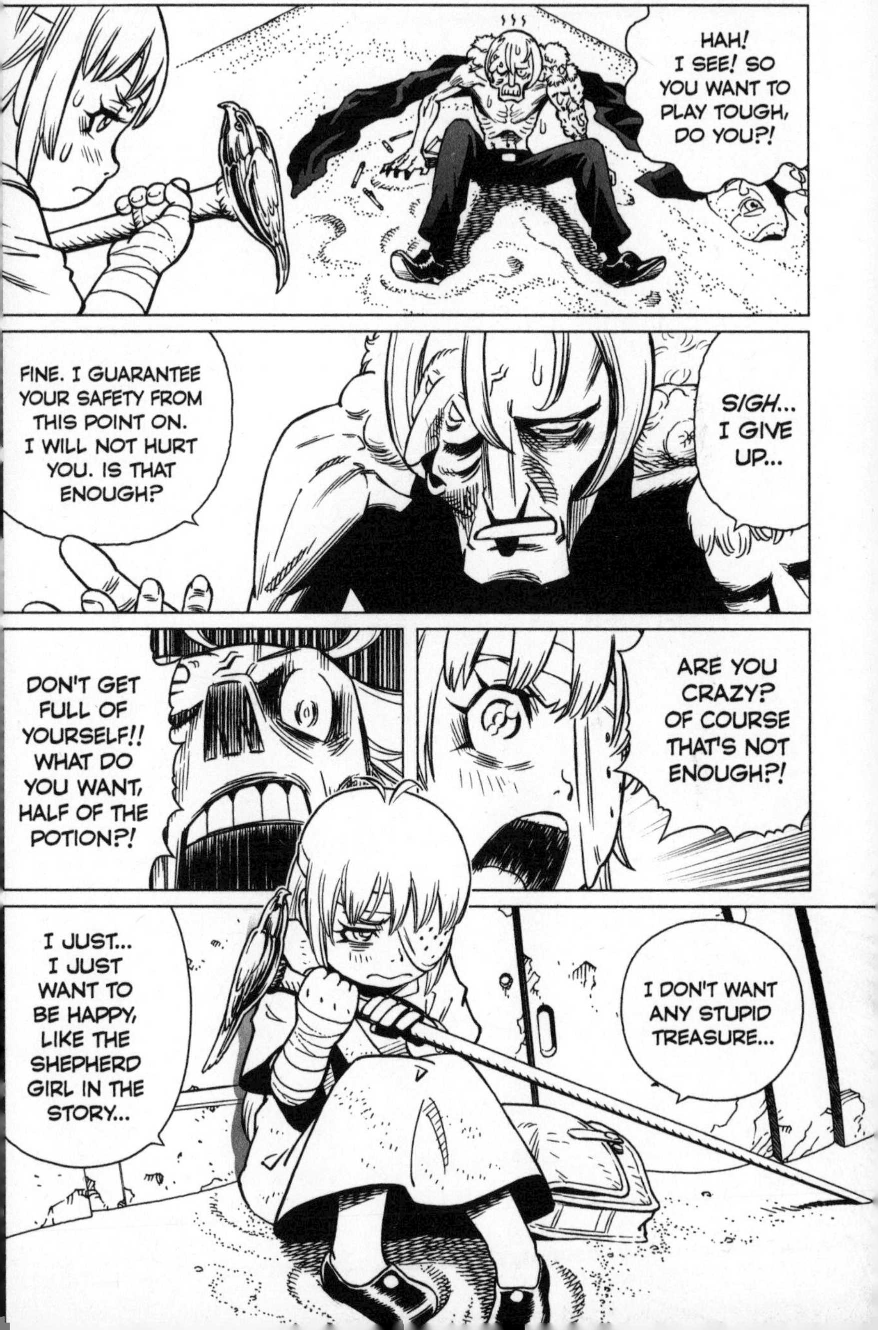
HAH! I SEE! SO YOU WANT TO PLAY TOUGH, DO YOU?!
SIGH... I GIVE UP...
FINE. I GUARANTEE YOUR SAFETY FROM THIS POINT ON. I WILL NOT HURT YOU. IS THAT ENOUGH?
ARE YOU CRAZY? OF COURSE THAT'S NOT ENOUGH?!
DON'T GET FULL OF YOURSELF!! WHAT DO YOU WANT, HALF OF THE POTION?!
I DON'T WANT ANY STUPID TREASURE...
I JUST... I JUST WANT TO BE HAPPY, LIKE THE SHEPHERD GIRL IN THE STORY...

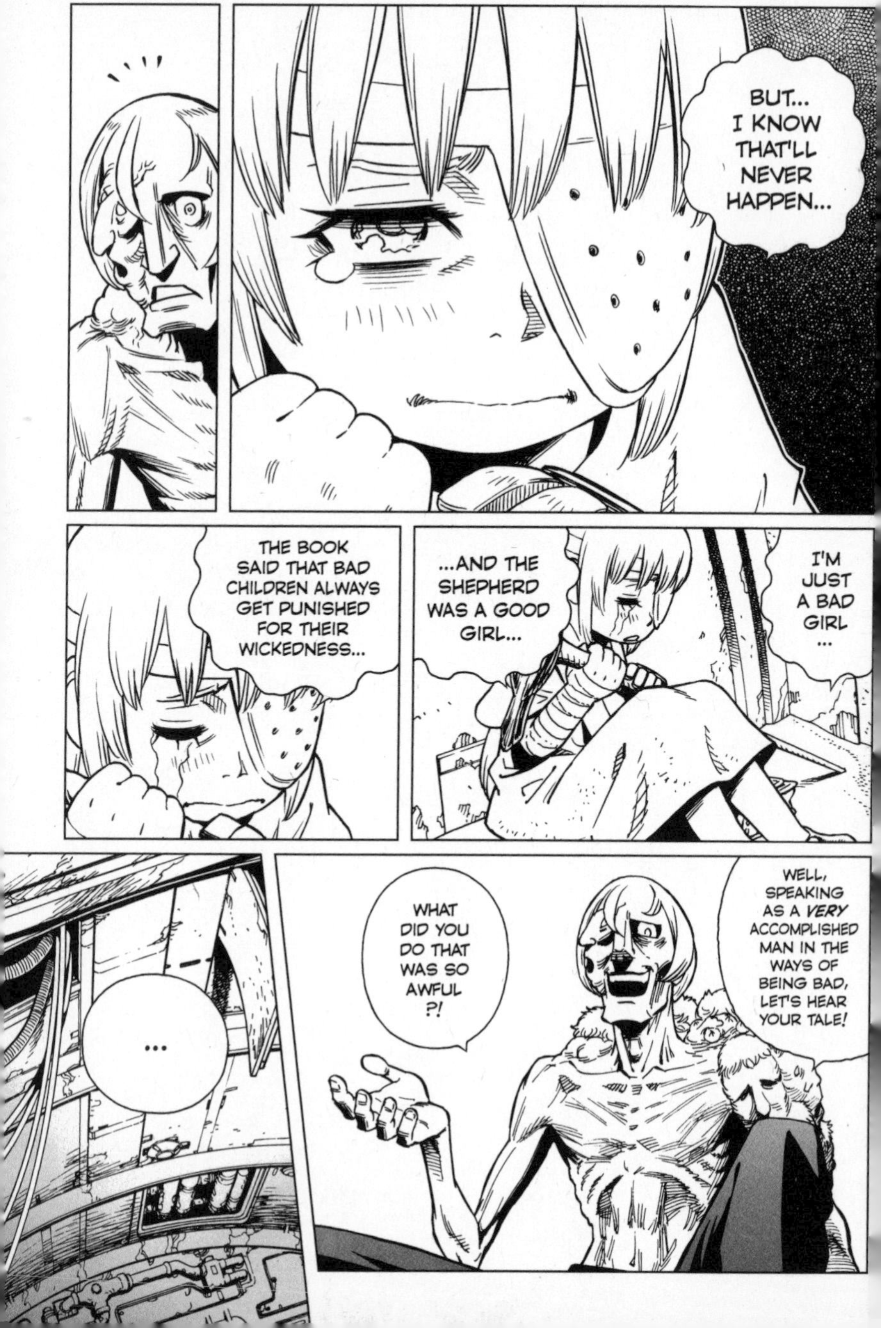
BUT... I KNOW THAT'LL NEVER HAPPEN...
I'M JUST A BAD GIRL ...
...AND THE SHEPHERD WAS A GOOD GIRL...
THE BOOK SAID THAT BAD CHILDREN ALWAYS GET PUNISHED FOR THEIR WICKEDNESS...
WELL, SPEAKING AS A *VERY* ACCOMPLISHED MAN IN THE WAYS OF BEING BAD, LET'S HEAR YOUR TALE!
WHAT DID YOU DO THAT WAS SO AWFUL ?!
...

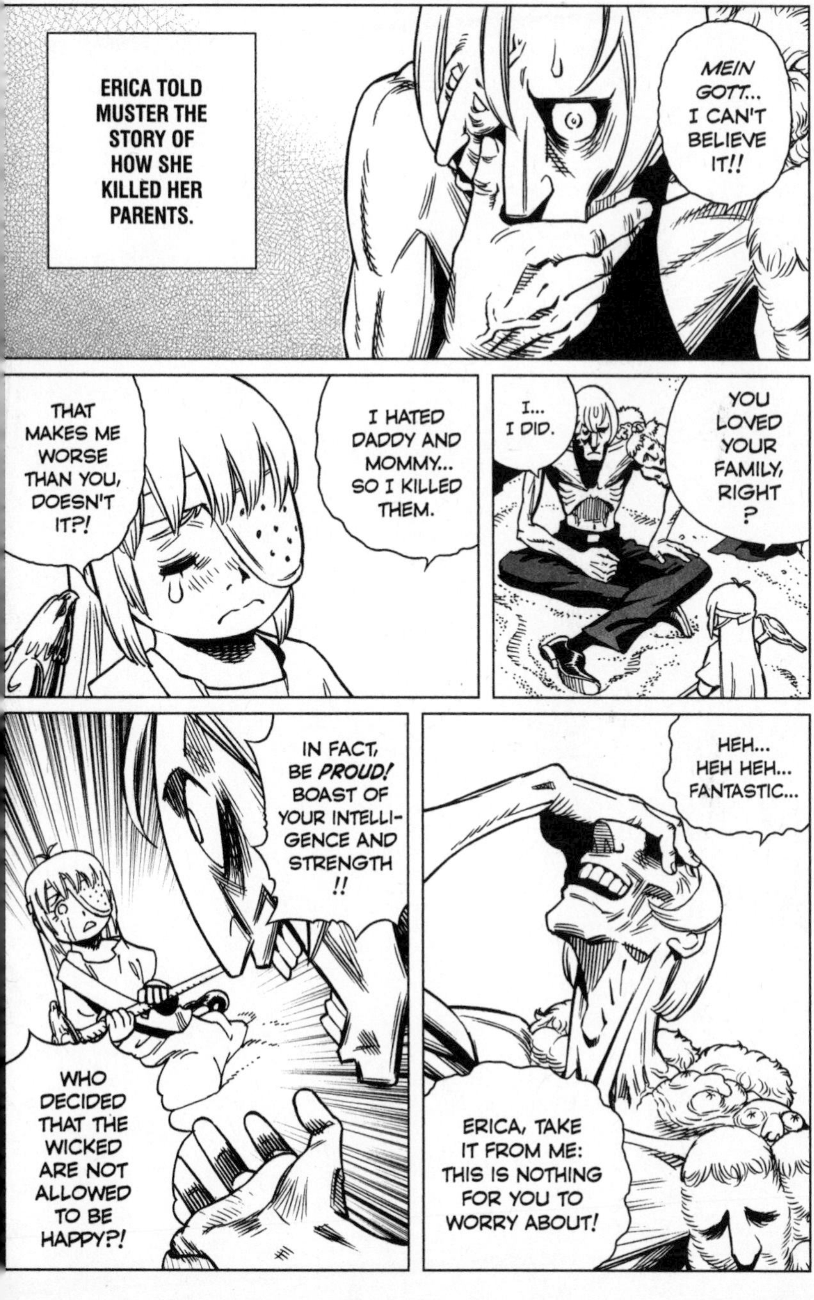

MEIN GOTT... I CAN'T BELIEVE IT!!
ERICA TOLD MUSTER THE STORY OF HOW SHE KILLED HER PARENTS.
YOU LOVED YOUR FAMILY, RIGHT?
I... I DID.
I HATED DADDY AND MOMMY... SO I KILLED THEM.
THAT MAKES ME WORSE THAN YOU, DOESN'T IT?!
HEH... HEH HEH... FANTASTIC...
ERICA, TAKE IT FROM ME: THIS IS NOTHING FOR YOU TO WORRY ABOUT!
IN FACT, BE *PROUD!* BOAST OF YOUR INTELLIGENCE AND STRENGTH!!
WHO DECIDED THAT THE WICKED ARE NOT ALLOWED TO BE HAPPY?!

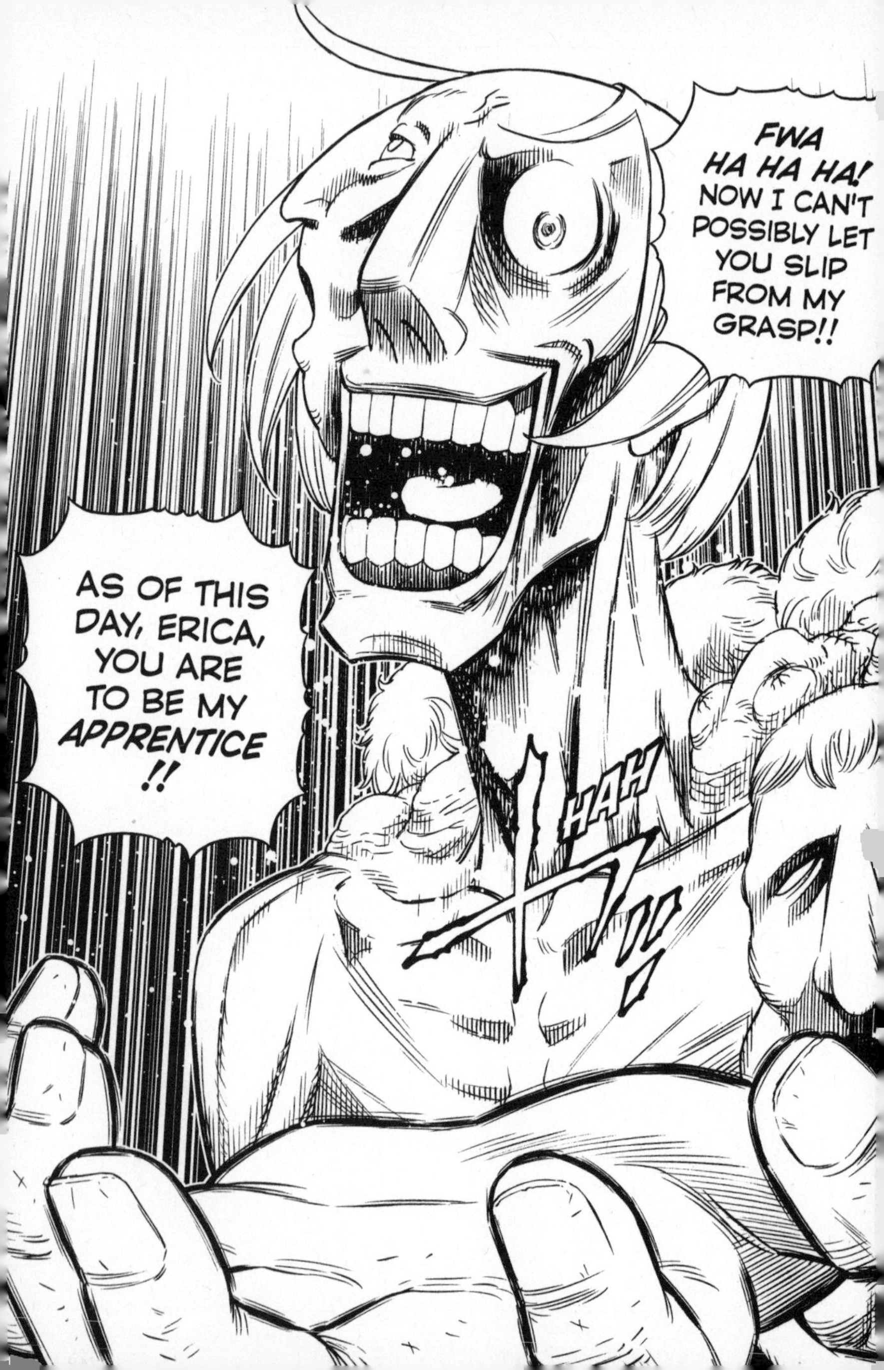
FWA HA HA HA! NOW I CAN'T POSSIBLY LET YOU SLIP FROM MY GRASP!!
AS OF THIS DAY, ERICA, YOU ARE TO BE MY *APPRENTICE* !!
HAH

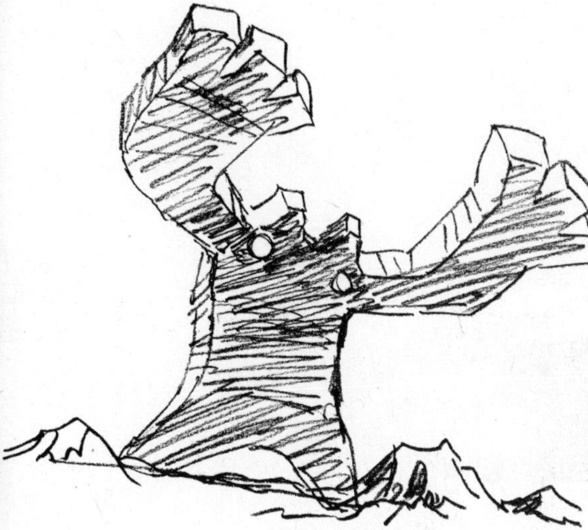

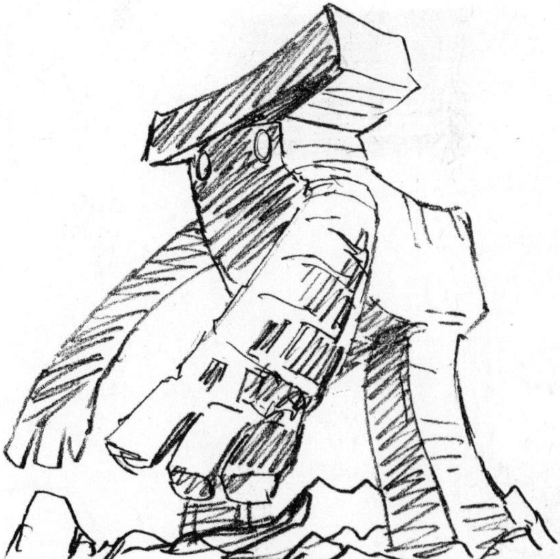

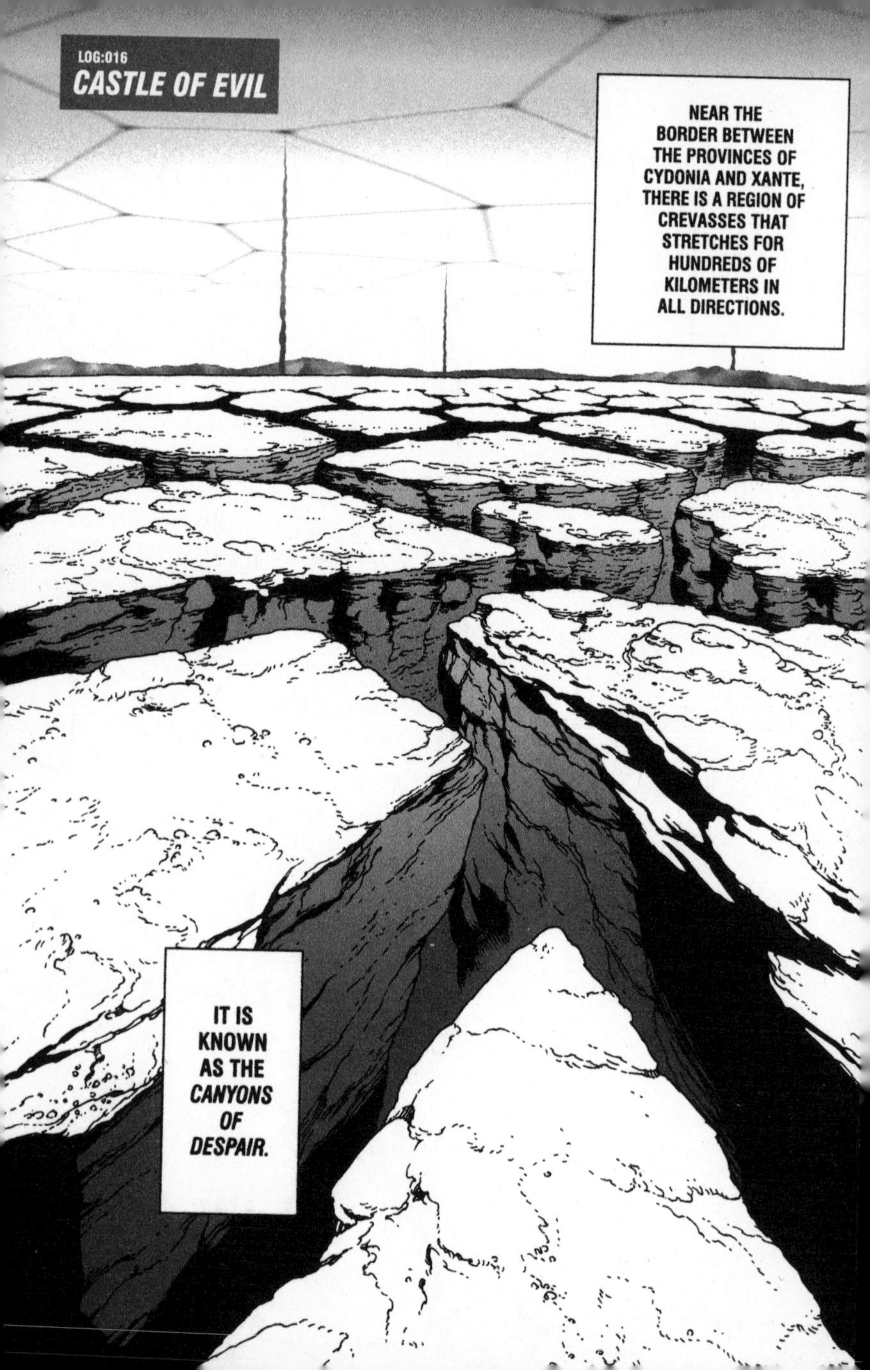
LOG:016
CASTLE OF EVIL
NEAR THE BORDER BETWEEN THE PROVINCES OF CYDONIA AND XANTE, THERE IS A REGION OF CREVASSES THAT STRETCHES FOR HUNDREDS OF KILOMETERS IN ALL DIRECTIONS.
IT IS KNOWN AS THE CANYONS OF DESPAIR.

LOG:016

CASTLE OF EVIL

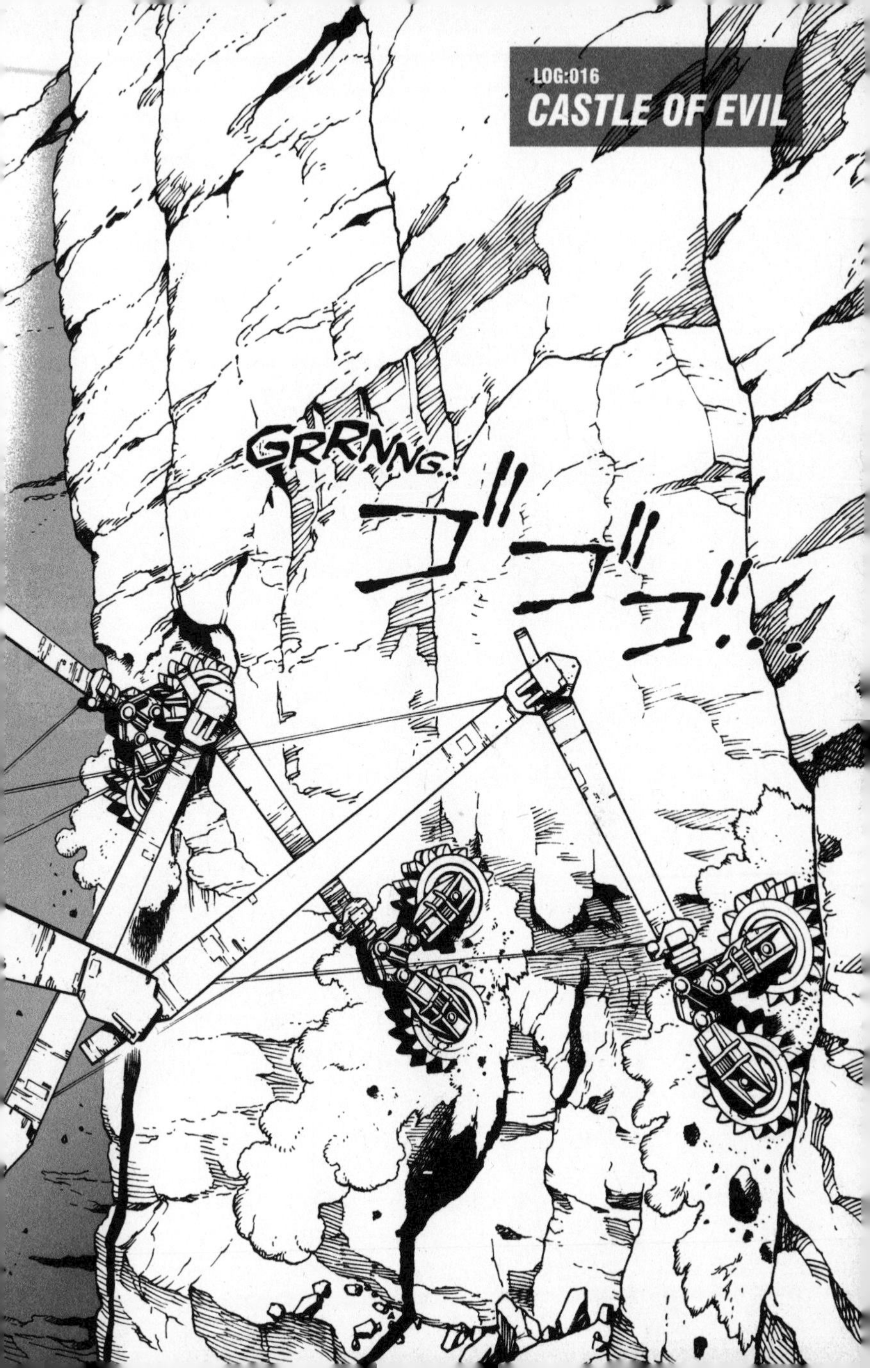
GRRNNG..
ゴゴゴ‥

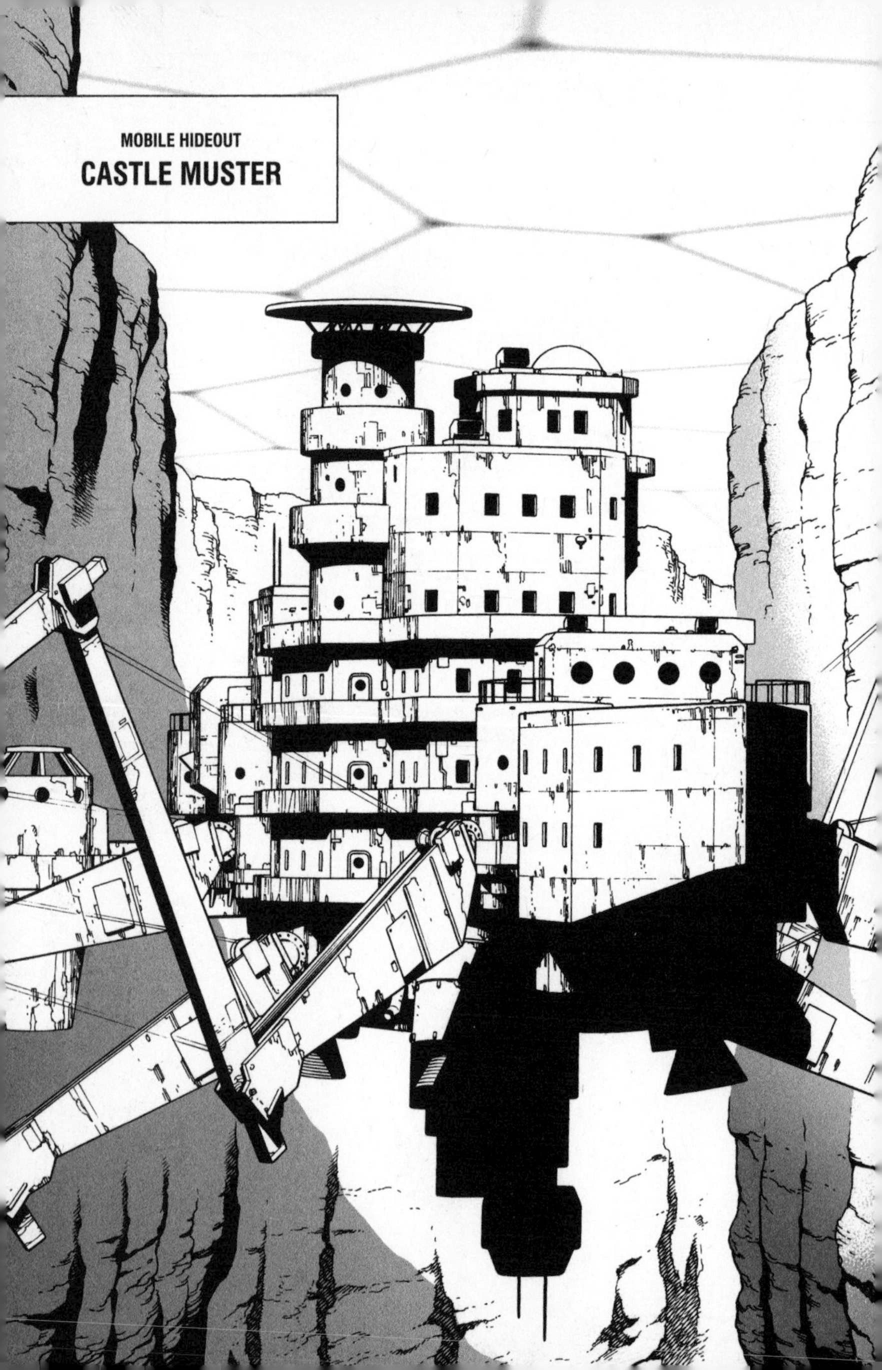
MOBILE HIDEOUT
CASTLE MUSTER

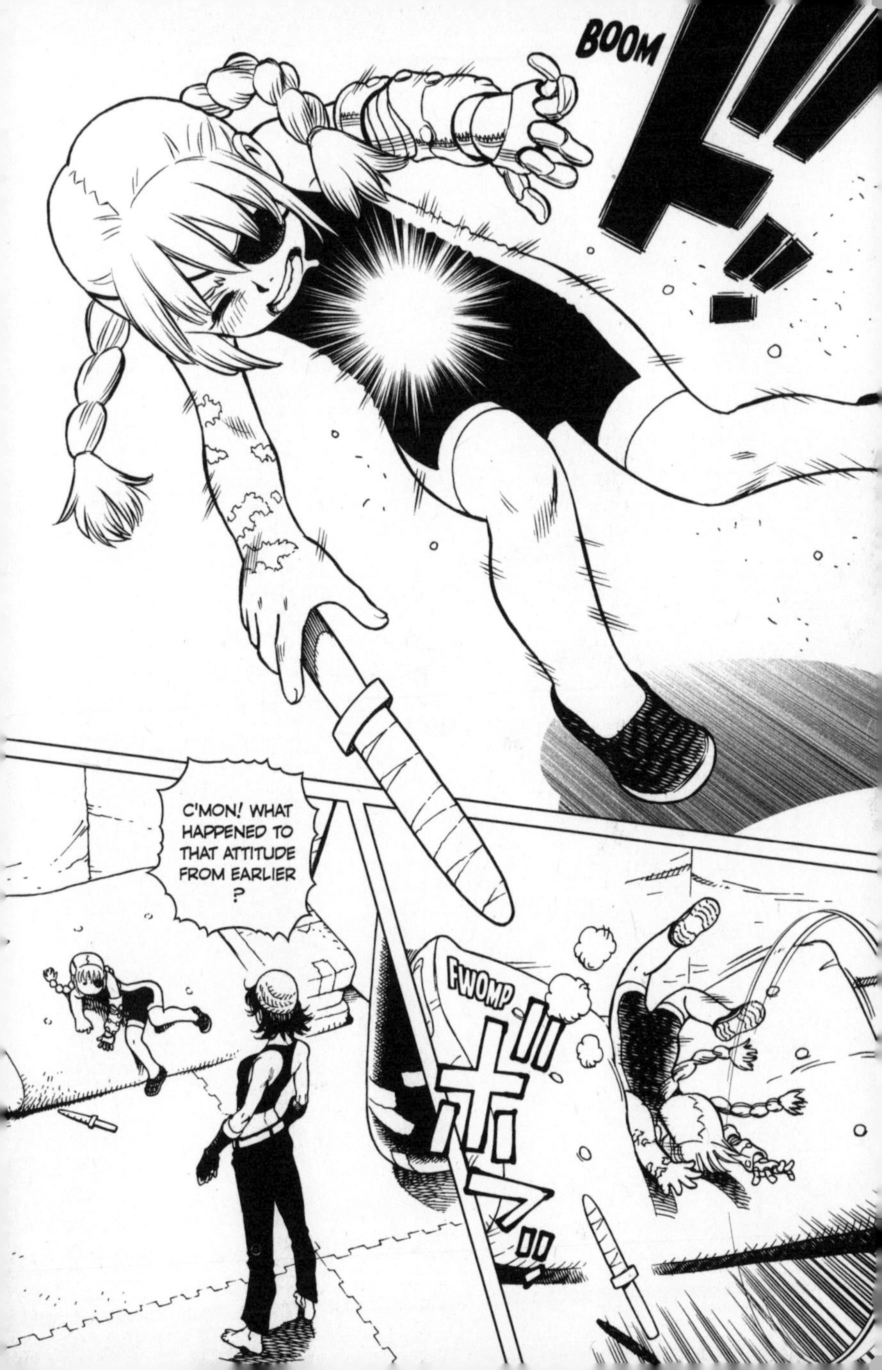
BOOM
FWOMP
C'MON! WHAT HAPPENED TO THAT ATTITUDE FROM EARLIER?

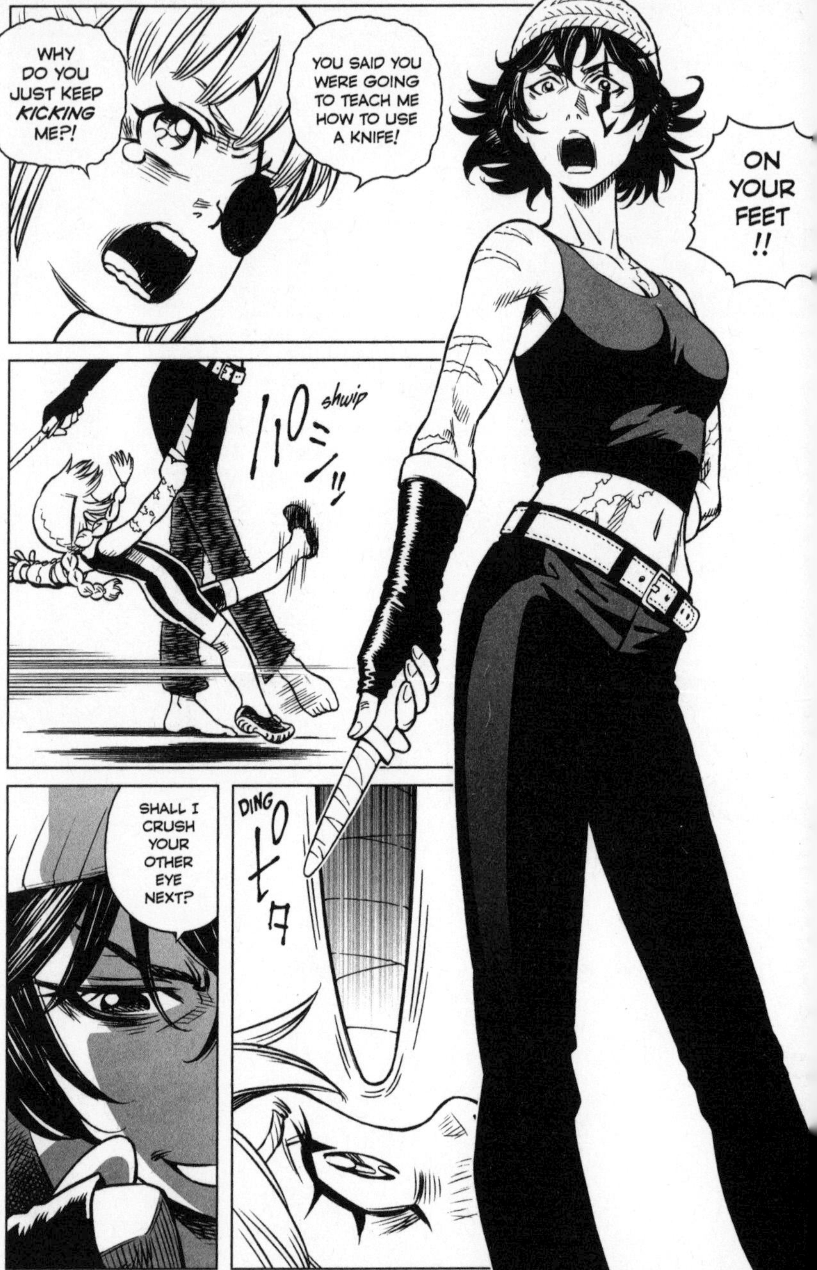
ON YOUR FEET !!
YOU SAID YOU WERE GOING TO TEACH ME HOW TO USE A KNIFE!
WHY DO YOU JUST KEEP *KICKING* ME?!
shwip
DING
SHALL I CRUSH YOUR OTHER EYE NEXT?

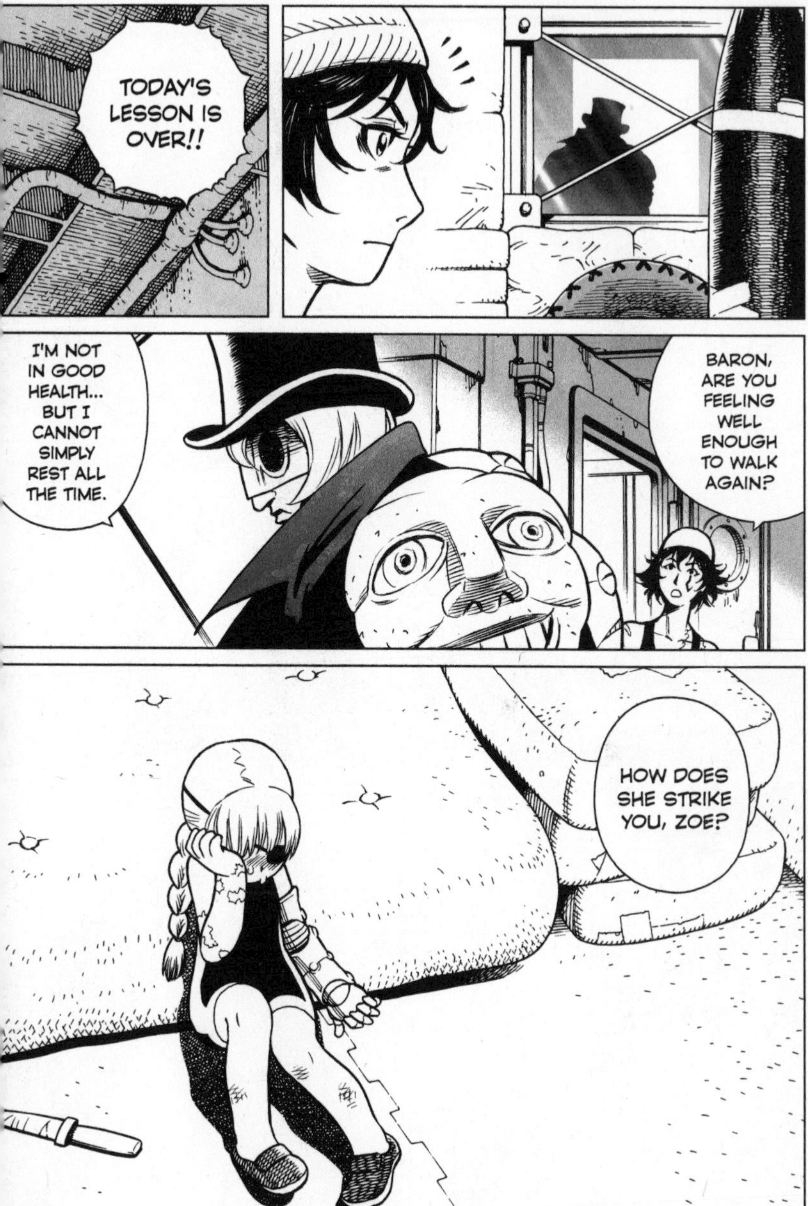
TODAY'S LESSON IS OVER!!
BARON, ARE YOU FEELING WELL ENOUGH TO WALK AGAIN?
I'M NOT IN GOOD HEALTH... BUT I CANNOT SIMPLY REST ALL THE TIME.
HOW DOES SHE STRIKE YOU, ZOE?

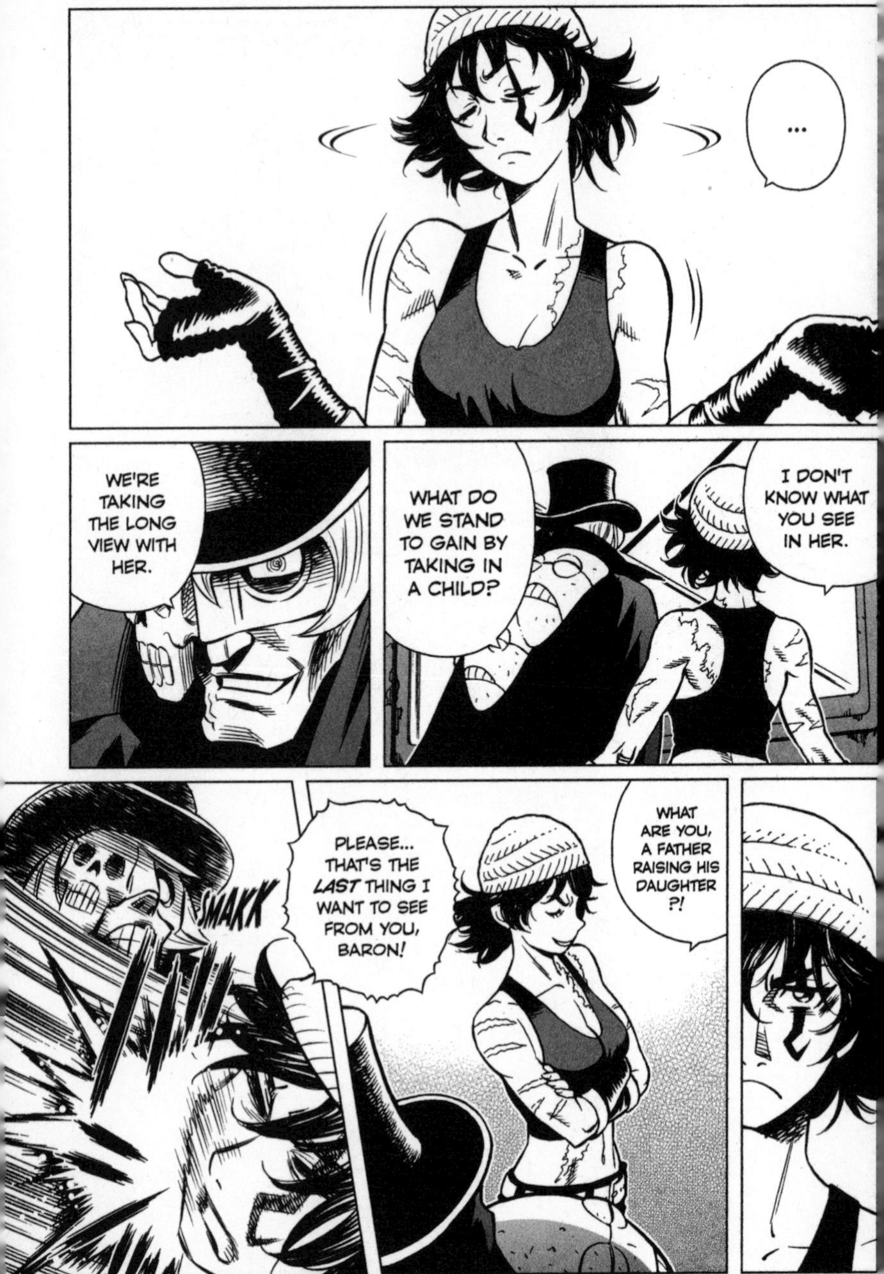
...
I DON'T KNOW WHAT YOU SEE IN HER.
WHAT DO WE STAND TO GAIN BY TAKING IN A CHILD?
WE'RE TAKING THE LONG VIEW WITH HER.
WHAT ARE YOU, A FATHER RAISING HIS DAUGHTER?!
PLEASE... THAT'S THE *LAST* THING I WANT TO SEE FROM YOU, BARON!
SMAKK

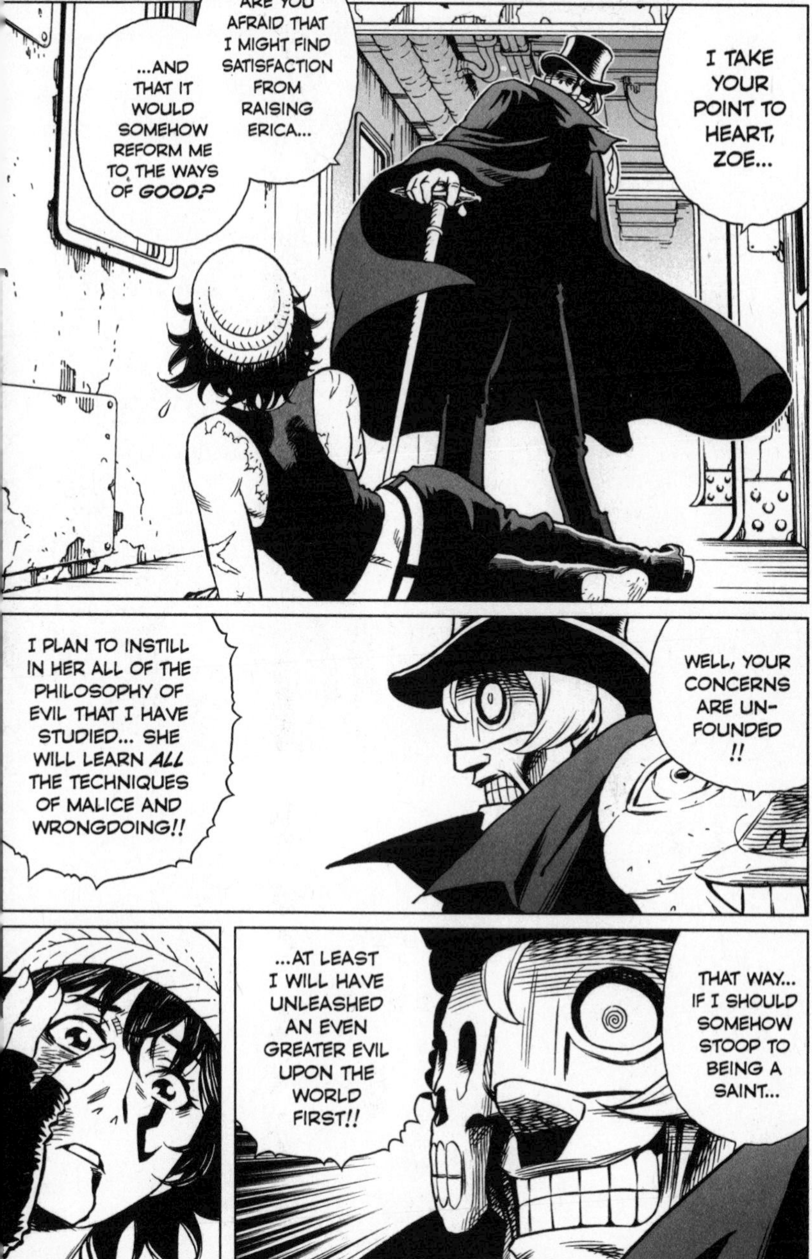
I TAKE YOUR POINT TO HEART, ZOE...
ARE YOU AFRAID THAT I MIGHT FIND SATISFACTION FROM RAISING ERICA...
...AND THAT IT WOULD SOMEHOW REFORM ME TO THE WAYS OF *GOOD?*
WELL, YOUR CONCERNS ARE UN-FOUNDED!!
I PLAN TO INSTILL IN HER ALL OF THE PHILOSOPHY OF EVIL THAT I HAVE STUDIED... SHE WILL LEARN *ALL* THE TECHNIQUES OF MALICE AND WRONGDOING!!
THAT WAY... IF I SHOULD SOMEHOW STOOP TO BEING A SAINT...
...AT LEAST I WILL HAVE UNLEASHED AN EVEN GREATER EVIL UPON THE WORLD FIRST!!

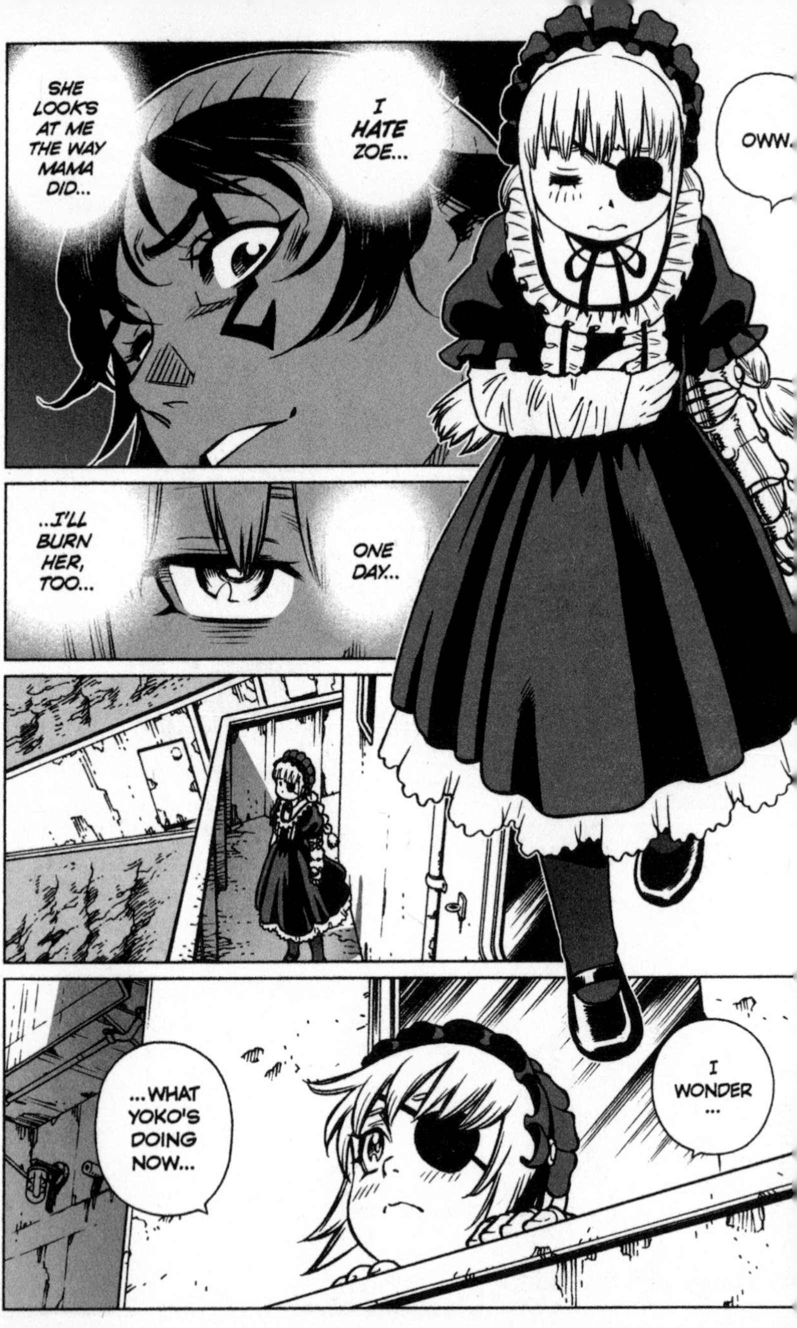
OWW...
I HATE ZOE...
SHE LOOKS AT ME THE WAY MAMA DID...
ONE DAY...
...I'LL BURN HER, TOO...
I WONDER ...
...WHAT YOKO'S DOING NOW...

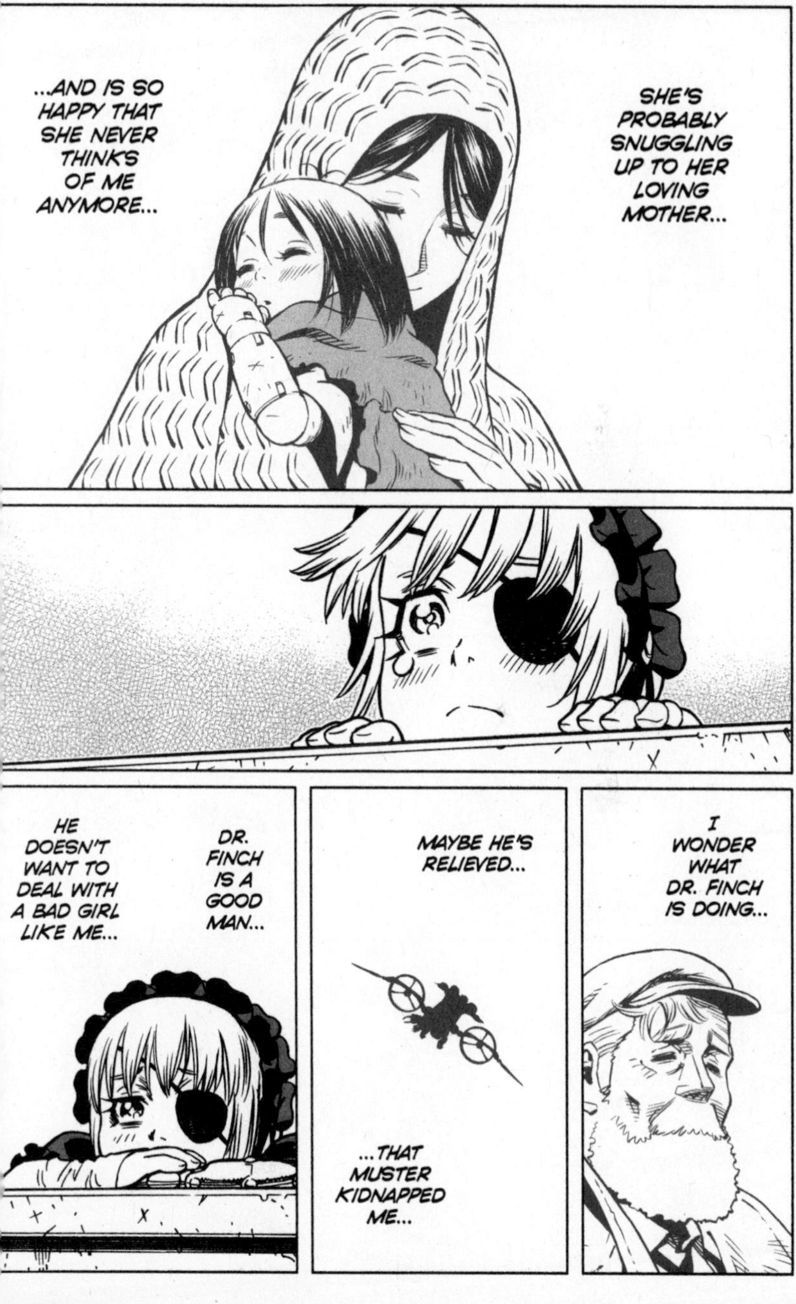
SHE'S PROBABLY SNUGGLING UP TO HER LOVING MOTHER...
...AND IS SO HAPPY THAT SHE NEVER THINKS OF ME ANYMORE...
I WONDER WHAT DR. FINCH IS DOING...
MAYBE HE'S RELIEVED...
...THAT MUSTER KIDNAPPED ME...
DR. FINCH IS A GOOD MAN...
HE DOESN'T WANT TO DEAL WITH A BAD GIRL LIKE ME...

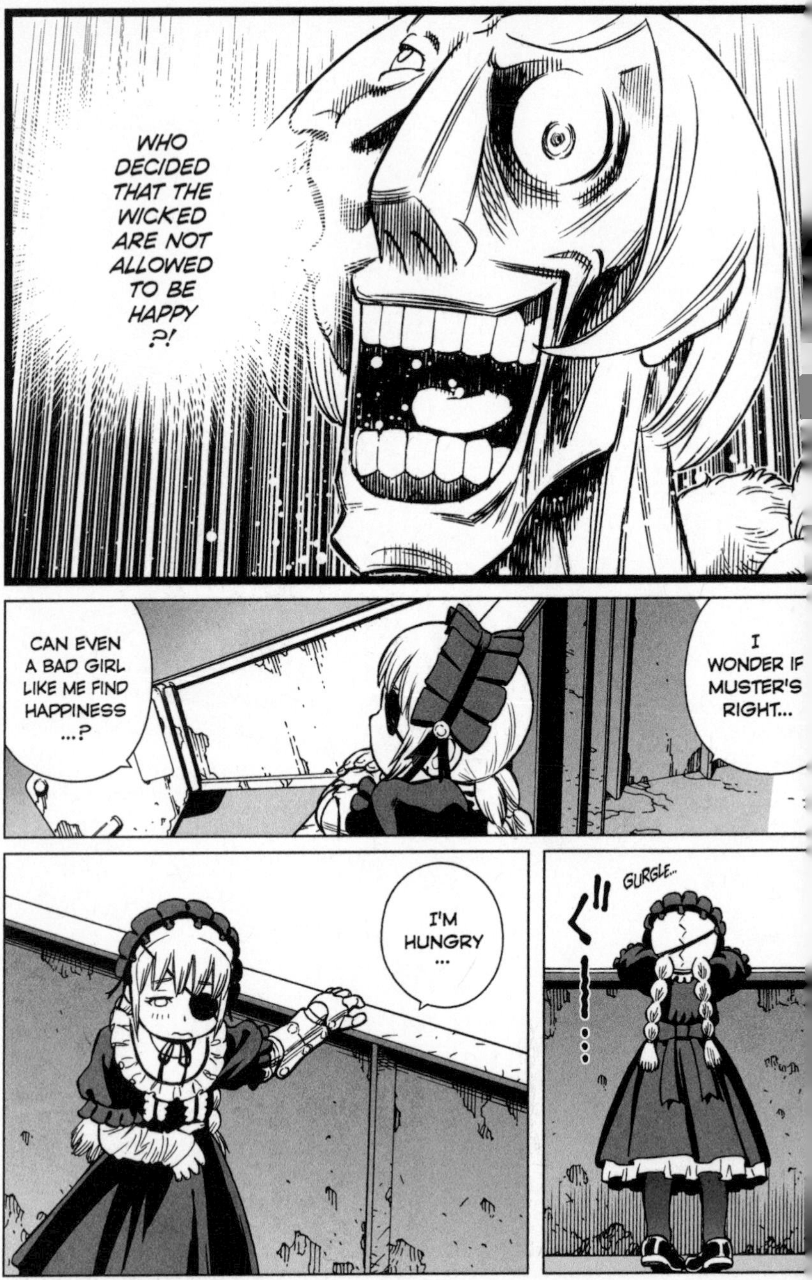
WHO DECIDED THAT THE WICKED ARE NOT ALLOWED TO BE HAPPY ?!
I WONDER IF MUSTER'S RIGHT...
CAN EVEN A BAD GIRL LIKE ME FIND HAPPINESS ...?
GURGLE...
ぐー…
I'M HUNGRY ...

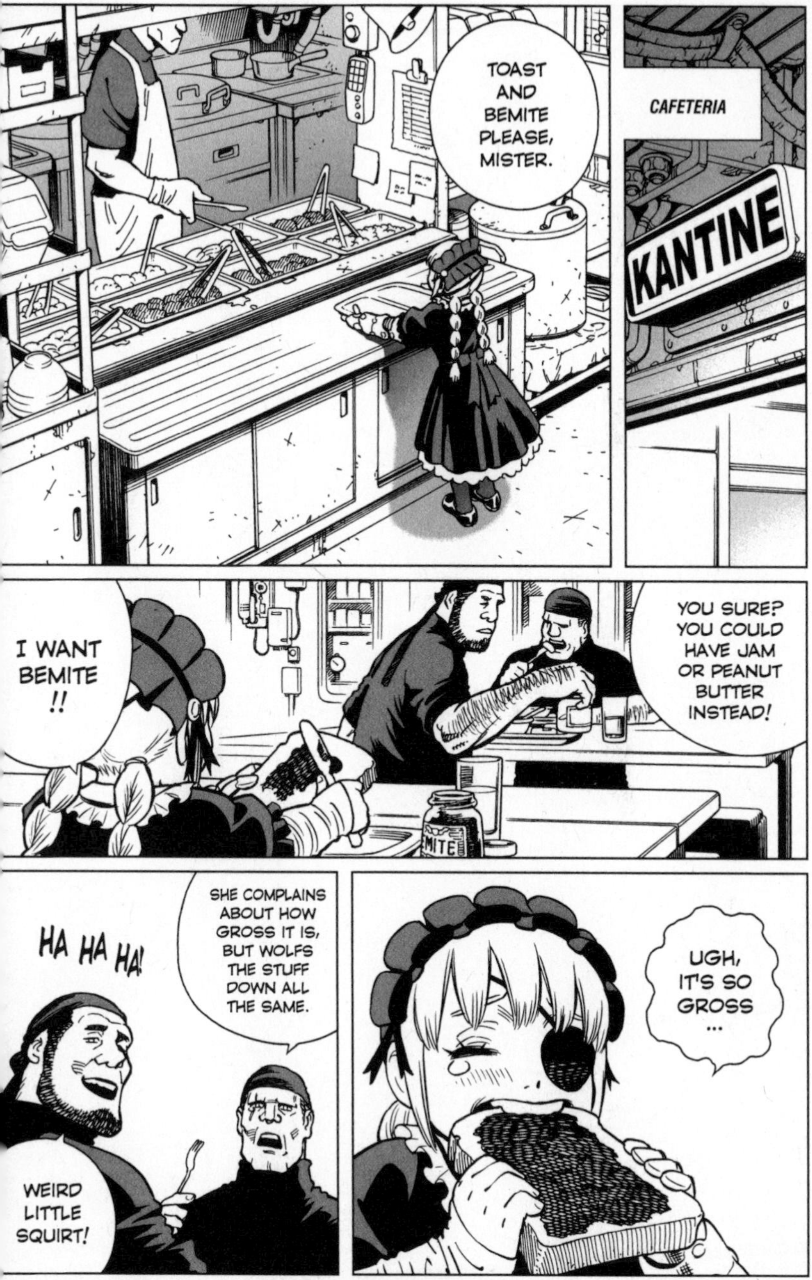
CAFETERIA
KANTINE
TOAST AND BEMITE PLEASE, MISTER.
YOU SURE? YOU COULD HAVE JAM OR PEANUT BUTTER INSTEAD!
I WANT BEMITE !!
UGH, IT'S SO GROSS ...
SHE COMPLAINS ABOUT HOW GROSS IT IS, BUT WOLFS THE STUFF DOWN ALL THE SAME.
HA HA HA!
WEIRD LITTLE SQUIRT!

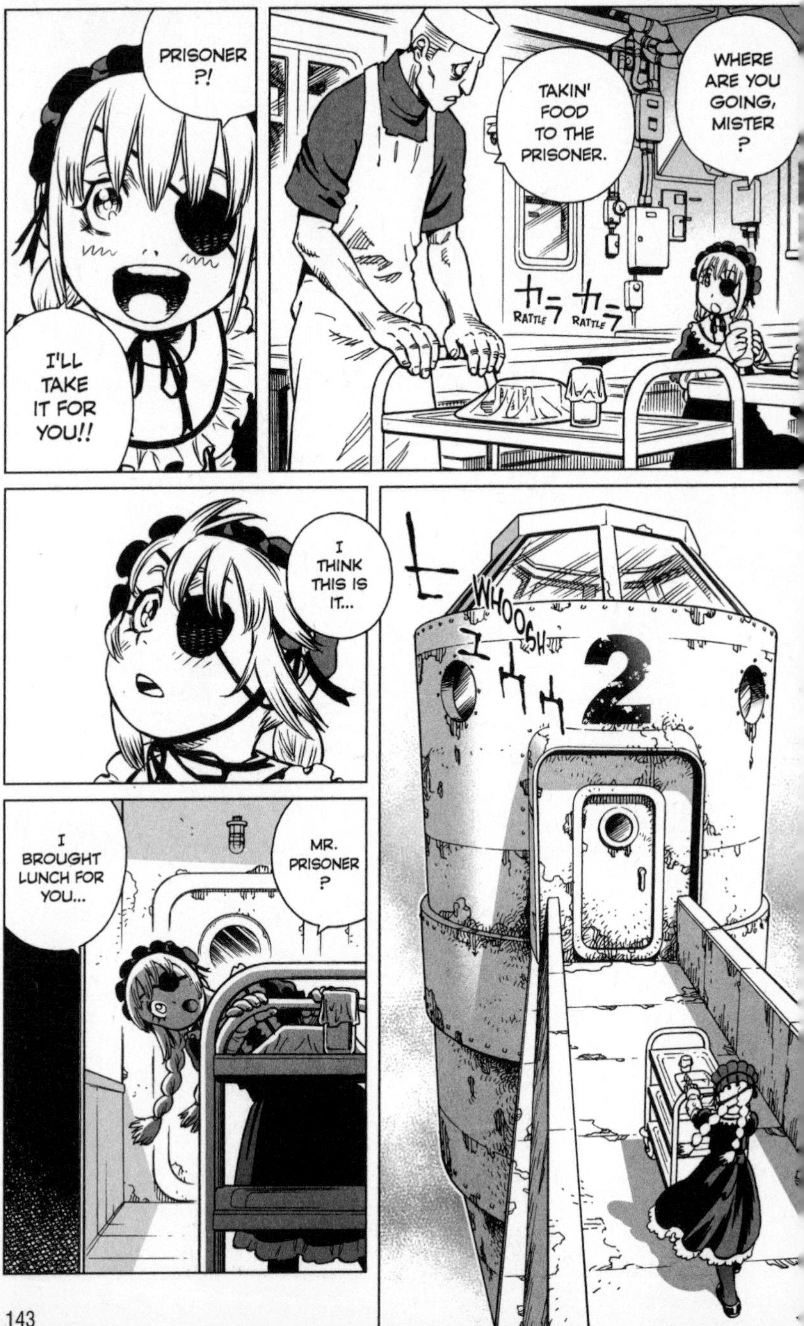
WHERE ARE YOU GOING, MISTER?
TAKIN' FOOD TO THE PRISONER.
カラ RATTLE カラ RATTLE
PRISONER?!
I'LL TAKE IT FOR YOU!!
WHOOSH
I THINK THIS IS IT...
MR. PRISONER?
I BROUGHT LUNCH FOR YOU...

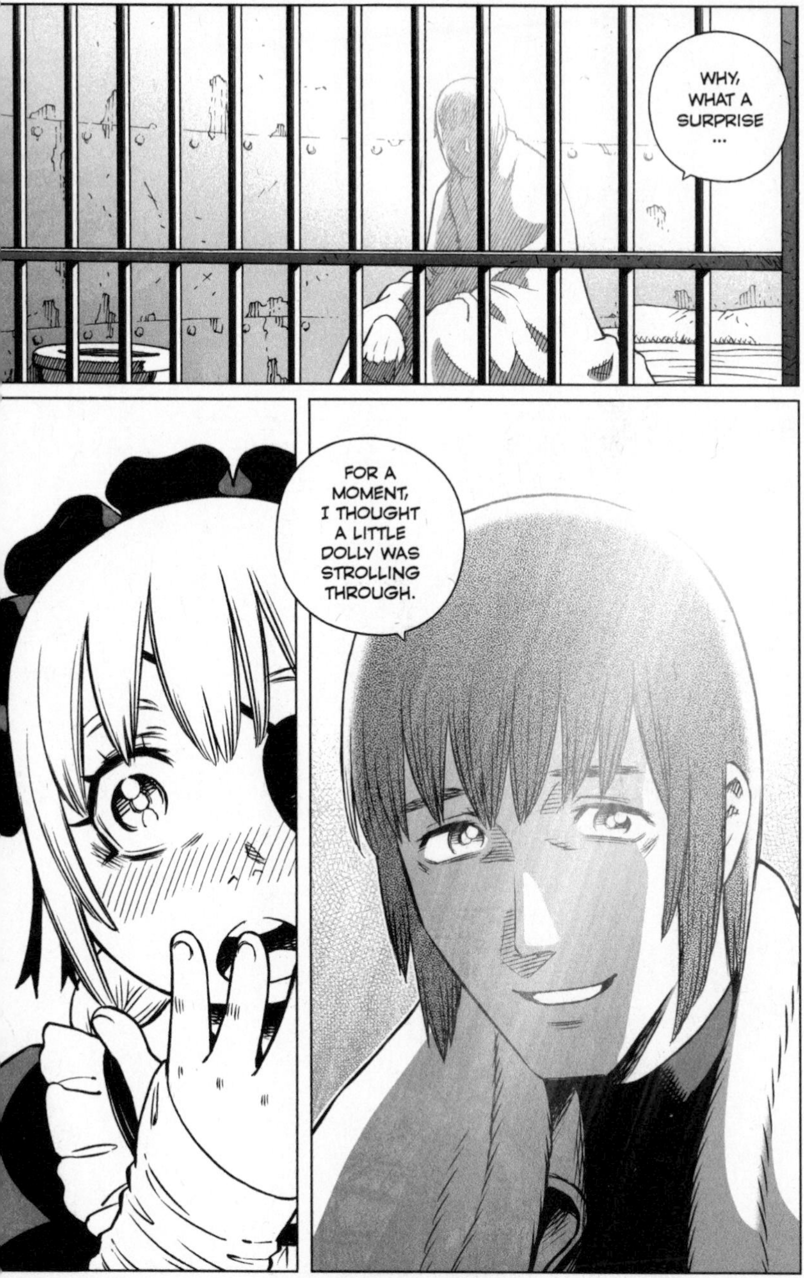
WHY, WHAT A SURPRISE ...
FOR A MOMENT, I THOUGHT A LITTLE DOLLY WAS STROLLING THROUGH.

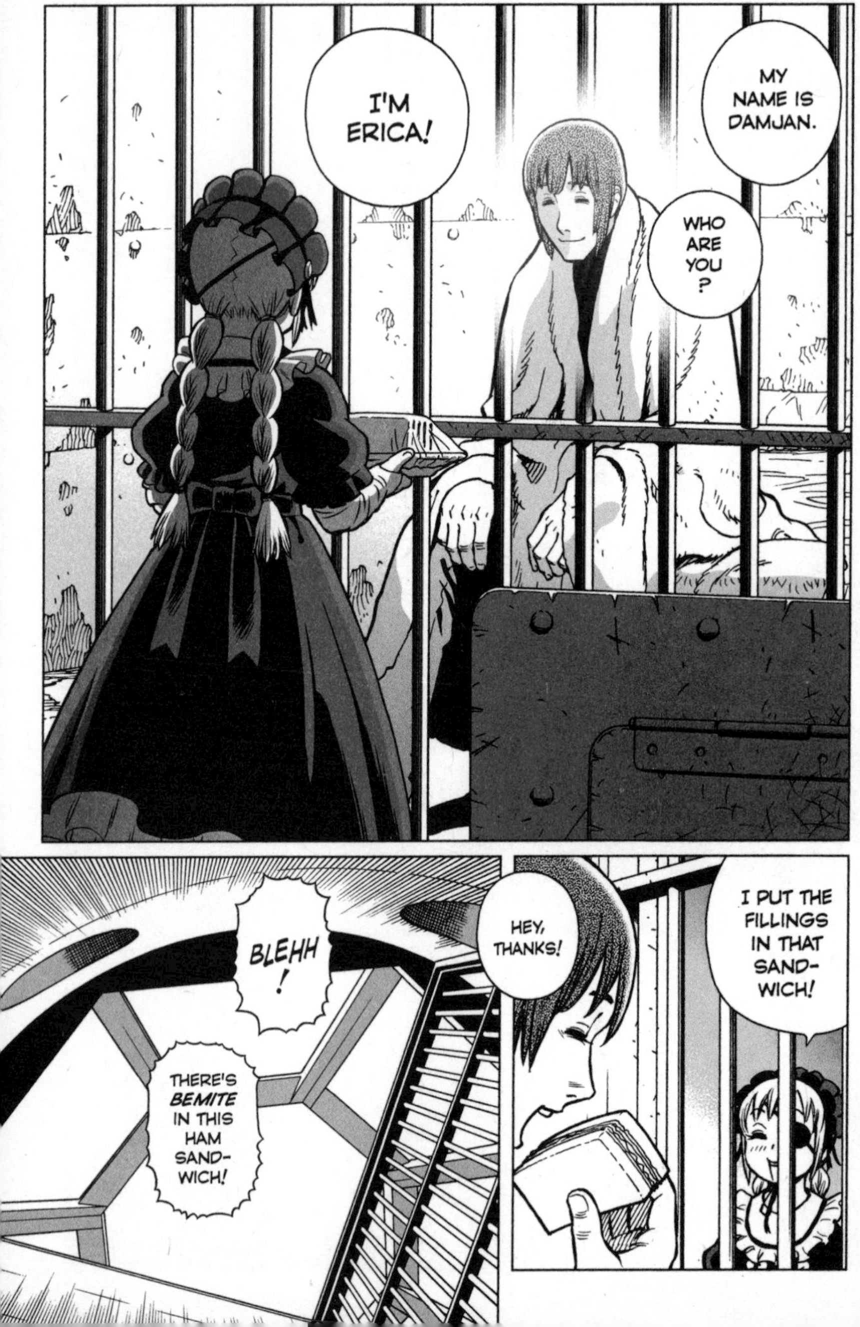
MY NAME IS DAMJAN.
WHO ARE YOU?
I'M ERICA!
I PUT THE FILLINGS IN THAT SANDWICH!
HEY, THANKS!
BLEHH!
THERE'S *BEMITE* IN THIS HAM SANDWICH!

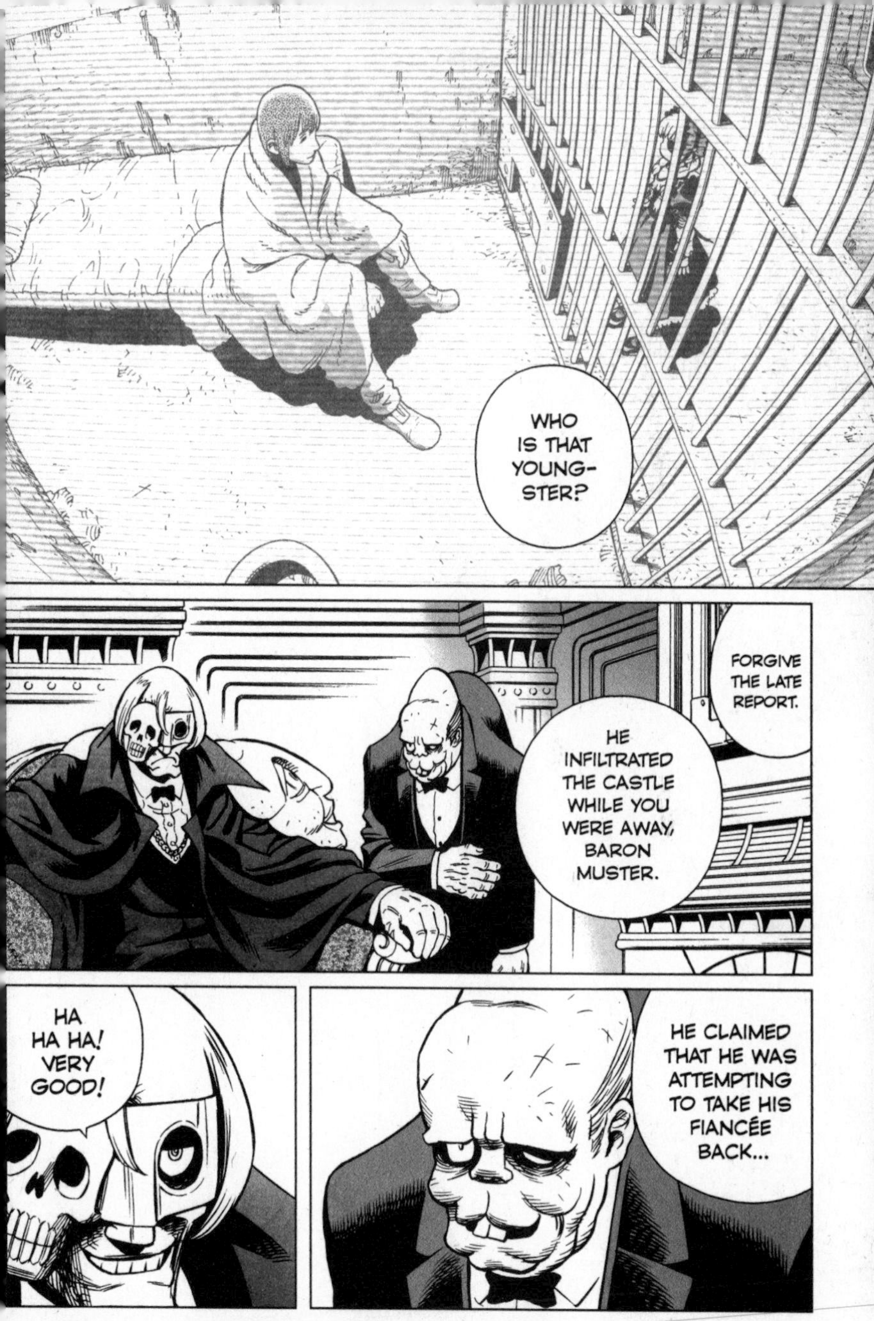
WHO IS THAT YOUNG-STER?
FORGIVE THE LATE REPORT.
HE INFILTRATED THE CASTLE WHILE YOU WERE AWAY, BARON MUSTER.
HE CLAIMED THAT HE WAS ATTEMPTING TO TAKE HIS FIANCÉE BACK...
HA HA HA! VERY GOOD!

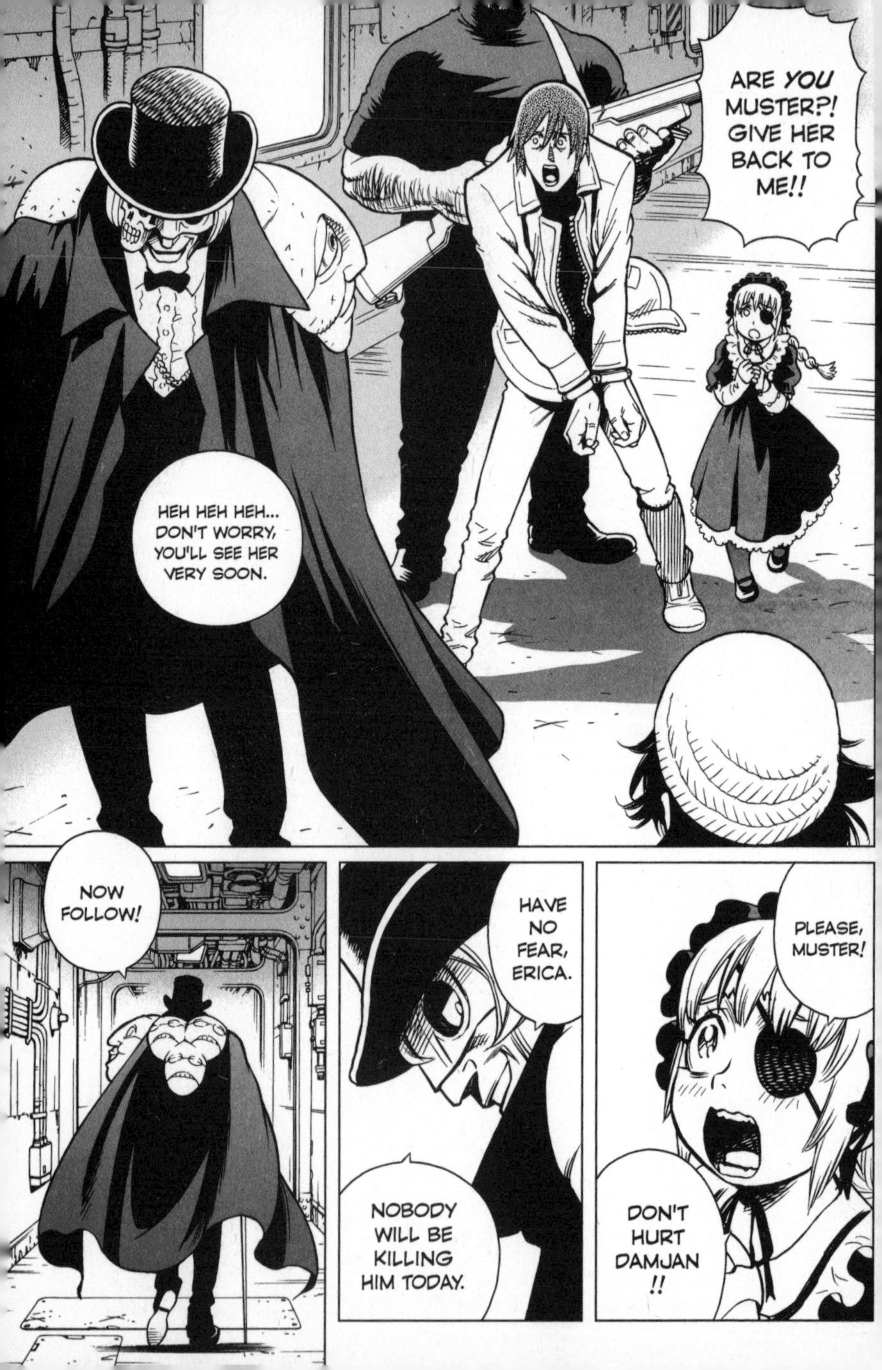
ARE *YOU* MUSTER?! GIVE HER BACK TO ME!!
HEH HEH HEH... DON'T WORRY, YOU'LL SEE HER VERY SOON.
PLEASE, MUSTER!
DON'T HURT DAMJAN !!
HAVE NO FEAR, ERICA.
NOBODY WILL BE KILLING HIM TODAY.
NOW FOLLOW!

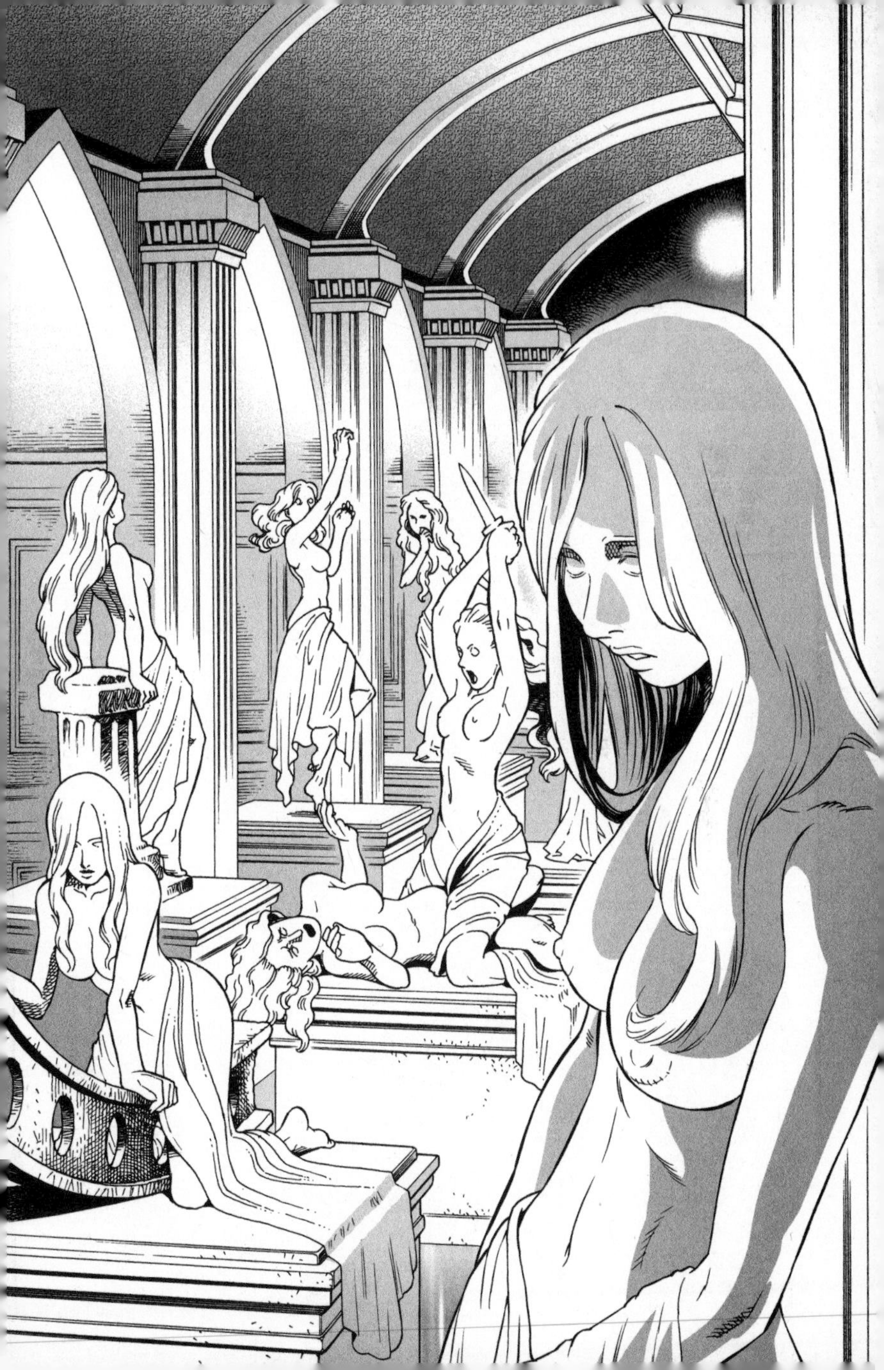

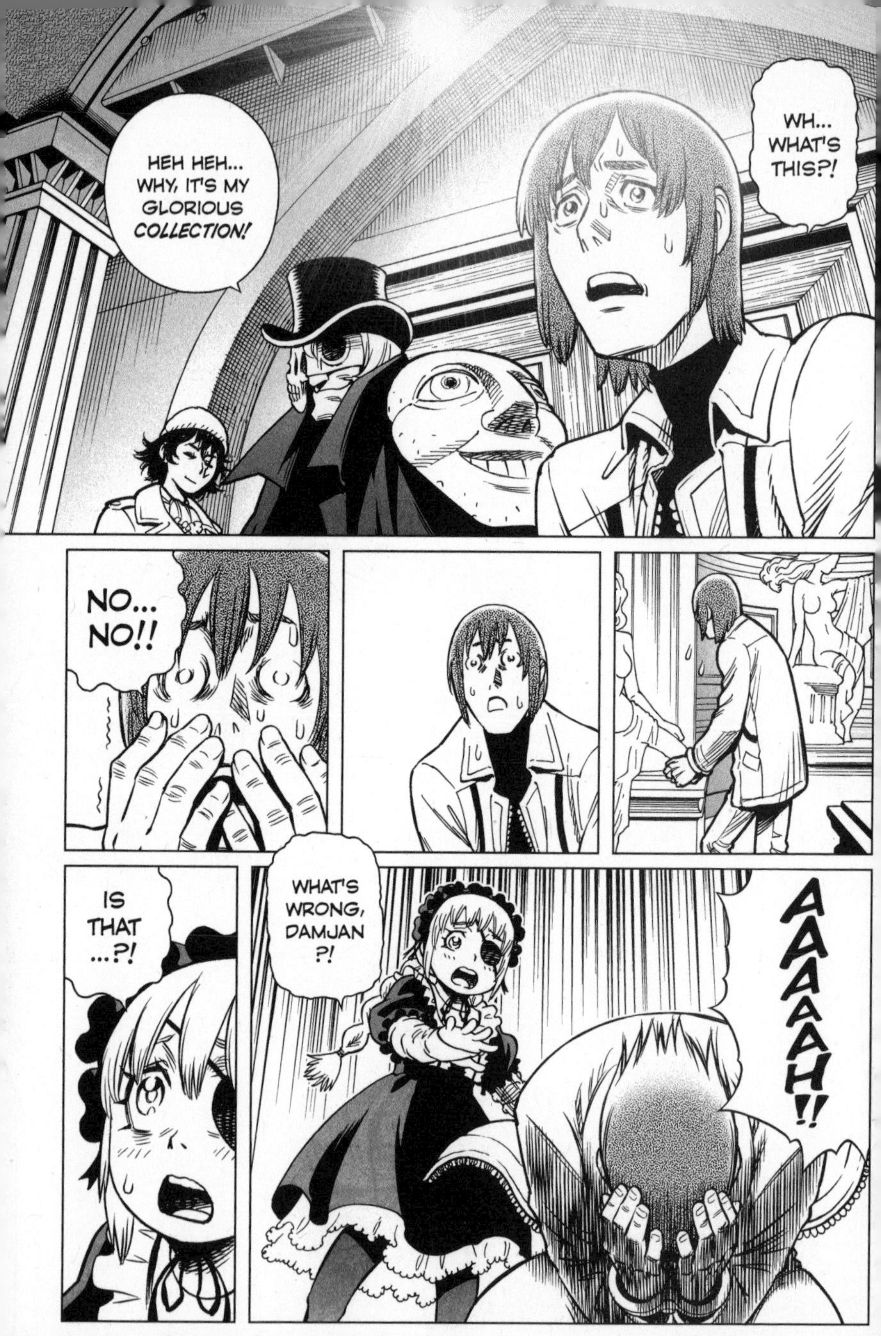
WH... WHAT'S THIS?!
HEH HEH... WHY, IT'S MY GLORIOUS COLLECTION!
NO... NO!!
AAAAAH!!
WHAT'S WRONG, DAMJAN ?!
IS THAT ...?!

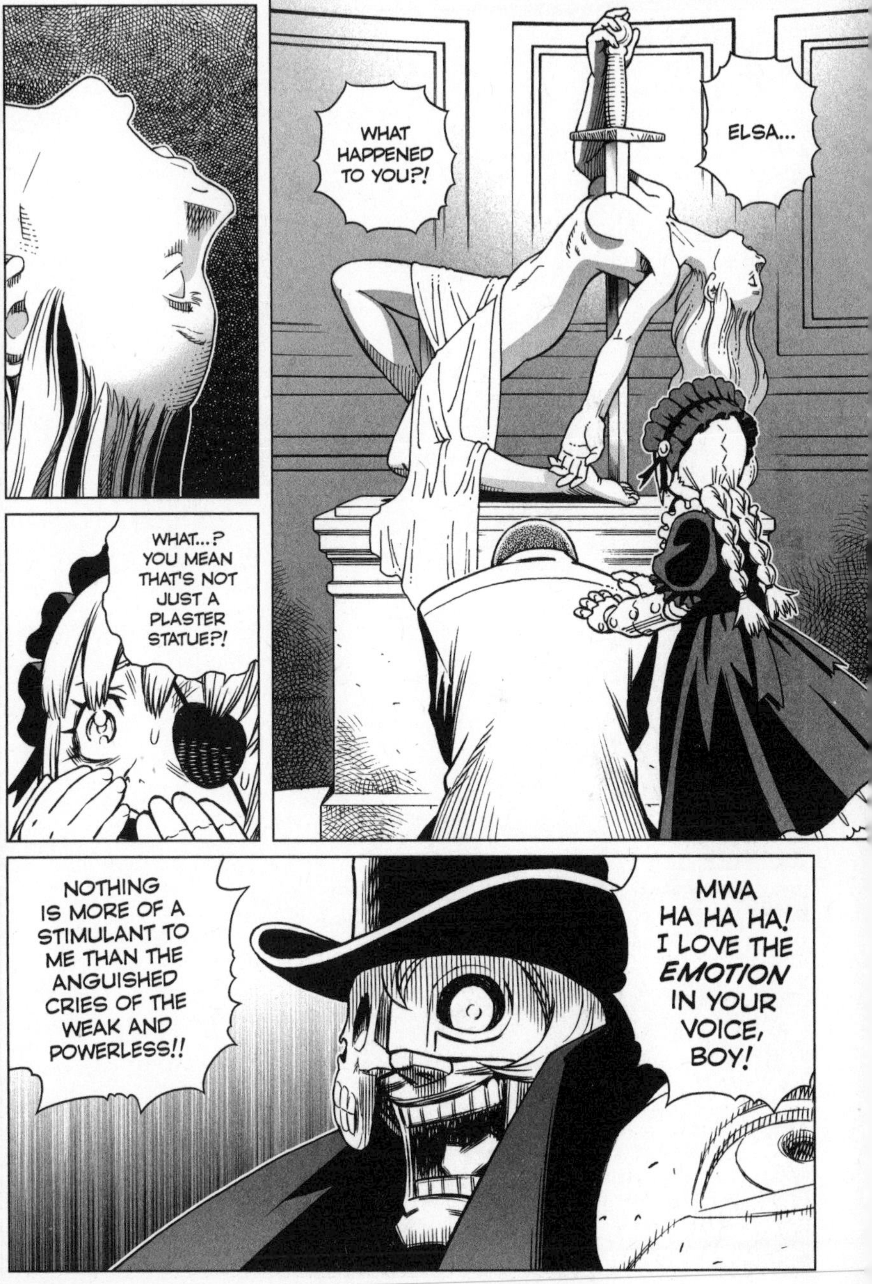
ELSA...
WHAT HAPPENED TO YOU?!
WHAT...? YOU MEAN THAT'S NOT JUST A PLASTER STATUE?!
MWA HA HA HA! I LOVE THE *EMOTION* IN YOUR VOICE, BOY!
NOTHING IS MORE OF A STIMULANT TO ME THAN THE ANGUISHED CRIES OF THE WEAK AND POWERLESS!!

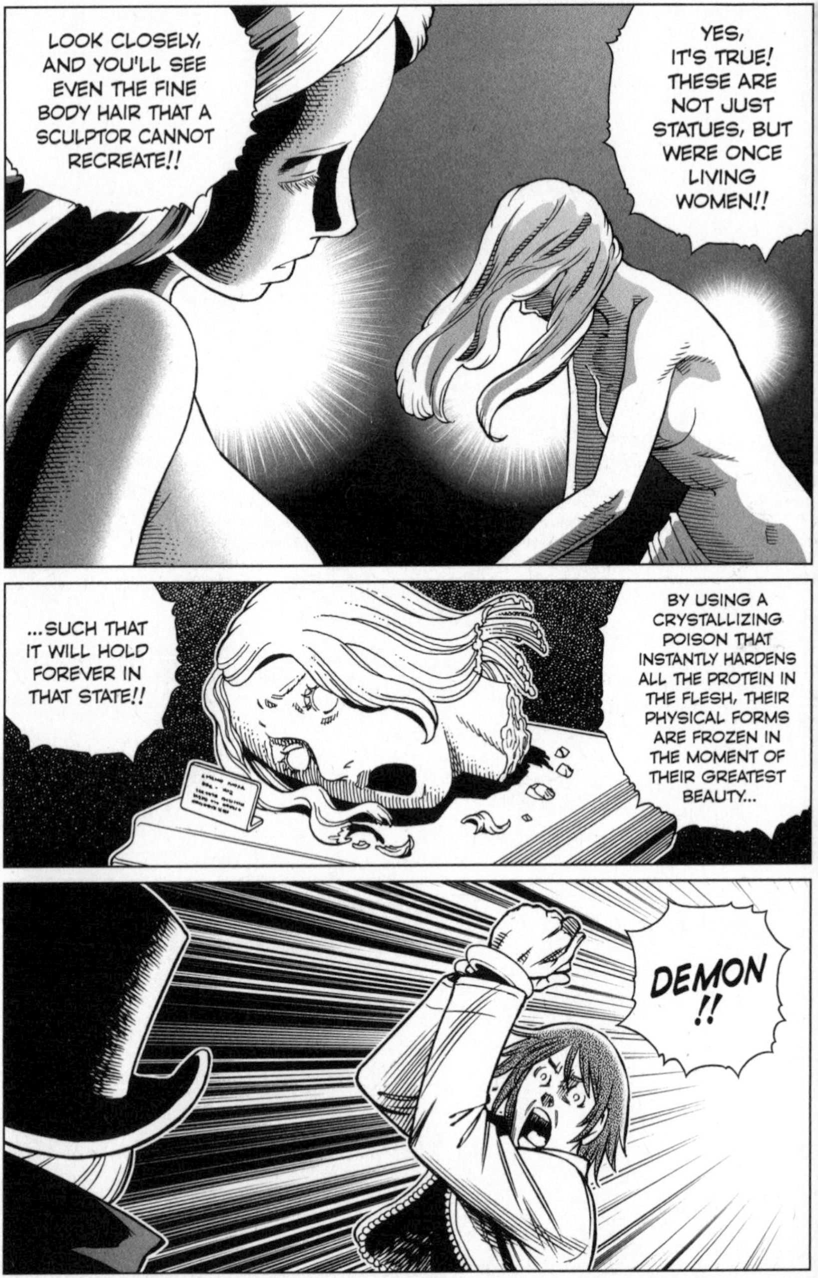
YES, IT'S TRUE! THESE ARE NOT JUST STATUES, BUT WERE ONCE LIVING WOMEN!!
LOOK CLOSELY, AND YOU'LL SEE EVEN THE FINE BODY HAIR THAT A SCULPTOR CANNOT RECREATE!!
BY USING A CRYSTALLIZING POISON THAT INSTANTLY HARDENS ALL THE PROTEIN IN THE FLESH, THEIR PHYSICAL FORMS ARE FROZEN IN THE MOMENT OF THEIR GREATEST BEAUTY...
...SUCH THAT IT WILL HOLD FOREVER IN THAT STATE!!
DEMON!!

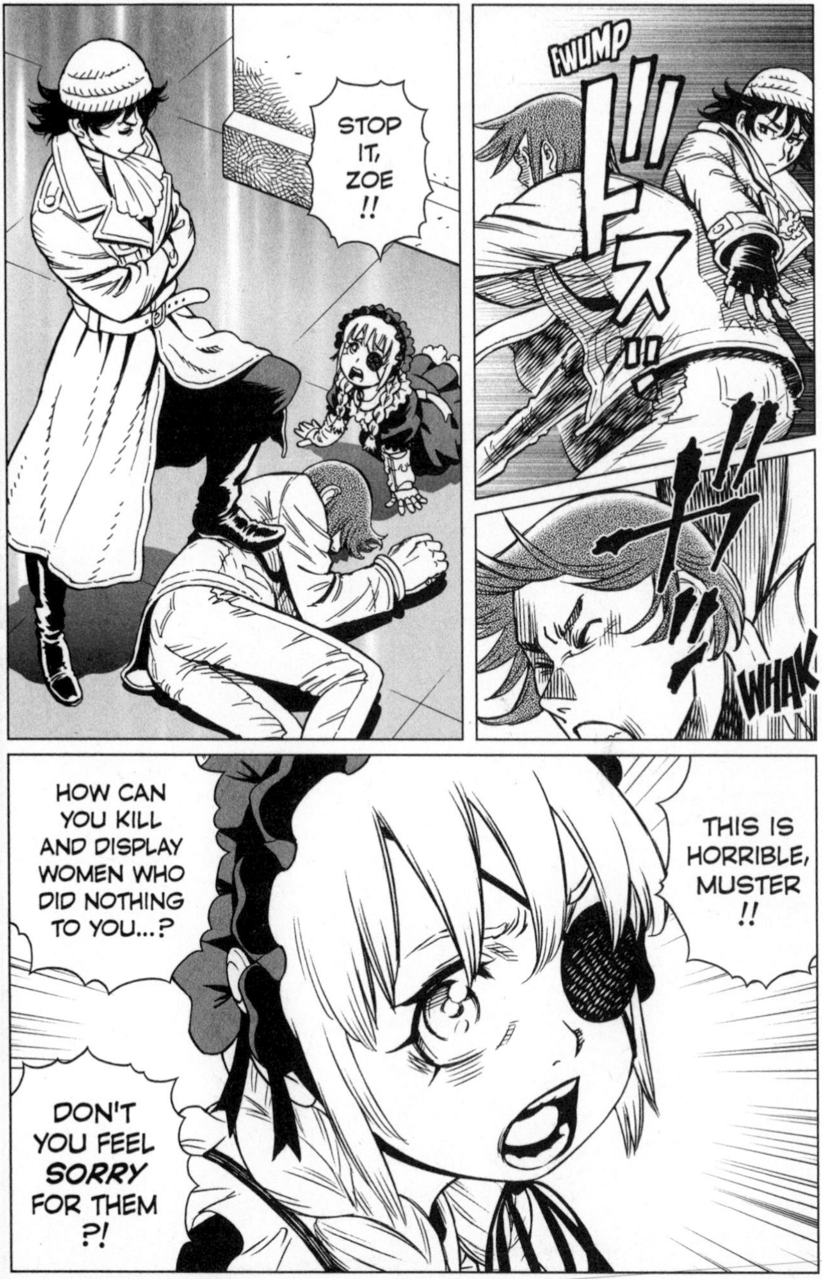
FWUMP
ドス
WHAK
STOP IT, ZOE !!
THIS IS HORRIBLE, MUSTER !!
HOW CAN YOU KILL AND DISPLAY WOMEN WHO DID NOTHING TO YOU...?
DON'T YOU FEEL *SORRY* FOR THEM ?!

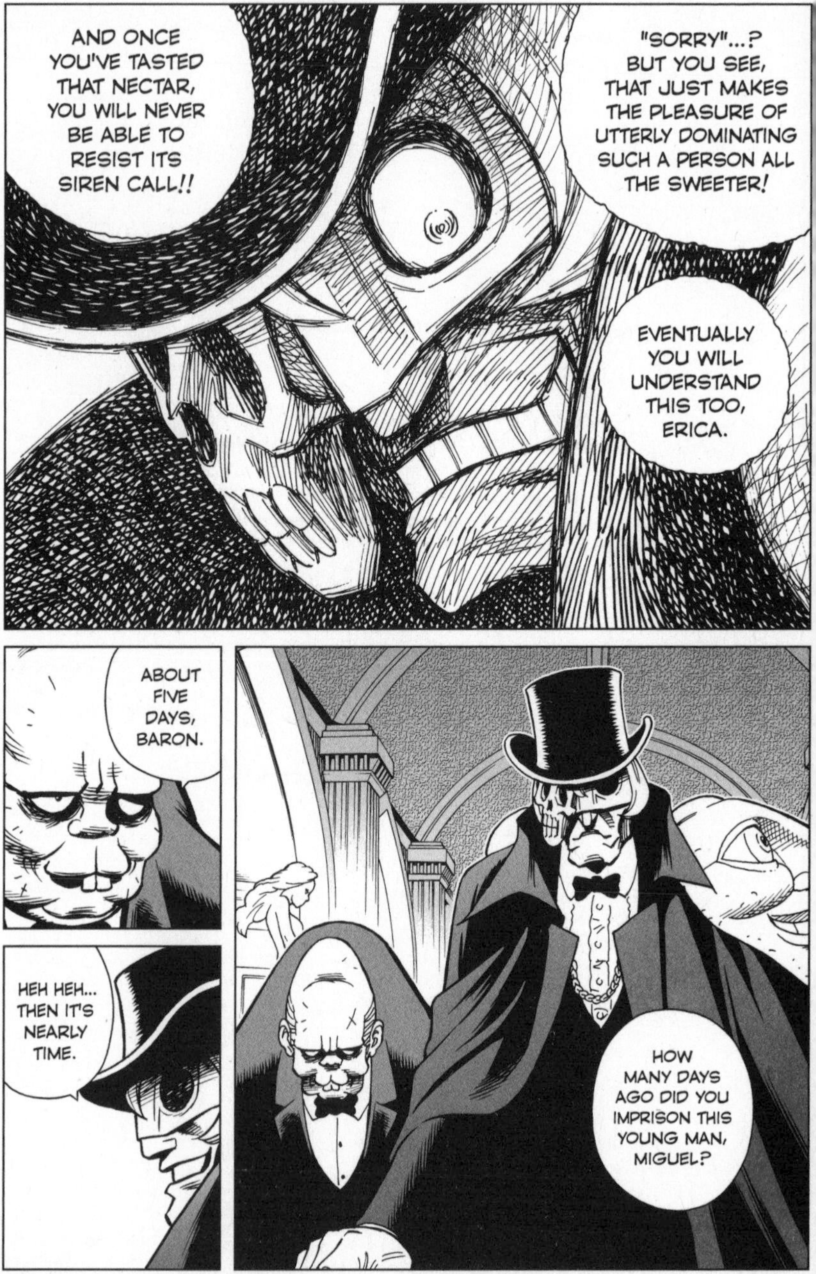
"SORRY"...? BUT YOU SEE, THAT JUST MAKES THE PLEASURE OF UTTERLY DOMINATING SUCH A PERSON ALL THE SWEETER!
AND ONCE YOU'VE TASTED THAT NECTAR, YOU WILL NEVER BE ABLE TO RESIST ITS SIREN CALL!!
EVENTUALLY YOU WILL UNDERSTAND THIS TOO, ERICA.
HOW MANY DAYS AGO DID YOU IMPRISON THIS YOUNG MAN, MIGUEL?
ABOUT FIVE DAYS, BARON.
HEH HEH... THEN IT'S NEARLY TIME.

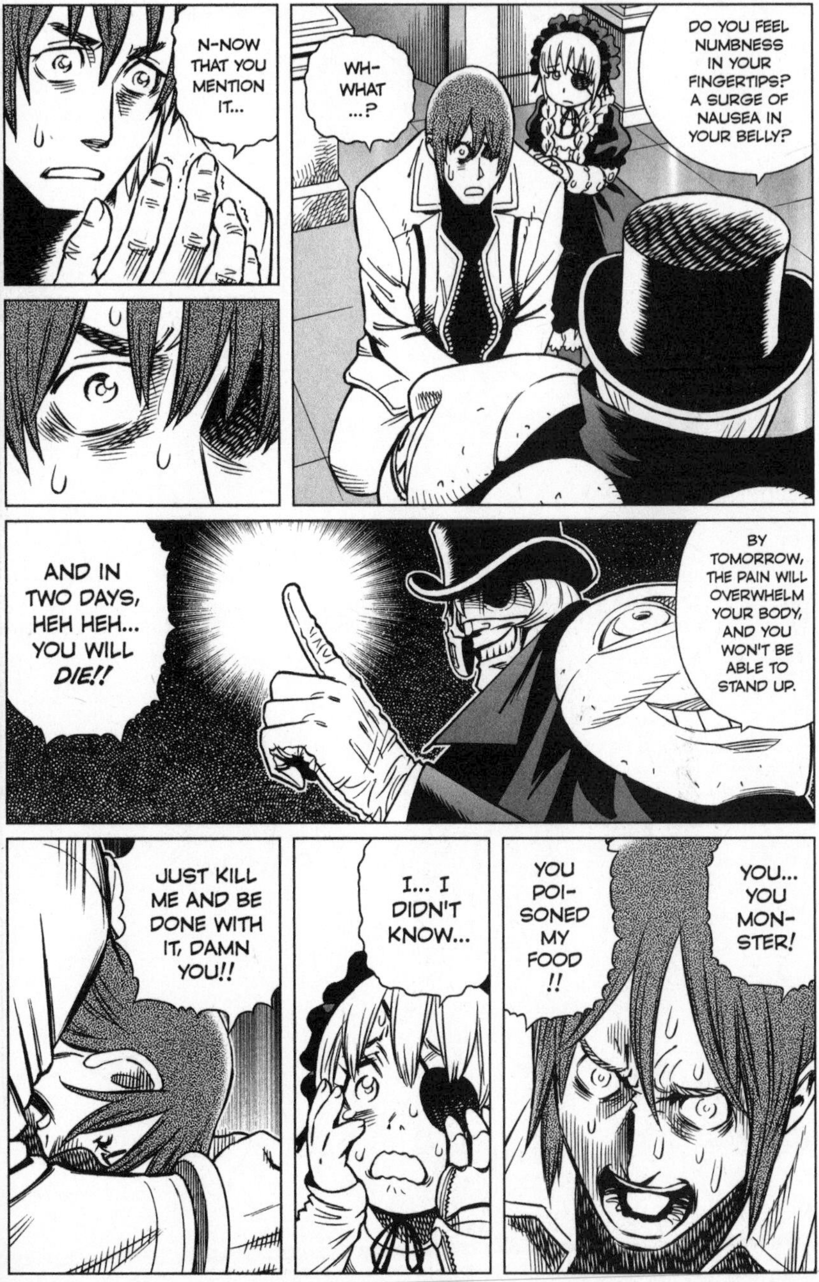
DO YOU FEEL NUMBNESS IN YOUR FINGERTIPS? A SURGE OF NAUSEA IN YOUR BELLY?
WH-WHAT ...?
N-NOW THAT YOU MENTION IT...
BY TOMORROW, THE PAIN WILL OVERWHELM YOUR BODY, AND YOU WON'T BE ABLE TO STAND UP.
AND IN TWO DAYS, HEH HEH... YOU WILL *DIE!!*
YOU... YOU MONSTER!
YOU POISONED MY FOOD !!
I... I DIDN'T KNOW...
JUST KILL ME AND BE DONE WITH IT, DAMN YOU!!

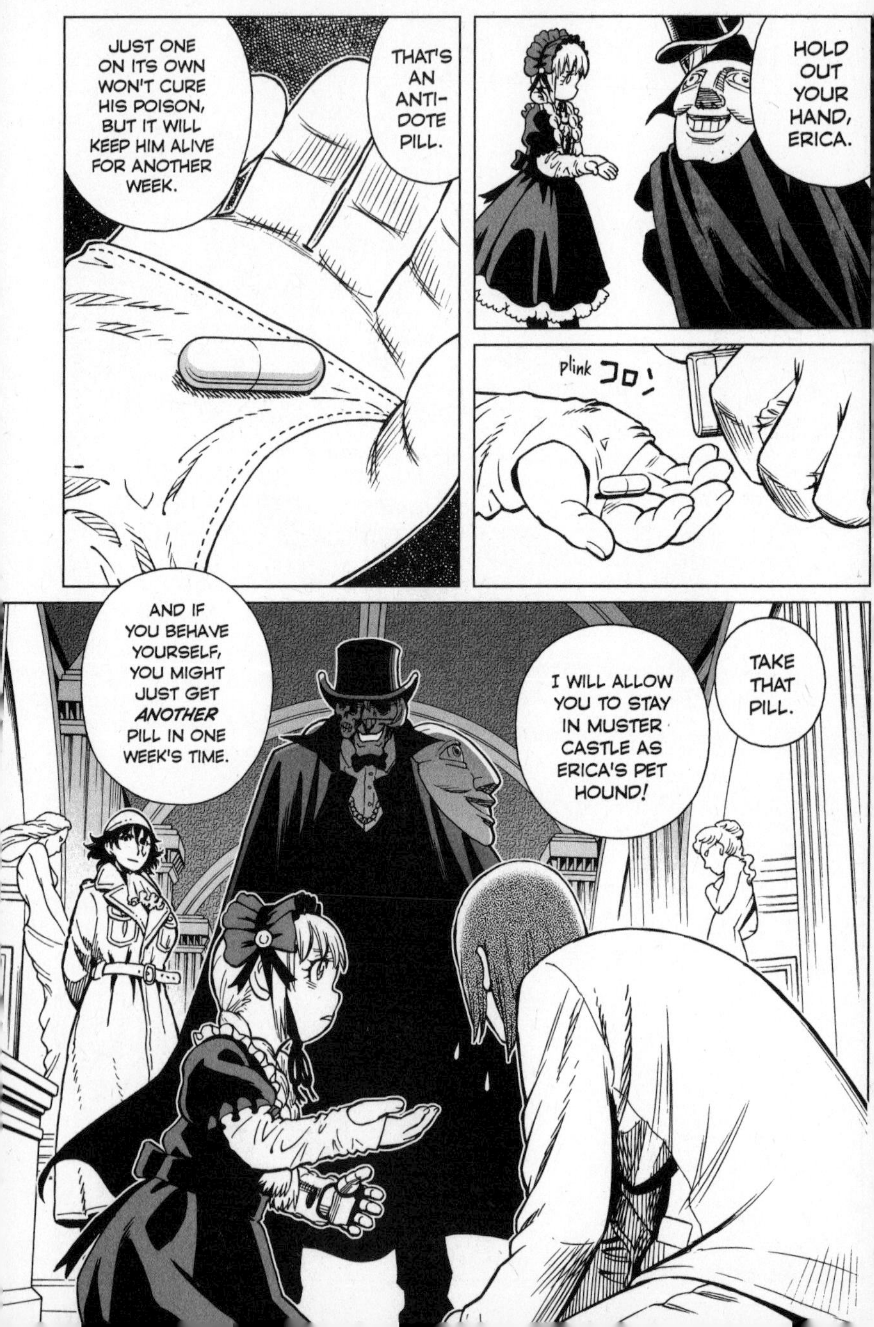
HOLD OUT YOUR HAND, ERICA.
plink
THAT'S AN ANTI-DOTE PILL.
JUST ONE ON ITS OWN WON'T CURE HIS POISON, BUT IT WILL KEEP HIM ALIVE FOR ANOTHER WEEK.
TAKE THAT PILL.
I WILL ALLOW YOU TO STAY IN MUSTER CASTLE AS ERICA'S PET HOUND!
AND IF YOU BEHAVE YOURSELF, YOU MIGHT JUST GET *ANOTHER* PILL IN ONE WEEK'S TIME.

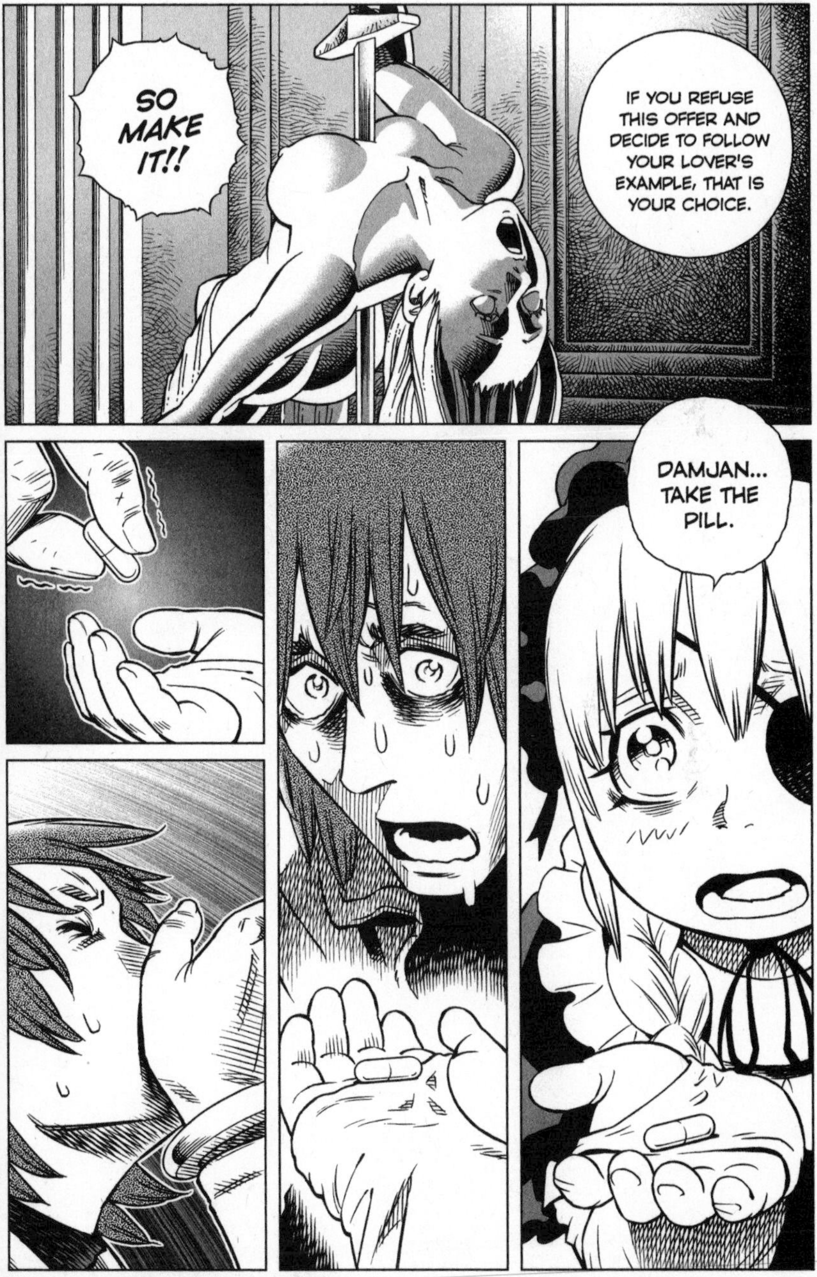
IF YOU REFUSE THIS OFFER AND DECIDE TO FOLLOW YOUR LOVER'S EXAMPLE, THAT IS YOUR CHOICE.
SO MAKE IT!!
DAMJAN... TAKE THE PILL.

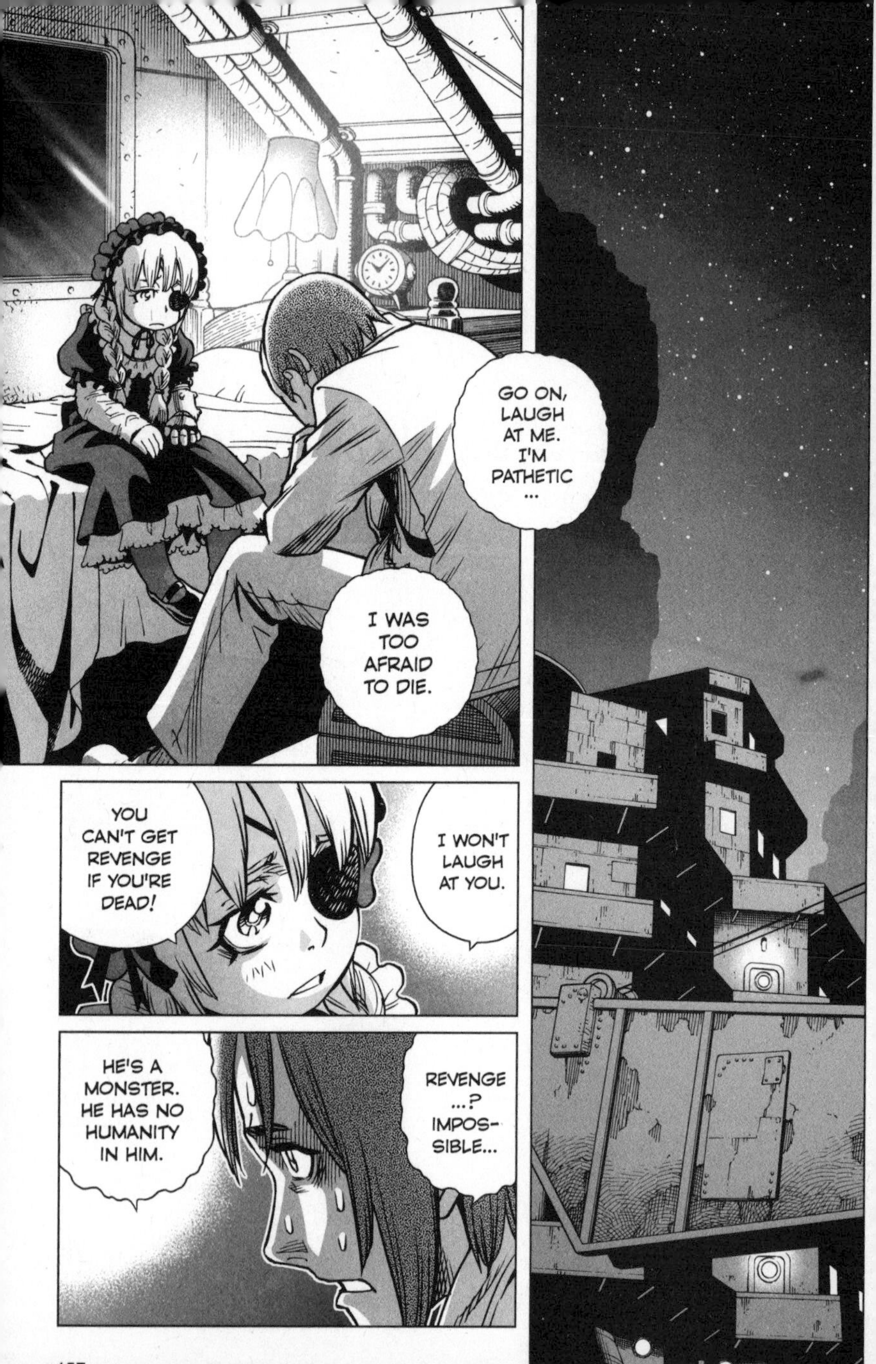
GO ON, LAUGH AT ME. I'M PATHETIC...
I WAS TOO AFRAID TO DIE.
I WON'T LAUGH AT YOU.
YOU CAN'T GET REVENGE IF YOU'RE DEAD!
REVENGE...? IMPOSSIBLE...
HE'S A MONSTER. HE HAS NO HUMANITY IN HIM.

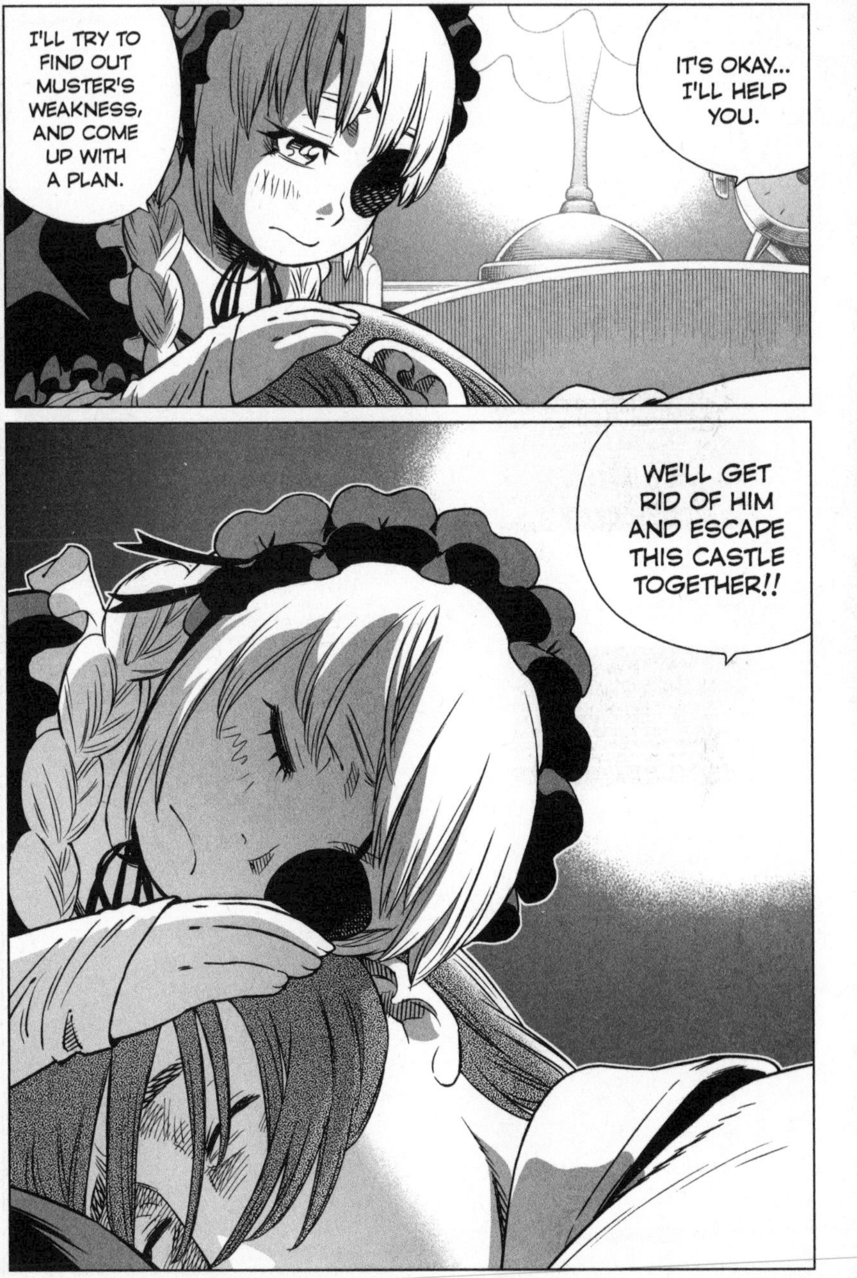
IT'S OKAY... I'LL HELP YOU.
I'LL TRY TO FIND OUT MUSTER'S WEAKNESS, AND COME UP WITH A PLAN.
WE'LL GET RID OF HIM AND ESCAPE THIS CASTLE TOGETHER!!

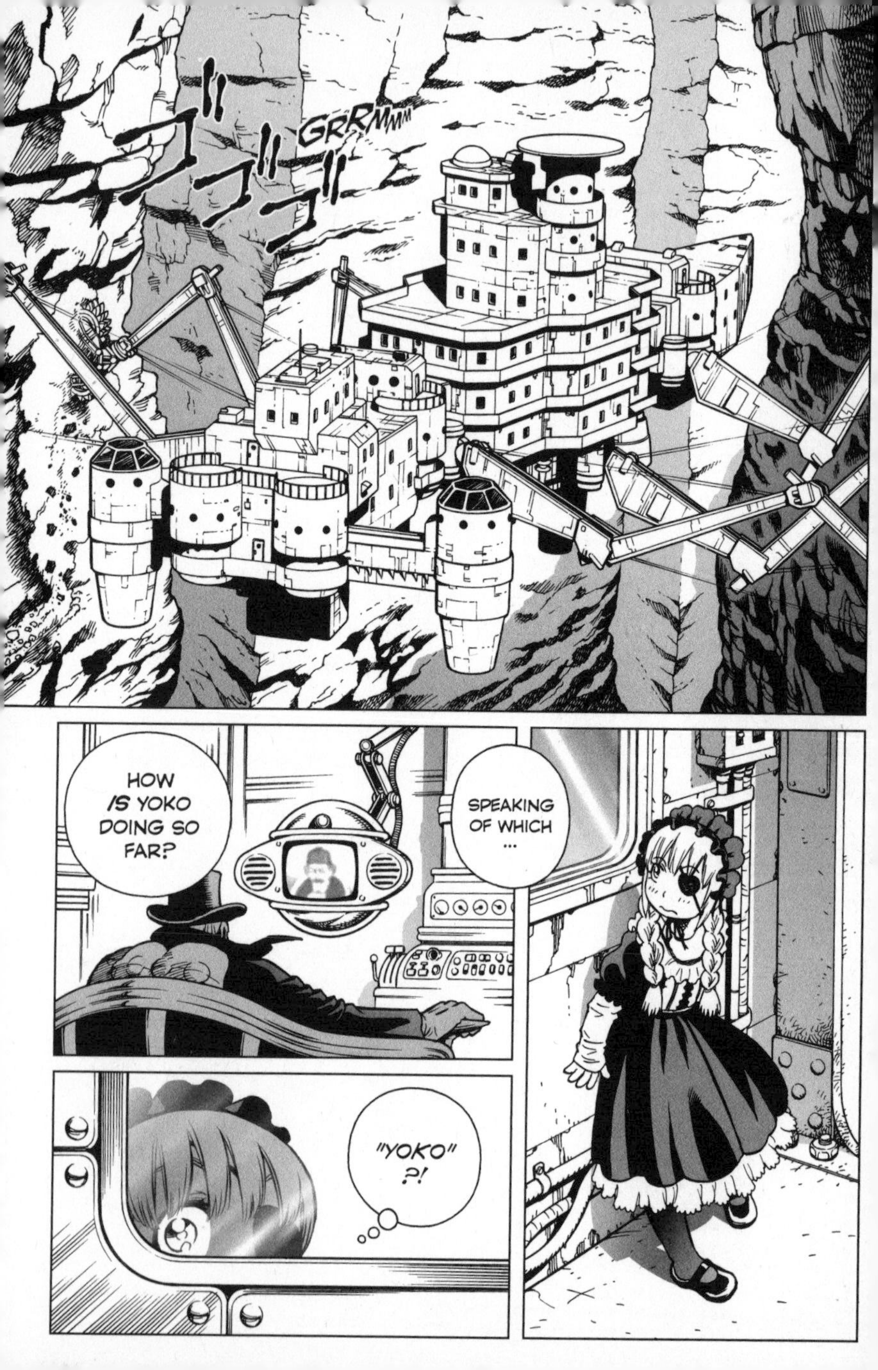
GRRMMM
SPEAKING OF WHICH ...
HOW *IS* YOKO DOING SO FAR?
"YOKO" ?!

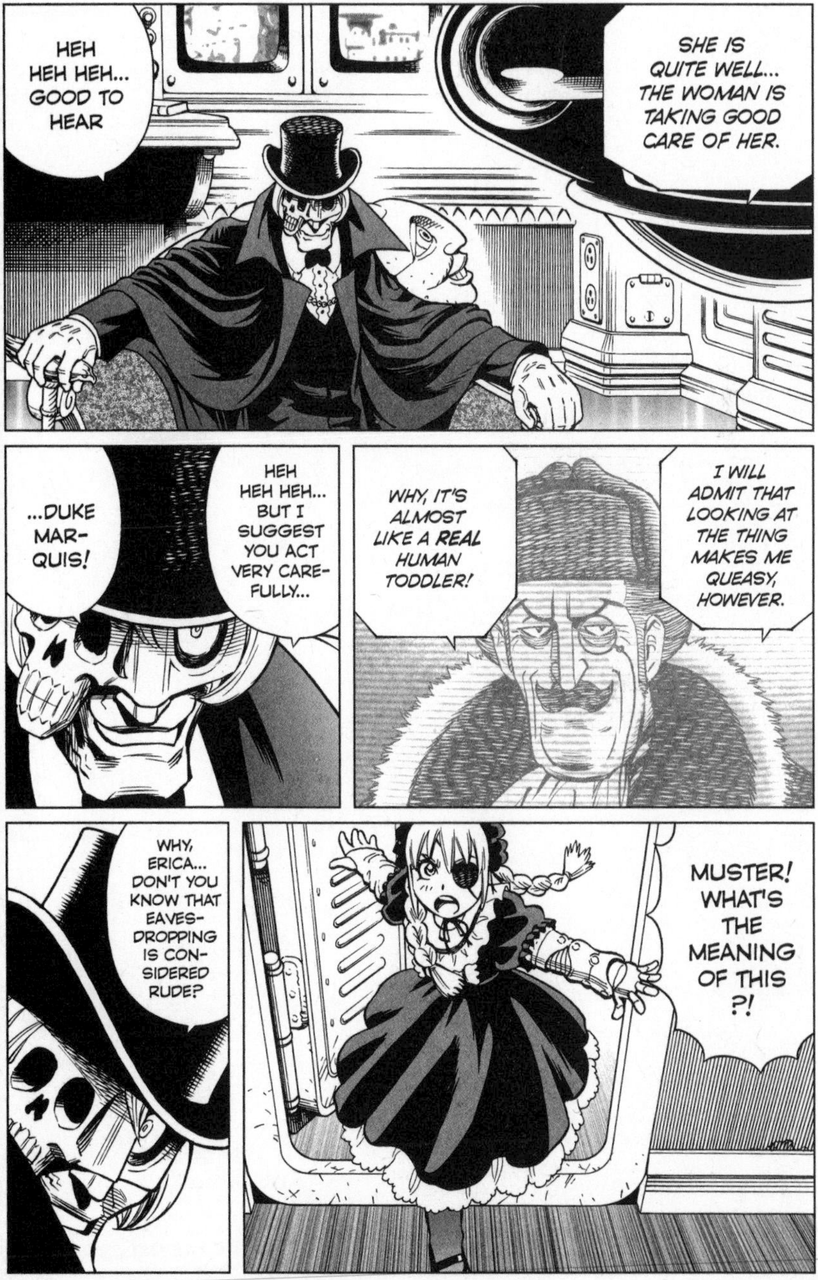

SHE IS QUITE WELL... THE WOMAN IS TAKING GOOD CARE OF HER.
HEH HEH HEH... GOOD TO HEAR
I WILL ADMIT THAT LOOKING AT THE THING MAKES ME QUEASY, HOWEVER.
WHY, IT'S ALMOST LIKE A **REAL** HUMAN TODDLER!
HEH HEH HEH... BUT I SUGGEST YOU ACT VERY CAREFULLY...
...DUKE MARQUIS!
MUSTER! WHAT'S THE MEANING OF THIS?!
WHY, ERICA... DON'T YOU KNOW THAT EAVESDROPPING IS CONSIDERED RUDE?

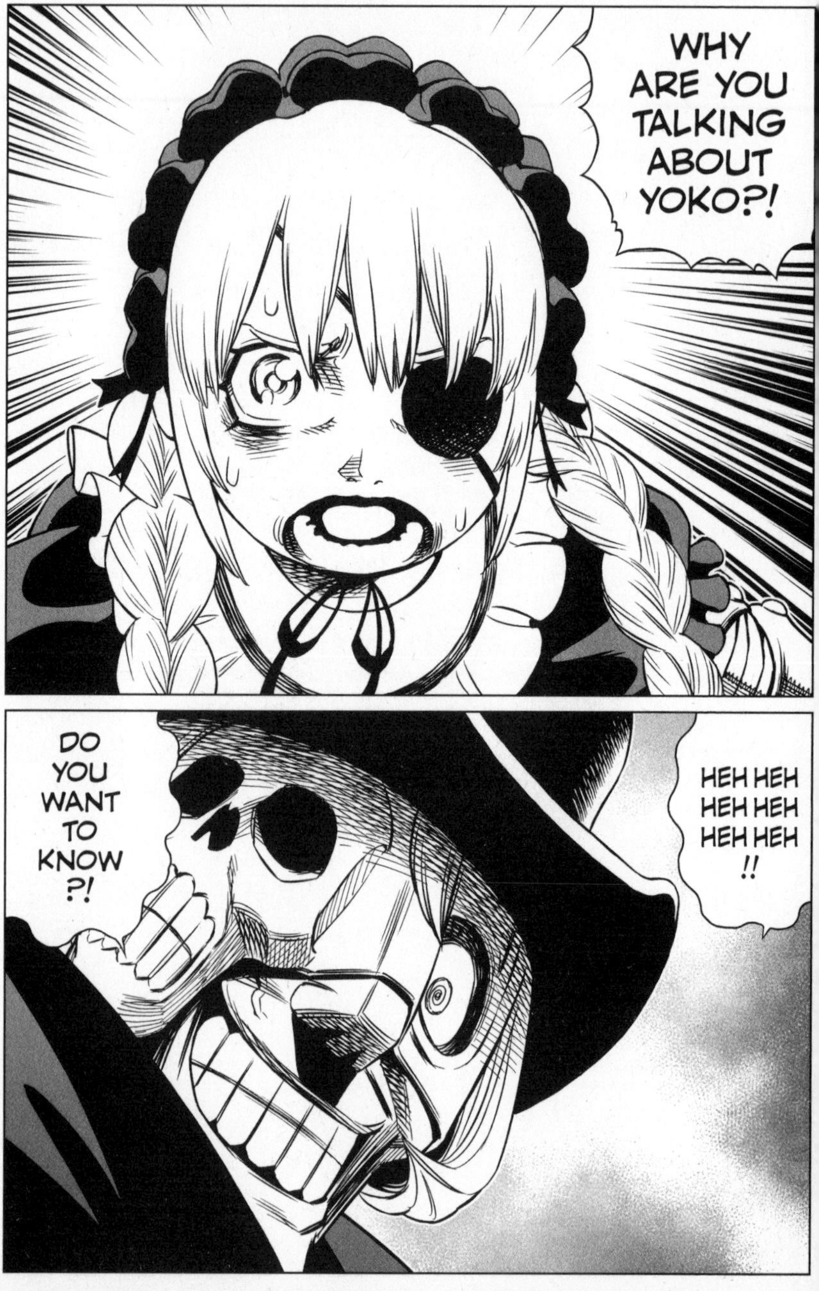
WHY ARE YOU TALKING ABOUT YOKO?!
HEH HEH HEH HEH HEH HEH !!
DO YOU WANT TO KNOW ?!

BATTLE ANGEL ALITA
MARS CHRONICLE

PRESENTED by YUKITO KISHIRO

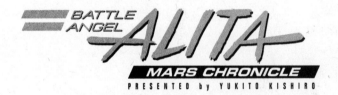

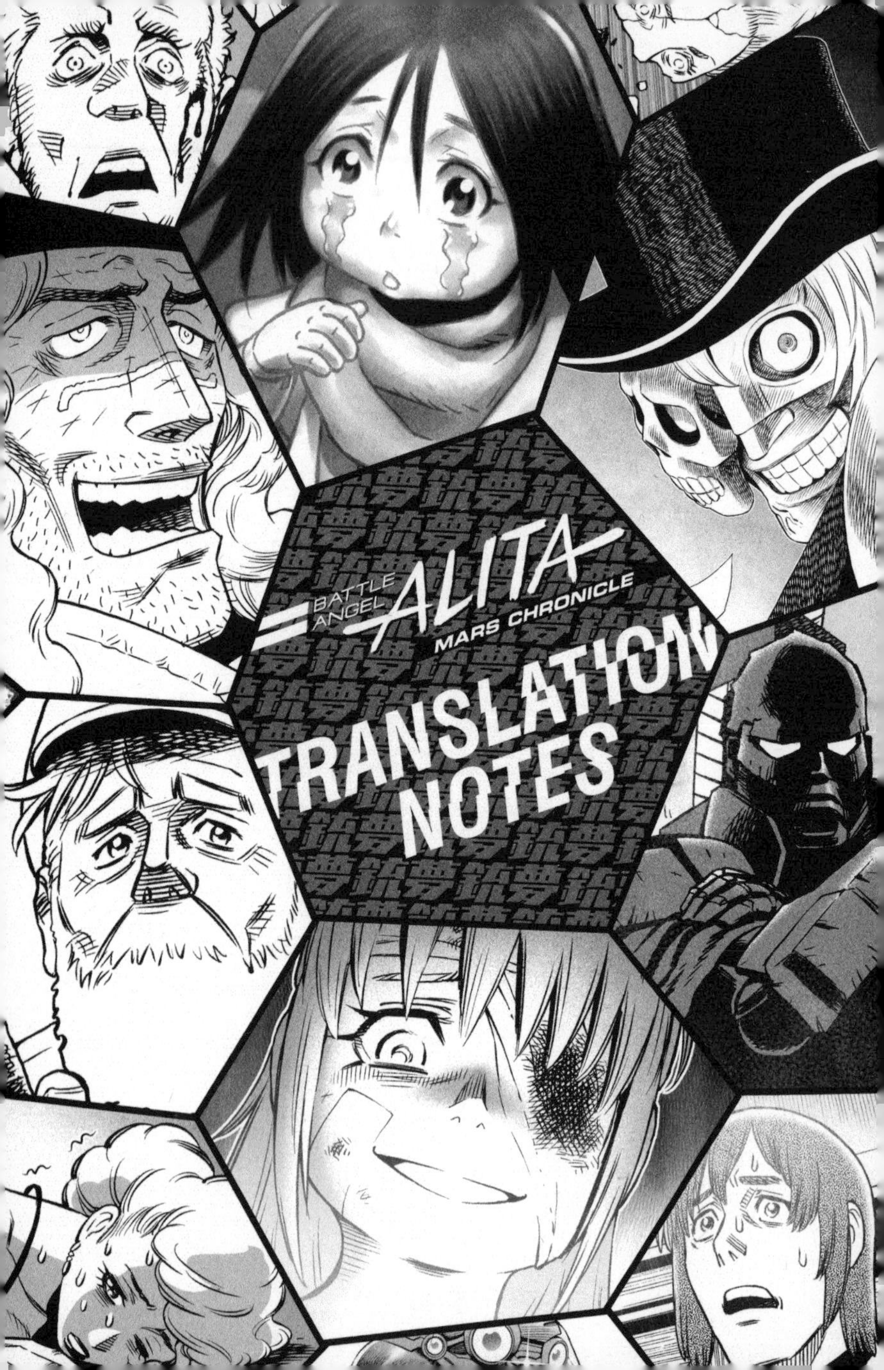
BATTLE ANGEL ALITA
MARS CHRONICLE
TRANSLATION NOTES

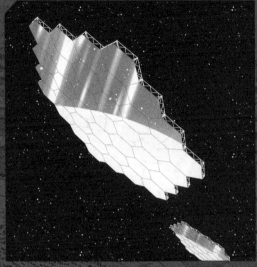

TIIDA KAGAN

pg. 35

The words "tiida" and "kagan" mean "sun" and "mirror," respectively, in the language of Okinawa.

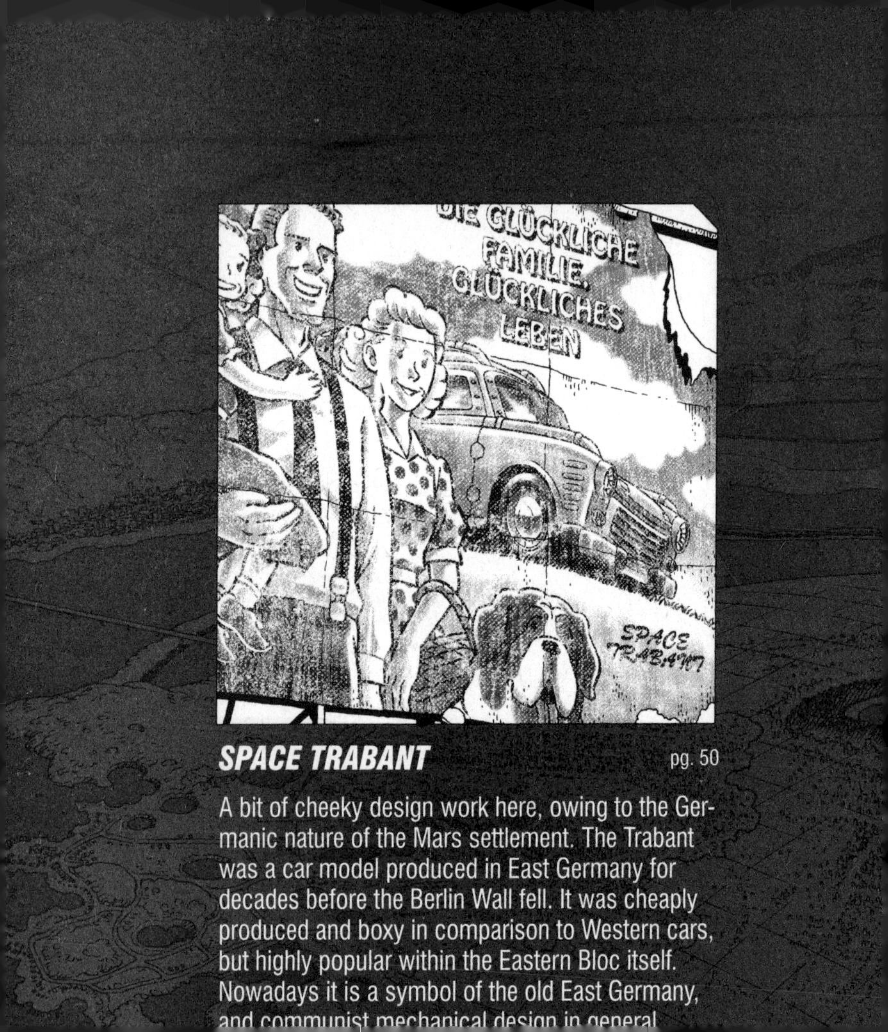
GLÜCKLICHE
FAMILIE,
GLÜCKLICHES
LEBEN
SPACE TRABANT

SPACE TRABANT

pg. 50

A bit of cheeky design work here, owing to the Germanic nature of the Mars settlement. The Trabant was a car model produced in East Germany for decades before the Berlin Wall fell. It was cheaply produced and boxy in comparison to Western cars, but highly popular within the Eastern Bloc itself. Nowadays it is a symbol of the old East Germany, and communist mechanical design in general

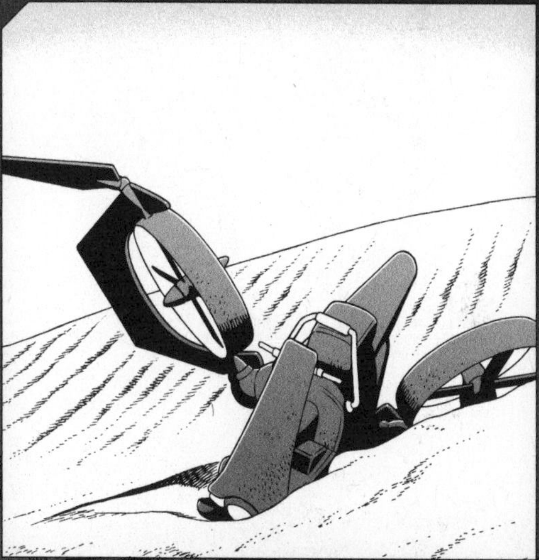

LIBELLE pg. 104

The German word for "dragonfly."

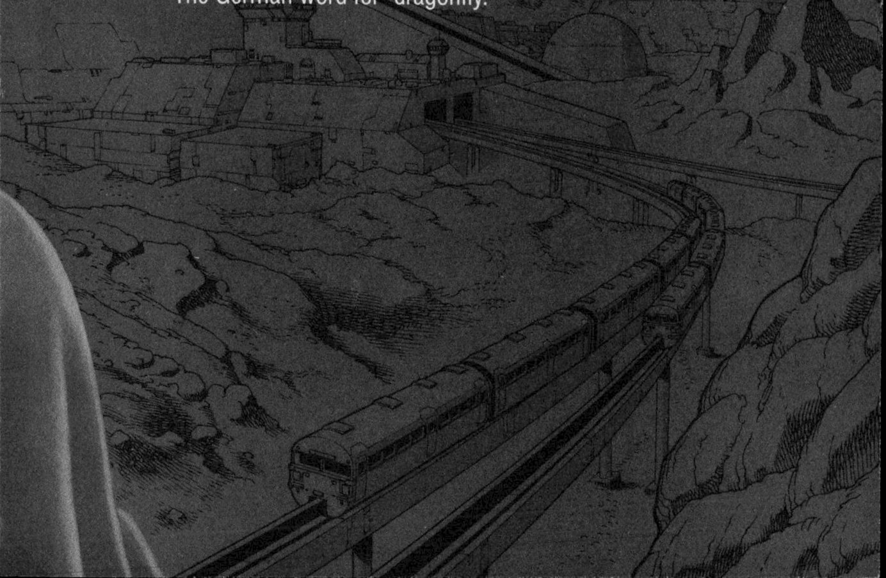

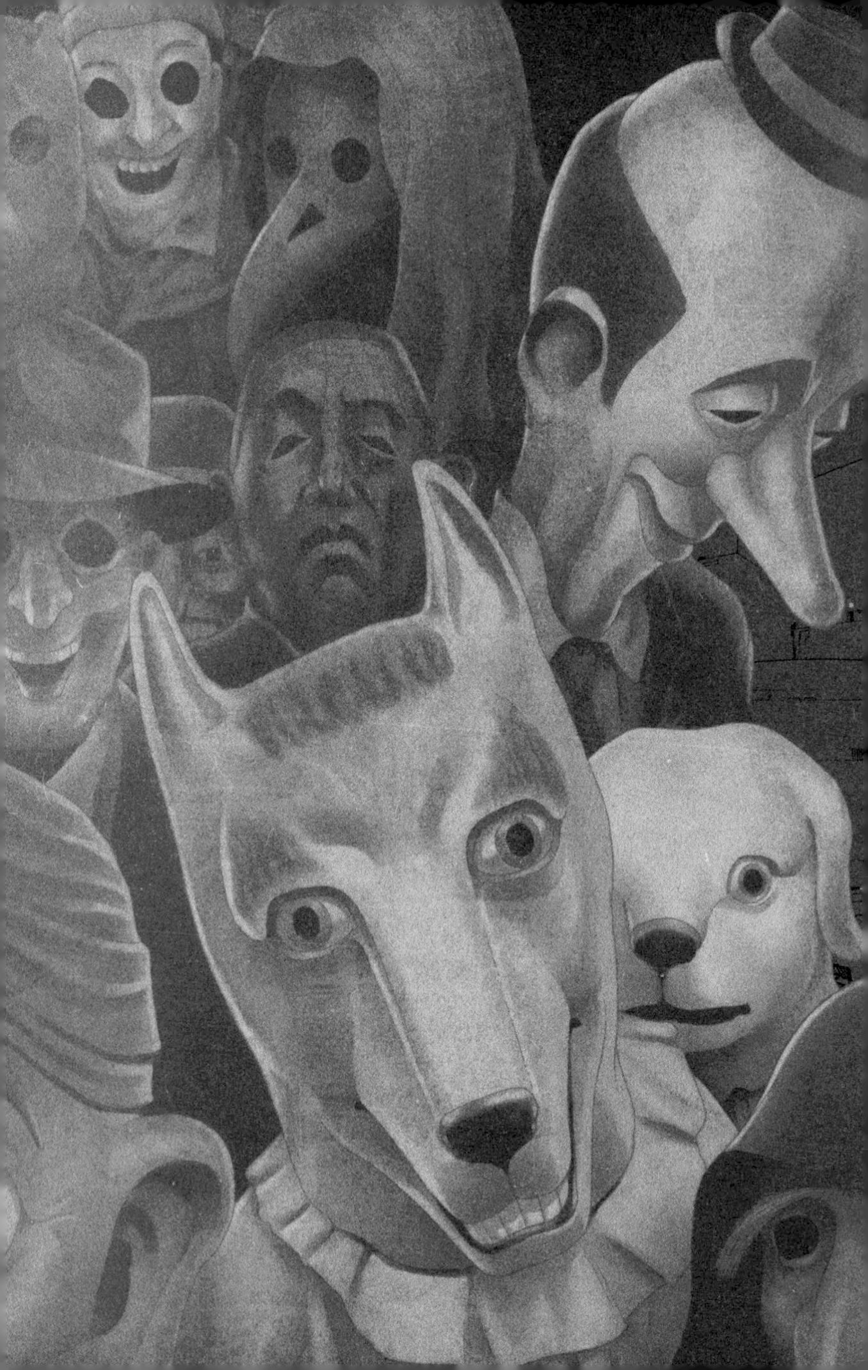

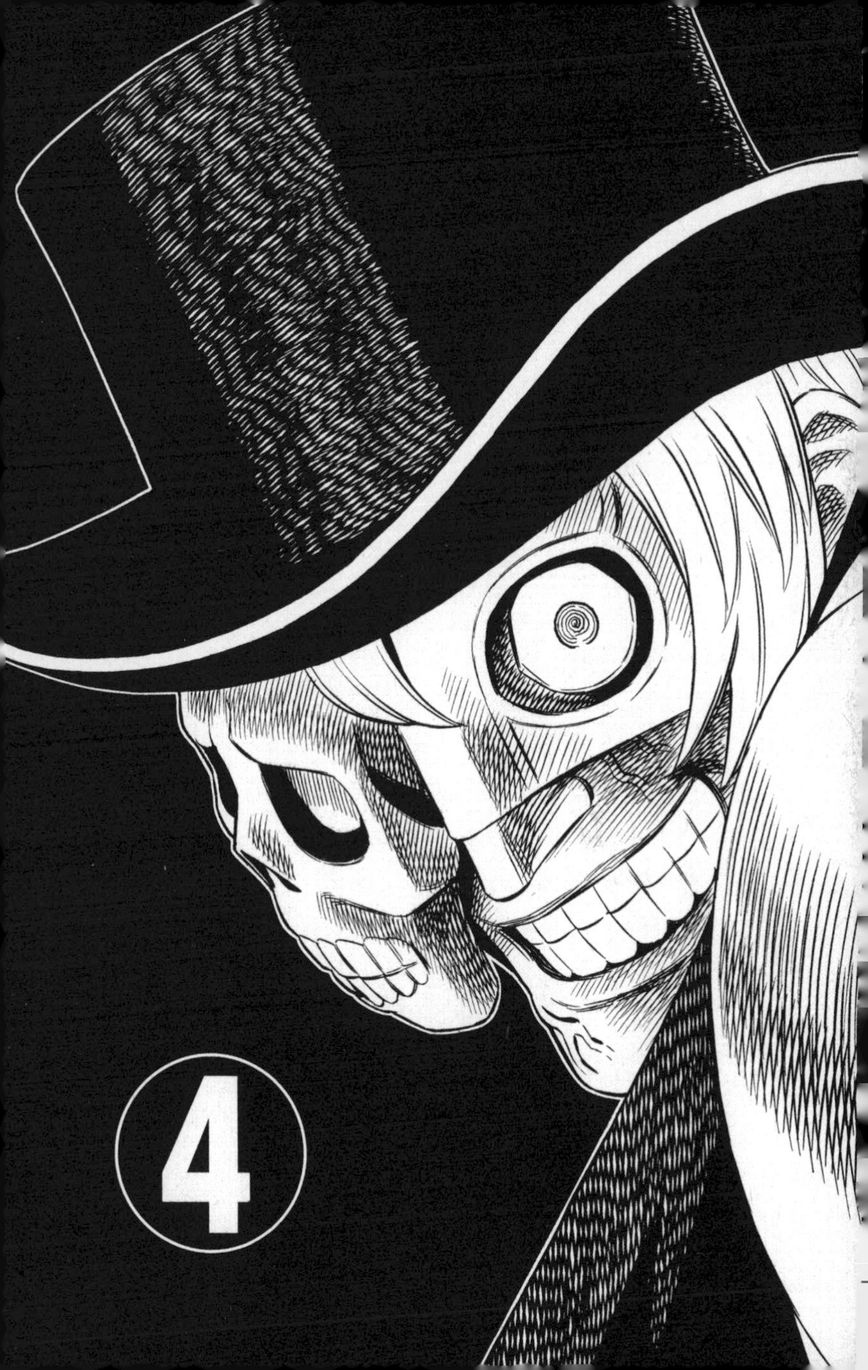
4

THE GIRL'S FATE IS SUBJECT TO THE WHIMS OF OTHERS.

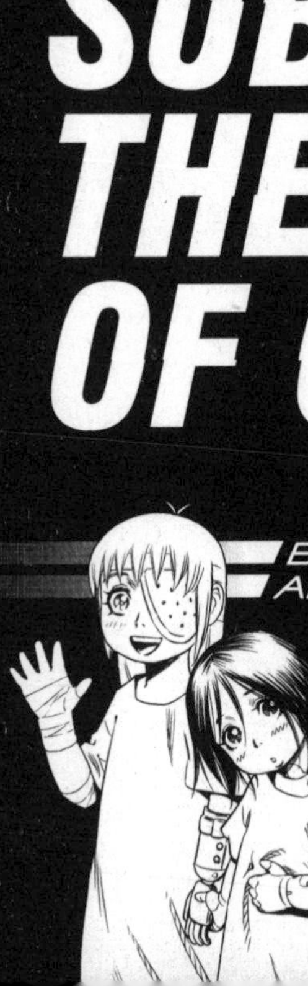

BATTLE ANGEL ALITA

MARS CHRONICLE

PRESENTED by YUKITO KISHIRO

BATTLE ANGEL ALITA: MARS CHRONICLE 4
GOES ON SALE SOON!!

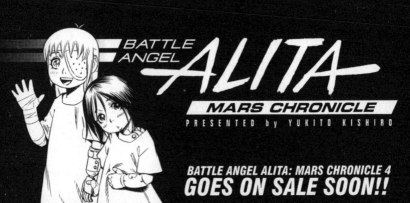

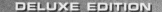

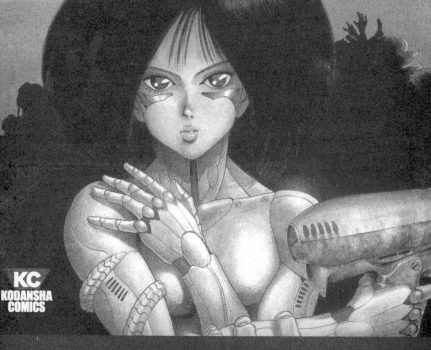

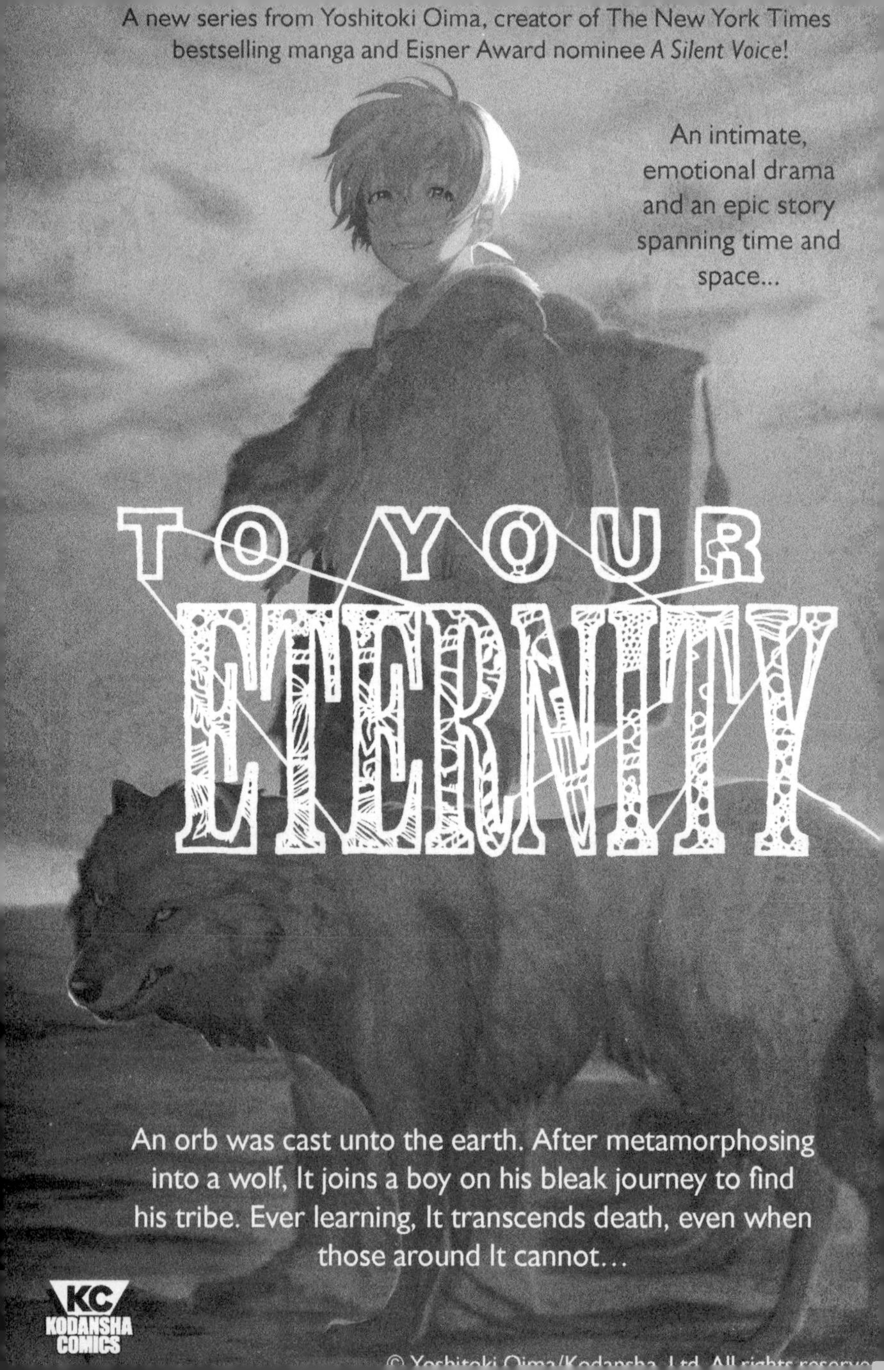

A new series from Yoshitoki Oima, creator of The New York Times bestselling manga and Eisner Award nominee *A Silent Voice*!

An intimate, emotional drama and an epic story spanning time and space...

TO YOUR ETERNITY

An orb was cast unto the earth. After metamorphosing into a wolf, It joins a boy on his bleak journey to find his tribe. Ever learning, It transcends death, even when those around It cannot…

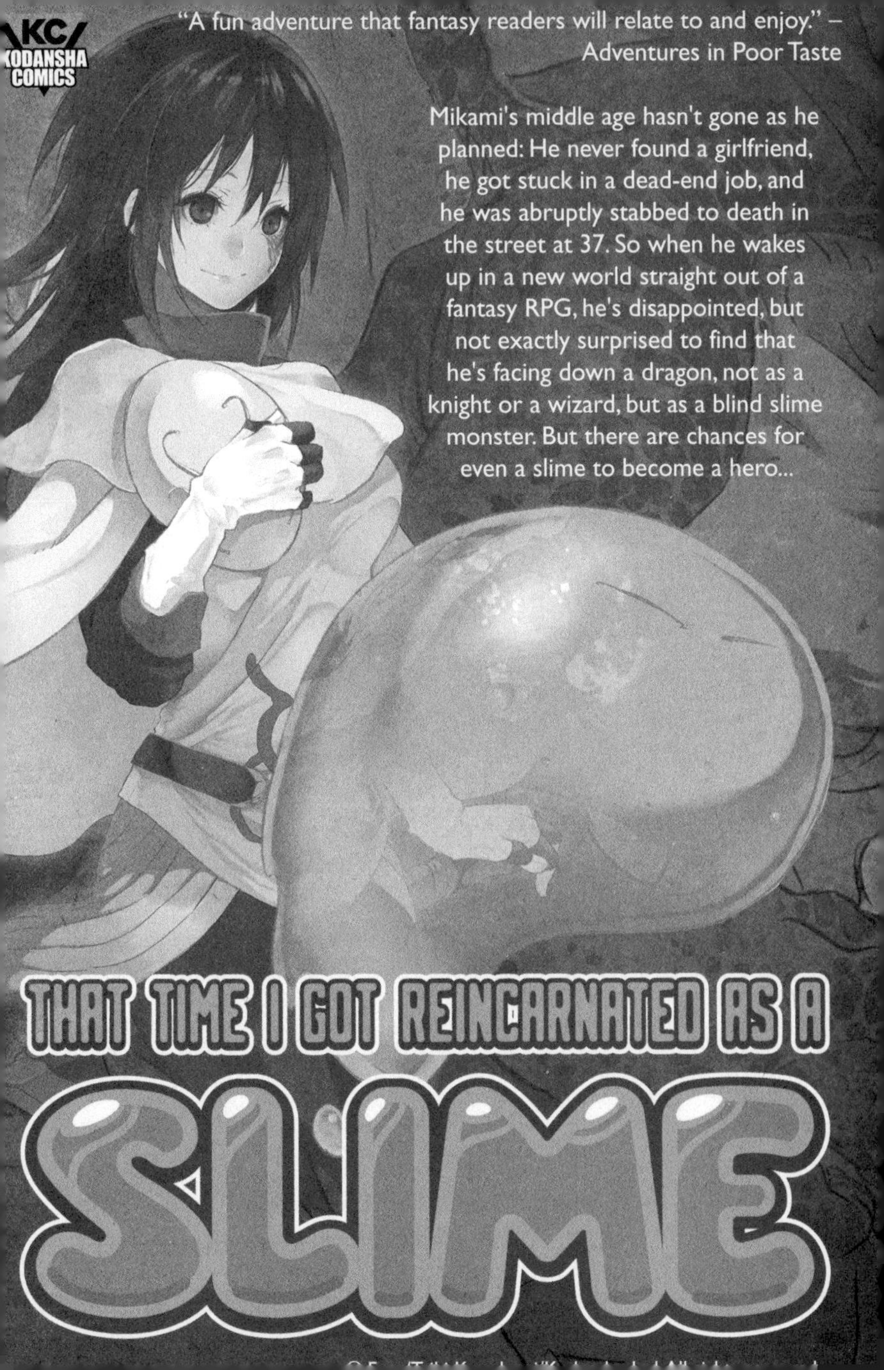
KC KODANSHA COMICS
"A fun adventure that fantasy readers will relate to and enjoy." – Adventures in Poor Taste
Mikami's middle age hasn't gone as he planned: He never found a girlfriend, he got stuck in a dead-end job, and he was abruptly stabbed to death in the street at 37. So when he wakes up in a new world straight out of a fantasy RPG, he's disappointed, but not exactly surprised to find that he's facing down a dragon, not as a knight or a wizard, but as a blind slime monster. But there are chances for even a slime to become a hero...
THAT TIME I GOT REINCARNATED AS A
SLIME

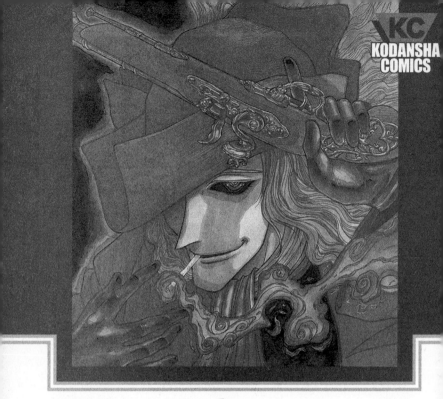

The Black Museum The Ghost and the Lady

By Kazuhiro Fujita

Deep in Scotland Yard in London sits an evidence room dedicated to the greatest mysteries of British history. In this "Black Museum" sits a misshapen hunk of lead—two bullets fused together—the key to a wartime encounter between Florence Nightingale, the mother of modern nursing, and a supernatural Man in Grey. This story is unknown to most scholars of history, but a special guest of the museum will tell the tale of *The Ghost and the Lady*...

Praise for Kazuhiro Fujita's *Ushio and Tora*

"A charming revival that combines a classic look with modern depth and pacing... **Essential viewing both for curmudgeons and new fans alike.**" — Anime News Network

"**GREAT!** The first episode of *Ushio and Tora* captures the essence of '90s anime." — IGN

Japan's most powerful spirit medium delves into the ghost world's greatest mysteries!

Story by Kyo Shirodaira, famed author of mystery fiction and creator of *Spiral*, *Blast of Tempest*, and *The Record of a Fallen Vampire*.

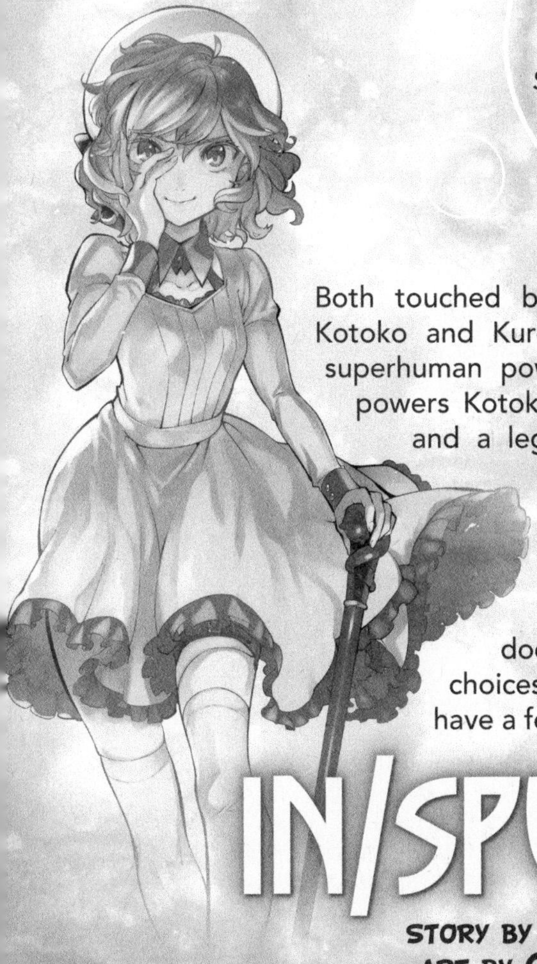

Both touched by spirits called yôkai, Kotoko and Kurô have gained unique superhuman powers. But to gain her powers Kotoko has given up an eye and a leg, and Kurô's personal life is in shambles. So when Kotoko suggests they team up to deal with renegades from the spirit world, Kurô doesn't have many other choices, but Kotoko might just have a few ulterior motives...

IN/SPECTRE

STORY BY **KYO SHIRODAIRA**
ART BY **CHASHIBA KATASE**

New action series from Hiroyuki Takei, creator of the classic shonen franchise Shaman King!

In medieval Japan, a bell hanging on the collar is a sign that a ca
has a master. Norachiyo's bell hangs from his katana sheath, but he i:
nonetheless a stray — a ronin. This one-eyed cat samurai travels across :
dishonest world, cutting through pretense and deception with his blade.

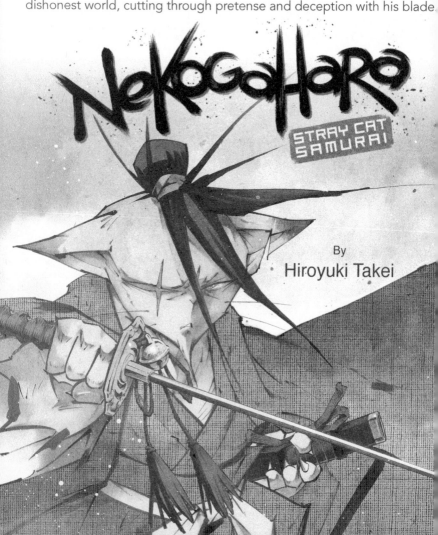

By
Hiroyuki Takei

HAPPINESS

——ハピネス——

By Shuzo Oshimi

From the creator of *The Flowers of Evil*

Nothing interesting is happening in Makoto Ozaki's first year of high school. HIs life is a series of quiet humiliations: low-grade bullies, unreliable friends, and the constant frustration of his adolescent lust. But one night, a pale, thin girl knocks him to the ground in an alley and offers him a choice.

Now everything is different. Daylight is searingly bright. Food tastes awful. And worse than anything is the terrible, consuming thirst...

Praise for Shuzo Oshimi's *The Flowers of Evil*

"A shockingly readable story that vividly—one might even say queasily—evokes the fear and confusion of discovering one's own sexuality. Recommended." —The Manga Critic

"A page-turning tale of sordid middle school blackmail." —Otaku USA Magazine

"A stunning new horror manga." —Third Eye Comics

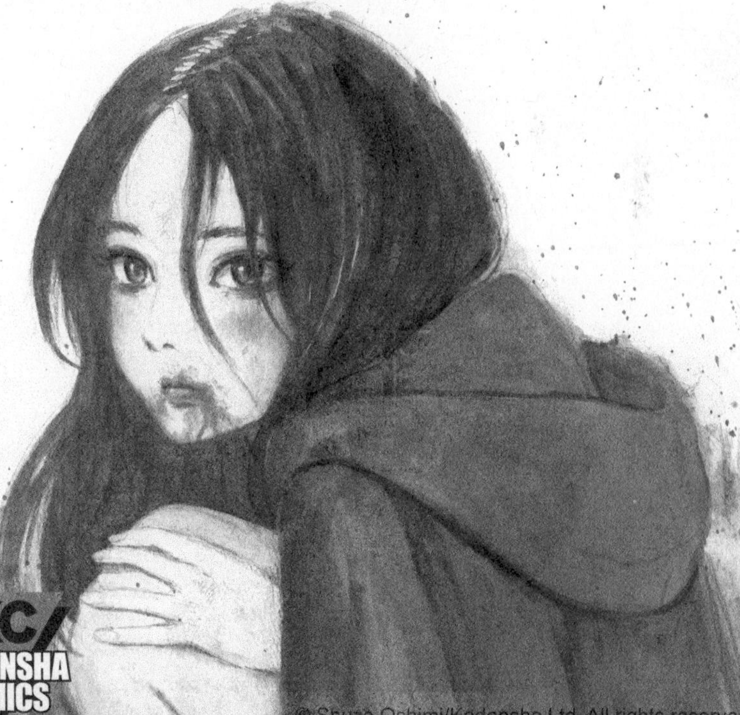

KC KODANSHA COMICS

"I'm pleasantly surprised to find modern shojo using cross-dressing as a dramatic device to deliver social commentary... Recommended."

-Otaku USA Magazine

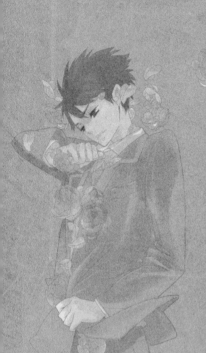

The prince in his dark days

By **Hico Yamanaka**

A drunkard for a father, a household of poverty... For 17-year-old Atsuko, misfortune is all she knows and believes in. Until one day, a chance encounter with Itaru-the wealthy heir of a huge corporation-changes everything. The two look identical, uncannily so. When Itaru curiously goes missing, Atsuko is roped into being his stand-in. There, in his shoes, Atsuko must parade like a prince in a palace. She encounters many new experiences, but at what cost...?

Battle Angel Alita: Mars Chronicle volum
characters, places, and incidents are the products of the author's imagination or are used fictitiously. Any resemblance to actual events, locales, or persons, living or dead, is entirely coincidental.

A Kodansha Comics Trade Paperback Original.

Published in the United States by Kodansha Comics, an imprint of Kodansha USA Publishing, LLC, New York.

Publication rights for this English edition arranged through Kodansha Ltd., Tokyo.

First published in Japan in 2016 by Kodansha Ltd., Tokyo, as *Gunnm: Mars Chronicle 3*.

ISBN 978-1-63236-617-7

Printed in the United States of America.

www.kodanshacomics.co

9 8 7 6 5 4 3 2 1

Translator: Stephen Paul
Lettering: Evan Hayden
Editing: Ajani Oloye
Kodansha Comics edition cover design: Phil Balsman